Acclaim for Misha Glenny's

McMAFIA

Shortlisted for the *Financial Times*/Goldman Sachs Business Book of the Year Award

"Glenny sets a fast pace as he races from one criminal hot spot to another, riding with marijuana traffickers in British Columbia, walking into pachinko parlors in Tokyo, visiting brothels in Tel Aviv and scoping out sex clubs in Dubai."
　　　　　　　　　　　　　　　　　　　　—*The New York Times*

"A vividly recounted journey through a dozen of the world's most potent gangs, cartels, and transnational mafias."　　　—*The Wall Street Journal*

"Engrossing.... Glenny has done the hard and sometimes dangerous work of identifying the criminal syndicates."　—*The New York Review of Books*

"Immensely informative and more than slightly scary."
　　　　　　　　　　　　　　　—*The Washington Post Book World*

"A fascinating primer on the crime and contradictions that lie just below the surface of the new world order."　　　　　　　—*The Oregonian*

"Eye-opening.... From the streets of Bombay (now Mumbai) to Bogotá to Tokyo, Glenny recounts criminal enterprises that, after a time, take on a sameness with their ruthless methods and motives." —*The Miami Herald*

"A startling tour of the new international underworld, documenting the hidden costs of an unregulated global free market."　　　　—*Salon*

MISHA GLENNY
McMAFIA

Misha Glenny was educated at Bristol University in
England and Charles University in Prague. He is also
the author of *The Rebirth of History*, *The Fall of Yugoslavia* (which won the Overseas Press Club Award
for Best Book on Foreign Affairs), and *The Balkans:
Nationalism, War and the Great Powers, 1804–1999*.
During the early 1990s he was the Central Europe correspondent for the BBC World Service, and in 1993 he
won a Sony Award for his coverage of Yugoslavia. He
has contributed to most major U.S. and European
newspapers and current affairs magazines and is regularly consulted by U.S. and European governments on
Balkan issues. Misha Glenny lives in London.

McMAFIA

McMAFIA

A JOURNEY THROUGH THE GLOBAL CRIMINAL UNDERWORLD

Misha Glenny

VINTAGE BOOKS

A DIVISION OF RANDOM HOUSE, INC.

NEW YORK

FIRST VINTAGE BOOKS EDITION, APRIL 2009

Copyright © 2008, 2009 by Misha Glenny

All rights reserved. Published in the United States by Vintage Books,
a division of Random House, Inc., New York. Originally published in
hardcover in slightly different form in the United States by Alfred A.
Knopf, a division of Random House, Inc., New York, in 2008.

Vintage and colophon are registered trademarks of Random House, Inc.

The Library of Congress has cataloged the Knopf edition as follows:
Glenny, Misha.
McMafia : a journey through the global criminal underworld /
by Misha Glenny.—1st ed.
p.   cm.
1. Organized crime.   2. Transnational crime.   I. Title.
HV6441.G54 2008
364.1'06—dc22   2007030522

Vintage ISBN: 978-1-4000-9512-4

Author photograph © Ralph Glenny

www.vintagebooks.com

Printed in the United States of America
7

For Kirsty

CONTENTS

FOREWORD TO THE VINTAGE EDITION

uhgedaboutit!" In May 2008, *Newsday* published this pithy response to my call in *McMafia* for increased regulation of the world's banking system. A few months later, almost everyone, including *Newsday*, had changed their tune.

By September 2008, insufficient regulation had brought capitalism to the brink of disaster. So we may feel inclined to "fuhgedaboutit," but we now know that doing so can seriously damage our health, not to mention obliterate our wealth. Banks and investment houses have not only shafted the taxpayer by handing their executives and shareholders hundreds of billions that were never theirs to give. The opacity of financial markets (further intensified by the desperate search for credit) has allowed all manner of criminals and corrupted individuals from across the world to realize the profits of their illegal business.

Last November, the British NGO Global Witness published a devastating report that investigated the complicity of the world's major banks alongside some of the most corrupt regimes around the world, coming to a stark and disturbing conclusion:

> *The subprime crisis and ensuing credit crunch have shown that allowing banks to self-regulate does not work. They consistently claim that they employ the cleverest people in the world and can be allowed to manage their own risk. But if, as they have shown, they cannot even manage the issue that is of greatest importance to them—making a profit—then it seems clear that they cannot be expected to self-regulate when it comes to ethical issues. . . . The establishment and constant expansion of anti-money-laundering regulations has been inextricably linked with the framing of money laundering as a security issue. . . . The irony behind the banking system's failure to adequately know their customers from corrupt shadow states is that it is precisely these environments that provide an ideal breeding ground for drug trafficking, organised and serious crime, and, most recently, terrorism.*

Foreword to the Vintage Edition

This book charts the rise of the McMafia, the many connected criminal groups and corrupt politicians that comprise what I call the Global Shadow Economy. Since the book was published, the McMafia has enjoyed some spectacular successes as it seeks to undermine new pastures.

Most ominous has been the assault on the coast of West Africa. In one of the unsung successes of the 1990s, the West brought to an end the terrible "blood diamond" wars in Sierra Leone and Liberia with judicious military intervention. Having invested money as well as military and political effort in saving these countries, we now appear to have abandoned them to the corrupting influence of the drug cartels. These fragile nations and several of their neighbors have now been targeted as the ideal transit countries for South American cocaine headed for Europe and the Middle East. The World Bank has sent out urgent messages to Western governments, warning them that international organized crime is strangulating West Africa's coastal states, but unsurprisingly in times like these, such an issue is low on the list of our priorities.

Chinese criminal syndicates continue their infiltration of the production chains of legitimate goods and replacing them with contaminated materials; toys, baby milk, and anti-cancer medicines are just three of the commodities that have spread death and illness from China's factories in the past year. The failure of China's leadership to establish institutions to combat corruption will mean that these poisonous money-making activities will continue to proliferate.

But northern Mexico provides the most distressing theater for McMafia activity. In little more than half a decade, this has become the fiery cockpit of America's futile War on Drugs. The power of the syndicates who make billions of dollars from the United States's policy of drug prohibition has transformed the region into a slaughterhouse where some 5,000 men, women, and children have been executed in the first three-quarters of 2008. The bloody consequences are now licking America's southern border region, intensifying gang warfare not just in Mexico, but also in Central America, Miami, and Los Angeles.

The greatest irony accompanying the rise of international organized crime has been the collapse of the most famous syndicate of all: the Sicilian Mafia. Readers were puzzled that I barely mentioned the original Mafia in this book, and they deserve an explanation. I was looking at the attempts of new criminal organizations to exploit the opportunities offered by globalization and the collapse of communism. In the 1990s and after the millennium, the Sicilian Mafia was one of the few crime syndicates whose influence started to wane even to the point of obscurity.

Foreword to the Vintage Edition

During the Cold War, the Cosa Nostra had prospered because of its links with the Christian Democratic Party (DC), Italy's dominant political force in the postwar period. Relied upon by the United States to keep the threat of communism at bay, the DC entered into a strategic alliance with the Sicilian Mafia in the 1940s. Whenever Italy's courageous but weak law enforcement agencies made a serious move against Mafia activities, the Dons picked up the phone to Rome and made the problem go away. And if they commissioned the murder of senior anti-mafia figures, the investigation would rarely result in the conviction of anybody other than *mafiosi* small fry. Come election time, Italy's middle classes, unhappy with the corruption but frightened by the communists, agreed to "hold [their] nose and vote for the Christian Democrats."

But with the collapse of the Soviet Union, the threat from communism in Italy disappeared. The Italian Right could no longer play the old game. Before long, the Christian Democrats were in free fall. Tumbling behind the party was its corrupt system of government, including the collaboration between Sicilian Mafia and the most senior politicians in Rome, some of whom were eventually convicted.

Giovanni Falcone and Paolo Borsellino, two resolute state prosecutors in the Sicilian capital, Palermo, sought to take advantage of the Mafia's growing vulnerability as its Christian Democrat protectors in the capital began to run for cover. The two anti-mafia prosecutors had already brought dozens of *capi* to justice in the late eighties in the so-called Maxi Trial. But just as they were preparing to administer the final blow against Sicily's legendary organized crime syndicate, they themselves were murdered in the early summer of 1992. The deaths provoked a huge outcry in Sicily as well as on the mainland.

Initially, the Mafia fought back. From May to August of 1993, they planted five bombs, not on their Sicilian turf but in Rome, Milan, and Florence, including one attack that damaged the fabled Uffizi Gallery in the Tuscan capital. This was too much for the middle classes of central and northern Italy to tolerate—it is one thing for the Mafia to strangle the impoverished *Mezzogiorno*, Italy's dusty southern provinces, but it is quite another to cause mayhem in the industrial powerhouses of the north. Anti-mafia politicians and police built upon this indignation to launch an attack of unprecedented efficacy on the bastions of Mafia power from which Sicily's clans have never fully recovered.

The Uffizi bombing and the spectacular assassinations of Falcone and Borsellino rank as perhaps the Mafia's biggest mistakes. In the 1980s, the organization had begun to make more money than ever before thanks to the pivotal role it carved out for itself in the global drug market. In the 1990s, with the collapse of communism and the advent of globalization, the drug trade went berserk, creating undreamt of wealth for those criminal organizations involved in it. Just as the Mafia was about to hit the jackpot, it overplayed its hand. The demise of la Cosa Nostra was typified by the arrests of its two bosses of bosses, Salvatore "Toto" Riina in 1993 and Bernardo "The Tractor" Provenzano in 2006.

Sadly, the crisis within the Sicilian Mafia has not ended the tyranny of organized crime in Europe's fifth largest economy. The Mafia was just one of several large regional organizations. The Sicilians were forced to cede power and influence, but there were others who were quick to fill their vacuum; the neighboring networks from Naples known as the Camorra, the 'ndrangheta from the province of Reggio Calabria, and the Sacra Corona Unità from the Adriatic coast of Apulia have now strengthened their position within the Global Shadow Economy. Their links stretch from Canada through Brazil to South Africa, and they now have very close relations with counterfeit goods syndicates in China.

The McMafia is alive and well across the globe. Knowing its ability to manipulate financial markets, its members could exploit the credit squeeze to its advantage; they control billions of dollars in cash and sought-after commodities. Now when banks are desperately short of capital, the temptation to take money from gangsters may prove irresistible.

At the same time, politicians around the world, under pressure from ordinary folk whose savings have been threatened by the shenanigans of the super rich, are ready to impose new regulations on the international financial markets. It is essential that they use this chance to tighten up the system of money-laundering controls and give some backbone to the feeble monitoring bodies currently responsible for challenging the economic power of the McMafia.

INTRODUCTION

I t was the evening of April 30, 1994, and spring had settled on Woking in Surrey. The Barnesbury Estate is not quite middle management, but there is no shortage of aspiration in this part of southern England. And as dusk fell on Willow Way, a quiet road of terraced housing, cars had already been garaged and families sat down for dinner and Saturday night television.

At nine o'clock, a man emerged from his red Toyota outside number 31. Carrying a flat blue and white box, he strolled up to the front door and tapped on it. Inside Karen Reed, a thirty-three-year-old geophysicist who analyzed seismic data for a living, was enjoying a glass of white wine and a chat with a friend when they heard the man's muffled voice through the window. "Have you ordered a pizza?" he inquired. Karen opened the door, whereupon the pizza deliverer drew a .38 pistol and shot her several times in the head with calm deliberation. The killer then ran back to the car and drove off.

Karen Reed was not the intended victim that night. There was a reason for the murderer's confusion, however. His real target was Karen's sister, Alison Ponting, a producer at the BBC World Service, who was living with Karen at the time but happened to be out that evening. The killing had probably been carried out at the instigation of Djokar Dudayev, president of the Republic of Chechnya.

In 1986, Alison had married a chubby Armenian charmer, Gacic Ter-Oganisyan, whom she had met a couple of years earlier while studying Russian at a university. The marriage triggered a chain of improbable events that eight years later unleashed the whirlwind of death, imperialism, civil war, oil, gangsterism, and nationalist struggle known as the North Caucasus upon the sleepy commuter town of Woking.

Eighteen months before Karen's murder, two brothers, Ruslan and Nazarbeg Utsiev, had arrived in London as envoys of President Dudayev with a brief to arrange the printing of passports and banknotes for the new Chechen state. Ruslan was the volatile Dudayev's most trusted adviser and a hard-liner in the faction-ridden administration. His brother was a martial arts expert and general muscle-for-hire. Along with their public mandate to print the documents of the putative Chechen state, they had a number of other missions: to secure a $250 million loan from an American businessman for the modernization of Chechnya's huge oil refineries; to conclude negotiations with the German energy company Stinnes AG for the quick sale of Chechen oil at world prices; and as investigators later discovered, to purchase 2,000 ground-to-air Stinger missiles. To embark on such complex negotiations, the Chechen government representatives needed a skilled interpreter and fixer. Ruslan remembered that he was once interviewed by a BBC producer, Alison Ponting, and he turned to her for help. She suggested her husband, Ter-Oganisyan, hoping, perhaps, that he would find gainful employment.

During his time in London, Alison's Armenian husband had developed into the consummate chancer. Ter-Oganisyan was ducking and diving: smuggling, setting up fake companies for money laundering, and also doing menial work when his tentative criminal activities dried up. Initially the macho Caucasian trio hit it off, holding raucous parties to which a stream of call girls were invited. Not surprisingly, Alison was increasingly unhappy at the behavior of her husband and the two Chechens, as were the wealthy occupants of Bickenhall Mansions, the apartment block a stone's throw from Sherlock Holmes's reputed domicile at 221B Baker Street in central London where the Utsiev brothers had found a flat.

At some point, relations between the Armenian and the Chechens soured. Later, England's Crown Prosecution Service insisted that Ter-Oganisyan had discovered that the Stinger missiles were destined for Azerbaijan to be deployed in the war against his home country, Armenia. There was a second theory: that the Stingers were indeed bound for Chechnya and that the Utsiev brothers and Ter-Oganisyan fell out over money. What is certain is that Ter-Oganisyan alerted senior members of the Armenian KGB to the Utsiev brothers' activities and a couple of hitmen were dispatched from Los Angeles, the center of the Armenian diaspora in the United States, to London.

The Utsiev brothers were murdered in gruesome fashion (Ruslan's body was dismembered and only discovered when it fell out of a packing case en route to the north London suburb of Harrow). Ter-Oganisyan is now doing life for their murders, while a codefendant, an officer of Armenia's KGB, hanged himself at Belmarsh Prison while awaiting trial.

I was appalled when reading about this case at the time, not least because I discovered that Alison and Karen's father was David Ponting, a lecturer in drama at Bristol University. His one-man show about Dylan

Thomas had made a great impression on me when I studied there. David had taught me radio production, skills I would later employ as the BBC's central Europe correspondent.

After Karen's murder, Alison accepted an offer to go into a witness protection scheme. Deprived of his children, David moved to the United States, where he worked for a while as an actor. Later, he too went underground.

The Pontings were gentle and unassuming. It is hard to imagine a family less likely to be involved in a political mafia killing from the former Soviet Union. But one of the officers involved in the Utsiev brothers' case pointed out at the time, "We were suddenly dealing with crime and politics from a part of the world that, to be honest, none of us in the Metropolitan or Surrey police had ever heard of. We knew nothing about the wars, about the crime, and about the politics—we were frankly all at sea."

It was 1994, and the failing state, an unknown concept to most, was visiting Britain for the first time.

The post–World War II order began to crumble in the first half of the 1980s. Its dissolution followed no obvious pattern, occurring instead as a series of seemingly disparate events: the spectacular rise of the Japanese car industry; Communist Hungary's clandestine approach to the International Monetary Fund to explore a possible application for membership; the stagnation of India's economy; President F. W. de Clerk's first discreet contacts with the imprisoned Nelson Mandela; the advent of Deng Xiaoping's reforms in China; Margaret Thatcher's decisive confrontation with Britain's trades union movement.

Individually, these and other events seemed to reflect the everyday ups and downs of politics; at most they were adjustments to the world order. In fact, powerful currents below the surface had provoked a number of economic crises and opportunities, especially outside the great citadels of power in Western Europe and the United States, that were to have profound consequences for the emergence of what we now call globalization.

There was one development, however, that had its roots firmly in America and in its primary European ally, Britain. The world was taking its first steps toward the liberalization of international financial and commodity markets. Western corporations and banks had begun to pry open markets that had hitherto maintained strict controls on foreign investment and currency exchange. Then came the fall of Communism in 1989, first in Eastern Europe and then in the mighty Soviet Union itself. Out of ideas, short of money, and beaten in the race for technological superiority, Communism fizzled out in days rather than years. This was a monumental event that fused with the processes of globalization to trigger an exponential rise in the shadow economy.

These huge economic and political shifts affected every part of the planet. In some areas, such as the United States, the early 1990s saw a dramatic increase in personal income. South Africa prepared for the end of apartheid, the most excoriated political system in the world. The people of the Soviet Union—effectively closed to the West for seventy years—had to adjust to a new life, one in which their government no longer exercised control over them from cradle to grave. In Latin America, the military regimes and their brutal abuse of human rights fell into disfavor, to be replaced by the immense political test of managing capricious national debt.

Overall, there was a significant worldwide upsurge in trade, investment, and the creation of wealth. The latter was, however, distributed very unevenly. Countless states found themselves cast into the purgatory that became known as "transition," a territory with ever-shifting borders. In these badlands, economic survival frequently involved grabbing a gun and snatching what you could to survive.

The fall of Communism was, of course, a great victory for the West, demonstrating the superiority of the world's democracies over Communist dictatorship in every respect. Europe celebrated the unification of Germany and the liberation of many East European countries. The new Russia was quite content, it seemed, to give up its military dominance of the region, disbanding NATO's erstwhile rival, the Warsaw Pact. Initially reluctant, Moscow then allowed the other peoples of the dying Soviet Union to form their own independent states, fulfilling their national aspirations. Looking back, this was the high point of my own life. In my teens, I had become involved in Western organizations supporting the beleaguered opposition throughout Eastern Europe, such as Poland's Solidarity or Czechoslovakia's Charter 77. I had done everything from translating documents to smuggling dismembered photocopying machines across the Iron Curtain to the dissidents. And so when I stood five yards behind Czechoslovakia's great moral leaders, Václav Havel and Alexander Dubček, as they addressed their public from a balcony above Prague's Wenceslas Square in November 1989, I felt both a sense of real achievement and cautious optimism about the future of Europe and the world.

This initial euphoria was soon dampened by indications, admittedly in rather obscure places, that the new world of peace and democracy might face some teething problems. In the Caucasus along Russia's southern border, sporadic reports emerged of fighting in obscure pockets of the region. In parts of Africa, such as Angola, wars that had started as proxy conflicts between American- and Soviet-backed forces did not mimic the cold war by coming to an end—if anything, they intensified. Then the former Yugoslavia dissolved into a murderous civil war, presenting the new united Europe with a challenge that it was entirely unable to meet.

The new circumstances bewildered old international institutions. All had to improvise and no party quite understood the implications of its actions or their unintended consequences.

One group of people, however, saw real opportunity in this dazzling mixture of upheaval, hope, and uncertainty. These men, and occasionally women, understood instinctively that rising living standards in the West, increased trade and migration flows, and the greatly reduced ability of many governments to police their countries combined to form a gold mine. They were criminals, organized and disorganized, but they were also good capitalists and entrepreneurs, intent on obeying the laws of supply and demand. As such, they valued economies of scale, just as multinational corporations did, and so they sought out overseas partners and markets to develop industries that were every bit as cosmopolitan as Shell, Nike, or McDonald's. The title of this book reflects this global reach, as criminal corporations aspire to penetrate markets the world over, mirroring the global goals of legal entities such as McDonald's.

They first became visible in Russia and Eastern Europe, but they were also exerting an influence on countries as far away from one another as India, Colombia, and Japan.

I spotted them in the early 1990s when I was covering the wars in the former Yugoslavia for the BBC. The booty paramilitary units brought home with them after destroying towns and villages in Croatia and Bosnia was used as capital to establish large criminal empires. The bosses of these syndicates became rich very quickly. Soon they established smuggling franchises that conveyed illicit goods and services from all over the world and into the consumer paradise of the European Union.

As a writer on the Balkans, I was invited to many conferences to discuss the political issues behind the disastrous wars in the region. It was not long before I received invitations to gatherings discussing security issues. Politicians, policemen, and nongovernmental organizations (NGOs) were all hoping to learn what lay behind the immense power of organized crime in the Balkans and beyond. However, most knowledge of the new wave of global crime was anecdotal at best. Nobody had connected the dots.

Introduction

Initially, I looked at the networks and motives of criminal groups in the Balkans but quickly realized that in order to understand crime there, I would have to extend my research to other parts of the world: the regions that produce criminal goods, such as Russia, South America, Africa, India, and China; as well as the regions that consume them, such as the European Union, North America, Japan, and the Middle East.

Among the many consequences of the Soviet collapse was the emergence of a thick belt of instability that began in the Balkans and stretched all the way across the Caucasus, the so-called *stans* of Soviet central Asia, and on to the western edge of China and the North-West Frontier of Pakistan.

This was the New Silk Route, a multilane criminal highway that linked the belt with other troubled regions such as Afghanistan and which permitted the swift and easy transfer of people, narcotics, cash, endangered species, and precious hardwood from Asia to Europe and farther to the United States.

This clutch of uncertain new states on the southern periphery of the former Russian empire was born as the pace of globalization accelerated. Countries in Western Europe and the Mediterranean proved a powerful magnet for those scrambling to seize power along the New Silk Route. Money translated directly into political power and vice versa. And so those harboring ambition in the failing states needed the New Silk Route for three related transactions: to transfer cash to the sanctity of Western banks and real estate; to sell illicit goods and services into the European Union, the United States, and eastward to Japan; and to buy and sell arms within the former Soviet Union and to export them into the world's trouble spots.

"In '93–'94 I started working in law enforcement, knowing that globalization was beginning to have an impact on a whole range of issues," said Jon Winer in his plush office a couple of blocks from the White House. The architect of the Clinton administration's organized crime strategy, Winer had spotted these new developments earlier than most. "The paradigm was El Salvador. After the war, people decided to use their arms caches to make money in criminal gangs. And then we saw that the right-wing paramilitaries and left-wing guerrillas began *working together*! Burglary, carjacking plus kidnapping, car theft . . ."

Winer had stumbled across something that still plagues peace initiatives aiming to stop wars that engulf failed states. When diplomats succeed in bringing the fighting to a halt, they are confronted with a wrecked local economy and a society dominated by testosterone-driven young men who are suddenly unemployed but have grown accustomed to their omnipotence. If you want lasting stability, you have to find useful jobs to occupy them. Otherwise these people find the temptation to retrain themselves as organized criminal units irresistible. In retrospect, Winer argued, the extent of this problem in El Salvador and other conflicts from the 1980s was a stroll in the park compared with what the 1990s had in store: "The main sources of revenue in Salvador was not carjacking or drugs. But when you got to the Balkans or the Caucasus, the main source of revenue in society *was* criminal. Now you had a very different model!"

The deepening links in a globalizing world magnify the impact of immense disruptions to the international order like the collapse of the Soviet Union. And for the first few years after the event, nobody had the slightest notion what the sudden injection of huge sums of mineral wealth and criminal profits into the legitimate and shadow economies actually implied. And those who did observe some changes in the way the world worked were frequently baffled by it. What was a cop on the beat in leafy Woking expected to know about the internecine struggles of the Caucasus?

Academics and researchers have channeled considerable energy into understanding the process of "licit" globalization, a process that is largely regulated and quantifiable, although hedge funds and private equity sometimes appear to have slipped their moorings. But since the liberalization of international financial and commodity markets on the one hand and the fall of Communism on the other, the shadow economy has shot up as a percentage of global GDP. According to figures culled from the IMF, the World Bank, and research institutes in Europe and North America, it now accounts for between 15 and 20 percent of global turnover.

Of course, this includes a multitude of sins, such as tax avoidance, that cannot be ascribed to a growth in transnational criminal conspiracies. But given that the shadow economy has become such an important economic force in our world, it is surprising that we devote so little effort to a systematic understanding of how it works and how it connects with the licit economy. This shadow world is by no means distinct from its partner in the light, which is itself often far less transparent than one might suspect or desire. In both banking and commodity trading, the criminal operates much closer to home than we think.

That vast unregulated economic area is a swamp that contains protein-rich nutrients for a host of security problems. International terrorism certainly feeds in these same grounds, but in terms of the death and misery caused, terrorism is a primitive and relatively insignificant species. Crime and the pursuit of money or political power have proved incomparably more damaging over the last two decades. The concentration of huge resources on fighting terrorism to the neglect of other security problems is the consequence of chronic mismanagement, especially under the administration of President George W. Bush. It is striking how all opinion polls in Iraq since the invasion have placed corruption and crime in equal first place with terrorism as the major concern for citizens. The impact of the former—not just in Iraq alone but across the Middle East—will last long after the latter has diminished.

From the Balkans, which I knew well, I embarked on a journey around the world in an attempt to trace the history of the astonishing growth in organized crime and the shadow economy over the last twenty years. On my travels, I met fascinating characters of great intelligence, vitality, courage, wit, and spirit. Many were criminals, some were victims, others were politicians, policemen, or lawyers. Almost all were happy to tell their strange, frightening, and even funny stories. The nature of the topic means that many were only willing to speak anonymously and names have often been changed.* I would like to thank all those I interviewed and consulted for their time and their profound insights.

I hope their stories contribute to solving the puzzle of how organized crime fits in to a globalized planet. I also hope they offer some clues as to how politicians and police might address these problems to prevent men and women, such as Karen Reed, from falling victim to this shadow world.

---

*Indicated by the italicization of a name on first appearance.

PART I

The Fall of Communism

CHAPTER 1

Death of an American

The bells tolled uninterrupted for fifteen minutes as they carried the coffin into St. Nedelya's Cathedral. At the head of the procession was Patriarch Maxim, head of the Bulgarian Orthodox Church, behind him were several thousand mourners. It seemed as if *le tout* Sofia had come on that blustery cold Friday in March 2003 to pay their final respects to Ilya Pavlov, the man who had defined the 1990s for them.

At the end of the service, thirty brothers from the dear departed's Masonic lodge, the Antient Free and Accepted Scottish Custom, closed the doors of the cathedral. Dressed in jet-black suits and clasping bouquets of white flowers, the men performed a secret ritual to speed "Brother Pavlov to the Eternal Orient." His overall, gloves, and the lodge's crest then "accompanied Brother Pavlov to the Grand Architect of the Universe."

A government minister bore a message from the prime minister, Simeon Saxe-Coburgotski. Formerly the king of Bulgaria, the lean and elegant Simeon had relinquished his claim to the throne in order to lead his country and its government out of the morass of the late 1990s after his political party had won a landslide victory in the elections of 2001. "We shall remember Ilya Pavlov," read the king's telegram of condolence, "because he created jobs for many families in a difficult period for the people. We'll remember him for his spirit as a businessman and for his extraordinary energy."

MPs, artists, the bosses of the most important oil companies and banks, two former Miss Bulgarias, the entire CSKA soccer team (to Bulgarians a fusion of Manchester United and the Yankees), all joined Pavlov's grieving family. There as well was another prominent group of his acquaintances, better known to the Bulgarian public by their nicknames: "The Skull," "The Beak," "Dimi the Russian," and "The Doctor."

The most conspicuous absentee was the American ambassador to Bulgaria, Jim Pardew. The embassy had made urgent inquiries five days earlier, on March 7, when a single sniper bullet felled Ilya Pavlov at a quarter to eight in the evening as he chatted on the phone outside the headquarters of his megacorporation, Multigroup. The death of such an eminent and wealthy American citizen on foreign soil would naturally raise serious concerns for the United States and its representatives.

Pavlov could never have made it to the White House, as he was not born in America. But he was still a proud foot soldier in that mighty army that has participated in the rich traditions of naturalized immigration to the United States. The only curious aspect about Pavlov's American aspirations was that two consecutive U.S. ambassadors to Sofia vigorously opposed them. Both diplomats made personal representations in Washington to try to prevent Pavlov from entering the country, let alone having U.S. citizenship bestowed upon him. But Pavlov also had his supporters in the United States. Despite an FBI investigation into his past activities, not to mention heightened security concerns after 9/11, Pavlov received his American passport.

In the 1970s and 1980s, Communist Bulgaria was topped only by Romania and Albania as the most miserably depressing place to live in Europe. I recall tramping through the fog-bound streets of Sofia, drifting from one shade of gray to the next in search of a restaurant or café to alleviate the boredom. As a foreigner and journalist, I always had included in my personal hospitality pack at least two minders from the DS (Bulgaria's KGB) who tracked my every footstep. Their presence ensured that on the rare occasion I persuaded ordinary folk to engage in conversation, the best I could hope for was a little chitchat about the weather.

But slowly I understood that beneath this moribund conformity there were eddies of activity, some quite vigorous, that nourished more interesting lifestyles—not the pained martyrdom of intellectuals and dissidents who fought courageously against the injustice of Communism but the serendipity or good fortune of some who found ways to mold parts of the system to their advantage.

As a teenager growing up in the 1970s, young Ilya Pavlov had one particular skill that marked him out from most of his peers: he was an accomplished wrestler, indeed the champion of Bulgaria in his weight class. Had he been very smart or a gifted rock guitarist, Ilya might have landed in trouble, as these talents usually led youngsters to a life of rebellion and disobedience. But in Bulgaria, the greatest heroes were not soccer or tennis players but musclemen. Before the fall of Communism, weight lifting, wrestling, and boxing were dominated by Eastern Bloc states, which routinely pumped their promising sportsmen and -women with gallons of steroids in the search for Olympic glory.

A pro in all but name, the successful wrestler could expect public acclamation (and fringe benefits such as casual sex on tap), money, an apartment, and a car (the latter two being out of the reach of all but the most feted youngsters). Pavlov would have anticipated this when he was picked out to attend the Institute for Physical Culture in Sofia, Bulgaria's elite breeding ground for future Olympians.

Ilya was doubly advantaged, because his father ran a restaurant and bar in Sofia, where his tough young son worked. "At that time, being a barman or waiter conferred considerable social status on you," explained Emil Kyulev, a graduate of the Police Academy and Pavlov's contemporary. "He hung out with a lot of tough guys and people looked up to him. That way he also came into contact with the security services."

For an uneducated young steer like Pavlov, the DS was not the Orwellian instrument of repression that people in the West perceived. For some Bulgarians, it was an avenue to status and influence. If, as many claim, Pavlov worked as an informant for the DS, then he could expect rewards. His most important came in the shape of a pretty young woman, Toni Chergelanova, who accepted his proposal of marriage in 1982. A greater catch than the girl was her father, Petur Chergelanov, who worked for state security. Ilya had wed into secret police royalty.

The Bulgarian state security service was held in special regard by its Soviet masters for its efficacy and reliability. Usually invisible, it never disappointed on those occasions when it did catch the public eye—the DS masterminded the death of a Bulgarian dissident who, when working for the BBC in London, was struck down by a poison-tipped umbrella as he strode across Waterloo Bridge in 1978.

The business of eliminating enemies of the state le Carré style was mere icing on the cake. The most important and lucrative trade of the Bulgarian secret service was smuggling—in drugs, in arms, and in high tech. "Smuggling is our cultural heritage," Ivan Krastev, Bulgaria's leading political scientist, explained. "Our territory has always nestled between huge ideologies, between Orthodoxy and Roman Catholicism, between Islam and Christianity, between capitalism and Communism. Empires riddled with hostility and suspicion for one another but home, nonetheless, to many people who want to trade across the prohibited boundaries. In the Balkans, we know how to make those boundaries disappear. We can cross the roughest sea and traverse the most forbidding mountain. We know every secret pass and, failing that, the price of every border guard."

Fortified by the might of the totalitarian state, the DS took full advantage of this romantic tradition. As early as the 1960s, it established a company called Kintex, which enjoyed a near monopoly on the export of arms from Bulgaria and sought out markets in trouble spots like the Middle East and Africa. At the end of the 1970s, the DS expanded Kintex by setting up the Covert Transit directorate. Its primary role was to smuggle weapons to African insurgent groups, but soon the channels were also being used for illegal people trafficking, for drugs, and even for the smuggling of works of art and antiquities.

Other companies specialized in the sale of an indigenous Bulgarian amphetamine, Kaptagon, to the Middle East, where it was a hugely popular drug due to its alleged aphrodisiacal properties. In the other direction, some 80 percent of heroin destined for the West European market would cross into Bulgaria from Turkey at the Kapetan Andreevo border point and into the hands of the DS. Not only did Bulgaria make big money out of this, but the trade helped to undermine capitalist Western Europe by flooding it with cheap heroin.

The DS enabled Bulgaria to play a pivotal role in the distribution of illicit goods and services between Europe, the Middle East, and central Asia. But it was resolute in preventing anyone else from muscling in on the trade. Bulgaria's border force was ruthless, and severe punishments were meted out to anybody caught smuggling drugs or weapons without authorization. This resolve was not born of a commitment to uphold the rule of law (a concept that was anathema to state security), but to underscore the DS's economic monopoly.

The trade in high tech was different. Until the revolutions of 1989, the Soviet Bloc maintained an unwieldy trade association, COMECON, which determined the "socialist international division of labor." In practice, this meant that Moscow ordered Czechoslovakia to concentrate on producing turbines for power stations while forcing Poland to produce fertilizer because that's what Moscow wanted. During the 1960s, the Soviet Union ordered Bulgaria to beef up its electronics industry.

As a consequence, in the late 1970s, Bulgaria (the most rural of all East European economies) flowered into an unlikely center of the magnetic disk and computer industries. The Pravets was born—Europe's first socialist PC, manufactured in the eponymous little town twenty-five miles northeast of Sofia, which (not coincidentally) was the birthplace of Todor Zhivkov, Bulgaria's long-standing dictator.

Moscow charged the DS with breaking the COCOM regime—this was the regulatory body set up by the United States, which included Western Europe and Japan, to prevent sensitive high-tech equipment with possible military usage from making its way through the Iron Curtain and into the Soviet Union.

The DS conscripted some of Bulgaria's most senior scientists with the goal of supplying Bulgaria and the Soviet Union with advanced technologies over which COCOM had imposed an embargo. Two years later, it established clandestine companies abroad into which revenues of about $1 billion flowed from the illegal sale of technology.

The most important spin-off from this arrangement was the Memory Disks Equipment company (known as DZU), in which Bulgaria began to build a team of gifted hardware and software engineers. It was a profitable business. "According to our clients' estimates," a former intelligence boss later admitted, "between 1981 and 1986, the annual profit of technological and scientific intelligence activities was $580 million; i.e., this would have been the price of technologies had we bought them."

All three industries—drugs, arms, and high tech—were deemed of immense strategic value to the Bulgarian state. At the heart of the smuggling operations lay Military Counter Intelligence, the Third Directorate of the DS, which controlled all of Bulgaria's borders. And the head of Military Counter Intelligence was General Petur Chergelanov, the father-in-law to Ilya Pavlov.

In 1986, as Mikhail Gorbachev consolidated his authority in Moscow, Western leaders were unaware that the Soviet Union's hegemony over its East European allies was coming to an end. The Bulgarian state security service had no such illusions about the system it policed. Experienced observers of the Soviet scene, the DS's leadership calculated that Communism did not have long to last.

Under pressure from Gorbachev, the Bulgarian Communist Party had passed Decree 56, which overnight allowed the creation of private enterprises in Bulgaria, known as joint-stock companies. Many in the party, still hard-liners, were shocked by this development, as it looked like the thin end of a capitalist wedge. But the state security services, which habitually subordinated ideology to the love of power, took it in their stride.

"When I looked at the trade register for 1986, it struck me," explained Stanimir Vaglenov, a Bulgarian journalist who specializes in corruption and organized crime, "the security services founded the first company a week after Decree 56 came into effect. And within the first year, members of the DS had founded 90 percent of the new joint-stock companies!" While the bulk of Bulgaria's long-suffering population was still being force-fed the rhetoric about socialism's bright and eternal future, the regime's most senior representatives were teaching themselves how to make money. Big money. Having spent forty-five years expounding the theoretical evils of capitalism to ordinary Bulgarians, the secret police were now keen to demonstrate those evils in practice.

In 1988, a year before the collaspse of Communism, Ilya Pavlov himself registered Multiart, a company dedicated to the import and export of antiques and high art (using the channels established by Kintex's covert directorate). Business flourished, and before long Pavlov had become the talk of the town, bursting into one of the new private restaurants with a team of stunning young women swinging behind him—the lizard had acquired a tail. "Multiart was in fact a big mess," Pavlov later conceded, describing his early days. "We developed a whole string of businesses without any structure." One of Multiart's codirectors was Dimitur Ivanov, boss of the Sixth Directorate of the DS, the political police, known with mock affection in Bulgaria as the Gestapo. Ivanov introduced Ilya to Andrei Lukanov, the country's leading reform Communist. Ilya Pavlov, a one-time champion wrestler, all-around toughie, and glitzy playboy, was on the verge of a new career.

Andrei Lukanov beamed mischievously as we surveyed the chaotic parliamentary proceedings in the last days of 1989. "This is all going rather well, don't you think?" I was perplexed. "But aren't you worried about ordinary people's reaction toward Communists like you?" I asked him. "Oh, no, Misha—you mustn't be alarmist," he retorted in impeccable English. "I have always wanted to change, and things are about to get much better."

Despite his slightly gnomish face, Lukanov was charm personified (in stark contrast to most other influential Communists). People, including me, took an instant liking to him. A polyglot with the smoothest political patter, Lukanov was born in Moscow, where he maintained a dense web of connections. He had assumed the role of prime minister after the overthrow of the dictator, Todor Zhivkov, in November 1989, and together with Ilya Pavlov and their friends in the DS, he was planning to hijack the Bulgarian economy. Almost all their bases were covered: Lukanov controlled the political machine; Dimitur Ivanov mobilized the security services network; Ilya and his wrestler friends provided the muscle.

The only thing missing was support from the democratic opposition. The newly formed Union of Democratic Forces, with unstinting financial and political support from the American embassy, had seized the moral high ground in Bulgarian politics after the 1989 revolution. It was bitterly hostile to the Communists for the destruction they had wrought on the country. Pavlov and his colleagues were all closely associated with the Communist regime, and so they needed to neutralize any opposition attempt to foil their business plans.

In 1990, Ilya came up with the solution. A good friend was the deputy head of Podkrepa, Bulgaria's fiercely anti-Communist independent trades union, which also received strong backing from the American government. Pavlov persuaded Podkrepa's bosses that the real enemies of ordinary workers were the Communist-appointed directors of the big state-owned factories.

"Ilya's game was simple." Boyko Borissov speaks with authority. In his mid-forties, the former operations director of the Interior Ministry is a black belt in karate. He also used to be involved in protection rackets before going straight and joining Prime Minister Saxe-Coburski as his bodyguard. The quintessential poacher turned gamekeeper, he has inside knowledge of the criminalization of Bulgaria:

> It was called the Spider Trap. Ilya walked into the office of the director of Kremikovtsi, one of the biggest steelworks in Eastern Europe. He was accompanied by a boss of the most powerful trades union, and then sitting there is Dimitur Ivanov, the man who until recently was head of the Sixth Directorate. And these guys tell the director of the enterprise—"You have a choice . . . work with us or we will destroy you!"

Pavlov told the director that from that point on, he would be buying raw materials not directly from the Russians at a subsidized price but from one of his companies at the world market price. And then instead of selling the end product directly to the consumer, the director would have to sell it at a knock-down price to another of Ilya's firms, which would then sell it on the open market. He controlled the entrance and exit to the factory—the Spider Trap.

The simplicity and efficacy of this system delighted Pavlov. The government run by Lukanov continued to provide subsidies to the company over many years. "The enterprise doesn't collapse immediately," said Emil Kyulev, one of Bulgaria's richest bankers before his assassination in October 2005. "You hang a goat on a hook and cut it at its foot and it will expire very slowly as the blood leaves its body, drop by drop—it agonizes over the years. Pavlov and friends created these holding companies in virtually every branch of the Bulgarian economy, in agriculture, in transport, in industry, energy—you name it. The holdings were parallel to the branch organizations of Podkrepa: wherever Podkrepa was, Ilya would create a holding company."

After the revolution of 1989, Bulgaria's social security system collapsed, leaving a trail of poverty and destitution in its wake. The country had been hit hard as it emerged from the cave-dwelling existence of socialist economics into the blinding sun of free market capitalism. Under Communism, factories had survived, thanks to massive state subsidies, while the Soviet trading bloc ensured their shoddy products a guaranteed sale on East European markets. When the Berlin Wall fell in 1989, Bulgaria's markets crumbled with it.

With industry in near terminal crisis, agriculture, the economy's traditional mainstay, assumed ever-greater importance, but this sector too ran into trouble. The European Union was unwilling to increase its minuscule imports of Bulgarian agricultural produce, as this would undermine its protectionist racket masquerading grandly as the Common Agricultural Policy (CAP).

As the world's major powers began to trumpet the revolutionary significance of globalization in the early 1990s, they skimmed over its inconsistencies. When countries opened up in the hope of greater cooperation with the mighty Western economies, the EU, the United States, and Japan demanded that these emerging markets accept the sale of European, American, and Japanese goods. At the same time, they insisted on low corporate tax rates in exchange for new investments as the vogue for "outsourcing" production to keep down labor costs took hold among Western corporations. Within months of the end of Communism, Snickers, Nike, Swatch, Heineken, and Mercedes had begun their irresistible march eastward, conquering in a matter of weeks those parts of Europe that had defied even Napoleon and Hitler. Entranced by the novelty and quality of these must-have Western goods, the peoples of Eastern Europe (and Africa and Asia, for that matter) dug deep to spend what little money they possessed to acquire the new status symbols.

It is a universally acknowledged truth of international trade that if you import goods and services into your country, you need to export others in order to pay for them (the poorer the country, the more urgent the need—it is much cheaper for rich countries like the United States to run up ludicrous debts). Bulgaria's high-quality soft fruits, cotton, roses, wines, and cereals could have played a vital role in restoring this battered little economy—such goods could perhaps have offset some of the cost of the new Western products flooding the market. Unfortunately, the opportunities were severely limited by arrangements like the CAP, blocking the sale of agricultural produce. Bulgarian consumer goods were still socialist in design and durability (i.e., they were ugly and did not work) and therefore were no competition for Western consumer products. So the problem of how to pay for the growing number of Western imports remained.

While most Bulgarians experienced a sudden collapse in living standards, a small minority was taking advantage of the chaos. By 1992, Ilya Pavlov had become a multimillionaire owning companies registered in Switzerland, Lichtenstein, and Bulgaria, by transferring the assets of the state into his private liquid capital using the Spider Trap. Still in his early thirties, he soon created a sister company in Vienna, Virginia, just outside Washington, D.C. Through Multigroup US, he bought two casinos in Paraguay.

Back home, Pavlov employed several PR firms to project an image of dynamic success and patriotism—he became the face of the new Bulgaria. The most high-profile businessman in the country, he had newspapers and TV shows slavishly following his exploits. Invitations to social events such as his annual birthday party every August 6—traditionally held at one of the most opulent hotels in the Black Sea resort of Varna—became prized possessions, as recipients had the opportunity to mix with the grandest members of the country's economic and political elite. A photo taken with Ilya was enough to secure large loans on easy terms. At first hundreds, then thousands, then tens of thousands of Bulgarians desperate for money and employment became indirectly dependent on the commercial operations of Multigroup and similar megacorporations springing up around the country. Naturally, many disapproved of Pavlov's methods. Many others were jealous competitors who conspired with and against him in the demi-monde of Bulgaria's nascent market economy, in which it was usually impossible to distinguish between the legal, the gray, and the outright criminal. But others regarded him as a genuine, energetic, and likable entrepreneur with the interests of Bulgaria at heart, providing jobs in areas where the state had unexpectedly and calamitously fulfilled Marx's prophecy by withering away.

The headquarters of Multigroup, his new corporation, was located outside Sofia in the mansion on Bystrica Mountain, where Bulgaria's top trade unionists had once spent their holidays. The building had been bought for a song by Robert Maxwell, the British media magnate who had been cultivating both the Soviet and Bulgarian Communist leaders for several years. The Maxwell connection demonstrated how quick some predatory Western businessmen linked up with proto-oligarchs from Eastern Europe to internationalize the asset stripping of the new democracies. Maxwell was in the vanguard of a criminal industry that would run out of control in the 1990s: money laundering. Together with Prime Minister Lukanov, Maxwell arranged the transfer of $2 billion from Bulgaria into Western tax havens—subsequent Bulgarian governments were unable to trace what happened to this cash, although we do know that it did not end up in the London *Daily Mirror*'s pension fund, from which Maxwell was also stealing hundreds of millions of pounds at the same time.

For most Bulgarians, the early 1990s looked grim: the country had lost its markets; Pavlov and friends were skinning the economy of all its valuables; nobody wanted to buy Bulgaria's goods; and furthermore, now that Bulgaria was a fledgling democracy, the United States and the International Monetary Fund wasted no time in demanding that Sofia meet its obligations and start paying off $10 billion's worth of debt run up by the profligate Communist regime. What could they possibly sell to finance this and the modest lifestyle of the overwhelming majority of the population?

On a bright, warm spring day in 1991, I pulled up in front of the Hotel Esplanade on Mihanoviceva Street in central Zagreb. The four-hour drive from Vienna had been a breeze in my black Audi Quattro. Without question the spiffiest car I had ever driven, it was a cut above the standard BBC issue, but I had insisted on a four-wheel drive after several hair-raising journeys through snowstorms on the ever-unpredictable tarmac of Eastern Europe during the revolutions of 1989. As I got out of the car, a new, slightly nervous porter asked for the keys so he could valet park the car. This was a regular procedure at the Esplanade and so I handed them over.

Everyone swung in and out of the Esplanade—mediators such as Cyrus Vance and Lord David Owen, and various ministers from the region, from the EU, and from the United States. They would dine next to mercenaries who were filling the rooms in anticipation of a profitable war, as well as young diaspora Croats from Edmonton or Cleveland, Ohio, who were ready to risk their lives for a fatherland they had never before laid eyes on.

Death of an American

Next morning, I went to find the Audi in the car park. It wasn't there. I didn't yet know it, but my car had embarked on a mystery tour that would end several weeks later at a used car market 200 miles away in Mostar, the capital of western Hercegovina. By then I had collected the insurance (fortunately the Austrian insurance companies had not yet scrapped coverage for Yugoslavia as they had done for Poland, Romania, Bulgaria, and Albania), and so I never again saw my dear Audi, which would almost certainly have then been commandeered by one of the emerging militias in Bosnia-Hercegovina.

Thus did I fall victim to Europe's fastest-growing industry—car theft. Every month thousands of cars would be stolen from the streets of northern Europe in preparation for their illegal export to Eastern Europe and the Balkans. In 1992, I watched a huge container ship regurgitate the contents of its hold into the decrepit Albanian port of Durres. Onto a quay of chipped stone and rust rolled dozens of BMWs, Peugeots, Hondas, and above all Mercedes, Mercedes, and more Mercedes, mostly the 200 series beloved of taxi drivers in Germany, the Low Countries, and Scandinavia. Customs officers barely awoke from their slumber as excited, dusty, and dirty men took possession of vehicles still with their original number plates, with their Christmas tree air fresheners and family photos dangling from the mirror, with old cigarette packets on the seats.

Cars were banned in Communist Albania except for official use; the roads were designed to accommodate a few trucks a day, and nobody except the small band of state chauffeurs learned how to drive. In the chaos of collapsing Communism, the floodgates opened and anyone able to get his hands on a (stolen) car hit the public highways with Mediterranean gusto despite never having sat behind a wheel. Mayhem! The country was transformed into a huge and deadly dodgem ride, while any vehicle was fair game for thieves (given that they were all stolen anyhow, it was difficult to construct a morally watertight case of ownership). The cars that didn't stay in Albania were sold in Macedonia, Bulgaria, Russia, the Middle East, the Caucasus, and former Soviet Central Asia.

At the time, I didn't appreciate the significance of my car being stolen. I could not see the iceberg of crime that was rapidly forming below the swirling sea of revolution, freedom, nationalism, and violence that had engulfed Eastern Europe. Many people were engaged in settling old scores. Others were working hard to preserve the privileges they enjoyed under the old system but in a society where *Communism* was suddenly a dirty word. Ironically, in Bulgaria the revolution was led by Communists such as Lukanov who were impatient to begin their new careers as capitalists.

Many of their fellow citizens were understandably keen to see the great machine of Communist repression dismantled. In an equally understandable bid to win popularity, successive governments started sacking thousands upon thousands of policemen. All manner of operatives lost their jobs: secret police, counterintelligence officers, Special Forces commandos, and border guards, as well as homicide detectives and traffic cops. Their skills included surveillance, smuggling, killing people, establishing networks, and blackmail. By 1991, 14,000 secret policemen were kicking their heels and looking for work in a country where the economy was contracting at an alarming rate. One sector, however, was experiencing an unprecedented expansion, and it was a line of work that was ideally suited to unemployed and disaffected policemen. This sector was organized crime.

Another recently disenfranchised group found themselves in a similar situation—the wrestlers, boxers, and weight lifters. As a budgetary crisis combined with the zeitgeist of freedom to reduce the state police to a skeletal force, sports societies throughout the country were transformed into small private security forces.

The distribution network for the stolen cars belonged initially to the wrestlers. Across the country, this tight band of comrades took control of motels along the major transit routes. With their superior muscle and high level of trust among themselves, they embarked on a violent spree of both intimidation and incorporation of petty thieves and street gangs. By 1992, the wrestlers enjoyed a near stranglehold on Bulgaria's major cities, although in some areas they faced competition from protection rackets run by ex-policemen and security officers. The brighter sparks among them combined the skills of the two professions—sportsmen for muscle, policemen for networking. The hybrid organizations grew to dominate the economy, and two groups, known by the acronyms SIC and VIS, became the overwhelming market leaders.

SIC and VIS presented themselves as insurance companies, legal businesses that emerged out of their criminal work as car smugglers. "I took possession of my Mercedes in June 1992," one Sofia taxi driver explained, "and naturally I took out insurance with the state company to reduce the bribes paid to the traffic cops. At the time, we were stopped every few miles and the cops just demanded cash for no particular reason. But if you were in violation of traffic laws, like driving without insurance, you'd have to pay double. Before long, however, I was approached by a bunch of hard guys—you know, cropped hair, tattoos, leather jackets—and they told me I had to take out insurance with SIC. So I did—I wasn't going to mess with them. But some of the drivers refused—within hours their cars were stolen. And they could only get them back when they had paid up their SIC premiums . . . with interest, of course!"

This was not just extortion. If your vehicle was stolen when already insured with SIC, the thugs would work hard to get it back. They were providing a genuine service (albeit with menaces), and they took a dim view of smaller operations trying to muscle in on their turf.

SIC, VIS, and later TIM became huge operations, diversifying into many branches of the economy, licit and illicit. It often seemed as if these people and not the government were in charge of the country. "We are not just talking about these thick necks with gold chains taking the best seats in one's favorite restaurant," exploded one European diplomat unable to contain his disgust. "They had the cheek and the confidence to block off entire thoroughfares in the center of Sofia just because they wished to lunch undisturbed by the traffic!"

Some oligarchs outsourced part of their security requirements to SIC and VIS. Others preferred to build up their own in-house goon squad. Later on, Ilya Pavlov was careful to dissociate himself from them. But earlier, he was close friends with several of the most prominent gangsters. Most notably, he worked with one of SIC's bosses, Mladen Mihailev, known to all as Madzho, not least because Madzho started his career as Ilya's chauffeur. To blame Ilya Pavlov for choosing this life that veered between gross corruption, grand larceny, frontier capitalism, and organized crime would be unfair. He was not an especially moral person. But he took his opportunity at a time when the Bulgarian state had all but collapsed. People were discovering all over Eastern Europe that when the country goes into freefall, the law is the first thing crushed under the rubble of transformation. Capitalism had not existed until 1989, and so the hopelessly weak states that emerged throughout the former Soviet Union and Eastern Europe had simply no capacity to define what was "legal" and what was "illegal." They had neither the money nor the experience to police the novelty of commercial exchange. Those who positioned themselves well in the first three years after the end of Communism were often in a position to make up the rules of their brave new world as they went along.

The cross-border nature of the stolen car trade ensured that the emerging Bulgarian syndicates established links with similar groups in other Balkan and East European countries. Each developed a reputation for being especially good in the trading of particular commodities. In the former Yugoslavia, for example, it was arms and cigarettes. In Bulgaria, it was cars. In Ukraine, it was the trafficking of migrant labor as well as women. Everyone shifted narcotics.

Hungary and Czechoslovakia had a special place in the new crime networks, thanks to the close economic and commercial links that they had established over the previous decade with their neighbors Germany and Austria. But as former socialist countries, they still maintained a visa-free regime with the rest of Eastern Europe. Kazakhs, Georgians, Bulgarians, Moldovans, Yugoslavs, and Latvians could settle temporarily in either country without difficulty.

So, of course, could the Russians.

An especially lively currency exchange market emerged in Hungary that became an early center for major money-laundering operations. Such was its appeal as a base for transnational criminal operations that the most powerful Russian mafia groups selected Budapest as their forward base in central Europe as they sought to expand their activities westward. "When the Russians came, they forced the new Bulgarian mafia out of Hungary and into Czechoslovakia," explained Yovo Nikolov, Sofia's leading expert on Bulgarian organized crime. "It started off with car smuggling but then the guys noticed something else."

That something else was the *silnice hanby,* or Highway of Shame—the highway that linked Dresden and Prague via the heart of Czechoslovakia's heavy industry complex, northern Bohemia. In a depressed and chaotic economic climate, young Czech women began selling themselves on the E55 for pocket money. For the price of a modest meal, the teenagers would satisfy the desires of the ceaseless column of sweaty BMW drivers and overweight truckers cruising between Bohemia and Saxony.

"People are coming from all over Eastern Europe to the 'affluence border' in order to offer young prostitutes to aging German men," noted *Der Spiegel* at the time. The national aspect to this sexual *Drang nach Osten* gave the sordid trade an added frisson, as many punters were East German (so there were a few sweaty Trabant drivers among the BMWs).

Women working on the Highway of Shame were, on the whole, exercising choice—to be sure, their economic circumstances compelled them to work as prostitutes, but they were not physically coerced. A minority was forced into the trade by individual pimps, but a majority worked voluntarily in order to earn a living in this way. A large percentage was made up of young Gypsy or Roma women who faced a double dose of prejudice as prostitutes and as Roma.

The Bulgarian heavies milling around Prague and northern Bohemia noticed the virtual absence of any effective policing of this spontaneous sex trade. The potential market was huge—it was well known how thousands of German men traveled every year to Southeast Asia and the Caribbean to indulge in sex tourism. Why not take advantage of that demand by offering them beautiful young women at low, low prices just over the German border, in slightly more relaxing surroundings than the rest stops of the E55? So Bulgarian gangs bought up, built, or rented cheap motels in north Bohemia. With the aim of maximizing their profits, they sought out pliant women who were not so well connected with the local community. So they sought out their compatriots. In contrast to the local Czech women, however, these Bulgarian women did not enter into the trade voluntarily—they had no idea what awaited them.

Nineteen-year-old Stanimira shared a dingy apartment in the polluted Danubian port of Ruse in northern Bulgaria when her flatmate suggested breaking out. "She told me she had a great job as a shop assistant and I could get one too with a wage of about 3,000 DM a month.* From Bulgaria we went straight to Dubi in the Czech Republic via Hungary and Slovakia. The first thing I noticed about the apartment building when we got there was that all the windows were barred."

The building in the northern Czech town of Dubi belonged to a former Bulgarian muscleman, and it was positioned just off the Highway of Shame. In his early forties, Tsvetomir Belchev had trod the familiar path of graduating from a sports academy in Razgrad, Bulgaria, before drifting into a life of crime. At nineteen, he was sentenced to twelve years' imprisonment for attempted murder, and not long after his release, he was back in prison. "From his prison cell, he then founded the political party Renewal in defense of the rights of prisoners," his file at the Bulgarian Interior Ministry explains, suggesting that he was an extremely intelligent inmate. "In this capacity, he organized prison strikes, riots, and protests throughout 1990. He then ran for president the following year." As his political career petered out, Belchev moved to the Czech Republic to investigate business opportunities away from the prying eyes of the Bulgarian police. His mother acted as scout for girls back home.

On arrival, Stanimira was told that she would not be working as a waitress but as a prostitute. At first she refused point-blank to cooperate. "Belchev beat me black and blue, hitting and kicking me, in the pavilion opposite the Sport Hotel. He kicked me with hobnailed shoes. He kicked my back, and used a chair too. He summoned his mates, Krassi and 'Blackie,' on the walkie-talkie, and ordered them to beat me too. I was taken

*About $1,500 at the time—a fabulous salary for any unemployed Bulgarian.

down to the cellar, where the two went on kicking and hitting me, mainly in the abdomen. Blackie clasped my head and struck me with fists. When I passed out, they poured water over me and when I came around they handcuffed me by one hand to the radiator pipe. I was in excruciating pain. I was handcuffed there all day. Belchev then raped me in one of the rooms in the country house."

When police finally raided the Dubi brothel in the summer of 1997, the forty women they rescued there had all been tortured and raped by Belchev and his henchmen. During their imprisonment, the women were required to earn a minimum of $3,000 per month (naturally, they never saw any of this money). Failure to do so resulted in beatings, as did any hint of insubordination (Belchev ran a system of informers among the women). A refusal to sleep with any of the gang led to both rape and beatings, and the Czech investigators' suspicion that at least one girl had been murdered was confirmed a few years after Belchev's arrest when they found a corpse buried in the brothel grounds. Invariably young and frightened, deprived of their passports, unable to speak the local language, and ostracized in any event as prostitutes, the women were entirely dependent on their tormentors.

The Belchev case was a rarity because he was actually busted, the racket broken up, and the women freed (astonishingly, Belchev continued to manage three brothels from his prison cell using a mobile phone his lawyer smuggled in to him). But elsewhere before the dust from the Berlin Wall had even settled, gangsters and chancers were laying the cables of a huge network of trafficking in women that reached into every corner of Europe. Bulgarian gangs quickly assumed a pivotal role in this industry due to their country's strategic position. Every border offered a lucrative trade. South to Greece represented the quickest route into the European Union—once across that border, the women could be transported anywhere in the EU (excepting Britain and Ireland) without having to pass a single police control. The southeastern route to Turkey was reserved for the burgeoning sale of women to the Middle East, in particular to the United Arab Emirates. The road west led to the traffickers of Macedonia and Albania (and then later Kosovo as well), where the demand side grew exponentially as soon as the first peacekeepers were deployed in 1994 as part of the UN Preventive Deployment (the bulk of the internal Balkan trafficking is based on UN peacekeepers and international civil servants). Traveling north, the gangs would transport women to the Czech Republic and Germany before making the return journey in a stolen car.

There was some overlap between the traffickers of women and the car smugglers. They certainly shared routes and expenses, but police have since identified them as separate enterprises. As a general rule, trafficking in women is performed by small cellular groups who pass their commodity on from region to region, unaware of where their buyer is taking them. Wide-scale car theft is more complex, requiring the direction of larger and better-organized syndicates. Despite the overlapping of most commodities and services (especially regarding the routes they travel), it is the commodity, its geographical origin, and its destination that usually determine whether it is traded and distributed by a large syndicate or by a small one.

Women are attractive as an entry-level commodity for criminals. They can cross borders legally and they do not attract the attention of sniffer dogs. The initial outlay is a fraction of the sum required to engage in car theft; overhead costs are minimal; and as a service provider, the commodity (a trafficked woman) generates income again and again. Just one woman can make between $5,000 and $10,000 per month for her trafficker. These calculations do not take into account the frightful reality of multiple rape and unspeakable exploitation. But neither the supplier (the gangster) nor the consumer (a rich West European) understands this relationship in anything other than economic terms. The former lives in an environment that is scarcely regulated or policed—if he does not sell this woman, somebody else will. The latter is apparently able to leave his conscience at the cloakroom with his hat and coat.

Police forces throughout Eastern Europe found the transition to capitalism exceptionally hard. Many people reviled them for their previous complicity in repressing opponents under Communism. The drudgery of policemen's lives in the new democracies contrasted with the playboy lifestyle that some former colleagues enjoyed as they helped to build huge criminal empires. In the new market conditions, a policeman's paycheck was risible—every time I drove through Bulgaria, Yugoslavia, or Romania in the years immediately following Communism's collapse, I would be forced to pay at least fifty dollars in informal fines levied by impoverished traffic cops. The rule of law, so crucial for building confidence in these embattled societies, was a fiction.

Then—and not for the last time—the West did something really, really dumb. On May 30, 1992, the UN Secretary Council in New York passed Resolution 754, which imposed economic sanctions on Serbia and Montenegro. The Balkans, war ravaged, impoverished, and traumatized, was about to be transformed into a smuggling and criminal machine that had few if any parallels in history. While the world wrung its hands and fretted over the terrible nationalist urges of the Yugoslav peoples and their leaderships, the Balkan mafias started putting aside their ethnic differences to engage in a breathtaking criminal collaboration. This would in turn reach out to counterparts across the globe, bringing together the mafias of Colombia, Russia, and the Golden Triangle, to name but the most influential. It took the "international community" years to get even an inkling of what was going on.

CHAPTER 2

Bloody Lucre

Five minutes, Dick," snapped Sandy Berger, national security adviser to Bill Clinton. "He gets five minutes with the president and no more." Dick Sklar was disappointed. He felt the president of Montenegro, Milo Djukanovic, deserved more time with his U.S. counterpart. But Berger was unequivocal.

Sklar had worked for several years behind the scenes as an indefatigable fixer on behalf of Clinton. He knew the president's views on the Balkans well, but he was taken aback by the short shrift given to the youthful Djukanovic. Admittedly, the president of Montenegro represented an obscure mountainous statelet in the Balkans, the butt of fictional jokes from John Buchan to Agatha Christie. But as Sklar pointed out, "Djukanovic had been our most courageous ally during the Kosovo campaign." And victory in that war was why Clinton and his team were in such a sunny mood that mid-June 1999 when they arrived in Slovenia, the Alpine state nestled between the Balkans and central Europe.

A couple of weeks earlier the Yugoslav military had sued for an armistice, to the palpable relief of Clinton and his closest advisers. It had been a tough war—not the one-week pushover that some senior administration officials had predicted in advance of hostilities. Now the president had traveled to Europe to express America's gratitude to its eighteen NATO allies and to other supporters for staying the course.

Montenegro was a younger sibling to Serbia's capriciously violent elder brother in the dysfunctional federal family called Yugoslavia. But although Montenegro's airports, harbors, and borders were controlled by the Yugoslav military during the Kosovo war, the willowy pro basketball player

Balkan smuggling routes in the 1990s

turned Montenegrin president had emerged as a thorn in the flesh of Serbia's dictator, Slobodan Milosevic. Not only did Djukanovic support Western policy (despite having suffered since 1992 under the UN's stringent economic sanctions), but he provided a safe haven for Milosevic's opponents, ensuring that dissent in Serbia was not stifled. Milosevic bullied and threatened Djukanovic, but the Montenegrin held his nerve—and that took guts.

Djukanovic's war had been uniquely awkward. NATO had bombed dozens of targets in Montenegro during the campaign, and yet he supported these attacks on his own republic by a foreign aggressor.

These risks taken on behalf of the West, Dick Sklar felt, had earned Djukanovic more than five minutes' chitchat at the Brdo Castle north of the Slovene capital, Ljubljana. But as soon as the two presidents sat down, Sklar was able to relax: Clinton warmed to Djukanovic immediately and they cast protocol aside, spending more than an hour talking on all manner of subjects—on Milosevic, on the war, on Kosovo, and on the future of the Balkans. Djukanovic later expressed his pleasure at Clinton's knowledge of Montenegrin history—as ever, the U.S. president had done his homework. But there was one subject they touched on about which Djukanovic was uncharacteristically coy: cigarettes. An odd subject, perhaps, for a nonsmoker like Clinton to raise. But he had been informed that cigarettes were Djukanovic's biggest vice, and he felt compelled to issue his Montenegrin counterpart with a health warning.

Throughout most of the 1990s, Djukanovic's country, Montenegro, with a population of just 650,000 (regarded by the rest of the Balkans as a legendarily indolent people), was the focal point of a multibillion-dollar criminal industry that generated income from America through the Middle East, central Asia, the Maghreb, the Balkans, and western Europe.

Week after week, several tons of illegal cigarette shipments would land at the country's two main airports before being transferred swiftly to the port of Bar. In the spring of 1996, I recall speeding along empty Montenegrin roads in keen anticipation of the view that would greet me when I hit the Adriatic coast just north of Lake Shkoder. The bright yellow cliff fell sheer hundreds of feet to the dramatic coastal road. The sea in this part of the Adriatic is a deep crystal blue, free from the green-black gunk that Italy's industrial behemoths spew out along the Adriatic's northwestern coastline. But when I looked down at the port of Bar on this occasion, I also saw dozens of tiny little speedboats cluttered closely in the marina. Packed with contraband cigarettes, they were all revving up for the short 130-mile hop across the Strait of Otranto and to their sister port of Bari, where the Italian Mafia group called the Sacra Corona Unità (SCU) was waiting to unload them.

Each carton of smokes was subject to what Milo Djukanovic styled a "transit tax." Milosevic in Belgrade had throttled the flow of federal funds to Montenegro to a trickle, and so, Djukanovic argued, the "transit tax" was the only way to keep his little state on its feet and free from Serbian pressure.

Everybody in the Balkans knew the region was a center of the illicit trade in cigarettes. Soon after the outbreak of war in the former Yugoslavia in 1991, little boys as young as six would sneak in and out of restaurants in Zagreb, Belgrade, and Sarajevo, the wooden trays hanging from their necks neatly stacked with the best-quality Western cigarettes. On the sidewalks, old men with the craggy features born of a lifetime of committed puffing were positioned every twenty-five yards, offering Winston and Marlboro in cartons of ten-packs. In London these would cost seventy-five dollars, in New York maybe forty. But all over the Balkans, they cost just ten bucks each. That price differential made smoking an entirely affordable bad habit, even in the harsh conditions of war. More than half of people in the Balkans smoked—this was a rich market.

I had a regular supplier, a cheeky lad from Belgrade called Micko, with tousled brown hair. (Dear readers, rest assured that I have since rid myself of the addiction.) It was important to build a relationship of trust with your smoke supplier because there were two types of illegal cigarettes, indistinguishable to the naked eye but very different. One was produced with low-grade local tobacco and then packaged as a Western product. It looked like the genuine article but it tasted like sawdust mixed with goat droppings—counterfeit.

The second cigarette was high quality, produced by Western tobacco companies as a duty not paid (DNP) item, designated for export. Purchased direct from the factories in America, Europe, and Japan, the merchandise was then sent to Europe's two free trade zones, Rotterdam in Holland and Zug in Switzerland. From here they would be sold on to a third country with high levels of corruption—perhaps Egypt, perhaps Uzbekistan. Officials and organized crime syndicates levied a tax at every step of the journey, and those aimed at the European Union market would make their final stop in Montenegro before reentering the EU by speedboat. Even with everybody taking a cut in this fashion (the customs officer in Egypt, the director of ports in Romania, and so on), the cigarettes were nonetheless more than 50 percent cheaper when sold on the black market in Italy or Britain, because taxation on tobacco in these countries is so high.

Bloody Lucre

After an eight-year investigation into the trade, European Union prosecutors finally filed a lawsuit in October 2002, accusing two U.S. firms, R.J. Reynolds and Phillip Morris, of complicity in the trade, although in 2004 Philip Morris struck a deal with the EU, releasing the company from any liability. It also agreed to work with the EU against mafia penetration of the tobacco trade. R.J. Reynolds denies any complicity. The charges leveled were wide-ranging, including the claim that the Balkan cigarette trade was linked to the laundering of Colombian drug money. The lawyers included a detailed breakdown of how President Djukanovic and his associates made hundreds of millions of dollars from smuggling. Two Montenegrin companies, both controlled by Djukanovic and the secret service, levied thirty dollars on each case transited through the country. "This money was divided up among various Montenegrin officials involved in this business and who controlled the licenses to ship cigarettes through Montenegro," said the EU court submission. The second company, with the disarmingly frank name Montenegrin Tabak Transit (MTT), was co-owned by Italians suspected of Mafia links. "MTT was created by certain members of organized crime in conjunction with Montenegrin government officials. The company was officially sanctioned by the Montenegrin Foreign Investment Agency and operated under the special protection of Milo Djukanovic," the EU document claimed.

As early as 1994, the EU had learned that the cigarette mafia with whom Djukanovic did his business was costing it an estimated $6–8 billion annually in lost tax revenue alone, largely in Italy and the United Kingdom. Italian prosecutors were desperate to indict Djukanovic on charges of smuggling and of maintaining links with the Mafia. Yet at the same time, the United States sent discreet messages to the government in Rome, requesting that the Italians lay off Djukanovic. Washington needed the Montenegrin president in its battle against Milosevic.

Djukanovic claims that the annual revenue from the tobacco trade was $30 million and that with this he was able to pay for most of the state's running costs. In 1998, when the Italians were looking to indict Djukanovic, Dick Sklar was sent to Rome to negotiate on behalf of the West's Balkan ally. Sklar posed the eminently logical question "Why don't you just pay him the $30 million and then he'll close down the trade?" The Italians refused (quite illogically), but by the time Clinton met Djukanovic in the summer of 1999, the Kosovo war had been won and so the Montenegrin president was no longer quite so valuable as an ally. Washington was now telling him that if he wanted closer relations with NATO and the EU, it was time to get out of the cigarette business. "After the meeting with Clinton, I told Milo that he had now put on a clean starched shirt and he had to stop getting those shirts messed up by the nasty company he had been keeping," Sklar explained. By October 2001, British intelligence finally reported that Montenegro had reined in the speedboat traders. Djukanovic had gotten the message and acted upon it.

During the 1980s and 1990s, a huge discrepancy in wealth had emerged between Western and Eastern Europe. Never before had so many West Europeans (about 75 percent) lived not only above the poverty line but in secure comfort. In the second half of the 1990s, there was much debate about whether the affluent countries of Western Europe could maintain their expensive welfare systems in the face of a rapidly aging population and a fatal antipathy toward labor migration into the EU. The appearance of dynamic young economies in Eastern Europe put this problem in a yet starker perspective as Poles, Czechs, Hungarians, and others proved willing to put in longer hours for less money as they sought to make up for half a century of consumer misery under Communism. Growth rates in Eastern Europe began shooting up after the fall of the Berlin Wall. Germany was busy outsourcing its industrial base throughout Poland, the Czech Republic, Slovakia, and Hungary, while the European Union accession program meant that huge sums in regional development funds were fighting poverty and assisting in the development of democratic institutions in Eastern Europe. Ordinary people still moaned about how difficult life was economically under capitalism, but after an initial dip, living standards began to pick up.

A very different fate awaited people in the Balkans. Here there was no light of prosperity at the end of the tunnel. The malign rule of nationalist leaders bent on war led to a grinding, debilitating collapse in incomes and lifestyles. They were surrounded by successful Europeans, and culturally they still felt like Europeans. They watched European television programs and took part in European sporting events, and they were aware of how rich their neighbors were. Furthermore, on those rare occasions when they were allowed to travel to their European Union neighbors, they faced frequent humiliation at the hands of immigration officers. Finally, they had to run the gauntlet of Balkan stereotyping, which presented them as natural-born killers and only happy when slitting throats. Juxtapose this miserable desert characterized by unemployment, stagnation, and violence to a boundlessly rich, fertile paradise, and should we wonder how powerful the temptation is to become involved in organized crime?

Djukanovic's entanglement with the mob was the rule, not the exception. More than in any other Communist country, politics and organized crime became tangled in a tight knot throughout the former Yugoslavia as it descended into a frightful fratricidal civil war at the beginning of the 1990s. Organized crime controlled dictators, opposition politicians, liberals, nationalists, and democrats alike, and vice versa.

Most shocking of all, however, is how the gangsters and politicians fueling war between their peoples were in private cooperating as friends and close business partners. The Croat, Bosnian, Albanian, Macedonian, and Serb moneymen and mobsters were truly as thick as thieves. They bought, sold, and exchanged all manner of commodities, knowing that the high levels of personal trust between them were much stronger than the transitory bonds of hysterical nationalism. They fomented this ideology among ordinary folk in essence to mask their own venality. As one commentator described it, the new republics were ruled by "a parastate Cartel which had emerged from political institutions, the ruling Communist Party and its satellites, the military, a variety of police forces, the Mafia, court intellectuals and with the president of the Republic at the center of this spiderweb . . . Tribal nationalism was indispensable for the cartel as a means to pacify its subordinates and as cover for the uninterrupted privatization of the state apparatus."

As a consequence of war, sanctions, and corruption in the Balkans during the first half of the 1990s, the states of the former Yugoslavia turned to and nurtured mafias to run the logistics of their military effort, and it was not long before the criminals were in control of the economy, the government, and the war. Anyone with any serious political ambition had no choice but to get mobbed up.

Eight years earlier, in February 1991, before Clinton met Djukanovic, before the term "ethnic cleansing" had been invented, and before the outside world had heard of Kosovo, I was sitting with friends in the elegant baroque center of Croatia's capital, Zagreb. Anxiety was written on their faces, as credible rumors were spreading that the Yugoslav military was about to launch a coup to stop Croatia from declaring independence. The anxiety turned to fear when the authorities in Yugoslavia's federal capital, Belgrade, announced the suspension of normal TV programming for two hours that evening. Instead, the main state channel would broadcast a film alleging a major criminal conspiracy inside the country. Along with the country's frightened, fragmenting peoples, I watched footage caught by a concealed black-and-white camera of three men mumbling inaudibly across a sparse wooden table in a modest kitchen. Subtitles had been helpfully added by Yugoslavia's military counterintelligence service, KOS, who had created the film. There was no mistaking the squat shape of the main actor in the film. It was the new defense minister of the proto-Croatian state and a close collaborator of the Croat nationalist president Franjo Tudjman.

The man selling the minister large amounts of illegal weaponry for the Croats was not a Hungarian arms dealer, as he claimed, but a Serb and an agent of KOS. He was also a founding member of Multigroup, Ilya Pavlov's megacompany in Bulgaria. In Eastern Europe, KOS had no peers; its penetration of the new criminalized structures of neighboring countries such as Bulgaria as early as 1990 was ample demonstration of its power and reach.

The film aimed to prove that President Tudjman was planning an armed uprising. In their wars for independence from Yugoslavia, the Croats and Bosnians faced one huge challenge: Yugoslavia boasted the Serb-dominated Yugoslav People's Army (JNA), the fourth-biggest military in the world, which possessed a sizable if aging arsenal. The great majority of Croat and Bosnian officers in the JNA went over to their local governments to fight for secession. But their nascent armed forces desperately needed weapons. This became all the more urgent when the United Nations imposed an arms embargo on all the Yugoslav republics three months after the fighting broke out in June 1991. In order to stand a chance of winning the war, first Croatia and then, a year later, Bosnia had to find ways of importing weapons despite the international ban.

The Croat diaspora in the new world has never been as prominent as that of its Mediterranean neighbors, the Italians, the Greeks, or even the Albanians, but it is quietly effective and fiercely patriotic, notably in central Canada, Ohio in the United States, Australia, and above all else in South America. The South American community is regarded as the most nationalistic of all, as many Croatian fascists fled here at the end of World War II. Immediately after the UN imposed the arms embargo in 1991, Argentina's president, Carlos Menem, signed a secret decree allowing the sale of 6,500 tons of weaponry to Panama. The shipment was in fact diverted to Croatia on vessels of the state-owned Croatia Line. Menem followed this up with a second secret deal, authorizing the sale of $51 million worth of arms to Bolivia. An official investigation in Argentina later revealed that the consignment was rerouted to Croatia: "8,000 automatic rifles, 18 155mm cannons, 2,000 automatic pistols, 211,000 hand grenades, 3,000 Pampero rockets, 30,000 rifle grenades, 3,000 mines, 60 mortars, and several million rounds of ammunition."

When a year later the Muslim-dominated government of Bosnia-

Hercegovina found itself squeezed between the two Christian armies of Croatia and Serbia, it appealed to its co-confessionals to break the UN weapons embargo and supply it with the means to defend itself. Between 1992 and 1995, Saudi Arabia, Iran, Turkey, Brunei, Pakistan, Sudan, and Malaysia deposited some $350 million into the bank account of a Muslim charitable organization in Vienna, and the money was then used to purchase weapons.

The arms embargo played a key role in establishing the smuggling channels to Croatia and Bosnia, and soon drugs were accompanying the guns along the same routes. But this was nothing compared with the Balkan-wide impact of the comprehensive UN *economic* sanctions imposed on the rump of Yugoslavia, comprising Serbia (including the troubled province of Kosovo, with a large Albanian population) and Montenegro. The UN imposed the sanctions in July 1992 because Serbia was aiding the Bosnian Serb military in violation of earlier Security Council resolutions.

Unlike the Croats and Bosnians, Serbia and its allies in Bosnia were not short of weaponry. But with the sanctions in place, Belgrade needed to guarantee oil supplies and it needed to find goods to export to pay for the business of waging war. Just as Serbia allowed weapons from Romania and Bulgaria to reach their enemies in Croatia and Bosnia via Serbian territory, so were the Bosnians, Croats, and Albanians more than happy to sell oil to their Serbian enemies because of the extraordinary profits that a sanctions regime generates. These profits were then split between the state, which purchased more weapons with them, and the deep pockets of the mafia.

In a darkened café, I listened to a former business partner of Vladimir "Vanja" Bokan, the man who as a thirty-year-old had opened Hannibal, Belgrade's first private clothes boutique, in 1985. My interlocutor warned me that if I identified him, he would soon be dead. "And they'll probably kill you too," Mr. X. added for emphasis. After this somber introduction, however, he warmed to his subject. "At first we would travel to Italy and buy designer clothes in bulk, which we sold in Hannibal. But then Vanja had a better idea—we called it the Dazzle," he explained. "He'd order the clothes from Romania—the dazzle. They were perfect—you couldn't tell them apart from the Italian original—and then he'd sell them as originals for an enormous markup in the shop. In order to get goods like these previously, people had to go on an expensive trip to Italy."

Bokan was restless, dynamic, and intelligent. His mother was a pediatrician and his father had worked as an engineering consultant to the

United Nations, so Vanja had grown up in such exotic places as Indonesia and South America. He was a talented linguist who spoke Greek, Italian, and English alongside Serbo-Croat. Full of ideas, Bokan was a natural-born entrepreneur. When he opened his boutiques in Belgrade and Novi Sad, and later his workshops across the Balkans, he was a model capitalist, seizing the opportunities that the collapse of Communism and the embrace of the West enabled. Even before the outbreak of the wars in the early 1990s, he had diversified the company, importing and exporting all manner of goods to and from Yugoslavia. His business was entirely legal; he was forging economic ties between a former Communist country and the European Union; and he was creating both revenue for the state and work for Yugoslavia's growing band of unemployed.

But in 1992 the war with Bosnia and UN sanctions intervened, altering his business environment. The vote imposing an embargo on Yugoslavia immediately rendered all Bokan's trade illegal in international law, as Serbia was the center of his trading empire.

Sanctions had a negligible impact on the European Union and America. Most Western companies could afford to stop trading with Belgrade, an insignificant market, especially as their governments threatened tough penalties if anybody violated them. Serbia lies at the heart of all Balkan trading routes—its roads and its markets are almost as essential for its neighbors as they are for Serbia itself. The UN, of course, issued warnings to the surrounding countries that they must break all links with Serbia and Montenegro. For Balkan countries, the sanctions were a catastrophe.

Even though the Bulgarian government could no longer officially buy and sell to Serbia, businessmen such as Ilya Pavlov felt less constrained. Yugoslavia's military counterintelligence, KOS, used its influence in Multigroup and encouraged Pavlov to borrow railcars from the government in order to send millions of gallons of gasoline into Serbia by train. They were accompanied by members of the SIC, one of the two largest protection rackets in Bulgaria, and waved through by customs officers whose measly pay packets meant that their allegiance was easily purchased. The then U.S. ambassador to Sofia, Bill Montgomery, remembers how the Bulgarian state was in fact deeply involved from the start: "An embassy officer was passing the western border by chance at night when he noticed there were a lot of police around with flashlights. He pulled over and just watched what happened. Along came 100 oil tankers—he counted them—rumbling through the night before being directed across the border by the Bulgarian police."

Bulgaria's main route to the rest of Europe was through Serbia. The United Nations Security Council had already told Sofia to kiss good-bye the $1 billion it was owed by Saddam's Iraq when it imposed sanctions on Baghdad. Now the UN was telling Bulgaria it could not send its trucks through Serbia. This was devastating, as the country's most important exports to Western Europe were perishable. "Bulgaria had a GDP of $10 billion and on the fruit and vegetables alone they lost $1 billion of income annually," explained Bill Montgomery. "I proposed that we allow the Bulgarians to send a weekly convoy through Serbia, which would be accompanied by a UN vehicle at the head and a UN vehicle at the tail. They would not stop but travel straight through. The UN signed off on this; the Europeans signed off on this; but Leon Furth, adviser to the vice president, Al Gore, was opposed and he blocked it. He was not to be moved and it was very frustrating." Frustrating, and furthermore a cheering boost to organized crime, which thrived on the economic distress such myopic policies promoted.

Not a penny of assistance or compensation was offered to Yugoslavia's neighbors—they were all expected to shoulder the costs of the international community's moral indignation about Serbia's behavior in Bosnia. So the only way they could pay pensions, wages, and health care was by allowing the mob to shore up its control of the country's main trading routes, and claim ignorance, helplessness, or both. As the crisis deepened, so did this damaging symbiotic relationship between politics and crime.

In Serbia itself, Vanja Bokan was quick to arrange shipments of oil and metals into Yugoslavia. Criminals and businessmen throughout the region worked feverishly to create a dense web of friendships and networks to subvert the embargo. Virtually overnight, the vote at the UN Security Council ordering sanctions created a pan-Balkan mafia of immense power, reach, creativity, and venality.

Some inside the U.S. administration had warned President Clinton of such dangerous consequences. One senior member of the U.S. Treasury told me, "We made it plain to our colleagues in the White House that you could never break Serbia with sanctions. The Serbs were self-sufficient in food, and given its centrality to the regional economy, the neighbors were bound to continue trading with them." Like so many warnings about the deleterious impact of sanctions, this one was ignored.

Soon everyone was following Vanja Bokan's example by selling oil to Serbia from wherever they could get their hands on it. The Romanians floated barges almost sinking under the weight of their appallingly low-grade oil. "In Albania," a U.S. intelligence report noted, "imported oil was shipped via pipeline across the northern border, by boat across Lake Shkoder, by caravans of cars with extra fuel tanks added, by donkeys carrying barrels of oil across mountainous regions. . . . The total oil flow was estimated to have brought Albania more than $1 million per day during 1993–1994." Despite being one of Serbia's harshest critics, Albania played a key role in supplying Belgrade with oil. "Barges were used to bring oil products from Ukraine," the report continued. "The volume of shipments along the Danube River attracted the interest of Serbian pirates who would cruise the Danube looking for fuel shipments to hijack. . . . Romanian oil products arrived by highway, by ship, and by an underground pipeline from the Romanian oil facility at Timisoara. Cars were refitted to carry as much as 500 gallons of fuel."

The sanctions-busting carnival was also, of course, an opportunity that Russian business could not let slip through its fingers. Gazprom, the oil and gas giant, agreed to a barter arrangement with Serbia. Using its surplus grain stocks, Serbia was able to exchange between $100 million and $250 million of oil a year from Gazprom.

By the time the gasoline reached the consumer in Belgrade, it was four times the price of fuel elsewhere in Europe. I would buy it by the side of the road in the district of Zemun. Petty traders sat on their jerricans and buckets full of gasoline (lit cigarettes hanging out of their mouth as a matter of course). Vehicles just pulled up beside them and the driver purchased two or three gallons of whatever was available. I developed a business relationship with a certain Stevo from Zemun, who for a consideration ensured that I got only high-quality gas from Hungary or Bulgaria and not the explosive low-grade mix from Romania, which, legend had it, would lead your engine to seize within hours.

The economies of the fragmented republics of the former Yugoslavia had been devastated—firms were often dependent on suppliers in countries they were now at war with; the export of industrial products to Eastern and Western Europe had collapsed. But still they were purchasing billions of dollars' worth of weapons, oil, food, consumer goods, and luxury goods every month. Although the majority of the population was becoming poorer by the day, a hugely wealthy new class of entrepreneurs and gangsters was visible on the streets of all Balkan cities. Ferraris, Porsches, and armored Mercedes and SUVs clogged up Zagreb, Belgrade, and elsewhere. Occasionally, the thick necks with shades would emerge from behind the smoked-glass windows. I well recall a terrified restaurant owner in Skopje, the capital of Macedonia, asking me to pay my bill and vacate my table in a hurry, as some special guests were arriving whom he did not wish to disappoint. As I saw the platoon of lobotomized bodybuilders stride into the establishment while I exited, I noticed that they weren't even Macedonian but Bulgarian—they treated foreign countries as their own.

These men carried guns with impunity and would sport the nationalist insignia of their particular tribe: the four Cs of Serbia, the lily of Bosnia, the eagle of Albania, or the checkerboard of Croatia. Because although they were quite happy to trade with their equivalents in enemy territories, most were hooked up with the vile militias that were busy slaughtering civilian populations in the war zones of Bosnia and Croatia. In Bosnia, the Serb forces who had locked Sarajevo in a siege were not the only thugs in town. Bosnia's own Muslim warlords controlled the entire economy of the city, trading with the Serb besiegers and then squeezing every last penny out of their compatriots by ratcheting up the price of basic foodstuffs, many of which were stolen from the United Nations and other humanitarian organizations.

Somehow this orgy of war and consumer excess had to be paid for. The former Yugoslav republics were no longer in a position to balance the books with their traditional exports, and so they decided to finance the war by other means. And because the industry of sanctions busting had now created a huge pan-Balkan network of organized crime (the members of which had no sense of ethnic loyalty when it came to trade), the easiest way of underwriting the affairs of state was through mafia business: drugs, arms, oil, weapons, women, and migrants. The foundations for a factory of crime had been laid.

Life as a sanctions buster and dodgy entrepreneur entailed risks. Competition for the illegal markets in the former Yugoslavia was tough, and spectacular assassinations of gangsters and businessmen became a regular feature of life in the capitals of Croatia, Serbia, Bosnia, and Montenegro. Bokan's wealth and market share were sufficient of themselves to make him a target. But he was still more vulnerable for another reason—he didn't like Slobodan Milosevic, the big boss of Serbia, and furthermore, he was not afraid of telling people.

Bokan's former partner, Mr. X., recalled one summer day in 1992 in Belgrade: "We were driving down Revolution Boulevard when a black Jeep drew up beside us. The passenger pulled out a semiautomatic and just started firing at us." Three of the five bullets lodged in Bokan's shoulder. It was time to lie low for a while, and so Bokan and his family moved to Greece. This proved an ideal base—Greeks were sympathetic to Serbs, and the country's northern port of Thessaloniki was by now one of the most important pivots of the growing sanctions-busting operation. "The Greek authorities did everything in their power to facilitate the violation of the embargo," Vanja admitted later. "For example, they never asked for Letters of Discharge. . . . They believed the embargo was unjust." Bokan secured citizenship in record time by using his contacts in Greek intelligence, and quickly established himself as a sparkling social light on the cosmopolitan stage that Athens had become since the fall of Communism. The Greek capital teemed in the early 1990s with Georgians, Hungarians, Albanians, Russians, Balts, and more. All were loaded, all were attracted by Greece's corruptible civil servants, and many claimed a Greek heritage and thereby an automatic right to a European Union passport.

Bokan also now turned his attention to Serbia's sister republic, Montenegro. In a curious echo of the experience of the Bulgarian Ilya Pavlov, Vanja Bokan's Montenegrin father-in-law was one of the top three generals of KOS, Yugoslav military counterintelligence. He introduced Bokan to Montenegro's leading politicians and businessmen, including the ambitious young prime minister, Milo Djukanovic. Linked by an entrepreneurial spirit, the two men were soon exploring possible areas of cooperation. The Black Pirate, as Bokan was known, had recently acquired two Ilyushin 76 transporter planes. At first, this looked like a poor investment, as NATO had imposed a no-fly zone over Serbia and Montenegro. But Bokan had uncovered a loophole that allowed planes to land in Montenegro "for technical purposes." With help from his new Montenegrin friends, Bokan came up with his billion-dollar idea—selling untaxed cigarettes to the Italian Mafia.

Bokan filled his cavernous Ilyushins with cigarettes imported to one of the free trade zones in Europe direct from the factories of all major tobacco manufacturers in America and Western Europe. Sometimes the planes would pick up the merchandise from airports in the Middle East or in central Asia, where their export paperwork was easily lost. They would then fly on to Malta or other apparently innocuous destinations in Europe but would be permitted the "technical landing" in Montenegro. "I get the cigarettes from America and dispatch them to Rotterdam using entirely legal channels," Bokan explained. "The cigarettes are formally destined for Romania but I divert them to Montenegro and then sell them to Italy," he added frankly. "The planes would be on the ground for the shortest time. They would land, unload, and then take off again while the cigarettes were taken off to storage or directly to the port."

At the harbor, they were packed on to the speedboats, and every night a swarm of tiny vessels buzzed across the Adriatic to the Italian province of Apulia. The province was home to one of the youngest and more chaotic but undoubtedly pugnacious Italian organized crime groups, the Sacra Corona Unità. "The Italian police and customs were in a hopeless position," said a Serb journalist who investigated the trade closely. "From the port of Ancona way to the north down to Bari, i.e., 300 miles of coastline, they initially possessed just *two* high-speed vessels capable of catching the Montenegrin speedboats of which there were dozens and dozens making the crossing every night!"

"Since 1992, Montenegro has become one gigantic marketplace for smuggled cigarettes," wrote the German state prosecutor who has been looking into the entire trade since 1994. Of course, the reason this impoverished state became involved is because men and women in the European Union don't like paying high taxes on cigarettes and are prepared to break the law themselves by buying them off the street. In north London one could buy stocks of untaxed cigarettes from a group of Kurdish and Kosovo Albanian sellers just outside the Safeway supermarket on the Holloway Road, a busy thoroughfare. A pack cost between £1.50 to £2.00, a savings of almost £3.00 on those sold with the tax included. Despite the tortuous journey these cigarettes had taken from the United States via Rotterdam, on to the eastern Mediterranean and then back through the Balkans, the dozens of people involved in the smuggling had all made a handsome profit, as the cost of cigarettes at the factory gate was a mere forty cents a pack. For many in the Balkans, this was the ultimate victimless crime—there is no opprobrium attached to the smoking habit in the Balkans, and the only people who lose out are the finance ministries of Europe. So who cares?

Bokan could run the cigarette business only with the approval of the government in Belgrade, which meant Slobodan Milosevic himself signed off on it even though the two men disliked each other. "He approved everything," Vanja's father-in-law, the KOS general, later admitted. So of course did Yugoslavia's mighty secret police forces, UDBA (civilian) and KOS (military). Unlike in all other East European countries, the establishment of nationalist dictatorships and the collapse into war in the former Yugoslavia meant that there was no campaign to strip the secret police of its power as happened in Bulgaria. Organized crime and secret police worked hand in glove throughout Yugoslavia; indeed, it was often impossible to distinguish one from the other. The criminalization of Yugoslavia thus surpassed all others in Eastern Europe. The consequences were violent and damaging.

. . .

Croats, Albanians, Macedonians, Montenegrins, and Serbs cooperated splendidly in shifting contraband, narcotics, and women from territory to territory. "Licensed" by governments and the security services, these were effectively horizontal cartels that stretched across several countries. One of the largest combined Turkish heroin gangs with Bulgarian, Serbian, Macedonian, and Albanian syndicates to shift the bulk of the heroin originating in Afghanistan into Western Europe. The cartel functioned smoothly during both the Kosovo and Macedonian wars at the turn of the millennium even though the front lines cut right across the smuggling route.

While collaboration with national enemies proved easy, the criminals faced serious threats from competitors on their home turf. In the hundreds of mob-associated murders between 1990 and 2007 in the Balkans, most were commissioned by compatriots of the victims—Serb-on-Serb or Croat-on-Croat violence was an everyday phenomenon.

One of the bloodiest episodes in Serbia was triggered by the "cigarette wars," breaking out when two new guys on the block decided they wanted to muscle in on Vanja Bokan's action. Both were very dangerous men. Stanko "Cane" Subotic, who had started a lowly tailor and an employee of Bokan's, eventually became the most powerful smuggler in Europe, residing in Switzerland with offices in Dubai. Cane exploited Bokan's reputed stinginess to move in on the Montenegro cigarette trade by offering co-conspirators higher cuts from his profits.

The second man was an amateur racing driver who built Bambiland, a faux Disneyland in his hometown of Pozarevac, Serbia. People treated this young gangster with utmost respect, as his name was Marko Milosevic, the son of the greatest Serbian capo, Slobodan Milosevic. The anti–organized crime unit in Serbia has detailed how Milosevic Junior ordered the bull-dozing of duty-free shops (a pivotal retail outlet for cigarettes) belonging to his competitors on Serbia's borders. It has also been uncovered that Slobodan Milosevic's wife, Mirjana Markovic, or the Lady Macbeth of the Balkans, persuaded the chief of customs to allow her son's contraband goods in and out of Serbia with impunity.

The emergence of these two competing syndicates was quickly followed in 1997 by the outbreak of political warfare between the presidents of Serbia and Montenegro, Milosevic and Djukanovic. Both men ruled over republics in which organized crime had usurped key positions in political and economic life; and both men used the security forces and gangsters to intimidate opponents. But Djukanovic realized that Milosevic's strategy of continually goading and challenging the West was unlikely to yield long-term dividends. Deploying his brisk, modern approach, Djukanovic announced that he wanted to emulate the other republics in the former Yugoslavia by leaving Serbia to become independent, and then strike out on a new, pro-Western course.

The political war soon degenerated into a real one. Within weeks, close associates of both presidents (almost all leading figures in the cigarette trade) were being whacked in broad daylight. Serbia's deputy interior minister was holding court in Belgrade's nouveau restaurant Mamma Mia, just a few yards from the British embassy, when he was pumped full of bullets from the submachine gun of an unknown assailant. The minister, an unreconstructed thug of whom Milosevic was especially fond, was murdered as he guarded DM 700,000 in cash (profits from cigarette sales). "He just got greedy," one of his colleagues in the Serbian security forces lamented. "He wanted to grab too much for himself and didn't cover his arse." Next it was the turn of Djukanovic's security chief, who, up to his neck in the business, was assassinated at his home. As his pistol was still in its holster (it was otherwise always cocked and ready to fire), most concluded that he fell victim to someone he trusted. "People were ordering murders like they were ordering cups of coffee," recalled one Serbian government minister after the fall of Milosevic. But while the roll call of corpses grew longer, the cigarettes kept moving and the money kept rolling in—and even though Milosevic and Djukanovic became the bitterest enemies, their representatives still managed to find a modus vivendi over distributing profits from the cigarettes. Arrangements were occasionally, however, complicated by unexpected funerals.

A mobbed-up country like Serbia is inherently unstable. Huge discrepancies between rich and poor become extremely visible; inefficiencies plague the economy; corruption becomes endemic; and leaders such as Milosevic are easily persuaded to engage in military adventures that eventually prove self-defeating. Defeat in the Kosovo war in 1999 unsettled Milosevic's criminal backers. There were signs that some major oligarchs and underground figures were tiring of the uncertainty their own mob rule perpetuated. And the rise of Milosevic's wife and son as the bosses of a major cartel generated widespread resentment among ordinary people and competitors alike. Then, six months after the Kosovo war had ended, an assassination took place in Belgrade, with immense consequences.

The cold in January 2000 would break records, and on Saturday the fifteenth, freezing fog had smothered the city for most of the day. Night had fallen and the temperature had begun a downward slide past zero. The blackness was pierced by the intense dark green light emanating from the Hotel Intercontinental, a desolate rectangular block that stands lonely over the Danube in New Belgrade. Just inside the building, a group of tough-looking men were slouched in the reception area's hideous 1970s leather sofa enclaves, discussing football and filling out betting slips. At 5:04 p.m. a former Belgrade cop, Dobrosav Gavric, emerged from the elevator and walked toward them. But as he reached the reception area he pulled out a gun and started shooting. Pandemonium reigned for about two minutes as the men sitting down returned fire. Gavric was hit in the back but saved from certain death by an accomplice who appeared from nowhere and hauled him through the entrance's revolving door and into a car, which the thick fog soon swallowed up as it sped toward a rendezvous with a second getaway vehicle.

Back inside the Intercontinental amid blood and wailing, the betting man who was known to his many admirers as the Commandant was breathing his last. He had received three bullets to the head, one of which had gone straight through his left eye into his brain. This was the pre-dictably inglorious end of Arkan, the most notorious crime boss in Bel-grade, who was wanted throughout Europe on charges of murder and armed robbery—"aggressive, armed and extremely dangerous," as the Interpol warrant described him. The Hague War Crimes Tribunal was also preparing a case against him for genocide, and even the thoroughly immoral Serbian dictator, Slobodan Milosevic, had a year earlier dubbed him "my greatest enemy," despite the fact that during the Yugoslav wars of the 1990s Arkan had soaked himself in blood on Milosevic's behalf.

But the Commandant had many friends, and indeed countless Serbs venerated him as the country's most glamorous celebrity. At the time of the killing, Zoran Djindjic, the opposition leader beloved by the West as a scourge of Milosevic and later as Serbia's first democratic prime minister, reacted to the assassination by declaring Arkan a close friend. "It was Arkan who warned me to flee to Montenegro during the Kosovo war because Milosevic intended to murder me," Djindjic explained later. (Indeed, with an eye to Serbia's democratic political future, Arkan had organized and paid for Djindjic's evacuation.) Gangsters, oppositionists, entertainers, supporters of Milosevic, opponents of Milosevic, soccer hooligans, the business fraternity, mourned Arkan in their hundreds of thousands. His reputation even extended to Italy. He had brokered the sale of some of Ser-bia's best soccer players to Lazio, and so fans of the Italian side had once rolled out a huge banner proclaiming HONOR TO ARKAN AND HIS TIGERS.

In 1995, Arkan had married Ceca, a buxom singer who had popularized

turbo-folk, the indigenous rock genre favored by Serbia's dissolute nationalist youth. The wedding saw Arkan emerge from St. Sava Cathedral in the
full-dress uniform of a First World War general. This image proved almost
as popular with photo editors around the world as when he had posed in
front of a tank in a paramilitary outfit holding a baby tiger (Milica, on hire
from the Belgrade Zoo) and presenting his cutthroat comrades from the
Serb Volunteer Guard, the "Tigers." The latter picture was carefully framed
to instill admiration and war fever in the Serbian masses and fear in the villagers of Bosnia and Croatia, whom he intended to kill or "cleanse." Early
in the Bosnian war, I remember being holed up in a hotel close to the Sarajevo airport under sustained attack from Serb forces. During this siege, we
noticed that all the Muslim villagers were packing their things and preparing to flee. "We've been told that Arkan and the Tigers are on their way,"
they explained to us hurriedly. Nothing was more effective in the business
of ethnic cleansing than the mere possibility of Arkan's imminent arrival.

Arkan was born Zeljko Raznatovic in 1952, the son of a Yugoslav air
force pilot. He enjoyed a relatively privileged upbringing but developed a
reputation as a tearaway in his teens, receiving his first prison sentence for
theft in Belgrade aged just seventeen. Unlike other East European countries
who were allied to the Soviet Union as members of the Warsaw Pact,
Yugoslavia professed neutrality in the cold war and permitted a small
degree of capitalist enterprise in its socialist system. Moreover, whereas
most citizens of the Soviet Bloc were imprisoned in their own countries,
unable to travel to the West, Yugoslavs enjoyed free access to Western
Europe. Hundreds of thousands traveled to Germany, Switzerland, and
Scandinavia to take up menial jobs, and this provided a milieu in which
less salubrious Yugoslav characters could take refuge and disappear from
the police if necessary. After his release from Belgrade prison in the early
eighties, Raznatovic decided to try his luck in this wider world. Throughout the seventies, his notoriety blossomed as he robbed, extorted, and
murdered his way across northern Europe. For these crimes, he was
imprisoned in Sweden, Holland, Belgium, and Germany, escaping at least
three times, often with the aid of false passports.

"When Bulgarian organized crime groups were emerging in the early
1990s, they came into contact with their Yugoslav counterparts for the first
time at the beginning of the war. And when they did, they had a big shock,"
explained General Boyko Borissov, the general director of the Bulgarian
Interior Ministry. "Our guys were just playing at being gangsters—the
Yugoslavs had been thieving and killing in Europe for real over decades.
They were seriously tough, and to this day, if you want to kill somebody in

Bulgaria and you want the job done reliably and cheaply, then you hire a Serb. They are the best assassins."

In 1983, Arkan was charged with the attempted murder of two Belgrade policemen. Under normal circumstances, this would have meant a lifelong lockup. But at his trial it emerged that he was an agent for UDBA, one of the most feared secret police operations in Eastern Europe. Arkan, it seems, had sold his outlaw's soul to Mephistopheles. The attempted murder charge was dropped and the two parties began a deep and fruitful relationship, which over the next eighteen years would bring Arkan great riches, beautiful women, power, and fame. Until, that is, Mephistopheles came to claim his soul on that cold winter night at the Intercontinental.

Arkan's killers were found, tried, and imprisoned, but they were simply hired hands. To this day, nobody has discovered who ordered the murder or why. But the consequences were profound, as the events that January afternoon triggered an unprecedented internecine battle among Serbia's gangs, known as Bloody Spring 2000. Less than a month after Arkan's death, the Yugoslav defense minister was exterminated while dining in a Belgrade restaurant. Thereafter assassinations and executions occurred on a weekly basis as Milosevic's final months began to resemble the fearful denouement of an Elizabethan revenge tragedy.

As he emerged from his Mercedes 500 in front of his villa in Athens early on the morning of October 7, 2000, Vanja Bokan's face was obliterated by twenty-nine bullets fired from a couple of semiautomatics. He too was a victim of the uncertain times. Two days earlier, the thirteen-year rule of Slobodan Milosevic had ended in the flames that engulfed Yugoslavia's parliament as half a million Serbs took to the streets of Belgrade in support of the opposition. Frustrated by the way he had been excluded from business in Serbia and Montenegro, Bokan had started to talk to the Greek press. In unprecedented detail, he had begun to reveal secrets of the cigarette trade, and he hinted that he was preparing to spill all the beans and name names. Gangsters are reluctant to wash their dirty laundry in public for understandable reasons—but Bokan had chosen an especially bad time to break the *omertà*.

Much of the killing that took place between Arkan's death in January 2000 and Milosevic's fall was in anticipation of the latter event. The leading mobsters, oligarchs, and secret police operatives were hedging their bets against a change in the regime. As Zoran Djindjic, the incoming democratic prime minister, admitted, several top bosses established discreet contact with him and his fellow opposition leaders in advance of Milosevic's demise. The new prime minister was characteristically frank about these events. "The mafia," he explained, "had lost the Milosevic state and so it was looking for a new one." Like all influential politicians, whether democratic or not, Djindjic commuted regularly between the gray and the black zones of the economy to fund his political activities—although his ultimate declared intention was to lead Serbia into the light. He was aware that a pair of clean hands and honest features were not sufficient to beat Milosevic and his criminal networks. So in the run-up to Milosevic's political collapse, Djindjic made deals with a number of criminal bosses who were not only involved in dirty business but also stained by complicity in war crimes in Bosnia, Kosovo, and elsewhere.

The rising kingpin in Belgrade was an extremely violent thug called Dusan Spasojevic, leader of the Zemun gang, which was named after a fashionable Belgrade suburb where he had built a preposterous nouveau riche mansion. Spasojevic hailed from south Serbia near Veliki Turnovac, a town with a majority Albanian population that had for decades been the Balkan pivot for the heroin smuggling industry. During the 1990s, Spasojevic had established a monopoly on the heroin trade in Belgrade so that according to the local police, "he was processing about 100 kilograms of hard drugs monthly—this was bringing him in tens of millions of dollars."

The chaos in Serbia at the turn of the millennium was mirrored by instability elsewhere in the former Yugoslavia. With a decade of brutal wars coming to an end, the region was now full of testosterone-fueled, unemployed young men, who were often well armed. The conflicts had also created hundreds of thousands of refugees, a majority of whom went to Western Europe, establishing efficient distribution networks for the illicit goods transiting the Balkans.

Naturally, cigarettes were not the only commodity traded across the Balkans and into the European Union. Neither did the Serbs and Montenegrins have a monopoly on these activities. Situated just below and across from the soft underbelly of Europe, the Balkan Peninsula has developed into the ideal transit zone for illicit goods and services from around the world from those seeking access to the most affluent consumer market in history—the European Union. Europeans could choose from a glittering array of consumer goods to ease their lifestyle and fill their leisure time. Despite the boundless choice of licit consumer goods, a significant section, including both the wealthy and the poor, sought to satisfy its needs outside the legitimate market. Organized crime is such a rewarding industry in the Balkans because ordinary West Europeans spend an ever-burgeoning amount of their spare time and money sleeping with prostitutes; smoking untaxed cigarettes; snorting coke through fifty-euro notes up their noses;

employing illegal untaxed immigrant labor on subsistence wages; stuffing their gullets with caviar; admiring ivory and sitting on teak; and purchasing the liver and kidneys of the desperately poor in the developing world.

With no wars left to fight, former paramilitaries became engaged full-time in the transit of heroin, cigarettes, labor migrants, and women into Western Europe. The Keystone Cops regime of the UN and NATO in Kosovo had no resources to combat the Albanian fighters from the Kosovo Liberation Army who had consolidated Kosovo as a new center for the distribution of heroin from Turkey to the European Union. Elsewhere, Bosnia and Hercegovina were mired in an early scandal involving UN peacekeepers and trafficked women and as the local money-laundering center. Macedonia was about to dissolve into a civil war that was provoked almost exclusively by a dispute between mafia groups over control of the illegal cigarette routes through the country.

Spurred by his success in moving heroin, Spasojevic wanted to expand his operations by trading in another drug—cocaine. "Cocaine is a rich man's drug—rich people, bigger profits, and Spasojevic wanted a piece," said Milos Vasic, Serbia's leading expert on organized crime. Spasojevic soon realized that he had hit a gold mine. Cocaine usage in Europe was rising everywhere, with significant new markets opening up in the former Communist countries of the East. Spasojevic quickly understood that he was not alone in wanting to exploit the Balkans' collapsing infrastructure. Another group of people had begun to monitor it very closely. These people lived far away in Colombia.

The 300-mile railroad ride west from the Brazilian border through dense Amazonian jungle in eastern Bolivia is known as *el tren de la muerte* because it is repeatedly targeted by bandits with scant regard for human life. Thieves perpetrate all manner of scams on this route; most notoriously they pass themselves off as Interpol officers in their efforts to mug unsuspecting foreigners. The relief on arrival in Santa Cruz is combined with shock, as much of the housing in Bolivia's eastern capital resembles the middle-class suburbs of Texas or California. Fueled by large gas deposits, which since the mid-1990s have attracted a host of multinationals into the region, the opulence of Santa Cruz seems a million miles from the desperate, inert poverty that affects most of Latin America's poorest country.

Apart from the energy sector, Santa Cruz is the center of Bolivia's commercial farming industry, which distributes vegetables and oils throughout the world. In late July 2003, managers of an import-export business in

Santa Cruz were finalizing the departure of two consignments, one bound for a clinic in Madrid consisting of 78 containers of medicinal clay. A second cargo, made up of some 770 boxes of powdered mashed potato, was being loaded onto trucks that were headed for Chile.

At nine-thirty in the morning, dozens of police from Bolivia's Special Force Against Narcotrafficking surrounded a Varig plane destined first for Brazil and then Spain. A few hours later, they stopped the trucks. The two tons of cocaine hidden among the medicinal clay was relatively easy to find. But it took two or three days for government chemists to discover that the mashed potato was infused with another three tons of cocaine. Even more baffling for the Bolivians was its destination—from Chile it was due to sail to the Black Sea port of Varna in Bulgaria.

The Santa Cruz bust was the culmination of Operation Moonlight, which included the cooperation of British intelligence, the Bulgarian police, Washington's Drug Enforcement Administration (DEA), the Spanish police, and the Bolivian Special Antitrafficking Force. Interestingly, the Bulgarian and Bolivian interior ministries had no idea of each other's role in the operation until the arrests were made. "This is the biggest transnational trafficking group we have ever monitored in Bolivia," said the government minister Yerko Kukoc at the time of the operation, "and the largest amount of cocaine ever seized."

The affair had begun just under a year before when a British intelligence officer passed on a mobile phone number to the Bulgarian police. "Frankly, it wasn't much to go on," said the officer in Sofia in charge of the case. But gradually, the Bulgarians pieced together an extraordinary story. A Colombian cartel (almost certainly from Medellín) arranged to smuggle a top chemist into Bulgaria, where he lived for several months. "The Colombian arrived in Greece using his real passport, then somebody from the group picked him up and brought him across the border illegally. His job was to train the Bulgarian chemists," added the policeman, "and he did a good job." It later emerged that a year before the mashed potato, the chemists had extracted 200 kilograms of cocaine from a shipment of soya oil that had arrived in Plovdiv via the same Santa Cruz–Varna route.

Ever since the collapse of Francoism, there had been two main centers for the import of cocaine into Europe. Spain had been the entry point of choice for South American coke smugglers as they cashed in on the habits of Europe's yuppies during the boom years of the 1980s. The reasons were obvious—the linguistic and cultural connections between Latin America and Spain allowed the establishment of a strong host community to receive and distribute the drugs. Spain also had a huge coastline, which is difficult to police. However, an improvement in cooperation between European police forces and the DEA, combined with a vigorous increase in the use of cocaine in Europe during the 1990s, meant that the Spanish route could no longer satisfy the demand.

Amsterdam, with a significant Colombian community, remained the pivotal distribution point for northern Europe, with the drugs arriving largely from Spain, Italy, and West Africa.

By the late nineties, the American cocaine market had reached super-saturation notwithstanding the billions of dollars pumped by successive U.S. governments into eradicating the coca industry. The price to the U.S. consumer dropped year on year, and so in response to these depressed market conditions, the Colombian producers sought out new marketing and distribution strategies. Not only did their research establish that the European markets were still underdeveloped, but they realized that with the collapse of the Berlin Wall, a new middle class, young and dynamic, was springing up in Eastern Europe and Russia. They wanted to increase their access to these markets by improving distribution. Like good global entre-preneurs, they took a leaf out of the corporate book and started to out-source production.

In the mid-nineties, the Colombian cocaine industry had experienced a thorough shake-up after the DEA and Colombian police destroyed the two main syndicates, the Medellín and Cali cartels. Unfortunately for the advo-cates of Washington's war on drugs, new, more effective syndicates soon emerged to replace the two dismantled cartels. Technology played a much greater part in the manufacturing, distribution, and security policies of the groups that filled the gaps left by Medellín and Cali. Younger and better-educated bosses were refining their marketing strategies, which they or their employees had learned at business schools in the United States. The poorly policed coastlines and corruptibility of Croatia, Albania, and Bul-garia represented a superb opportunity to ratchet up sales in Europe. In addition, the Colombians could make use of the high levels of education that were the legacy of Communism in the Balkans. Yugoslavia and Bul-garia abounded in highly qualified chemical engineers, and so the process-ing of cocaine could now be completed much closer to its final destination.

Since the end of the Kosovo war in 1999, the Balkans' role in the indus-try had been transformed. "Spain still accounts for almost half of the coke imported into Europe," the Bulgarian officer explained, "but in the past four years the Balkans has absorbed much of the rest of the traffic." The three tons of cocaine headed for Bulgaria in the mashed potato was a vast quantity, and altogether Operation Moonlight's catch was worth more than $300 million.

This was a truly transnational operation. The British and Italian police uncovered three tons of acetone on a ship harbored in Trieste en route to the Albanian port of Durres. "There's only one thing you use acetone for in those quantities," said the head of the Balkans unit of the National Crime Intelligence Service in London, "and that's processing coca paste into powder."

Then in 2003, a leading Bulgarian gangster had his head blown off in the crowded foyer of the five-star Sonesta Hotel on the Caribbean island of Aruba. The murder was caught on the hotel's CCTV, revealing the killer to be Latin American in origin, according to the Oranjestad police. Bulgarian police suspected that the gangster had been killed for having in 1999 stolen 600 kilograms of cocaine that belonged to one of the Serb coke bosses. Evidently it had upset some Colombians on Aruba as well.

In the Balkans itself, major gangsters from all the former republics were involved in the trade and either making huge amounts of money or getting killed. In the summer of 2002, French police and the DEA thought they were getting close to finding the main channel between Colombia and the Balkans when they set up a complex sting operation. But French and American officers looked on aghast when Dusan Spasojevic, the Zemun gang boss, was taken off a plane about to leave Paris for Bogotá because the Serbian government had ordered his extradition on suspicion of murder. By now Croatian paramilitary generals, Slovene businessmen, and half of the Bulgarian underworld had become involved in this wild new industry with profits that outstripped the traditional Balkan narcotic contraband, heroin, and amphetamines. Most made considerable sums from the trade, although most are now dead. The business, of course, continues.

The Balkans played and continues to play a very specific role in the global shadow economy that has emerged since the mid-1980s: it is the chief transit zone for goods and services from around the world aiming to reach the European Union.

Atyrau and the Caspian center of Kazakhstan's oil and caviar trades

CHAPTER 3

The Mafiya:
Midwives of Capitalism

Astride the great Ural River, the city of Atyrau is distinguished by the nonporous soil that lies beneath it, blocking all natural drainage. In winter, the river water rises, covering the paved roads and sidewalks in mud. For the first fifteen minutes of my visit to this town of 60,000 people, I tiptoe along the streets with trousers hitched in the hope of keeping them clean. Then, like everyone, I yield to the gunk that has already plastered my shoes, socks, jeans, and coat. The yellowy-brown walls of the Soviet-era housing appear to have been designed with the color scheme of mud in mind. Inside, the grubby, decaying hallways and elevators give off a powerful stink of urine.

This dilapidated architecture is familiar to hundreds of towns in the former Soviet Union, but in Atyrau it comes to an abrupt halt as one approaches the center. Suddenly rows of pristine white houses stand in place of the socialist projects. Guards in slick blue uniforms patrol this displaced American suburbia laid out behind imposing fences. Opposite the gated community stands a postmodern office structure with a façade dominated by glistening slanted windows. The district emanates efficiency, progress, cleanliness, and wealth. Yet somehow the new Atyrau seems as soulless as the aging Soviet slum it is replacing.

For all these bleak first impressions, Atyrau in Kazakhstan's far northwest is no ordinary post-Soviet wasteland. In economic terms, it is probably one of the ten most important areas in the former Soviet Union. The chief reason for this (and for the invasion of Western offices and housing) is the huge reserves of oil and gas, about 50 percent of Kazakhstan's voluminous capacity, which sit 100 miles and more away at the bottom of the Caspian Sea. The coast is a mere twenty miles distant at the delta of the Ural River. And yet, as most Atyrauans remind you, 90 percent of the city's inhabitants have never seen the Caspian—the entire region around Atyrau was a restricted military and economic zone in the Soviet Union and remains one today.

Kazakhstan achieved its independence in 1991 through no effort, fault, or desire of its own. The Soviet Union fell apart and Russia relinquished its direct political control over huge swathes of Europe and Asia. One such area was this little-known central Asian country, which is larger than Western Europe but home to a tiny population of 15 million. To most people, the country's only claim to fame is Borat, the outrageous fictional Kazakh TV presenter invented by the British comedian Sasha Baron Cohen. Borat's Kazakhstan is a land of donkeys and prostitutes. In reality, it is a land of great geostrategic importance, wooed by Russia, America, and China alike. Independence coincided with the dawning realization that Kazakhstan's potential oil wealth might be immense, and it was not long before the great powers and great corporations were hovering over Atyrau, sniffing the riches and offering the technological know-how to extract as much of the mineral resource as quickly as possible.

The question facing Kazakhstan today is whether its new/old elite (former Communists turned Kazakh patriots) possesses the wisdom to circumvent the "curse of oil," or whether any nascent institutions of democratic accountability will be swamped by the tidal wave of human greed that accompanies the discovery of mineral treasure. The alternatives to these institutions is a system that is regulated chiefly by corruption. Such has been the fate of countries recently afflicted, such as Angola, Nigeria, and Indonesia, although Saudi Arabia remains the original, probably unbeatable model.

So far there are few signs that the electoral dictatorship of President Nursultan Nazarbayev has the capacity to distribute the money equitably, although with such a small population, he and his oligarchic friends have a real opportunity to do so.

The corrupt system of governance the oil revenues have fostered also generates a permissive environment in which flourishes one of the world's most destructive criminal industries. I had traveled to Atyrau to investigate not the petroleum billions but the other "black gold" for which the city is renowned. The Ural River is home to the only remaining spawning grounds of the beluga sturgeon. As one approaches the river's delta, Atyrau quickly peters out and what remains of the road merges into a barren moonscape. Visibly poor fishermen shuffle glumly in their wading boots around the few desolate villages. They are reluctant to talk about the sturgeon trade, but one reveals, "We receive three dollars per kilo from the state when we sell them the caviar. But it gets more difficult each year. Fewer fish." When the dead female's eggs have made the long journey from the Ural to the finest dining tables in New York or Paris, they will be worth between $6,000 and $7,000 per kilo. This markup of more than 100,000 percent is the sort of price hike that can tempt even the most law-abiding citizen. And there is no expensive drilling equipment involved. The only initial investment needed to harvest caviar is a net and a knife.

The availability of caviar in the Caspian had prompted the growth of one of the most profitable mafia operations in the former Soviet Union. In the last fifteen years, the Caspian Sea's sturgeon population has fallen dramatically. In 2004, only 760 tons of sturgeon were caught by the Caspian nations, down from 26,000 tons in 1985. This is a consequence of human beings engaging in a frenzied program of extermination against an ancient species that until 1989 had faced most evolutionary challenges since the dinosaurs with equanimity. Before the collapse of Communism, there were only two Caspian littoral states: the Soviet Union and Iran. But the breakup of the Soviet Union divided the coast among four new countries— Azerbaijan, Turkmenistan, Kazakhstan, and the Russian Federation (which includes the frenetically unstable province of Dagestan). Unless the five custodians of the Caspian introduce drastic remedial measures, the five main types of sturgeon of the former Soviet Union will be close to final extinction by 2010.

Officially, visitors to Atyrau are permitted to purchase 100 grams of caviar from the modest personal quota agreed on between the government of Kazakhstan and CITES, the Convention on International Trade in Endangered Species. Officers at the local Fish Protection Squad insist that it is impossible to find caviar for sale apart from what is in special shops regulated by the government. Entering one of these is like stepping through a time portal that whisks me back twenty years to an authentic Soviet retail experience. The paltry selection of goods projects a peculiar sadness—it is as if the merchandise is hiding from the attention of desperate-looking customers. In the display cabinets, a few sheets of parchment turn out to be desiccated carp scattered around four of five tiny pots of caviar. In the government shops, the system is clearly working—you cannot buy ludicrous amounts of top-quality caviar for next to nothing.

But one hundred yards away, I wander down the narrow channels of the city's main bazaar. Here dozens of stalls boast richly colored vegetables, sausages, and cheese. Barking excitedly, traders extol the virtue of their goods as I am led into a bare room where five aging Kazakh women sit and gossip. I ask the most craggy-faced of all if she has any caviar to sell. "Sure," she replies tersely as she lifts a cloth covering a table to reveal buckets of fresh but illegal caviar. "What do you want? Fresh beluga, seasonal sevruga—we've got most in at the moment." I gape at her stocks, which are worth tens if not hundreds of thousands of dollars in the West. "I'll take a kilo of the fresh beluga, please!" As she shovels my hoard of "black pearls" into a square plastic salad container, I ask her, "Can you give me a receipt to get this through customs at the airport?" She explains irritably that this is out of the question, but is busy writing down a number nonetheless. "Here, call this man—he's called Nurlan, the director of customs at the airport."

Later in the day, I transfer my contraband from its container into a sturdy glass jar with a tightly sealed lid. Like most internal Kazakh flights, my return to Almaty, the country's commercial capital 100 miles from the Chinese border, is scheduled inexplicably for two o'clock in the morning. Despite my exhaustion, I still want to discover what will happen if I do not invoke Nurlan's protection, so I place my luggage with the caviar through the X-ray machine before calling him.

The unfriendly policeman scanning the bags stops the machine as mine goes through.

"What's this?" he asks suspiciously, pointing at the caviar.

"It's some caviar I bought."

"Wait here," the policeman says, pocketing my passport and ticket. He invites me into a back room and is on the verge of arresting me when I decide the time has come to call the cavalry and dial Nurlan's cell phone. The policeman takes the call and smiles after three seconds, then hands me back my phone, passport, and boarding pass. "Have a nice flight, Mr. Glenny," he bids me in his excellent English.

And that was it. Included in the price of 23,000 Kazakh tenge (about $175 for a kilo of the most sought-after caviar in the world—although note the markup from the river of $3 per kilo to the market ten miles away) was a free if corrupt passage through Atyrau customs, courtesy of its director. And that is how it works—from the fisherman right up to the Parisian restaurant buyer: everyone is on the take except the wretched sturgeon.

My little kilo was a pebble on the Everest of caviar that the world had consumed since the early nineties. (I say the world, but the United States accounts for one third of the total, while Western Europe consumes some

38 percent and the Middle East—especially the Gulf States—absorbs much of the rest). Until the 1970s, the two Caspian states—Iran and the Soviet Union—were producing caviar at sustainable levels. Then in 1977, "the Soviet government decreed a massive increase in the production and export of caviar because they desperately needed hard currency and this was an easy way to get it," explained Artur Shakhnazarian. Gaunt, serious, and with penetrating blue eyes, Shakhnazarian is an unlikely anti-mafia campaigner, although since he has fought in two wars on the periphery of the Soviet Union as it was breaking up, his courage should not be underestimated. Together with his energetic wife, Oksana Martinuk, he has been fighting to prevent the extermination of the sturgeon for more than a decade. "They were overfishing to such a degree that they ran out of rail trucks to export the stuff. To his credit, Mikhail Gorbachev put a stop to this overfishing and strengthened the Spetznaz [Special Forces] teams who were charged with protecting the sturgeon," Oksana said.

In a short time, the armed protection and a new restocking program had a demonstrably positive impact on sturgeon numbers. But after 1989, the police state that had cowed so many people for seven decades appeared to shrivel and die. "At first the poachers came at night, shooting their way to the river. And then the boats started to appear off the coast and the fishing assumed an industrial scale," remembers Artur. Gangsters began exporting caviar to Turkey, to the Middle East, and to Moscow—truckloads, boatloads, trainloads, and even planeloads to Dubai. Azerbaijan was plunged into bitter conflict with Armenia and needed to finance their war effort. The Azeri oil fields were either underdeveloped or obsolete, and so caviar became the most important provider of foreign currency. The Republic of Dagestan in the Russian Federation descended into lawlessness, which saw the Russian customs and border guards fight a losing battle against one of the most ruthless branches of the caviar mafia. Per year, 20,000, 30,000, and then 40,000 tons of caviar were fished as the new rich in Moscow gorged themselves on the black pearls, selling on the excess to the West for huge profits.

In 1998, the oligarchs in Russia had been plundering the state and polluting the financial system to such a degree that the banks went into meltdown. Tens of millions of Russians found themselves below the poverty line overnight as their savings were eaten up by hyperinflation. The ruble was worthless; the dollar was king but only available to those already bloated with wealth through criminal enterprises or through the stripping of state assets (if indeed these were discrete phenomena). Caviar, with its unsinkable hard currency value, became even more prized.

Caviar seeps out of the Caspian region across every border and in every direction. At the port of Novorossiysk on the Russian Black Sea coast, the mafia sends hundreds of individuals by ferry to Samsun in Turkey every day. They all carry their personal export entitlement of 250 grams of caviar. Once in Turkey, the caviar is recognized internationally as a legal *Turkish* product and can be exported without weight restriction. As a return ferry ticket costs about ten dollars, there is plenty of profit for everyone and nobody is breaching the letter of the law. A little of this caviar finds its way to the fish restaurants around Istanbul's Taksim Square, but the bulk is sent on to the United Arab Emirates to be enjoyed by wealthy Westerners and Arabs in the preposterous hotels that have set new standards in unnecessary opulence. But the southern route pales in comparison to the real hub of the trade—Moscow. Eighty percent of illegal caviar is transported to the Russian capital for local consumption or export.

The collapse of the Communist superpower, the Soviet Union, is the single most important event prompting the exponential growth of organized crime around the world in the last two decades. Almost overnight, it provoked a chaotic scramble for riches and survival that saw virtually every citizen sucked into a vortex of violence. From the bitter wars of the Caucasus to the shoot-outs in towns and cities, this was a deadly environment as a new class of capitalists exploited the vacuum of power by seizing whole industries and raiding the state coffers. Accompanied by an orgy of consumption and decadent behavior last witnessed a century ago under Czar Nicholas, even such mighty organizations as the KGB and the Red Army became quickly embroiled in this spectacular nightmare. The transformation traveled well beyond the Soviet Union's borders into all continents of the world as money poured out of the country, looking for safe havens, some legal but most decidedly dodgy. Throbbing at the heart of these extraordinary events was Moscow.

Shocking, terrifying, and threatening, Moscow in the early 1990s was also, unless you got on the wrong end of a bullet, thoroughly exhilarating. By 1993, when I made a short visit, the shootings had begun, the knockout prostitutes were already soliciting in public with equanimity, the most exotic food and expensive wines were being piled high in the restaurants catering for the New Russians, the casino lights dazzled at night. I had by then become used to the chaos of the Yugoslav war, with its bloody logic comprehensible if repellent. But Moscow? From the first time I visited the Soviet capital in the early seventies, I was always struck by how joyless it was. The grandiose buildings were the same in 1993 as they had been twenty years earlier, but the sudden energy and the suppurating wealth were too much to grasp. I spent an entire evening at a brand-new restaurant eating food that would have garnered three Michelin stars. I was flabbergasted by each mouthful, simply unable to conceive that this was indeed reinforced-black-breaded, rubbery-boiled-egged, and watery-souped Moscow. This was a fantasy Russia. Only the overweening brusqueness and a cheerful indifference to anything non-Russian remained constant. Like Americans, Russians live in a country that is so vast and blessed with such a huge, complex economy that there is little compulsion for ordinary people to be interested in anything other than their own country. And Muscovites were scarcely interested in anything beyond the boundaries of their extraordinary city—even in Soviet times. In the two years since my previous visit in 1991, it had been transformed into a breathtaking Babylon of guns, enterprise, money, violence, and fun.

General Vladimir Rushaylo shook his head and smiled sympathetically at the businessman sitting opposite him.

"I can't pick him up, Artyom Mihailovich."

"And why not?"

"For one thing, nobody's issued a directive telling me to, nor has anyone paid us to do so. And secondly, unless he were caught red-handed, then we'll have to carry out a long and tedious investigation, which would probably lead absolutely nowhere." The head of Moscow's anti–organized crime force, Rushaylo was apologetic but couldn't see that it was any of his men's business to get mixed up in this case. "When he shoots you or kidnaps you," one of Rushaylo's subordinates chipped in helpfully, "then we'll go after him!"

Artyom Tarasov understood the message clearly enough: blood on the sidewalk was sometimes enough to get the cops involved. But threats? If the desperately overstretched police had investigated mere threats, then the bewildering circus that was Russia in the early nineties would quickly have dissolved into genuine anarchy.

Tarasov sighed. It seemed he must continue his uncomfortable dispute with a former business partner who was demanding a payoff of several million dollars. He was just one among tens of thousands of Russians targeted by an extortion racket.

Looking back, Tarasov believes he was blessed with naïveté. "Sharks only move in for the kill when they can taste the fear of their victims," he mused, "and I don't believe I understood quite how serious things stood with the gangsters at this time, so I wasn't as scared as perhaps I should have been."

Tarasov's affable manner belies his exceptional business acumen, which transformed him from Communist bureaucrat into Russia's first million-aire after Soviet leader Mikhail Gorbachev's reforms had opened a window on private enterprise. "Our first business was fixing Western television sets. There were no spare parts so we had to improvise with Russian ones. And they worked, although if people had looked inside them, they would have seen a rather monstrous apparition—we couldn't get the genuine parts so we had to bodge them ourselves. After that I started a dating agency. I made thousands of dollars in a single week, but the police closed it down almost immediately for supposed immorality. It dawned on me that the market for these services was enormous."

In 1988, Gorbachev promulgated his Law on Cooperatives, which per-mitted characters such as Tarasov to set up a business in Russia for the first time in sixty years. Entrepreneurs discovered that as soon as a business was up, running, and making money, it attracted competition. "And rivals would employ any method to muscle their way in to your market," he explained, "including violence."

Appealing to the police for protection was futile. As General Rushaylo's frankness in conversation with Tarasov demonstrated, the police force (traditionally the imposing front line of the Russian state's authority) was giving up the ghost. It had neither the intellectual nor the financial resources to adapt to the emergence of capitalism. And so the state, slowly but momentously, started to concede its monopoly on violence to so-called *gruppirovki*, or street gangs. But far from being harbingers of anarchy, these groups of men—Afghan veterans, street toughs, martial arts experts, for-mer KGB officers, and every one of them terrifying—were the indispens-able midwives of capitalism.

Businessmen like Tarasov understood that the *gruppirovki* were in fact privatized law enforcement agencies. In contrast to their state-run coun-terparts such as the Interior Ministry (MVD) and the KGB, these flexible, self-organized gangs had an instinctive appreciation that there was a vibrant demand for their "protection" or insurance services among the new business class. Instead of paying taxes to the state (which had no idea *how* to tax the new small-scale private enterprise), businessmen willingly handed over between 10 and 30 percent of their turnover to local thugs who would ensure in exchange that they could continue trading, free from the violence of *gruppirovki* working on behalf of their competitors. "We are prepared to work with the racket because it charges 10 percent," a business-man from Omsk noted at the time. "The state takes 90 percent in taxes and even more in fines."

The emergence of the protection rackets was the first phase of a three-stage development that saw Russian organized crime steer a passage from petty criminal origins to its position as a powerful transnational force that sought a fixed berth within the global economy.

With the state in collapse and the security forces overwhelmed and unable to police contract law, cooperating with the criminal culture was the only option, Tarasov explained. Above all, he stressed, most business-men had to find themselves a reliable *krysha* under the leadership of an effective *vor*.

The two words are as essential to understanding Russia of the 1990s as *glasnost* and *perestroika* were to the Gorbachev era. *Krysha* literally means "roof" and is the Russian word for a protection agency or racket, the purest meaning of the Sicilian word *mafia*. The *vor-v-zakonye* or "thief-in-law" refers to those criminal (as opposed to political) prisoners in the Soviet period who were "crowned" leaders by their peers. They were subject to a peculiar code of behavior (*vory* were not supposed to marry, for example), and subordinates considered their word final in the resolution of disputes between prisoners. "Most of the *vory* were also run by the KGB, whether knowingly or not," according to Peter Grynenko, a New York cop who spe-cialized in Russian organized crime before setting up his own consultancy in Latvia. "It was a means by which the state monitored and controlled the criminal world."

Some of the *vory* were tough, but others were there just for show. When the largest Slav protection racket in Moscow, the Solntsevo gang, was first emerging as a force in 1991, they invited a *vor*, Dzhemal Konstantinovich Khachidze, to join them. Dzhemal was nominally Solntsevo's boss but brought little else to the party apart from his status as a *vor*. "This guy is a drunk and a drug addict but they clean him up and teach him how to use a knife and fork although they don't get him off the coke," said Bobby Levin-son, who ran the FBI's Russian Organized Crime desk in the 1990s. "But they build him up for PR purposes and promote him as the *vor* behind the throne, as it were. And he begins to control the narcotics dealers on a pro-tection racket basis." So the *vor* proved a useful branding for nascent pro-tection rackets but he was not necessarily an effective operative. "All they'd ever done was sit around in prison being *vory*," Grynenko said. "None of them had actually done any serious killing or anything like that."

And until the winter of 1991, it was indeed very tame stuff. The mob was largely a collection of inchoate street gangs who still had to watch their backs for the cops and the KGB. The latter suffered a huge blow to their prestige and room for maneuver with the failure of the hard-line coup in August 1991 that saw Gorbachev toppled by hard-liners but who themselves were compelled to make way for an even more ambitious reformer, Boris Yeltsin. It was not long before Yeltsin was moving beyond even the most radical of his youthful team of disciples by announcing that before January 1, 1992, the Russian government would free all prices (with some crucial exceptions). With this single act, seventy years of centralist discipline in which the writ of the state penetrated the dustiest nooks of people's lives went into hibernation for a decade. It took just months for Russia to descend into a surreal anarchic capitalism, the Wild East.

In 1992, President Yeltsin's team of enthusiastic reformers were bent on introducing capitalism overnight, and Yeltsin obliged. The pilots of the president's self-styled "kamikaze cabinet" were two young economists, Yegor Gaidar and Anatoly Chubais. Guided by the watchword *deregulate,* they flew their planes into the engine room of the Soviet social contract that had ensured a stable if grim course for seventy years. "We dismantled everything," explained Oleg Davydov, a key official at the Ministry of Trade. "We began liberalization in the absence of any controls."

Price liberalization, a dry economic term, was the starting gun for a roller-coaster ride into the unknown. For the American economists and advisers who swarmed to the government in Moscow, this was a unique opportunity. Russia's economy was a giant petri dish of Chicago-school market economics, but among the cultures they were busy cultivating was a Frankenstein that slipped out the door of their laboratory almost unnoticed.

This was partly because the reforms contained a number of catastrophic anomalies.

The prices that mattered to millions of ordinary Russians, for bread and rent, for example, were liberalized, while those prices that mattered to a tiny enterprising minority were not. In what Gaidar once referred to with gentle understatement as "a mistake," the reform team inexplicably held down the prices of Russia's vast natural resources—oil, gas, diamonds, and metals. A new class of traders could still buy these commodities at the old Soviet-subsidized price, often as much as forty times cheaper than the world market value. This was a license to print money.

At the same time, the government agreed to privatize the state monopoly that the Soviet Union had imposed on the import and export of all goods and commodities. This monopoly compelled foreign companies to conduct their business with the Foreign Trade Ministry in Moscow as an intermediary. When it came to settling the contract, foreign companies did not deal directly with the individual enterprises who were buying or selling. The ministry would buy from the diamond mines or oil fields in Siberia at the subsidized prices, for example one dollar a barrel for oil. It would then sell on to the foreign buyers at the price of diamonds or oil on the global market, pocketing the difference and channeling the profits back into the state coffers.

By exploiting the discrepancy between the high cost of raw materials on world markets on the one hand and their subsidized domestic prices on the other, this regime ensured that huge foreign currency earnings afforded some compensation for the witless inefficiencies of the Soviet planned economy. The ministry's monopoly was one of the few things about the Soviet Union that actually worked. It was a supporting wall of the economy: remove it without first installing a replacement and the house collapses. The "kamikaze cabinet" just removed it.

The coupling of a privatized foreign trade mechanism with the retention of rock-bottom subsidized commodity prices gave birth within months to an entirely new species of robber baron—the Russian oligarch. The logic of this life-form is simple: buy Siberian oil for a dollar a barrel and sell it for thirty dollars in the Baltic states and before long you become a very, very rich citizen. The state was no longer getting its cut from the deal. Instead, that vast profit was going to a few individuals.

Within a matter of four years, a group of several hundred fabulously wealthy men and women had evolved, while an inner clique of mega-billionaires formed a cortex that exercised ever-more decisive political influence over President Yeltsin. Between the oligarchs and tens of millions who had fallen into penury stood a small, fragile, and exasperated middle class.

This process of enrichment was quite simply the grandest larceny in history. As the new Russia dressed itself up to look like a responsible capitalist economy attractive to foreign investment, its most powerful capitalists were raiding its key commodities, trading these for dollars, and then exporting the funds out of the country in the biggest single flight of capital the world has ever seen. Because of the almost incalculable value of these mineral resources on the global markets, this process stands no historical comparison. As the IMF shoveled billions into Russia to stabilize the economy and prop up the ruble, the oligarchs sent even larger sums to obscure banks in every corner of the world, from Switzerland to the Pacific island of Nauru, to be swallowed almost immediately in bafflingly complex money-laundering schemes. The whole process was dramatic testimony to how venality and myopic stupidity are always likely to triumph in the absence of regulatory institutions.

The Soviet bureaucrats who still administered the state did not understand how to monitor, regulate, or adjudicate the principles of commercial exchange. The result was that "for all practical purposes the law enforcement agencies themselves abandoned their task of safeguarding private commercial structures," as Olga Kryshtanovskaya, the leading sociologist of the new Russia, explains. The police and even the KGB were clueless as to how one might enforce contract law. The protection rackets and mafiosi were not—their central role in the new Russian economy was to ensure that contracts entered into were honored. They were the new law enforcement agencies, and the oligarchs needed their services just as they needed remuneration from the oligarchs in return. And because the state's legal system had all but collapsed, the oligarchs and mafia groups defined the justice system of the new Russia. Between 1991 and 1996, the Russian state effectively absented itself from the policing of society. In any event, there were no hard and fast definitions of organized crime, money laundering, or extortion, and by implication, all commercial transactions were illegal and legal at the same time. This applied as much to drugs and women as it did to cars, cigarettes, and oil.

The oligarchs and organized crime were intimately linked. It is important to reiterate that from 1992 to 1999, the most abnormal circumstances prevailed in Russia (and much of the rest of the former Soviet Union) whereby a distinction between legality and illegality, morality and immorality, barely existed. But had the rule of law prevailed at the time, then there is no question that the oligarchs' behavior would have warranted severe punishment.

Some of their practices were straightforwardly criminal by any standards. The critical transfer of the state's financial assets into the oligarchs' pockets took place in the first half of the nineties through the newly corrupted banks. This is the period known as "easy money."

Some bad seeds were germinating within this fiscal culture. The institutions of state were falling apart, but individuals in the administration were learning how to cohabit and collaborate with the new business conditions. The old Soviet criminal justice system had no capacity to regulate the rampant commercial activity that flourished from 1992. But individual bureaucrats could go a long way to facilitate it by rubber-stamping a timely loan from the Central Bank, or by granting a crucial export license. The key word at the time was *resources*—the gangster's "resource" was his ability to wield convincing violence. The oligarch could charm his way into the ownership of whole factories for a song and then use this "resource" as leverage for further funds. The bureaucrat's "resource" was his rubber stamp, ever ready in the desk drawer. Each group sold its "resources" to the other. "In Soviet times," explains Lev Timofeev, a mathematician and economist who was a prominent dissident in the Brezhnev period, "the bureaucrat would initiate a deal. He well understood that he operated in a market—there were always shortages in the Soviet Union and a bureaucrat could sell his influence to help individuals overcome that shortage. The key shift in the 1990s comes when the individuals, that is, businessmen, approach the bureaucrat and offer a deal."

This simple triangular conspiracy between oligarchs, bureaucrats, and organized crime was happily concealed from most by the intense drama being acted out on the streets of Moscow and other major cities: assassinations, unbridled sexual activity, outrageous displays of wealth, and impenetrable political intrigues. Above all, it was shrouded by mob wars.

"There were a number of *vory* who turned up that day—most of them Georgian. They had a clear mission: extract several million dollars from me or failing that kidnap me." Artyom Tarasov smiled as he described one of his first *strelky,* or gangster meets. *Strelky* were organized affairs whereby the *krysha* of one businessman would consult with the *krysha* of another in order to settle a contractual dispute. In 90 percent of cases, the *strelka* would finish with an agreement and both businessmen were obliged to follow the advice of their respective *kryshy.* On this occasion, however, Artyom Tarasov had a narrow escape.

> A veritable army emerged from both sides—thirty to forty men. This bunch of inveterate cutthroats had occupied the Club Volodya Cemago in Moscow's Taganka district. They were brandishing their weapons in a way that would have terrified any normal person.

Tarasov was sent next door with his personal bodyguards to wait while his *krysha,* Malik and Shamad, negotiated with the *vory* from the other team.

Suddenly there was this wild screaming:

"Why did you come here? What are you doing mixed up with this bastard?" our boys were shouting at the *vory.*

"He's just dirt. And who do you think you are, anyway?"

"We are *vory-v-zakone!*" they screamed back.

Given that all were armed to the teeth, it was only a matter of minutes before they started shooting. I was brought into the hall. It was just like a gangster movie—totally unreal.

Weighing up the situation, Tarasov made the right decision by fleeing. Perhaps the first oligarch, or at least proto-oligarch, Tarasov was lucky to escape from this *strelka* alive. It was unusual for one of the businessmen at the center of the unresolved dispute to be present at a meet. Meetings between protection rackets or *kryshy* to hammer out contractual difficulties between the businesses they represented were a daily affair. The vast majority of these meets were harmless—protection rackets were rational operations that sought to avoid unnecessary loss of their personnel. But by its very nature, there was a danger that the *strelka* might develop into a *razborka,* or shoot-out. Vadim Volkov, Russia's foremost student of "violent entrepreneurs," as he describes them, explained:

> One cannot ignore or miss a *strelka.* Not only does failure to show up for a *strelka* automatically mean defeat; it also damages one's reputation. . . . The most remarkable feature of the *strelka* is its semiotics. When setting up a *strelka,* participants do not negotiate many details, but there are subtle signs. . . . All violent entrepreneurs are remarkably sensitive to these signs and know how to read them, since those who fail do not live long. Most important, one has to be able to predict the probability of a violent outcome and to prepare accordingly. How many people should be taken to the *strelka*? Should they all be armed and ready for a shoot-out? . . . Is it worth the risk?

Tarasov's relationship with his *krysha* mirrored the links between oligarchs and organized crime rackets in general. The millionaires and billionaires could not make and then hold on to their money without the protection of the rackets, and the gangsters flourished, thanks to the oligarchs' demand for security. The richer the oligarch, the bigger and wealthier his protectors—mutually assured wealth creation.

The Russian protection rackets of the 1990s differed in three ways from the classic mob families of southern Italy or New York and Chicago.

The Mafiya: Midwives of Capitalism

a) The Russians were indispensable for the transition from socialism to capitalism.

Despite the murders and the shoot-outs, the Russian mob actually ensured
a degree of stability during the economic transition. Of course, by normal
standards one might perceive extortion, kidnapping, and murder as consti-
tuting a rather harsh policing regime; and most people would probably
find it hard to approve of car theft, narcotics, or sex trafficking as a legitimate business enterprise. Yet Russia was not in a normal situation. No societies are free from organized crime except for severely repressive ones (and
although North Korea has undoubtedly very low levels of organized crime,
its state budget is decisively dependent on the trading of narcotics to criminal syndicates in neighboring countries). But when you replace one set of
rules (the Five-Year Plan) with another (free market) in a country as large
as Russia, with as many mineral resources, and at a time of epochal shifts in
the global economy, then such immense change is bound to offer exceptional opportunities to the quick-witted, the strong, or the fortunate (oligarchs, organized criminals, bureaucrats whose power is suddenly
detached from state control) that were absent hitherto. It is certainly true
that the Yeltsin government made some appalling errors. But they were
under considerable economic pressure at the time, as the crumbling Soviet
system was no longer able to guarantee food deliveries to the people and
inflation (even before the freeing of prices) had hit at least 150 percent and
was still rising. Something had to be done.

By the mid-1990s the Russian government estimated that between 40
and 50 percent of its economy was in the gray or black sectors, and it is
within this context that Russia and the outside world needs to understand
the phenomenon of organized crime: it emerged out of a chaotic situation
and was very brutal, but its origins lie in a rational response to a highly
unusual economic and social environment.

b) Unlike the traditional American and Italian mafias, members of
   the gangs were not strictly bound by family loyalties. The codes
   of the *thieves' world* (which conferred honor and recognition on
   the *vory*) only survived a matter of months in Russia's primitive
   capitalism.

Before long the title of *vor* was up for sale. Instead of earning it in the only
manner possible by spending many years in prison, you could simply buy
it. This devalued the authority of the *vor,* and the strict hierarchy of thieves

that had pertained in Soviet prisons crumbled in the face of street gangs and operational criminal networks.

One of the most violent and feared groups to emerge in Moscow and elsewhere was the Chechen mafia. Their mere reputation for being both fearless and gruesome was often sufficient to cow an opponent or persuade a businessman to take them on as his *krysha*. But their members were not drawn exclusively from the Caucasus, let alone from Chechnya: "The Chechen mafia, who should not be confused with the guerrillas fighting in the Chechen war, became a brand name, a franchise—McMafia if you like," explained Mark Galeotti, who has devoted the last fifteen years to studying the Russian mob. "They would sell the moniker 'Chechen' to protection rackets in other towns provided they paid, of course, and provided they always carried out their word. If a group claimed a Chechen connection but didn't carry out its threats to the letter, it was devaluing the brand. The original Chechens would come after them." So the Russian mafia as it developed was not guided by family loyalties but solely by transactions. How much? Who for? What's in it for me? This meant that they were unpredictable, fluid, and dangerous.

c) Third, in contrast to the five families of America's Cosa Nostra, there were thousands of these organizations in Russia.

By 1999, there were more than 11,500 registered "private security firms" employing more than 800,000 people. Of these almost 200,000 had licenses to carry arms. The Russian Interior Ministry has estimated that there were at least half again as many firms that remained unregistered. Not surprisingly, this proliferation in arms translated into a proliferation in murders and assassinations. By 1995, thousands of murders were being committed throughout Russia every year, especially in Moscow, St. Petersburg, Ekaterinburg, and other major centers of commerce. The cost of taking out a rival in 1997 was "$7,000 for a 'client' without bodyguards and up to $15,000 for one with bodyguards." Paradoxically, if you were not involved in business or the protection industry, you were much safer in Moscow than in most other major cities. "Solntsevo was one of the safest places in Russia," explained Alexei Mukhin, Moscow's most fastidious chronicler of organized crime groups. "You wouldn't get mugged there because that was the home base of the Solntsevo gang and they were genuinely proud of their origins."

There were about twenty major gangs in Moscow and dozens of minor gangs, some of them Slav and some Caucasian. Although there were tensions between the so-called ethnic groups and the Slav groups, both sides were wary of each other's influence and firepower. Within the first five years, Solntsevskaya Bratva (the Solntsevo Brotherhood) emerged as the biggest Slav organization. Like its competitors, the Ismailovskaya and Lyubertsy, this brotherhood evolved at an early stage from the first phase of organized crime, the protection racket, into the second phase, monopoly controller of goods and services. This was the shift from privatized law enforcement agency to a full-fledged organized criminal syndicate.

Just outside the bleak center of the Solntsevo (Sunnyside) district of Moscow, a small road leads to the village of Fedosinye—physically very near the buzzing metropolis but spiritually closer to the peasant world of Tolstoy. Life here revolves around a modest but well-kept and brightly colored church with bells that ring out with exceptional clarity. At the center of the nine bells (a huge collection for such a small community) is the sonorous bass dome on which is engraved FROM THE SENIOR PRIEST-HOOD, THE CHARITABLE FOUNDATION UCHASTYE, THE FIRM CB-HOLDING, AND THE SOLNTSEVO BROTHERHOOD.

The latter three organizations were all the brainchild of Sergei Mikhailov, born into a modest working-class family on the outskirts of Moscow in February 1958. As a young man, Mikhailov trained to be a maitre d'hotel at the Sovietski Hotel in central Moscow, just south of the Dynamo Moscow soccer stadium. The job brought with it certain influence, because as a registered hotel for foreigners, it was one of the very few places in Moscow where alcohol could be purchased after nine p.m. "Remember," said an erstwhile colleague of Mikhailov's, "this was a country where collecting empty Western beer cans was considered chic. Actually having access to real alcohol after hours not only offered a certain prestige; it was a way to make money as well."

In 1986, Mikhailov spent several months in custody for falsely claiming the insurance on his motorbike. After receiving a conditional jail sentence, he returned to Solntsevo and devoted himself to his other passion—wrestling. He hooked up with another former prisoner, Viktor Averin, and together they began to take control of Solntsevo's streets. A map of the Moscow district shows how a majority of the most influential gangs emerged from the postwar working-class districts that sit immediately outside the M-KAT, Moscow's equivalent of the Beltway or the M25. Solntsevo grows like a wart off the southwest of the M-KAT. The cosmopolitan inhabitants of the city center never considered these depressing zones an integral part of Moscow. But in the late eighties the gangs started encroaching inward as they sold their services of violence to businesses or destroyed those who refused to purchase them. The working class, in whose name the Communists ruled, were never especially visible in Moscow's city center. Once the Communist Party was swept away, its nominal supporters were curious to see what they had been missing. And of course, Solntsevo and similar areas possessed the key resource for the development of protection rackets—lots of tough, unemployed, aggressive young males easily identifiable by their beloved uniform of loose-fitting tracksuits (sometimes accompanied by a baseball bat), cropped hair, and elaborate tattoos.

But Solntsevo offered more than just goons. Two kilometers to the west lies Vnukovo, one of Moscow's biggest airports. A little farther around the M-KAT is another airport, Domodedovo. And, equally enticing, a little farther down there lies Southern Port (Yuzhny Port), the huge river docks through which goods from all areas of Russia pass into Moscow. The roads leading into Moscow via Solntsevo linked the Russian capital with Ukraine and the ports of the Black Sea. More commerce was concentrated here than in any other part of the city, and it was not long before the Solntsevo Brotherhood had established monopolies with an important ally in the two airports, as well as Yuzhny Port. This proved especially advantageous when the Brotherhood was developing its first enterprise outside of the protection business—the import of cars. As the oligarchs started to funnel huge amounts of cash into their pockets and organizations, there was a sudden rise in the demand not just for Western cars but for luxury cars. In a short time, the Mercedes 600 had become the status symbol of the New Russians and Solntsevo controlled much of the vehicle traffic into the capital. By the mid-1990s, Moscow had the highest number of Merc 600s registered anywhere in the world.

In December 1989, Mikhailov, Averin, and two other key leaders were arrested and held in custody for more than a year on suspicion of extortion. As in most similar trials of the time, witnesses just dropped their allegations or disappeared long before the case actually came to court. But the Solntsevo leadership had been imprisoned at a crucial time, just as the market was about to open up. On their return, they discovered that other groups were moving in on their territory. The Chechen mafia posed the greatest threat to Solntsevo. Hooked up to a network of tribal militias in the Caucasus, the Chechens had weapons, recruits, money, and a reputation as fearsome fighters.

The Slav-Caucasian gang war that engulfed Moscow for about two years beginning in 1992 is often portrayed as driven by national antipathy between the two groups. According to this widely held view, the bloody shoot-outs between the Chechens and Solntsevo in particular (although there were also battles featuring other Caucasian groups such as the Armenians, Azerbaijans, and Georgians, as well as other Moscow Slav brotherhoods) represented an attempt by the Slav groups to demonstrate their patriotism at a time of rising tension between the Russian army and insurgents in Chechnya itself.

There may have been elements of genuine nationalist ill will between the Caucasians and the Slav gangs, but behind the heady rhetoric there lay the predictable motive of economic interest. From 1988 to 1990, the Chechens had succeeded in wresting partial control of the Southern Port from the Solntsevo Brotherhood, as well as some of the key car dealerships. The most notorious clash between the two gangs took place in the summer of 1993 when Solntsevo became involved in a shoot-out with Chechnyan gangsters at the Kazakhstan Cinema. One of the Solntsevo legends, Cyclops, was killed in the battle, but slowly Mikhailov and his men were reasserting themselves as Moscow's top dogs. "Solntsevo operated differently from other groups, and here lies the key to its success," said the FBI man Levinson. "Every brigade with its own leader was autonomous, earning its own money. Each brigade organized its own protection rackets and its own scams. The cash was not funneled up to the leadership—it was a loose confederation and allowed people leeway. The top leaders, who included Mikhailov, were known as the Big Four. They also ran their own businesses but they split the profits four ways. But as membership dues, as it were, the smaller guys provided their services gratis. If there was a problem between brigades that required the intercession of one of the Big Four, then there had to be a split of profits between Mikhailov and those in dispute as the price of conflict resolution."

The Solntsevo empire grew. From car showrooms and bars it expanded into hotels and supermarkets. It also controlled three major markets in the center of Moscow and at least three major railway stations. Mikhailov seemed to understand instinctively that he must distance himself from the group's overtly criminal activities. He refused to assume the crown of *vor*, insisting instead that he be described simply as a businessman.

As early as 1992, the organization decided they needed to assume control of one or two banks. "Most Russian banks at this time were not banks in any recognizable or meaningful sense," explained Mark Medish, who under President Clinton worked at the U.S. Treasury as an expert on the Russian economy. "They did not take deposits or make credits; instead they made easy money by handling government transactions, borrowing state funds at low interest rates then buying high-yield, short-term government bonds, making super profits."

The move into banking brought Solntsevo and the top criminal syndicates still closer to the oligarchs. Together they set new exuberant standards in tastelessness as they celebrated their newfound status among the world's superrich.

One of the many ways they liked to flaunt their wealth was by throwing extravagant parties. A prominent oil executive threw a Soviet Union nostalgia party in a château outside Paris in the summer of 2004. It was a spectacularly ironic celebration of the system whose downfall had garnered the oilman's unbelievable riches. French peasants dressed as Soviet collective farm workers from the 1930s were driving their tractors around the fountain in front of the mansion. Heroic Soviet-era songs exhorting the working class to increase their production norms boomed out of loudspeakers. Underneath their fancy dress of greatcoats and Soviet Komsomol uniforms that blended in with the party's theme, the guests were clothed in finest designer garb. Welcoming them into the main hall was an imposing hammer and sickle carefully positioned between two enormous red banners that covered most of the château's façade.

Inside, skipping between the fountains of champagne and lines of coke (carefully chopped and ready for use), women with miniskirts split to reveal their buttocks would writhe occasionally to the marching beat of "Defenders at the Siege of Leningrad" or some such. Paintings and busts of Lenin, Stalin, and Brezhnev glared down with staunch disapproval on the unproletarian bacchanalia that satirized their memory.

The hire of the château and the party alone cost several hundred thousand dollars—a large sum to most of us but an unimaginable fortune to all but a tiny clique of Russians. On top of that, there was the cost of two large passenger aircraft chartered to bring most of the guests in from Moscow that day and back two days later. There was a hierarchy within the party, with most guests having access to a variety of entertainments in different rooms but only a privileged few allowed into the inner core. At the doors of this sanctum, the photographers stopped snapping and the videos stopped whirring as the oligarchs inside contemplated their billions and how to multiply them further.

The Soviet Union Nostalgia Party was a mere side order in the movable orgiastic feast in constant preparation for the oligarchs and their entourages—family, friends, lawyers, heavies, PR associates, politicians, entertainers. To this day, they slide from Marseilles to Miami, from Athens to Ashkelod, from Tokyo to Tahiti, in search of ever more outrageous kicks.

The oligarchs' rape of Russia's assets enjoys pride of place in the boom of the global shadow economy during the 1990s. Not only did these men succeed in turning Russia upside down, but their actions had a huge economic and social impact on the United States and on countries throughout Western Europe, in the Mediterranean (above all Cyprus and Israel), in the Middle East and Africa, and in the Far East. Unable even to claim that they were helping to police the transition to capitalism (as protection rackets undoubtedly were), they have had an overall influence more destructive than most of Russian organized crime.

Those organized crime bosses who survived the 1990s settled well into Putin's Russia. Several have Interpol red notices on them, wanted for crimes committed in Western Europe or the United States, but the government in Moscow shows no inclination to extradite them. Sergey Mikhailov has insisted that he is a legitimate businessman who conducts much of his work now in China. Chasing down alleged members of a global mafia is low on Beijing's priority list. Other mobsters now make their living broking major gas and oil deals between Russia, its neighbors, and Western Europe, recording handsome profits for their clients and themselves. Many remain in the opaque world of private security. President Putin has restored the power and prestige of the KGB (in its novel guise as the FSB), where he spent most of his career before his unexpected political elevation as Russia's prime minister in the late 1990s.

Under Putin, the Kremlin has clipped the wings of several of the most powerful oligarchs. From exile in the West or from inside prison, oligarchs like Boris Berezovsky and Mikhail Khordokovsky warn that the new president is the reincarnation of Stalin. But he isn't. He has fashioned a novel system that brings together aspects of capitalism and Soviet socialism—market authoritarianism. The oligarchs' desperate attempts to portray Putin as the new Stalin seek to conceal the primary responsibility they bear for the mess they and Russia find themselves in after their venality reached unprecedented levels in the late 1990s.

After the period of "easy money," the oligarchs could offer such attractive rewards that they were able to buy whoever they wanted. Corruption and organized crime are intimately linked—the former spawns the latter with a resolute determinism. More directly, the oligarchs needed to purchase the services offered by the private protection agency, or mafia, to protect their interests. When senior members of the KGB/FSB and MVD (Interior Ministry) observed how their influence was sinking as the wealth and power of the oligarchs grew, many decided to switch horses. The Russian security services have experienced fluctuating fortunes since the Gorbachev period. Some members were establishing companies abroad as covers for industrial espionage and money laundering. Others were less fortunate, and in 1992 the KGB's financial situation deteriorated to such an extent that officers were forced to sell lightbulbs and toilet paper stolen from their headquarters in the Lyubyanka Prison (as sacrilegious, surely, as priests nicking candlesticks from St. Peter's in Rome).

Almost all major oligarchs and business empires started to employ former KGB men to advise them on security. Vladimir Gusinsky, the media magnate and one of the most influential early oligarchs (before he fell foul of Putin), appointed Filip Bobkov as the boss of his security. Bobkov achieved notoriety in the 1980s as the former head of the KGB's Fifth Directorate, which was responsible for combating dissidents in the Soviet Union. "These days everyone is doing it!" Artyom Tarasov told me in his Moscow office. "I was talking to my old employee Viktor Vekselberg—you know, the one who bought the Fabergé eggs for Russia—who's one of the men behind the oil consortium TNK-BP. He was telling me the other day that he currently has twenty former KGB generals on his payroll!"

The death of Alexander Litvinenko, the former senior KGB officer poisoned in his London exile in late 2006, revealed how confused the relationship between the KGB and private security services had become. In the late 1990s, Litvinenko himself had been assigned to protect the oligarch Boris Berezovsky while still working for the KGB, and one of the prime suspects in his murder was another former KGB officer who ran his own private security firm and had once also provided protection to Berezovsky.

Through such characters, the oligarchs were in a position to exercise influence over the residual forces of law and order in what is known as the "deep state," the mighty forces of political influence that operate behind the scenes even in ostensible chaos. It went further, though: the integration of high-ranking KGB and MVD personnel into the paid retinues of the oligarchs triggered the privatization of Russia's security forces. During the 1990s, these two iconic institutions of Soviet power became simply another competing private law enforcement agency—in one fundamental sense, they were no different from the Solntsevskaya Bratva: their services were available to the highest bidder.

As a consequence, different branches of Russia's security service would find themselves fighting against each other on behalf of warring oligarchs. On December 2, 1994, Vladimir Gusinsky noticed he was being followed by a group of large, intimidating masked men as he drove to his offices on Novy Arbat. These also housed the offices of his chief political sponsor, Yuri Luzhkov, the mayor of Moscow and a political rival to Boris Yeltsin. As the owner of NTV, the most popular independent television station, Gusinsky was among the most influential oligarchs and one who excited jealous outbursts among his peers.

Boris Berezovsky, the first among equals in the oligarchy, persuaded President Yeltsin that Gusinsky needed to be taught a lesson. In late November, an article in a pro-Yeltsin newspaper called "The Snow Is Falling" had claimed that Gusinsky's Most company was "planning to force its way into power." If this was a shot across the bows, December 2 witnessed a full-scale broadside. The masked men started roughing up Gusinsky's bodyguards in the oligarch's car park. Watching from his office and feeling increasingly alarmed, Gusinsky was calling his contacts inside the counterintelligence unit of the KGB. These guys turned up and a *razborka* (shoot-out) erupted. Before blood was spilled, however, one of the KGB men realized that their opponents were from the presidential security service. They decided to withdraw. The more powerful the oligarchs became, the more damaging their rivalry. This both parodied and accentuated the rivalries that existed within Russia's security forces.

"All of us from the intelligence networks sat up when the shoot-outs between the KGB and the Interior Ministry began," the former head of a Balkan intelligence service told me. He had grown up with a profound admiration for the KGB and observed the events in a state of shock. "We then realized that the situation in Russia had run out of control. We could no longer rely on them—it was like losing a father."

The KGB officers and networks who had outsourced their services formed the middle belt of a pyramid supporting the opulent oligarchs at the top. The security service provided a crucial link with the state. But at the bottom of the pyramid, bolstering the entire structure, was a diverse group of people known as the *zashchita,* or "defense." This included a host of professionals—lawyers, PR companies, journalists (and in the case of a few oligarchs entire newspapers or television stations)—and anybody who might contribute to the defense of the oligarchs' interests. But at the core of the *zashchita* was the protection racket or mob. "Russian organized crime is thus characterized by at least three seamless webs," explained Jon Winer, deputy assistant secretary for International Enforcement (or Drugs and Thugs, as it is known colloquially in Washington), "between extortionists and security companies ... between licit and illicit business ... and between criminals on the one side and political and bureaucratic elites on the other. Out of these seamless webs has emerged a triangle of crime, business, and politics [which is] extremely strong and resilient."

But the final link between the oligarchs and the most powerful mafia groups was forged through a common interest—the need to launder money. Solnstevskaya and the Chechens in Moscow and other huge syndicates such as Tambovskaya in St. Petersburg or Uralmash in Ekaterinburg had reached phase two on the path toward a global mafia status: they were all whole or partial monopoly controllers of specific goods and services. Across the world, the trade in narcotics was one of the most profitable criminal activities. All the major criminal groups in the former Soviet Union had built up extensive business interests in the manufacture of amphetamines and ecstasy, in the importation of cocaine into Europe, and above all in the distribution and sale of heroin from central Asia into Eastern and Western Europe and the United States.

The oligarchs understood instinctively that Russia was a capricious and dangerous environment and that their billions of dollars were not safe there. They overestimated their ability to control President Putin, the man whom they chose to replace the weak and easily manipulated, alcoholic president Yeltsin. Yet their instincts served many of them well—as an insurance policy, they needed not just to get their money out of the country. They needed it to be clean once it arrived at its destination. So did the organized crime groups. Everybody needed to launder his cash. But before they could establish a worldwide launderette, they all—oligarchs and mobsters alike—needed to establish themselves abroad. The criminal groups now entered the most challenging stage of their development: phase three—overseas transplantation.

CHAPTER 4

Spreading the Word

I mmediately on arrival at Prague's Ruzyne Prison in August 1999, Tomas Machacek put in a request to the governor that he be placed in solitary confinement. "I had no choice," he explained. "They would have killed me. No question. There were a lot of Russians there."

It had been a hard fall for Machacek. Five years earlier, he had been recognized as one of the most promising young policemen in the Czech Republic when at the age of just twenty-six he was appointed leader of ALFA, the new anti–Russian organized crime unit. Now he was incarcerated in the same isolation block where Czechoslovakia's erstwhile Communist leaders had once locked up Václav Havel. An honest cop in a corrupt system, Machacek is a real-life Arkady Renko, the quietly intelligent detective in Martin Cruz Smith's novels *Gorky Park* and *Stalin's Ghost*, engaged in a quixotic struggle with much more powerful and darker forces.

Machacek's downfall could be traced to the moment of his greatest success. In May 1995, working on a tip-off that a murder was being planned, Major Machacek coordinated fifty officers for a raid on the restaurant U Holubu (The Doves) in the once dowdy working-class district of Andel. Two hundred and fifty guests were dining on sushi when Machacek ordered his men to break up the fortieth birthday celebration for Viktor Averin, deputy boss of the Solntsevo Brotherhood.

As the raid got under way, Machacek noted disconcertedly that the Russians appeared neither surprised nor worried. "None of them resisted— they all knew what was happening and lay on the ground obediently," he said. "None of them had guns and we knew from our intelligence that their security guys were always armed." Machacek went cold. "We had decided to go ahead only a few hours beforehand. And yet somebody had tipped them off." The implication was clear—a senior figure in the Czech police was working with the Russian mafia.

No charges were preferred against any of the guests, but the anti–organized crime squad did gather sufficient evidence to ban the key Russian mafia figures, such as Sergey Mikhailov of Solntsevo, from the Czech Republic for ten years (most promptly moved to Hungary). "At least we were able to send them a message that they could not use Prague as a springboard from where they could travel the world and manage their various narcotics and arms businesses," explained Machacek. "Thank you very much, gentlemen!"

This was both a blow and an insult to the Russians, as Prague and in particular the spa town of Karlovy Vary (Carlsbad) had become the top leisure destinations for the New Russians in central Europe (four-fifths of Carlsbad's splendidly pompous Habsburg properties are now Russian owned).

Police forces around Europe hailed Machacek's achievement, and on a working trip to Washington he was feted by Louis Freeh, the head of the FBI. Freeh pointed out the raid on U Holubu had provided the world's law enforcement officers with the first detailed documentation and photographs of the Solntsevo Brotherhood and its associates. Still in his twenties, Machacek looked set for great things.

But although U Holubu was renowned as a meeting place for Russian and Ukrainian mafia and businessmen, they were not the only ones who enjoyed the facilities there. Adorning the restaurant were photographs of the owner, Antoly Katrich, "with Czech politicians, Czech businessmen, actors, and other celebrities," as Machacek recalled. "For example, there was a photo of Katrich with the then minister of justice, Jiri Novak, and other ministers. . . . At our request, Jan Ruml, the interior minister, told the cabinet that they should desist from frequenting U Holubu and associating with these people. They ignored him."

An anonymous letter had prompted Tomas Machacek to launch the raid on U Holubu in May 1995. Its author claimed that the Solntsevo leadership was planning to murder a certain Semion Mogilevich during the birthday celebrations that night. Machacek knew that Mogilevich was a powerful man and a close associate of Solntsevo. But it was also rumored that Mogilevich and Mikhailov had fallen out over a payment of $5 million.

Yet that evening Mr. Mogilevich didn't turn up. Or at least, he turned up only after Machacek had launched the raid. "By the time I arrived at U Holubu, everything was already in full swing," said Mogilevich later, "so I went to a neighboring hotel and sat in the bar there until about five or six in the morning." If Mogilevich is—as most police forces in Europe and America claim—the true *capo di tutti capi* of Russian organized crime, then he is always two steps ahead of everyone else in the game. Effortlessly.

Not long after Averin's birthday party, a few local politicians and newspapers began questioning the motive behind the raid. This developed into a campaign. Commentators and opposition politicians claimed the storming of U Holubu was "an outrageous assault on legitimate businessmen enjoying a night out." A myth developed (still readily available on the Internet) that the police had carried out the raid Rambo-style, crashing through the ceiling and abseiling into the main hall. Rumors spread that Machacek and his close colleagues were unreliable and on the take.

"I used to just ignore the anonymous threats and telephone calls. And I dealt with the obscene letters sent to my wife," he explained. But one August morning when things seemed to have settled down, an officer of the police's internal investigation unit arrested Machacek out of the blue as he was arriving for work. He was disarmed and taken into custody, accused of malfeasance by a corrupt customs officer whom he had never met, in a location where he had never been.

Prague was the primary inspiration for Franz Kafka's two great fictional nightmares, *The Castle* and *The Trial,* in which an omnipotent and amoral bureaucracy without mercy and without apparent reason pursues a frightened individual known simply as K. Kafka's fiction came to life in his home city after Stalin installed the Communist Party as the "leading force" in Czechoslovakia in 1948. Throughout much of the forty years that Prague endured Communist control, people were kept in fear that this administrative leviathan could came knocking at their door with an arrest warrant. The Velvet Revolution in November 1989 was meant to put a stop to all this.

But though Kafka's bureaucracy may have moved into the shadows after the revolution, it still lurked discreetly. Soviet structures had penetrated deep into the fabric of Eastern Europe—through the Communist Party, the military, industry, the secret police, cultural associations. For the great majority who did not engage in political protest, life in this system was tedious but stable, and that stability enabled many personal and institutional links to bind together the elites of the Warsaw Pact members.

With his arrest, Machacek felt the full force of these opaque structures as he was publicly vilified. But so did the Czech state. His computers and files were stripped when he was put in jail, compromising his entire network of informers and undercover agents. Disillusioned with his treatment, Machacek's close colleagues began leaving the organized crime unit and other intelligence branches to seek work in the private sector.

Eventually the courts recognized that Machacek had been stitched up and he was offered any job he wanted. "I declined. I couldn't go back to an office where I would bump into people who I know had betrayed me, who were corrupt, and about whom I could do nothing."

Organized crime and corruption flourishes in regions and countries where public trust in institutions is weak. Refashioning the institutions of Kafkaesque autocracy into ones that support democracy by promoting accountability and transparency is a troublesome, long-term process. The task is made doubly difficult if economic uncertainty accompanies that transition. Suddenly people who have been guaranteed security from the cradle to the grave are forced to negotiate an unfamiliar jungle of inflation, unemployment, loss of pension rights, and the like. At such junctures, those crucial personal networks from the Communist period become very important. The Red Army evacuated its bases in Eastern Europe, but the equally effective yet more seductive force of favors owed and promises once made stood its ground to exert a strong influence over the transition.

Poland, the Czech Republic, and Hungary were the most sought-after destinations of Russian oligarchs and organized crime syndicates like Solntsevo. They knew the terrain, and in the former two, language barriers were less formidable than in Western Europe. There was one thing that distinguished these three states from the rest of Eastern Europe—they were all fast-tracked to join the European Union, and that was the quickest route to the gold at the end of the rainbow. "These countries were the gates to the West," noted *BusinessWeek*. "Their growing economies and borders with the EU offered firms located in this region the most precious commodity—legitimacy." Moreover, there was money to be made in these countries, and one commodity proved especially lucrative—oil.

Trained under Communism and hence used to obedient civilians, the police bemoaned the lack of respect they now encountered. "We are underpaid and have no resources—the criminals have faster cars, much more money, and contacts higher up if things go wrong," one said.

Tamas Boros, known as the Giant or Big Tom, was walking in Budapest with his lawyer past a Polish Fiat 500 just before midday on July 2, 1998, when somebody detonated the eight pounds of TNT attached to the vehicle's underside. The blast literally sliced him in two. The explosion and consequent deaths shook Hungary badly. Until this point, the dozens of mafia murders committed in the Hungarian capital since the early nineties had resulted in no collateral casualties—the assassins had proved strikingly accurate. The public response to mafia killings was even one of muted approval, along the lines of "One fewer gangster in the world, so what?" But this was different. It took place in broad daylight just yards away from Vaci Utca, Budapest's most fashionable shopping street, packed with people. Three innocent bystanders died with Big Tom, while twenty more, including foreign tourists, were injured as several vehicles were obliterated, causing carnage. The public was outraged and it wanted some answers.

Detectives at the Hungarian organized crime squad had several leads to work on. If anything, their list of suspects was too long. For the past year, Big Tom had been dishing the dirt to them about his colleagues in the criminal fraternity. There were at least six Hungarian organized crime groups who made a bid for Big Tom's territory after his murder, and several became key suspects as the investigations dragged out over years.

Initially the Hungarian police looked east toward Russia. Big Tom himself had told them in his confession. "It all started," he'd told them, "when this Russian guy called Uncle Seva turned up." By the time of Boros's murder, "Uncle Seva," a.k.a. Semion Mogilevich, had already been declared a persona non grata in Hungary and received a ten-year entry ban from the Czech Republic's Interior Ministry (slapped on him after the bust at U Holubu). Describing him as "one of the most dangerous men in the world," the British government had barred him from the United Kingdom following an extensive investigation into his business activities, while the FBI was preparing to place him on its Most Wanted list, where he can be found to this day.

Tamas Boros was involved in the biggest single criminal scam to hit Europe during the 1990s: the heating oil scandal. Suppliers of heating oil from Ukraine and Romania to the Czech Republic, Slovakia, and Hungary were exempted from paying duty on the product, so it was considerably cheaper than fuel for petrol engines. But once it was across the border, the gangs put the oil through a simple chemical treatment that rendered it compatible with motor vehicles. The petroleum was then sold to the gas stations, but the gangsters would pocket the tax revenue. "The heating oil scandal could have been solved with just two extra sentences in the law concerning the dyeing of oil products," the Czech Republic's then deputy interior minister, Martin Fendrych, told me. "We pointed this out to the Finance Ministry and they sat on it for two years. Why? Go and ask them!"

The scam sucked billions of dollars from the exchequers of the three countries over a three-year period. The industry was so lucrative that it caused dozens of murders in all three countries as businessmen, customs officers, cops, and politicians scrambled for a share of the profits. According to Hungarian police, Boros's claim that Uncle Seva had moved in on the industry in Hungary was probably his death sentence.

Unfortunately, speculation is often what the police are left with when dealing with Seva (or Papa, as Russian criminals call him). Law enforcement agencies around the world have been seeking to prosecute Mogilevich for more than ten years now, but the man has a knack for never being in the wrong place at the wrong time. In a Tel Aviv café, Ze'ev Gordon, one of Mogilevich's key lawyers, told me, "Mogilevich may be guilty and he may be innocent. I don't know. But in order to establish the truth, you have to produce evidence that stands up in a court. And so far nobody has done that or even come close."

There is a wealth of material about Mogilevich's supposed evildoings on the Internet, but the legal case against him is flimsy. He is no longer sought on charges of arms dealing and running prostitution rackets as he once was. The FBI has a warrant for his arrest only in connection with a large-scale fraud in which he is alleged to have fleeced Canadian investors of tens of millions of dollars, perpetrated through a variety of companies and known as the YBM Magnex scandal. The feds do warn that Mogilevich is armed and dangerous, but they are not seeking him on counts of arms and drug running, for which in private they claim he is responsible.

Indeed, most Western law enforcement officers engaged in anti–organized crime work insist in private and in public that he is probably the most powerful Russian mobster alive. "I can tell you that Semion Mogilevich is as serious an organized criminal as I have ever encountered," insisted Jon Winer, the anti–organized crime czar under President Clinton, "and I am confident that he is responsible for contract killings." "Who did he kill?" I wanted to know. "I cannot address the issue of who," Winer replied with uncharacteristic coyness.

This implies that Western governments rely on intelligence material that is not admissible in court. For all the periodic warnings about Mogilevich, Mikhailov, and other big Russian mafia dons, Western police appear to have limited capacity to prosecute these men in courts of law. In 1996, the Swiss prosecutor Carla del Ponte (later made famous, or notorious, depending on your viewpoint, at the Yugoslav War Crimes Tribunal in the Hague) oversaw a major case against Sergei Mikhailov for money laundering. Despite having some first-class witnesses (including a Russian law enforcement officer since compelled to go into witness protection in Switzerland), the prosecution made a dog's breakfast of the case. Not only was Mikhailov acquitted of all charges, but Switzerland paid him half a million dollars in compensation for wrongful imprisonment.

Spreading the Word

Neither Mikhailov nor Mogilevich travel to the West anymore (although Mogilevich still retains his Israeli passport). But they putter happily around Moscow, seemingly unconcerned and apparently untouched by the Russian state.

Who knows how many thousands of punters tried their luck when casino capitalism opened up in Eastern Europe? Most left the game empty-handed. For every story of a dazzling entrepreneur creating a business empire in half a decade, there were dozens who gave it their best shot but had to return in the end to the job market with not a penny to show for their endeavor.

Most business analysts would have placed Eural Trans Gas (ETG) in the no-hoper category when it set up shop in December 2002. ETG had few resources and the tiniest of premises in Csabdi, an anonymous village twenty miles west of Budapest. The nominal shareholders were hardly business school material. Louise Lukacs was an unemployed actress from the Transylvanian city of Cluj. Her career had peaked almost twenty years earlier when she starred in *Tears of a Girl,* Romania's entry at Cannes, which was short-listed for a prize. Louise explained that she had agreed to become an ETG shareholder because the company might pay her. "At least to cover my phone bill," she said. "I have to pay more than thirty-five dollars a month for the phone."

Louise recruited two similarly unlikely pioneers to the venture in this emerging market: an IT worker and his partner, a nurse, who lived with her mother in a cramped flat. Like Louise, they were on the breadline.

A fourth shareholder, Ze'ev Gordon, Mogilevich's Tel Aviv lawyer, was clearly the odd one out. What was he doing there? What was anyone doing in this company that had registered assets of $12,000 and an unmanned office in Csabdi? "I was merely asked to act as a shareholder for a Ukrainian businessman, Dimitry Firtash. It was a service, that's all," he told me.

He certainly did Firtash a good turn. In its first year of business, ETG went from being a $12,000 business to recording a $2 billion turnover, posting pre-tax profits of $180 million. Not bad, eh?

But then there was the CEO, one Andras Knopp, a former Hungarian minister of education during Communism whose most recent job had been as the senior representative in Moscow of Reemtsma, the huge German tobacco concern. In an interview after the extent of ETG's success became clear, he confessed, "Strictly speaking, the shareholders remain three Romanian citizens and an Israeli but the real parents are Gazprom and Naftohaz Ukrainy [NAK]." The Russian and Ukrainian gas conglomerates, he suggested, had not received the requisite paperwork to register the company in Hungary before December 31, the cutoff point for new businesses in Hungary to qualify for offshore status (and greatly reduced tax liabilities). Instead, in order to secure the tax break, the unwitting Transylvanian trio and Ze'ev Gordon were parachuted as intermediaries to form the company earlier.

This explanation was not implausible: instead of paying 18 percent company tax, ETG would pay only 3 percent company tax until 2005, coincidentally the date when its only two contracts would run out—one with Gazprom, and one with NAK to transport gas from Turkmenistan (the Caspian's most outrageous dictatorship) to Western Europe across Russia and Ukraine. A legal tax dodge—fair enough.

But why then did Gazprom and NAK flatly deny their parentage of ETG? NAK publicly stated that ETG was a "Gazprom contractor." Gazprom responded by saying NAK selected ETG. And why did they sign a contract for a job that they could do themselves without difficulty? And why did they deny the fruits of this revenue to themselves and their shareholders and hand them instead to a shoebox operation from a Hungarian village?

Gazprom is a monster. With an annual turnover of just less than $30 billion, it accounts for nearly a third of global gas production, 8 percent of Russia's GDP, and almost a quarter of Russia's tax receipts. Gazprom aspires to and may well become the single most influential energy company in the world (if it isn't already). As minister for the Soviet gas industry just before the collapse of Communism, Viktor Chernomyrdin, later to be appointed prime minister of Russia, channeled the USSR's immense natural gas resources into a single state company in 1989. Four years later, the company was partly privatized. It has an effective monopoly over the Russian gas pipeline system. Any gas coming out of Turkmenistan, Uzbekistan, or Kazakhstan that seeks a home on the West European markets must travel through Gazprom's pipelines, giving the Russian giant considerable leverage over its direct competitors. In recent years, it has become a brutal tool in Russian foreign policy, its clout used to exert pressure on former Soviet republics such as Georgia and even on its largest client, Western Europe.

Why, then, would Gazprom pay another firm with which it had no ostensible connection to transport gas that Gazprom owns through Gazprom's pipelines? Gazprombank loaned ETG $70 million and guaranteed a $227 million commercial loan. It made no sense whatsoever—unless, perhaps, those strangers were friends in disguise.

Spreading the Word

By 2000, when Vladimir Putin succeeded Boris Yeltsin as Russian president, the patience of Gazprom's small but vocal private investor shareholder group was running low. Their main irritation concerned the influence of a mysterious offshore company with offices in Jacksonville, Florida, called Itera International Energy Corporation.

The most tenacious private investor was William F. Browder, the grandson of America's wartime Communist leader, Earl Browder. Browder's company, Hermitage Investment, had invested in Gazprom, and he wanted to know why the energy giant was putting billions of dollars' worth of work Itera's way that Gazprom itself could do perfectly well. Using public sources, he researched unusual payments between Gazprom and Itera. He discovered that senior company officials were organizing huge transfers—and not just to players along the pipeline route. "The arrogance was so extreme that there was no cover-up whatsoever," Browder remarked. "But that was helpful to us, because it enabled us to paint a very accurate picture."

One of Itera's most lucrative contracts concerned the transport of gas from the fields of Turkmenistan to Ukraine, which landed them $120 million in profit annually. But Gazprom's small shareholders, like Bill Browder, wanted to know why they should be deprived of these dividends. Furthermore, nobody could ascertain who was benefiting from those profits.

As soon as he assumed power, President Putin let it be known that he was not going to tolerate such arch theft, and he singled out Gazprom as a specific target for his attention. To the surprise of many, Putin was quick to make good on his promise, replacing the company's discredited CEO with a friend from his St. Petersburg KGB milieu.

Itera's days as a Gazprom protégé were numbered. At the beginning of 2003, Gazprom announced it would not renew the contract, specifically for the transit of Turkmen gas to Ukraine. "Why should Itera make super profits using the facilities of Gazprom?" thundered the deputy chairman of Gazprom. The company, he continued, would henceforth run the transit operations itself.

Except it wouldn't.

Two months prior to Gazprom's renewed public commitment to transparency and propriety, its bosses had signed a secret deal with the tiny ETG, the day after it was registered in Hungary. Similarly, Gazprom's Ukrainian equivalent, Naftohaz Ukrainy, had also signed up with the new company, giving the latter exclusive rights for the transport of Turkmen gas across Ukrainian territory to Western Europe.

Over the next year and a half, ETG's curious relations with shadowy companies in Cyprus, Turkmenistan, Moldova, the Seychelles, France,

Britain, and elsewhere emerged. And several of these companies were connected with associates of Uncle Seva Mogilevich as an internal memo of the Paris-based Organization for Economic Cooperation and Development indicates (see page 81).

Ever since news about ETG became public, Western journalists and police forces have been furiously seeking a smoking gun that might link Mogilevich to the scam. Roman Kupchinsky, a tenacious journalist who writes on organized crime for Radio Free Europe, came close when he published a letter by the deputy head of Russia's organized crime unit that explicitly linked Andras Knopp with Mogilevich in an alleged cigarette-smuggling racket. Within weeks, however, ETG had produced a sworn affidavit from the cooperative Russian lawman that stated that the letter was a fake. The case collapsed.

Whether or not proof emerges of Uncle Sevo's involvement is immaterial in two respects. First, huge sums of money went into a company with an entirely opaque ownership structure and which should not have been offered the contract in the first place. Second, this company ETG had a turnover of $2 billion per annum—with no proper oversight of these accounts, all manner of funds could be channeled through the company that were not necessarily the product of the Ukrainian gas trade. In other words, ETG could have been a huge money-laundering vehicle. Although the company has since lost the Turkmen-Ukrainian contract, its role has been replaced by another unnecessary intermediary, RosUkrEnergo, which is also part owned by Dimitry Firtash, the man who Ze'ev Gordon explains was behind ETG.

For this perverse business operation to succeed, ETG (whomever it represented) required the absolute support of the Gazprom and NAK leaderships. But it also required protection from both the Russian and Ukrainian states (and indirectly from the notoriously vain, now deceased dictator of Turkmenistan, Saparmurat Niyazov, whose insatiable appetite for cash was one of the main motors behind the scam), as these two gas giants are at the very heart of the energy policy.

The ETG scam remains a mysterious, inscrutable affair. Whoever conceived the idea was determined to remain anonymous. It is hard to ascertain whether it was gross corruption or simply criminal, or, indeed, where the boundary between the two lies. But what it does demonstrate beyond doubt is that if a syndicate persuades a powerful state to acquiesce or cooperate in its schemes, then it has found the magic password to Aladdin's cave. For no organized criminal is as successful as the one who enjoys the backing of the state.

Eural Trans Gas: a complex cobweb (Q1 2004)

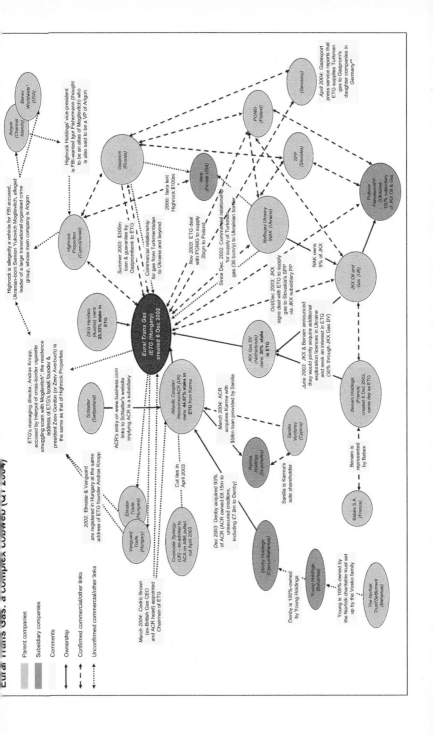

Conversely, a criminal master who loses the backing of the state becomes vulnerable. Mogilevich himself discovered this in January 2008 when bundled unceremoniously into a police van in the centre of Moscow. He was detained for several months on charges of tax evasion. However, there was an avalanche of speculation in both Russia and the United States that Mogilevich's sudden fall was related to power politics in the Kremlin. Most commentators argued that Mogilevich, the gas broker, was a supporter of the Kremlin hawks, the *siloviki*. They elaborated that once Vladimir Putin had anointed the liberal former boss of Gazprom, Dmitry Medvedev, as his successor that Mogilevich and his less than transparent business practices were a primary target. Other significant players with track records similar to Mogilevich were also picked up before and after his arrest.

The impact of this event, symbolic and practical, should not be under-estimated. In the 1990s, the oligarchs and gangsters quite clearly controlled the Kremlin. Under Vladimir Putin who systematically used popular hostility to the oligarchs to strengthen his political position as president, the situation was reversed: criminal and oligarch interests were subordinated to state interests. It does not follow that Putin and friends persecuted criminals or dispensed with corrupt practices. On the contrary, they flourished as before but they are now much more carefully controlled. Of course, it is often difficult to tell who is truly running the show—the chicken or the egg!

Serhiy Shushkov remembers that winter came late to central Ukraine in 2000. By early November, snow would normally be covering the fertile fields and forests near the town of Tarashcha, which lies some ninety miles south of Kiev.

Had the snow fallen as usual, then he and his father would not have noticed the hand sticking out from a pile of fresh earth on the edge of a beech wood forest as they were returning to their village that Thursday.

A local coroner, Ihor Vorotyntsev, established that the victim had first suffered a severe beating. It was hard to know, however, whether the flaying of his legs was the result of torture or of animals scavenging once the body was buried. Nonetheless, the coroner noted how "the skinning revealed the leg muscles like in an anatomical illustration, and suggested that sadists had been at work."

The corpse bore the marks of a gangland killing. Identification was made all the more difficult by its headless state, but matters were complicated still further when the coroner received an order from Kiev not to transfer the body to the capital. He protested that he had no refrigeration facilities in Tarashcha, but Ukraine's Interior Ministry insisted the corpse remain in the provinces. This was followed by a visit from Ukraine's chief coroner, who removed some organs and then ordered the local coroner to dispose of the corpse.

By now, Vorotyntsev knew that he was in the middle of a very sensitive case. This was not a conventional gangland killing: in this instance, the mafia organization was the Ukrainian state itself. According to Hryhory Omelchenko, the MP who heads the Parliamentary Investigative Committee into Organized Crime and Corruption, Ukraine's chief capo was none other than the president himself, Leonid Danilovych Kuchma. A former boss of the Yuzhmash missile factory in the industrial city Dnipropetrovsk, Kuchma was known as a leading "red director," that is, a Communist who actually worked for a living as opposed to those who just made their way up the Party's greasy pole. Western embassies in Kiev hoped that Kuchma's relative youth and energy would drag Ukraine out of the torpor characterized by its first post-Communist leader, Leonid Kravchuk, who was indeed a Communist Party boss from central casting. Like many others, the Western embassies were very wrong.

"It was a period in which the state was converted into a criminal political mafia," said Omelchenko, the combative and impressively mustached MP. "The political system and the state institutions were under Kuchma's control in order to secure absolute power, an authoritarian regime that could exploit its power for the boundless enrichment of Kuchma's family and those oligarchs closest to him. To achieve these goals, he and his closest circles didn't shy from using any method, including the dirtiest ones, even physical assault of the most violent kind."

Like most other Ukrainians, Tarashcha's local coroner was fully aware of the lawless nature of the state he lived in. So it took considerable courage to defy the orders he received from Kiev. But he did: he kept the body when ordered to dispose of it even though without refrigeration it had begun to decompose rapidly. He was relieved when some days later a team of journalists pitched up from Kiev to identify the body as that of Georgi Gongadze, who had disappeared two months earlier.

The investigative articles by the dead man, a thirty-one-year-old, half-Ukrainian and half-Georgian journalist, had begun to pry open the lid on Kuchma's maggot-infested administration. Its members had commandeered the judiciary, the police, the military, the security services, and industry—in short, the central mechanisms of state—as vital assistants in the amassing of wealth and power by a federation of regionally based cliques. Of course, just as in any other cabal of "families," there were frequent fallings-out, and indeed the system eventually came crashing down in December 2004 when former allies of Kuchma's, Viktor Yushchenko and Yulia Tymoschenko, led the Orange Revolution, which sought to replace venality with popular legitimacy as the guiding philosophy of the state.

But until then, the Ukrainian experience was unprecedented. Even in Russia under Yeltsin, when the influence of the oligarchs over the Kremlin was at its highest, a certain distance existed between political and economic processes, not to mention personal ambition. But at the turn of the millennium, the oligarchs and government became one in Ukraine, fused together by the adamantine bonding property of the SBU, the post-independence KGB. But occasionally even the SBU would slip up, and one whistle-blower decided to take a chance and shed some light on the Gongadze killing.

Mykola Melnychenko was most fortunate that the SBU was having a rare off day on October 30, 2002, when he applied for a passport to travel abroad. Perhaps its officers were too busy wondering where they should dispose of Gongadze's body. Whatever the reason, the day Serhiy Shushkov noticed a hand sticking up on the edge of a beech forest, Ukraine's Interior Ministry issued Melnychenko with a passport, which before long contained a visa for the Czech Republic, whither he left with his family three weeks later.

The SBU should have been interested in Melnychenko's intentions, because just a week before receiving his passport he had left its employ where he had worked as a presidential guard who spent most of the day close to or in Kuchma's presence. And for the previous twelve months, Major Melnychenko had been illicitly recording conversations that took place in the presidential office between Kuchma and his most senior colleagues. They had discussed all manner of subjects (including the troublesome Georgi Gongadze). When Melnychenko left for the Czech Republic via Warsaw, he packed 1,000 hours of digital recordings in his luggage. They were to prove very uncomfortable for Kuchma and his friends.

Surprisingly, when Melnychenko teasingly released just a few hours of the tapes, the former president conceded that the voice recorded was his own. But Kuchma argued that somebody or some organization had doctored the conversations or taken them out of context. Kuchma refused to allow a parliamentary inquiry into the tapes affair but did commission Kroll Inc., the New York risk consulting firm, to undertake an independent investigation into Gongadze's death.

The Kroll report barely mentioned the Gongadze murder (which it was in theory investigating) but did claim that it could prove that the tapes had been doctored. When journalists and Melnychenko scrutinized the Kroll report, they refuted its key scientific assertions about the recordings. The FBI agreed with Melnychenko—the tapes were for real.

The contents of these tapes are so explosive that they were bound to provoke a furious debate about authenticity in which both sides mobilized powerful allies. But Kuchma's admission that it was his voice is in one respect all one needs to know. More instructive than the contents (which like most ordinary conversations assume prior knowledge and so sound disjointed) is the language that Kuchma and his colleagues use. A simple cultural transfer and we could be listening to a clip from *Goodfellas* or an episode of *The Sopranos*. Kuchma is not the first president to use expletives on tape, but he makes Richard Nixon sound like the principal of a Swiss finishing school:

> KUCHMA (*on the phone*): Listen, now they just showed me the newspapers. Crap—all these bollocks that is published. Well, Hrysha Omelchenko is continuing to publish a paper. [*pause*] Well, what are you bullshitting? Eh no, right now the fifteenth of September he put out a paper. [*pause*] . . . *Svoboda* [*a newspaper*] and shit is being published. . . . There are such caricatures there, and also insults, crapping totally on the president. [*pause*] So invite Yulia [*Tymoshenko, later coleader of the Orange Revolution*]! Fuck your mother! You invite Yulia, and ask her: "Dearest, what the crap are you doing, bitch? Do you want us to screw the crap out of you completely or what?" And you can add: "Why are you financing Omelchenko, why are you doing this and that?" You don't know the basics of your job or what? How things are done the rest of the world over? So if they aren't one fucking bit afraid of you, then fuck your mother. Well, why are you this way? Why should you be feared? It is our service that they are afraid of. . . . It was I who appointed you. . . .

And on Gongadze—Kuchma may not have ordered his unknown interlocutor to murder the journalist, yet one cannot but detect a certain appeal to rid him of this troublesome reporter:

> KUCHMA: Ukrainska Pravda, well, this is completely already, crap, insolence. Bastard, shit. The Georgian, Georgian whore.
>
> UNIDENTIFIED INDIVIDUAL: Gongadze?
>
> KUCHMA: Gongadze. Well, who could be financing him? . . .

UNIDENTIFIED INDIVIDUAL: Well, he actively works with this, with [*member of parliament*] Moroz, with the newspaper *Hrani*.

KUCHMA: To court, maybe. Here, people's deputies. Let the lawyers take him to court. This goes to the prosecutor, right? It's just, crap . . . there is some kind of limit, son of a bitch, shit . . . Deport him, whore, to Georgia and throw him the fuck out there.

UNIDENTIFIED INDIVIDUAL: Drive him out to Georgia and throw him there.

KUCHMA: The Chechens need to steal him and throw him away.

The language reveals utter contempt for state institutions and the need for institutional control over individual ambition. Kuchma and his cronies had seized the state and now wielded power and money beyond the comprehension of most of Ukraine's 50 million inhabitants. For Kuchma and his pals, the state was nothing more than a mechanism to facilitate their personal aggrandizement. But not surprisingly, it created a serious long-term problem for the country as a whole. To compete on the world market, Ukraine needs to foster good relations with Russia above all but also with the European Union, the United States, and China, where it sells huge quantities of steel and other raw materials. And with so many competing economic demands, the primitive mafia system of government is inherently unstable. It actively discourages the emergence of a strong class of small and medium entrepreneurs who are the key to a diverse and flexible economy of a country in transition. Greed, incompetence, and oligarchic feuding eventually triggered if not a breakdown then a changing of the guard.

The Gongadze murder and the Melnychenko tapes accelerated the demise of the Kuchma regime. But it is far too early to conclude that the new rulers of Ukraine will succeed in persuading more democratic practices and institutions to take root. Less than a year after the Orange Revolution, which was supposed to do away with the mafia state, the new government had collapsed in a flood of mutual recriminations between the revolution's leaders. The oligarchs, in the meanwhile, recovered to fight against encroachments on their wealth and influence. Indeed, some Western intelligence officers claim the evidence is mounting that the decision to investigate the Eural Trans Gas scandal led to the fall of Yulia Tymoshenko's government.

Organized crime is deeply entrenched in Ukraine, and away from Kiev, where the spotlight of domestic and international scrutiny shines brightly, powerful criminal interests continue to dominate. Henry Hill, the main character in *Goodfellas*, remembered that his mob's wealth grew from the moment one of the biggest ports of entry on America's eastern seaboard came into operation in New York. "The real money started coming in when they opened up the airport at Idlewild," as JFK was originally known. Idlewild had a maritime equivalent in 1990s Ukraine—Odessa.

As I stroll along Primorsky Boulevard from Sergei Eisenstein's famous steps toward the Opera House, Odessa looks magnificent as it hugs the northern Black Sea coast. Indeed, the recent reconstruction of the center is so evocative of a glamorous past that I can imagine Anton Chekhov, Isadora Duncan, and their fashionable friends sweeping in and out of the Londonskaya Hotel, where they used to stay. A century ago a visit to Odessa was de rigueur for the moneyed classes of Russia and Europe alike.

This elegant illusion is maintained as I walk up Derebasovskaya Street, where peddlers are wooing tourists by performing with live snakes and crocodiles (less harmful than some of the other reptiles that creep around here). The high street takes you past the house, now sadly under scaffolding, where the painter Vassily Kandinsky grew up. Just visible underneath the crumbling plaster is a golden key painted above the door. This puts most Ukrainians and Russians in mind of Karabas Barabas and the story of Buratino and the golden key. Alexei Tolstoy, a distant cousin of the great novelist, adapted the Pinocchio story in the 1930s to create a Russian version. Buratino, the little puppet boy in possession of the key, is hounded by Karabas, an evil puppet master who will do anything to possess it, as it opens the door to the Kingdom of Happiness.

Myths and fairy tales are popular in Odessa, and by a strange coincidence, decades after Kandinsky had left, a man called Karabas actually moved into the House of the Golden Key. But the trail of this once living and breathing Karabas took me a few hundred yards beyond Derebasovskaya, to where the fairy tales cease and happy endings disappear in short wisps of gunsmoke—nineteen of them, to be precise.

Above Derebasovskaya Street, the ornate late-eighteenth-century façades are still ubiquitous but the elegance fades: these French-designed buildings have clearly fallen on Soviet times even before sinking into the mire of gangster capitalism. On Astashkina, a small, quiet street, I wander into Steam Baths number 4. The exterior is modest but the inhabitants have spruced up the courtyard with hanging baskets. The stairs at the back, painted a rich green, lead to the Russian sauna on the first floor. But before I reach the baths themselves, I come across several bunches of fresh flowers on the ground. Two plaques are attached to the wall above—the first engraved with the image of a man in his mid-forties, sporting cropped hair and looking sleek in a suit over a T-shirt; the second has on it a poem written by his closest friends after he, Viktor Kulivar "Karabas," was felled on this spot by nineteen bullets from an unknown assassin's semiautomatic:

Kulivar
Viktor Pavlovich
To Your Eternal and Sacred Memory
Karabas!
April 21, 1997

Naveshchayut kladbishche starushki	*The Old Cemetery Proclaims*
I druzya, rodnye v skorbnyi chas,	*To friends bereft in these sad times*
Predan zdes' zemle vozle tserkvushki	*The sacred clay holds the remains*
Viktor Pavlovich, nash dobryi Karabas.	*Of Viktor Pavlovich, our dear*
	Karabas

Banknotes are nestled inside the flowers. Money lying untouched in a public place suggests profound respect for its late recipient, as in Odessa poverty and begging are readily visible.

The people of Odessa have a history of romanticizing their city and themselves. Known for its self-deprecating, almost Schweykian, humor, its British equivalent would be Liverpool. Founded just over two centuries ago, the Pearl of the Black Sea has a rumbustious history in which crime, politics, and a joyous licentiousness have always been further fueled by large itinerant populations: seafarers, political refugees, and commercial adventurers. Furthermore, it was until recently the most ethnically diverse of all Russophone cities. Until Odessa's Jews fled in the face of Axis Romania's military advance of 1941, they amounted to 30 percent of the population. Most of those who remained were massacred, but like the Jews in a sister port, Thessaloniki in northern Greece, they did not conform to the stereotype of East European Jews as poor rural dwellers or prosperous businessmen. Instead, they comprised much of Odessa's tough working class, from whom the city's legendary criminal community emerged, as chronicled during the early twentieth century in the stories of the great Isaac Babel.

Although not Jewish, Karabas fit perfectly into the role of local criminal idol—and the more I spoke to Odessites of any nationality, the more convinced I became that he really was indeed a heroic gangster who prevented social collapse and lawlessness.

No mobsters controlled a post-Soviet city with as much popular support and quite so effectively as Karabas did. But his primary instrument was not violence but trust. "He was a local boy and he was fiercely proud of Odessa," argued Leo Zverev, a charity and social worker. "And he maintained order. The bulk of our narcotics problem, for example, used to be based in the part of the city that we call Palermo because there is so much criminal activity there. Karabas allowed the dealers to operate inside Palermo, but he blocked them from plying their trade anywhere else in the city. He was determined to hold down drug consumption in this city."

As economic breakdown and chaos spread across Ukraine following its independence from the Soviet Union in 1991, Odessa suffered a dramatic social seizure, with funds from Kiev largely drying up. Predators began stalking the city, and in particular the port and oil terminal at the foot of the Potemkin Steps. Relying on a brigade system similar to the one operated by Solntsevo in Moscow, Karabas responded by asserting his authority in establishing some ground rules. It took me some time to persuade members of Odessa's underworld to speak—at times they seemed more obstructive than Soviet bureaucrats. But eventually they talked under the strictest condition of anonymity. Their opinion of Karabas differed little from that of civilians. "He was a man of principle," one leading mobster told me. "Rarely carried a gun and often went out without bodyguards. As far as he was concerned, violence was a last resort for a racketeer. And as he was recognized by all of us as the *avtoritet,* a don, even by people like me who didn't work with him, this meant that levels of violence in Odessa were much lower than in other Ukrainian and Russian cities."

"Any firm, and there were a lot of them, considered it an honor to be under Karabas's protection," one local businessman explained. "This was a guarantee of total security not only from outside attacks by rogue rackets, but also not infrequently from encroachment by the authorities. Besides this, he was in his own way a city arbitrator, acting as judge in commercial disputes between various 'structures.' The value of his services cost firms a tenth of their net profits. The payout took place every month—even if there had been no need to seek out his services. And it would never have entered anyone's head to deceive him or attempt to conceal anything. Unthinkable. If someone was having problems, say, with tax auditing, not only might he reduce or postpone payments, but he would even write off the debt altogether. 'What is our gain in killing the goose laying the golden eggs?' he used to say."

But Odessa, even in the calmest times, is an irresistible magnet for criminality and corruption. Despite Karabas's benign rule, every imaginable contraband passed through the city. As a port, it was a hub of human trafficking. "We'd open up containers and find hundreds of people packed into them," described one former customs officer in the city. "The stench was indescribable, as they had sometimes been sealed in for weeks with no toilet facilities, and rotting bodies were also common." As the migrant laborers from Asia who survived the trip continued the journey toward Poland in the hope of entering the European Union illegally, their place in the containers was taken by women from Ukraine, Belarus, and Moldova en route from Odessa to brothels around the Middle East and Europe.

But more than that, Odessa and Ilichevsk, ten miles from Odessa, are the most important export terminals for Russian oil. And equally significant, during Communism the bulk of the Soviet Union's refinery capacity was concentrated here. Overall, economic and political control of the city translates into billions of dollars, especially since President Putin's foreign policy was based on Russia's immense influence in the global energy industry. Moscow had no intention of allowing Ukraine to develop its port and refinery system independent of its own policy goals.

The Russians found a pliant partner in Leonid Kuchma. Less accommodating, however, was the mayor of Odessa, Eduard Gurvitz. An energetic entrepreneur with great ideas for the rejuvenation of the port, Gurvitz backed a plan to transform the Odessa region from being merely an exporter of Russian oil to being an importer of Caspian and Middle Eastern oil, which it could then send by pipeline to Poland and the European Union. The logic behind this lay in freeing Ukraine from overdependence on Russian oil, and it involved the construction of a giant new terminal to the south of Odessa called Yuzhny (the South Port) that unlike Odessa could import oil as well as export it.

Although there was occasional friction between Mayor Gurvitz and Karabas, their goals for Odessa generally coincided. "When the Chechens first tried to muscle in on the oil industry, Odessite business consulted Karabas," said a local mobster, "and Karabas had a clear strategy: 'Leave Moscow to the Muscovites and Chechnya to the Chechens. Odessa belongs to the Odessites.' And he blocked their entry into the market."

Heroic though Karabas's strategy might have been, he was naïve according to Leonid Kapelyushny, who knew both Gurvitz and Karabas well. "Karabas had to go because he had one dumb idea," he said. "He believed in national organized crime and rejected the idea of transnational organized crime. And that's what did for him—every imaginable force in this country and from outside wanted control of the oil, and so Karabas and his Odessa patriotism had to go."

The gunning down of Viktor Kulivar "Karabas" in April 1997 triggered a series of bloody political murders over the next year and a sustained period of gang warfare as various mafia outfits fought over the huge territory that Karabas had controlled. When he heard the news of Karabas's death, Mayor Gurvitz turned to Kapelyushny and said, "Odessa doesn't yet understand what sort of man has been killed. Nor what consequences will now follow." His death deprived Odessa of the one man capable of policing the city—which was precisely the point. "After Karabas's death, the third force came into play," explained a retired investigative detective who declined to be identified. By the third force, he meant a fearful alliance of gangsters, ex-Communists, oligarchs, military intelligence, and KGB, which even Darth Vader would think twice about confronting. Gurvitz himself survived two assassination attempts in this period, but, despite widespread intimidation, he was reelected in February 1998, only to be stripped of the post soon after in a bizarre intervention by a court in Kirovgrad, a city hundreds of miles away with no jurisdiction over Odessa municipality. Leonid Kuchma, however, welcomed the court's decision.

In the next few years, Kuchma's preferred strategy for the terminals and ports of Odessa region sailed through unopposed, to the satisfaction of both Ukraine's oligarchs and Russia's industrial and political elite.

Like all key murders in the former Soviet Union, Karabas's is still entirely unsolved. Some clues might be found in the subsequent attempted murder of Leonid Kapelnyushy in February 1998, when he was the head of the city's Electoral Commission. Three men emerged from a car and gunned him down, leaving Kapelyushny for dead. "Before losing consciousness," the somber Kapelyushny told me, "I at least noted that the car was registered in Transnistria."

Odessa is only sixty miles from the border with the Republic of Moldovan Transnistria, which looks and sounds like the perfect setting for a Tintin adventure. The small breakaway province from the Republic of Moldova is the quintessential gangster state whither many criminals would scuttle, having carried out their mission in Odessa. This thin sliver of territory has been a problem ever since the Transnistrian authorities proclaimed independence from Moldova, triggering a bloody, dirty little war in 1990 that lasted for two years. Its president, Igor Smirnov, a former red director of a factory in the capital, Tiraspol, has relied for support on a coterie of KGB officers and oligarchs, as well as an uncharacteristically forgiving attitude of Gazprom to the huge debt Transnistria has run up with the energy giant.

During the conflict with Moldova, Transnistria held its own in large part because it happened to host both Russia's Fourteenth Army and its mighty arsenal of 42,000 pieces of stockpiled weaponry ranging from pistols to tanks and a handy supply of surface-to-air missiles. After the collapse of the Soviet Union, the Fourteenth Army in Transnistria was separated from the Russian motherland by the proclamation of an independent Ukraine. The army could have organized its return but preferred instead to remain in Transnistria as a "peacekeeping force." But although the Fourteenth Army offered de facto support to Smirnov and the breakaway republic, Russia, like the rest of the world, refused to recognize Transnistria—it is a pariah state.

The oil industry was the most lucrative industry in Odessa, but not far behind was the trade in illegal weapons from Ukraine and Transnistria. This had begun at the end of 1991 when Ukraine's then president, Leonid Kravchuk, decreed the establishment of a commercial department at the Defense Ministry that would have a main aim of turning the vast store of Soviet weapons inherited by Ukraine into cash. It wasn't long before an Odessa company, Global Technology Inc. (GTI), was dispatching the *Jadran Express* (despite its Croatian name a Nigerian-registered ship) to the former Yugoslavia packed full of arms in defiance of the UN weapons embargo. Given the oft-proclaimed solidarity between Russians, Ukrainians, and their Orthodox Slav brethren, the Serbs, it is astonishing how many Russian and Ukrainian citizens and companies were involved in supplying the Croats, Bosnians, and Albanians with guns. But as we shall see, it was states and groups from Africa who sent the greatest number of envoys to Ukraine to broker arms shipments from Odessa.

Leonid Kuchma presided over the total criminalization of the Ukrainian government and civil service. Most people understandably associate organized crime with drugs, prostitution, people trafficking, and similar activities. But the biggest bosses of Russia and Ukraine understood that if you wish to strike the really big money, you should invest in two "legitimate" businesses—the arms industry and the energy sector. The Eural Trans Gas and Itera scams saw the fusion of crime and state in the gas industry; in Odessa, a battle over oil exports broke the city in two. Karabas had a conscience, but he was still a mafia boss. But not even the mafia can compete when the full weight of the state becomes involved in transnational corruption and criminality as happened in Kuchma's Ukraine. Yet even Kuchma and his friends projected a semblance of order and propriety in contrast to the neighboring republic of Transnistria.

As Pavel Ciobanu ushers me into his Audi, I notice that he shares Karabas's dress sense, sporting a black jacket over a black T-shirt. The late autumn sky darkens as we speed from Chisinau, the Moldovan capital, toward Tiraspol, capital of Transnistria. Instinctively, I clutch my wallet. Three days previously while traveling through Transnistria, I had been relieved of fifty dollars by the border guards, who were happy to keep me in illegal custody until I coughed up. "Par for the course," diplomats in Chisinau assure me cheerfully.

But as head of the Moldovan Football Association, Mr. Ciobanu is a welcome guest in Tiraspol, and so the selfsame border guards who had previously extorted me now wave us through accompanied by obsequious salutes and nary a glance at our passports. Ciobanu speeds us toward the most unlikely top-of-the-table clash in European soccer, FC Sheriff Tiraspol versus FC Zimbru Chisinau.

As well as a criminal revenue-raising post, the Transnistrian border also acts as a time machine. As you enter Tiraspol, Lenin rises on a pillar in front of the parliament building while slogans remind people, "Our Strength Lies in Unity." We are indeed back in the Soviet Union, and people have that unforgettable Soviet combination of boredom and exhaustion etched on their faces as they trudge along the bare streets. The vision of this social anachronism doubles the shock on arrival at the astonishing home of FC Sheriff Tiraspol.

Regularly rented out by the most powerful teams from Kiev and Moscow, the Sheriff complex has two full-size soccer stadiums, an arena licensed for international meetings of any indoor sport, a five-pitch training ground, a sports academy, and a hotel, restaurant, and bar. I learn from UEFA, the governing body of European soccer, that it includes the only stadium in Europe that "conforms to every single safety and security measure that [they] stipulate." As a lifelong fan of soccer, I can testify that I have never seen so sophisticated a training and playing complex in Eastern Europe. And for those Transnistrians with time on their hands and money to burn (a rare breed), there is even a Mercedes showroom on the grounds.

In 1997, Victor Gusan decided to use his wealth to found a soccer club that could aspire to the final stages of the Champions League, the zenith of European sporting achievement. Having led a rich and varied life as the former deputy chief of Tiraspol Militia, Gusan turned his hand successfully to business in the early 1990s. While clearly a man with a razor-sharp acumen, Gusan was probably aided by his friendship with Vladimir Smirnov on his rise. Reputed to be Sheriff Football Club's biggest fan, Smirnov must have expended much effort in persuading the government of the self-styled Republic of Transnistria to go ahead with the construction of both the stadium complex and the team. After all, Transnistria's annual budget amounts to just under $250 million. The stadium, in contrast, cost around $180 million. But then, Mr. Smirnov is both the head of the Customs Service of Transnistria and son of the president, Igor Smirnov.

But not even the might of the president and his Communist Party could overcome the second hurdle facing FC Sheriff. In order to participate in any soccer competition, Sheriff must belong to a recognized member of UEFA. But that's been a problem ever since the Transnistrian authorities declared independence from Moldova—Tiraspol, capital of Transnistria, did not belong to a recognized UEFA country.

So how would Transnistria be able to put FC Sheriff on show? They spent all that money on the stadium complex, and brought in some first-class players from Africa, the Balkans, and Russia to cobble together a decent team by regional standards.

The Football Federation of Moldova was, of course, recognized by UEFA. A deal was struck. Although Transnistria refuses to have anything to do with Moldova on any other official level, in matters soccer it concedes the sovereignty of Chisinau. The government in Chisinau thus maintains a rather feeble lever over the government in Tiraspol. FC Sheriff wins the Moldovan league at a canter every season. As the Moldovan/Transnistrian equivalent of London's Chelsea Football Club, it can buy better players than all the other teams put together. It is then able to play in the qualifying rounds of the European Champions League.

Of course, all this begs a large question: From where does FC Sheriff get its money? Apart from the stadium, the other striking thing about Tiraspol is the number of Western Union signs hanging outside shops. In transitional countries and the developing world, such high visibility of Western Union means one thing—a significant level of emigration to better economic climes. But I wonder if the world has ever seen anything like this. Grigory Volovoy speaks in a wry monotone. As editor of *Novaya Gazeta,* he is one of the very few who dare raise their voices in Transnistria's living gulag. "In the early 1990s, the population stood at 750,000. Now it is about 450,000. We have about 150,000 able-bodied people of working age left here."

So notwithstanding the lure of the stadium, almost half of Transnistrians left to seek their fortune abroad in the last decade. A stroll around the streets of Tiraspol makes it crystal clear that there is not much trickle-down from Sheriff.

There is, however, the phenomenon of trickle-up. In addition to the soccer club, Sheriff owns the biggest supermarket chain in Transnistria, as well as every single land and mobile phone line in the country (a snip in 2002 for $2 million). Although Russia is too coy to recognize Transnistria, Gazprom has been subsidizing gas supplies to the territory to the tune of $50 million a year for more than a decade. And Itera, the Florida-based company with links to Solntsevo, is the majority shareholder of the metallurgical plant in Ribnitsa, the highest export earner in Transnistria.

But still you can't help wondering whether all this could conceivably finance FC Sheriff and the stadium. Remember that stockpile of Russian weapons? And, indeed, the estimated two to three factories that produce weapons unmonitored? These spew out of Transnistria via Odessa and into the worlds of war—the Caucasus, central Asia, the Middle East, western and central Africa.

Occasionally, President Putin suffers a crisis of conscience regarding Transnistria. "Maybe it is time to close down this black hole," he told Georgi Purvanov when the Bulgarian president pleaded with Putin to dam the lava of criminality that flows down from Transnistria and spreads throughout the neighborhood. Bulgaria is used by various groups as an important staging point in the smuggling of weapons from Ukraine and Transnistria, and Purvanov understandably considers this most damaging for his country's image.

Putin mulled it over but decided against closing it down. A few years back, the Russians agreed to allow an international agency to supervise the transfer of the Fourteenth Army weapons to Russia. At the time of writing, half of those have been returned. "Of course," said one Western intelligence officer, "we don't know how many of those made it to Russia and how many found their way elsewhere." Western governments are particularly concerned by the leakage of the Russian surface-to-air missiles, the Igla. In December 2003, 320 of these weapons were withdrawn, but the original inventory showed that there had been 394 pieces. Somewhere around the world in unknown hands are 74 highly accurate missiles that can bring down a 747. Each one is worth about $50,000. "There is enough kit in Transnistria to supply an entire army," the officer said. "It is worth millions and it is deadly."

Transnistria is tiny—the size of Rhode Island. But it affects and debilitates countries across large parts of the globe. Its rogue border regime has a deleterious impact on both Ukraine and Moldova. This is why soon after the Orange Revolution in Ukraine, the new administration turned its attention to the problem. "If the border is securely sealed, the illegitimate authority in Transnistria will soon lose the economic foundation of its existence," said the foreign minister Boris Tarasiuk in June 2005. Accusing the former president Kuchma of complicity, Tarasiuk continued, "The previous government used Transnistria as a springboard for contraband because the money chiefly flowed to Kiev. The situation has changed now. Ukraine is not interested in the existence of a 'black hole' on its frontier; neither is Ukraine interested in capitalizing on the conflict in this neighboring state."

Boris Tarasiuk was foreign minister for only a few months before the first Orange government collapsed in a welter of mutual accusations and a deteriorating economic situation, encouraged in no small part by energy "sanctions" imposed from Moscow. One perceptive analyst of Transnistria has suggested that the capacity of Moscow to dictate the politics of its "near abroad" (and thereby sustain rogue regimes like Tiraspol) has been shorn up since President Putin consolidated his control over the Russian energy sector as a means to project Russian foreign policy power. "As the EU is 60 percent energy dependent on the Russian Federation and has higher priorities in its agenda than conflict settlement," the analyst wrote, "the prospects of somehow strong-arming Russia are unrealistic."

As head of the Moldovan Football Association, Pavel Ciobanu is, strictly speaking, neutral when it comes to the big game between Sheriff and Zimbru. But he is smiling as we head back to Chisinau after Sheriff's convincing 3 to 0 victory (10 wins out of 10 for the season so far). "Gusan's aim is to get Sheriff into the final rounds of the European Cup," he explains to me. "I think we'll do it in a couple of years." This is bold ambition indeed, especially given the paltry attendance of just 4,000 spectators at the grandiose stadium, which can seat five times as many for what is supposed to be the biggest game of the season. "Mr. Gusan is very happy today. It is his birthday; he went hunting and killed a wild boar. And now he wins three to zero. He is doing great things for Moldovan football."

PART II

Gold, Money, Diamonds, and Banks

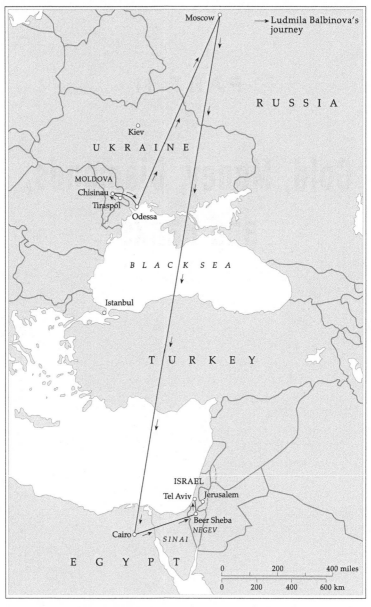

Sex trafficking from the former Soviet Union to the Middle East

CHAPTER 5

Aliyah

The border that separates Israel and Egypt is barely noticeable. Staring down at the flimsy wire fence separating the Negev Desert from northern Sinai, I am surprised how a country as concerned with its security as Israel permits such open access onto its territory from an Arab land. The police assure me that they patrol the border regularly, but I don't see a soul when driving up the northern half toward the southern tip of Gaza.

Until, that is, two camel heads rear up imperiously some two hundred yards in front of me. They are heading from Egypt into Israel, piloted by a group of four young teenagers, two jockeys and two guides. The camels are packed to the humps with smuggled goods, most probably cigarettes or narcotics, the bread-and-butter cargo for these cross-border traders. Seized by fear at the sight of my car, the boys urgently whip the great beasts, which bolt in the direction of an unlicensed pickup truck before the undulating Negev swallows all three—riders, vehicle, and camels.

Criminals in the eyes of the Israeli state, these smugglers nonetheless bear the torch of nomadic tradition, which has been all but extinguished among the Bedouins of the Negev. To be sure, theirs is a distorted inheritance. At the founding of Israel in 1948, 90 percent of these Bedouin were involved in nomadic or semi-nomadic economic activity—almost entirely pastoral. But in fits and starts since then, Israel has tried to corral the roughly 100,000 Bedouins from across the Negev into seven urban settlements in the desert's northwestern quarter. As a consequence, that statistic has been inverted—90 percent now work in low-wage industrial branches such as construction or the settlements' growing if impoverished public sector. A significant number of the 10 percent who don't now work instead as smugglers (there is no contest between this cash-rich trade and subsistence farming).

By regional standards, Israel can call upon immense security resources, but these are not limitless. And so the Bedouin farmers use their unparalleled knowledge of the desert terrain to refashion themselves as a critical cog in the industry of purveying illicit goods and services to the Israeli consumer.

Most tribally organized communities coming into contact with the modern state over the past half century have witnessed their traditional lifestyle come crashing down around them. The Bedouins are an excellent example. Like the Bushmen of southern Africa, the indigenous peoples of Irian Jaya, or the Inuit of the Arctic, the Bedouins of the Negev retain a powerful cultural memory that no longer bears any proper relationship to their social and economic circumstances. How can you be a nomad in a desert that is home to huge private farms such as the one that belonged to the former Israeli prime minister Ariel Sharon? The results are uniform across the world—indigenous communities record relatively high rates of birth, infant mortality, and illiteracy.

And so it is the young Bedouin smuggler jockeys who nurture the flickering flame of their people's collective memory. The job is certainly more interesting and varied than any of the limited opportunities available in the settlements, and it means continued contact with their cousins across the border in the Sinai. This profession is also growing, as the increasing incidence of drug abuse among the Bedouins testifies. Communities from whom land-based narcotics smugglers are drawn—Albanians, Bedouins, and Tajiks, for example—usually suffer chronic rates of drug abuse. But the reasons behind the development of the illicit sector in the Negev do not lie primarily with the Bedouins but among a group of immigrants to Israel who started arriving only fifteen years ago: the Russians.

When the Soviet Union collapsed and the economies in the successor states went haywire, the future looked both frightening and uncertain for the great majority of citizens. If the gangster capitalism in Moscow seemed scary, spare a thought for ordinary folk who lived on the periphery, especially in the Caucasus, where war, civil conflict, and sheer thuggery made even such mundane tasks as grocery shopping a hazardous activity.

Alexander Gentelev, a documentary film maker, hurried home from work one freezing winter's evening in 1991. Makhachkala, the capital of Dagestan, where he lived, was as wild as it gets. He was still shaken up following the assassination twenty-four hours earlier of a good friend who had left his job as a doctor to become involved in local politics. "He was getting into his car and they opened fire from both sides. They shot him sixty times," Gentelev remembered. "But I had no reason to expect they would come after me. I was wrong."

They came for him two days later. But Gentelev was lucky. "I was most fortunate that evening for two reasons," he told me in a café in Tel Aviv. "First, I had a bad flu and was wrapped up very warmly. And second, I had just been paid for a job. At the time, inflation was going mad and so this was a huge thick wad of notes." Out of the shadows stepped a couple of gunmen who opened fire. "I was knocked to the ground and lost consciousness, but the bullet aimed at my heart was cushioned by the cash and so didn't penetrate my body!"

He was still very seriously wounded. "As I lay in hospital in Makhachkala, I was warned that they would return," he said. "I didn't even know who 'they' were and so I asked my brother to evacuate first my family and then me to Moscow. And at this stage, my wife said, 'Right! Enough is enough! We are not going back!' "

Fortunately, Alexander was Jewish. Apart from when Stalin had a vicious anti-Semitic spasm just before his death, being Jewish in the postwar Soviet Union was not usually much worse than being anything else. As a Jew, one's professional ambition was often circumscribed in a way that did not affect Slavs and some other minorities, but in many respects all peoples in the Soviet Union were shat upon in equal measure. From 1989 onward, however, the Jews of the former Soviet Union enjoyed one valuable and exclusive privilege—they were eligible for Israeli citizenship and could get the hell out of Belarus, the Caucasus, Siberia, or wherever else with no questions asked.

And many didn't wait to be the victim of an assassination attempt like Gentelev. They took the passport and ran. Soon hundreds turned into thousands, thousands into tens and hundreds of thousands until within a decade 1 million Russian Jews had pitched up in Israel, amounting to more than 15 percent of the total population.

"Most came because the gates were open and they knew that they could be closed again at any moment," said Marina Solodkin, who after her arrival in Israel in 1991 went on to become the deputy minister for immigration in the Sharon government. "For Jews like me who were active in the underground in the 1970s, this was the Return Home—aliyah as it is called. But it was very important for the mixed and secular families as well. Nobody knew how things would develop in the former Soviet Union— would there be pogroms or no pogroms? None of us wanted to play Russian roulette, as it were."

It was not just the latent aggression of Russian anti-Semitism that triggered the exodus. There were positive reasons to come as well. The prospect of an Israeli passport and hence visa-free travel to most Western countries was a big bonus, as was the escape from the appalling Russian weather and the allure of the Mediterranean and Red Sea coasts.

Israel, of course, is a country that has been built on immigration since its inception in 1948. The country boasts an impressive record in the absorption of large groups long before the former Soviet Jews came—the Moroccan and Iraqi immigration of the fifties and more recently the immigration from Ethiopia. But it had never dealt with anything on this scale from such a well-defined and powerful culture. The Moroccan, Iraqi, and Ethiopian Jews had no choice but to learn Hebrew and submit to Israeli culture in order to survive. But the Jews from Russia and Ukraine were very different—they came in huge numbers in a short space of time, and they had a strong *Russian* cultural identity that was often more ingrained than their Jewishness. In the profoundly secular Soviet Union, Judaism and Zionism remained a minority interest at best among Russian Jews. "The former Soviet immigrants perceive themselves as the bearers of European culture in Israel, and 87% of them would like cultural life in Israel to be similar to that of Europe," noted one study on the sociology of the immigration based on extensive surveys. "However, only 9% believe that this is indeed the situation in Israel."

Israel, it seems, was a foreign country for these Russians. "The immigrants perceive Russian culture and language as superior to Hebrew. 88% of immigrants evaluate the impact of immigration on cultural life in Israel as positive or very positive, while only 28% evaluate the impact of cultural life in Israel on the immigrants as positive or very positive," the report said. Israeli culture was frequently zealous (unappealing for those who were once compelled to weather Soviet zealotry) and defined by a conflict with an enemy, the Palestinians, who did not excite Russian Jewish sensibilities. But it was also Mediterranean, which in the eyes of Russified Jews meant indolent and hence inferior. And then there were economic issues. "In addition to its size, another unique aspect of the Russian immigration was that many of the Russian immigrants were highly educated," the economists Sarit Cohen and Chang-Tai Hsieh have written. "About 60% of the Russian immigrants were college-educated, compared with only 30 to 40% of native Israelis." This led to social tension and real resentment between the indigenous population and the newcomers—Russian professionals wanted to muscle in on the labor market in large numbers. Not the dirty, poorly paid jobs traditionally reserved for immigrants but the well-paid posts for highly trained men and women.

Russian immigrants in Israel very quickly established a complex society that developed in parallel to the existing community. The state showed little inclination to become involved with the Russians, nor really had the capacity to do so. So as the Russians poured in during this first phase of integration, the two communities barely interacted at all—language and culture led to a period of mutual exclusion.*

It was the police who first noticed something odd happening. "At the time, I was head of the intelligence in Jerusalem," said the retired police commander Hezi Leder, "and we started getting reports from my colleagues in Haifa and the north of Israel of a dramatic rise in the amount of criminality among young people. These were kids who were thirteen and fourteen, maybe fifteen years old, but they seemed to be outside the education system. And they were almost all Russian."

By the mid-1990s, there were more than 700,000 Russians in Israel. Most were entirely honest, like Alexander Gentelev from Makhachkala. His was the familiar immigrant impulse from around the world—the search for sanctuary from a troubled environment and a better life for his children. "But if you have a million Russians here and just one percent is a criminal element," explained the former cop Gil Kleiman, "that's still a hell of a lot of bad boys!" Soon after Leder alerted his colleagues to the phenomenon of the youth gangs, police started to observe an increase in murders and assaults involving unprecedented brutality. The crime wave centered on Tel Aviv—or Sin City, as the tabloids refer to it—but almost always contained within the Russian-speaking community.

After receiving an anonymous tip-off in September 1996, Kleiman and his squad were shocked to discover the fresh corpse of a pimp called Oleg "Karpits" Karpachov. It was lying in a pool of blood in a high-rise apartment building. The autopsy report stated that he had been stabbed in both the forehead and the neck. "The knife went through the skin, the veins, and

---

*Although the two communities are now becoming closer and more intertwined, I spent a pleasant evening in Putin, a bar in the center of Jerusalem with a low-slung ceiling, where second-generation Russian teenagers conversed only in Russian; where there is no Hebrew script, only Cyrillic; and where the DJ plays only the latest songs from Moscow. Without doubt the most bizarre manifestation of this cultural stubbornness is the emergence in 2005 of a political grouping in Jerusalem, Tel Aviv, and Haifa called the Russian National Center. Its members are Russian *Jewish* teenagers whose avowed goal is to seek the "cleansing from mother Russia of all Yids, Chechens, and other minorities."

the windpipe all the way to the spine which was severed," read the report. He was also hit by a blunt object and stabbed in the shoulder and back. "The bulbs on his floor alone had been deliberately unscrewed so there would be no light," continued Kleiman, "so we knew that this was a seriously planned job. And later we discovered that when the murderers were coordinating the murder, they never used their cell phones for longer than a minute in case they were being tracked."

More shocking than the circumstances of Karpits's death was what Kleiman and the special investigative team discovered about the deceased's world. They began to unravel a network of pimps, brothels, protection rackets, counterfeit documents, and kidnapping. Apart from the sleaziness of this underground community, its most surprising aspect was its invisibility. This was an internal Russian affair that never impinged on the rest of Israeli society. Except, that is, in one respect—the single largest business these street-level Russian syndicates were running was prostitution, and the clients were by no means exclusively Russian.

Embracing globalization, Israel was becoming more permissive. Or rather, parts of Israel were. Jerusalem may have registered a growth in the number of devout Jews moving there and crowding out the secular inhabitants, but the inverse was occurring in Tel Aviv, the center of foreign investment and the boom in 1990s Israel. The success of Israel's high-tech industry in particular accelerated the emergence of a yuppie class bent on conspicuous consumption, including an extensive use of designer drugs, notably cocaine and ecstasy. The contrast between the endless glitter and thudding beat of Tel Aviv's nightclubs and just forty miles away the austere garb and somber mumbling of the Hassidim in Jerusalem is almost as eye-popping as the contrast between life in Israel and that in the bedraggled Gaza Strip. Moreover, a temporary reduction in tension with the Palestinians in the 1990s saw a return of mass tourism to Israel, and these factors combined to turn Tel Aviv into one of the two major hubs of prostitution in the Middle East (the other being Dubai). Brothels catering for every male pocket also began to flourish in tourist centers such as Netanya and Eilat. Like most other advanced developing economies, Israel came under American pressure to liberalize its markets and investment policies in the late eighties and nineties. And along with increased inflows and outflows of capital and goods came the personal acquisitiveness that underpins globalization and which presumes that money can fulfill any whim or desire. Combined with the ubiquitous images of male and female sexuality, this consumerism encourages the sense (certainly among men and increasingly, it would seem, among women too) that sex is less an expression of intimate relations and more a marketed commodity subject to the same rules governing the sale of hamburgers or sneakers, as one academic study argued:

> The concept of prostitution as a consumer activity is clearly evident on the Internet. One brothel Website boasts that it offers Israeli consumers the latest technology for "on-line orders for call girls right to your home, and all in Hebrew!" The site even offers potential clients a service agreement stating that they, like any client, will have the right to complain about the "services" rendered, since, after all, "The customer is always right." "Blazer," an Israeli magazine for men, was duly impressed: "What can I tell you? You've got to hand it to organized crime for really being organized. They learned from Domino's Pizza how to take orders. They asked me ... with mushrooms? Without? I asked them ... if it's not too hard, a natural blond, tall, with basic command of Hebrew."

Demand was rising rapidly, and the Russian underground in Israel knew how to supply it.

In early summer 2002 as Sheriff Tiraspol celebrated its fourth Moldovan soccer championship in a row, across the city *Ludmila Balbinova* was packing her suitcase. She was excited about her first trip abroad. Ludmila knew Israel was sunny and by the sea but not much else. She was going to meet an old friend who was working as a waitress in Israel. "You'll love it here," Victoria told Ludmila. "I've got you a job—the work's easy, the pay's good, and it is real fun." What Ludmila didn't know was that at the other end of the phone, Victoria had a gun pointed at her head.

Ludmila was not unhappy in Tiraspol, but like many young people she yearned for some adventure and fun. She thought herself fortunate that an acquaintance of her close friend had been so helpful in arranging both her documentation and her travel. It is complicated for residents of Tiraspol, because their own country, the self-styled Republic of Moldovan Transnistria, is not recognized internationally and so they must apply for passports thirty-five miles away in the capital of their supposed archenemy, the Republic of Moldova.

In fact, this accommodating acquaintance was a "recruiter." A majority of women trafficked out of Moldova and Transnistria are groomed and recruited by other women. The recruiters are motivated above all by money, but there are often other forces at work. Some are former prostitutes who have succeeded in buying themselves out of the trade by agreeing to work as recruiters back home. "Sometimes the mothers of trafficked women act as recruiters," explained Alina Budeci of La Strada, an NGO in Chisinau that assists trafficked women. "We had a case where a mother was contacted by traffickers who said that if she ever wanted to see her daughter again, she would have to recruit three new women to replace her."

The use of women is critical in order to reassure the victim. Trust is essential to the smooth functioning of any organized criminal activity. Except, that is, when the commodity being traded is a human being. In this instance, deceit must masquerade as trust. To reinforce the deception, the recruiter often accompanies the young woman (aged usually between fifteen and thirty) on the first leg of her journey. After her recruiter had secured Ludmila a passport, she was put on a train to Odessa and then to Moscow in the company of ten other women. Once in the Russian capital, she was taken to an apartment near the Moscow River. "This is when I first became very suspicious, because they confiscated our passports and locked the apartment," she said. "We were imprisoned."

From then on, whenever Ludmila was taken outside she was always accompanied by at least two thugs. After a week she and three other women were driven to Domodedovo Airport. At passport control, she had a final chance. In a compassionate outburst rare in Russian state officials, the officer at passport control pleaded with her to reconsider. "Do you really know where you are going?" he asked. "Are you sure you want to do this?" With one of the heavies literally breathing down her neck, Ludmila had little choice but to dismiss the officer's kind appeal. It was like the sound of the prison cell door slamming shut and the key being turned.

On arrival in Cairo, she was met by some Egyptian men who took her to a hotel, where she and the ten other girls waited for three days. In the early hours one morning, she was bundled into a Jeep and driven for several hours. "The Bedouins took charge of us and immediately put us into a cave." Although there are frequent reports of Bedouin smugglers raping the women they traffic (and indeed withholding them if they do not receive payment for their smuggling services), in Ludmila's case the girls were given a choice. If they offered sexual services to their temporary captors, "then the girls were allowed out, to eat properly, and to have a break. About three of the girls did this but I didn't," said Ludmila.

Just before they were due to leave for the next leg of their journey, one of these terrified women made a break for it. "The Bedouins captured her and then in front of us, they shot her in the knees." As victims of kneecapping in Northern Ireland well know, being shot in the knees is one of the most painful punishments that can be inflicted. But this young Moldovan woman's fate was even worse. "They just left her there in the desert to die."

By now Ludmila and her companions were terrified when the Bedouins again threw them in a pickup truck in the dead of night. "We drove for some time and then we were forced to crawl under a fence one by one. There were some other Bedouins meeting us on the other side, but then we were spotted by an Israeli border patrol, which came racing toward us. I was desperate for the border guards to reach us, but the Bedouins started shooting at our feet so we had to run as fast as we could to the next pickup truck. We were hurled into the back and a tarpaulin was thrown on top of us. It was simply terrifying." Having cut their teeth bringing contraband across the Egyptian-Israeli borders like their younger brothers I saw on the camels, these more experienced Bedouin men have now adapted their skills to traffic women. They frequently rape and brutalize the women—it is a depressing degeneration of their traditions.

In a hotel in the Negev capital, Beer-Sheba, Ludmila was paraded in front of potential purchasers. "The men spoke Hebrew most of the time so we couldn't understand, but then they would order us about in fluent Russian." At first Ludmila refused to get undressed. One of the Russians looked at her grimly. "The word *refuse* doesn't exist here. Understand?"

By the time she arrived in Tel Aviv, she had been passed through the hands of Moldovan, Ukrainian, Russian, Egyptian, Bedouin, Russian Jewish, and indigenous Israeli hands, half of whom had threatened her with violence. Her nightmare was only just beginning.

On a Friday evening in October as Shabbat approaches, I set out with two male friends to visit the brothels of Tel Aviv. Sitting under the fraying awning of the Banana VIP Club, a sickly yellow light illuminates a thick Russian neck against the dark street. Unlike the guards at almost every public establishment I've entered in Israel, he does not check for bombs or weapons but insists, in a touchingly Soviet fashion, on seeing our passports. He finally makes do with our driving licenses and we walk three floors up a thin stairwell past several apartments. We enter the reception lounge, where a couple of tense young men sit smoking and tapping their fingers against the armrests of cheap red sofas (along with red, the favored color of Tel Aviv brothels seems to be a dark nicotine yellow). Opposite the sofas on a slightly raised platform sit two women, occasionally exchanging some quiet words in Russian. One is dressed in a small pink top and taut bikini bottoms from which her buttocks stick out when she totters around on the four-inch heels that seem to be a de rigueur accessory here.

Behind the desk an exceptionally good-looking woman in her early twenties shares the look of infinite boredom that I note is as essential to whorehouses as the high heels. On either side of the lounge are corridors leading off to small rooms that, I can just make out, are large enough to accommodate a single bed and are decorated in red with dim red lighting. Conventional wisdom suggests this to be the color of romance, but this being my fourth brothel of the evening, I've already worked out that it effectively hides the filth on the carpets and beds. I have also discovered that it is regarded as normal for men to sit in the lounge, saying nothing and waiting till the mood strikes (or not). They then approach one of the women quietly and the two disappear (the woman effortlessly snatching a towel on the way). Dead face. No emotion.

Three brash American teenagers stroll in and break the silence. The one Hebrew speaker among them asks the girl behind the desk for the price. "Two hundred thirty shekels for half an hour; two-fifty for forty minutes." "Hey," replies his friend, "chill out a bit. Wait and see if they have any girls who are hotter than these," he says, gesturing toward the two women.

Although barely eighteen (if that), this guy was not a novice in this house. Raised on McDonald's and with an apparently sluggish metabolism, he was pug-ugly to boot and I couldn't help thinking that he would have found it difficult getting laid through more conventional methods. But I was still unable to account for such an inhuman attitude to these women in one so young. My friend Gideon leaned over to me and spoke softly: "You see them all the time," he said. "Their parents pack 'em off from the Upper West Side to Israel with a book filled with the phone numbers of synagogues, rabbis, and shuls, and a wad of cash. And then the minute they get here, they head for the whorehouses."

Earlier that evening, we had seen much worse. We had started our tour near the Old Bus Station, which is where some of the tens of thousands of foreign workers hang out in Israel. Since the last intifada, the Palestinians no longer carry out the dirty and dangerous jobs that are the preserve of immigrants elsewhere in the industrialized world. Their places have been taken by Romanians, Uzbeks, Thais, Filipinos, Turks—you name it. The importation of labor into Israel is a corrupt business in which organized crime also engages: globally, the International Migration Organization has identified the trafficking of indentured or slave labor as the fastest-growing sector in the industry.

Aliyah

The men who hang out at the Old Bus Station are not trafficked—although dirt poor, they are still probably the elite among this lumpen class. By any standards, though, this place is the pits. The buildings and streets are in disrepair, brightened up only by the odd, flickering neon sign of a heart or a naked woman pointing to a hovel behind the shop fronts. The brothels themselves are the bottom of this mucky heap. I can barely describe the pathetic aging women listlessly chain-smoking in rooms seven feet by three, ready to service any passerby for ten bucks (yes, ten bucks).

It is impossible to ascertain which of these women are compelled by traffickers and which by economic circumstance, as everybody in the trade, including the women, is wary of careless talk. It may be that high-class call girls enjoy the economic freedom their work affords them. But my short tour around Tel Aviv's brothels made it clear that for most women in the industry, the happy hooker is a preposterous myth. Similarly, it brought home how relentless the male sex drive is. Streams of men of different race, age, and class trotted in and out of the brothels as I was visiting them. The Jews are both secular and Orthodox; there are Palestinians from inside Israel and from the West Bank; there are a large number of Americans, West Europeans, and Japanese. Their faces indicate that they have overcome any qualms they may once have felt about their purchase of these services. I wonder if they were told the real stories behind the women they are abusing—women like Ludmila—how many would think again.

Instead of getting the holiday experience of a lifetime, Ludmila was kept locked in an apartment from six-thirty in the morning. At five-thirty in the afternoon, she was driven to a brothel above a pizza parlor on Bugashov Street, where she was forced to work for twelve hours in the high-volume second shift. "I worked seven days a week and had to service up to twenty clients per session," she explained. That is a euphemism. Ludmila was raped twenty times a night.

In Israel, as in most Western countries, it is the trafficked woman and not the client who is the object of law enforcement procedures. When Ludmila first succeeded in escaping, she was handed back to her pimp by the duty sergeant, who happened to be a client of the brothel. In response, she was beaten senseless by her "owner." The second time she got away, she handed herself in to a police station in another part of town. As is habitual, she was charged with being an illegal immigrant and thrown in a detention center for several months as her deportation order was processed.

When she finally arrived back in Chisinau, destitute and traumatized for life, Ludmila could not return to her home, partly for reasons of shame but above all for fear of being found by her traffickers. Hers is an everyday story of life in Moldova, Ukraine, Russia, Egypt, and Israel.

The day after I had spoken to Ludmila, her caseworker called. "I forgot to mention," she said, "Ludmila is now HIV-positive." Unsurprisingly, combination therapy is not readily available in a country such as Moldova.

A few months after Brigadier General Hezi Leder had identified the growth in Haifa street gangs, he received a tip-off that Grigory Luchansky was due to celebrate his birthday in Eilat. What is it about the Russian oligarchs and birthday parties? One of Russia's first superrich, this once respected vice rector of a university in Latvia had founded Nordex, a successful Vienna-based company, which police forces in Europe and America suspected relatively early on of involvement in large-scale money laundering. Still more sensitive were the allegations that Nordex had been shifting nuclear weapon components around the globe. "We didn't know who he was at the time, but the Americans were crazy about him because of Nordex and because he had met Clinton on some fund-raising thing and there was a photo of this," Leder explained. "I hesitate to use the word *mafia,* but if you saw how the guests approached Luchansky with such respect and kissing his hand, you see the strength of the hierarchy. This is a kind of mafia, and this was the beginning for us."

"We didn't know who these people were," explained one of Israel's most senior intelligence officers tasked with mapping Russian organized crime, "and we had to start from scratch. There were the low-level criminals—and we learned all about them; about the *vory-v-zakone,* the thieves-in-law; about their tattoos; we had people who learned how to speak their slang. And then there were the big guys. They were hard, but we went for them all."

The guests at Luchansky's party and at subsequent summit meetings in Tel Aviv read like a Who's Who of Russian business. The problem is that nobody knew Who exactly was Who. And Who was Not. Maybe.

Testifying to the House Committee on Banking in 1999, the former director of the CIA, James Woolsey, illuminated this conundrum when he asked the congressmen and -women to consider the following hypothetical situation.

If you should chance to strike up a conversation with an articulate, English-speaking Russian in, say, the restaurant of one of the luxury hotels along Lake Geneva, and he is wearing a $3,000 suit and a pair of Gucci loafers, and he tells you that he is an executive of a Russian trading company and wants to talk to you about a joint venture, then there are four possibilities. He may be what he says he is. He may be a Russian intelligence officer working under commercial cover. He may be part of a Russian organized crime group. But the really interesting possibility is that he may be all three—and that none of those three institutions have any problem with the arrangement.

A staggering number of Russians took out Israeli citizenship in the first half of the nineties, among them prominent members of Yeltsin's inner circle, known as the Seven Stars, such as Boris Berezovsky and Vladimir Gusinsky. Then there were budding industrial magnates such as the Ukrainian Vladimir Rabinovich or the Russian Mikhail Chorny, whom Western intelligence agencies suspected of criminal activities. And then there were others who had been barred from entering Britain and the United States, such as Semion Mogilevich and Luchansky himself.

There was even a scattering of gentiles, such as Sergei Mikhailov, the boss of Solntsevo, who just came along for the ride. "Mikhailov has as much to do with Judaism as I have with ballet!" guffawed the ursine Alexander Gentelev, "but he got his citizenship—no problem." It has since been revoked and the corrupt Israeli officials responsible for granting it have been prosecuted.

None of these Russians had a criminal record except for misdemeanors during the Soviet period. All had the outward appearance of successful businessmen with track records that on paper bespoke dynamism and guts. Why would Israel want to turn them away?

For their part, the oligarchs and organized crime bosses started colonizing Israel for a number of reasons. It was an ideal place to invest or launder money. Israel's banking system was designed to encourage aliyah, the immigration of Jews from around the world, and that meant encouraging their money to boot. Furthermore, Israel had embraced the zeitgeist of international financial deregulation and considerably eased controls on the import and export of capital. And, like most other economies around the world in the 1990s, it had no anti-money-laundering legislation. Laundering money derived from criminal activities anywhere else in the world was an entirely legitimate business.

Israeli police have estimated that these Russians laundered between $5 and $10 billion through Israeli banks in the fifteen years since the collapse of Communism. This is a significant sum for a small country such as Israel. But it is less than 5 percent of the huge capital flight from Russia during the 1990s, and it pales beside that of comparable countries such as Switzerland ($40 billion) or the perennial champions of the Mediterranean league, the Republic of Cyprus, which as early as the end of 1994 was processing $1 billion of Russian capital *a month*.

The main reason for Israel's popularity was the simplest—many of these iffy businessmen were Jews, and in Israel they were not treated like dirt but welcomed as valuable and respected additions to the family.

A disproportionate number of the most influential Russian oligarchs and gangsters were Jewish. Before the huge wave of immigration to Israel, Jews made up only about 2.5 percent of the population of Russia and Ukraine. But they were hugely influential in the vanguard of gangster capitalism during the 1990s. A cursory search of the Internet will reveal countless racist sites fueling the theory that the pillage of Russian assets during decade was borne of the World Jewish Conspiracy, once so beloved of the Nazis and (when it suited him) of Stalin. By contrast, many liberal commentators simply overlook the issue of Jewish involvement in Russia and Ukraine's chaotic transition, presumably to dodge accusations of anti-Semitism. In fact, by avoiding any mention of the elephant in the living room, they facilitate its portrayal by anti-Semites as a jackal.

Although the Soviet Union was renowned for its antipathy toward most national identities that threatened its idealized image of *homus sovieticus*, it did construct one specific barrier for Jews—the glass ceiling. In virtually all the central party and state offices, in almost all industrial branches, and in most places of learning, Jews were systematically prevented from reaching the top. There were exceptions to this rule—Kaganovich (one of Stalin's unloved Politburo colleagues) and, in the 1980s, Evgeni Primakov emerged as an extremely influential political figure, having prophylactically discarded his birth name, Yonah Finkelshtein. But on the whole, if you were Jewish, the key promotion would elude you.

In consequence, there were a lot of smart Jews who felt frustrated in their pursuit of intellectual challenges and entrepreneurial opportunities. Where better, then, to exercise those skills than in the world's toughest market (which officially didn't even exist!)—the Soviet planned economy. Over seventy years, they honed their business skills in this grim totalitarian world where huge industrial behemoths would seek to produce goods without regard to the laws of supply and demand. Instead, enterprises would follow the targets (or norms, as they were known) set down every five years by the State Planning Commission. These rarely bore any relation to the available materials, raw or processed, and so each factory would be engaged in a relentless and exhausting struggle against shortages. Factories were often reliant on suppliers based thousands of miles and several different time zones away and with which there were no functioning communications. The only way to meet those targets was to employ wheelers and dealers who could hustle the right materials from any source anywhere. These people were known as *tolkach,* and without the ingenuity of the *tolkachi* in sustaining the wobbly edifice, the Soviet Union may have buckled earlier than it did. And just as there were a disproportionate number of Jews among the oligarchs, so there were among the *tolkachi.*

"Being Jewish I couldn't study medicine as a matter of course," Vladimir Rabinovich, one of Ukraine's most notorious oligarchs, explained. Rabinovich was then subject to another burst of casual anti-Semitism and expelled from technical college. He was then compelled to begin his three-year military service. "I had been with my unit for just twenty days. The commander addressed us by asking 'Who can get hold of five tons of steel tubing with a three-quarters-inch diameter?' I had absolutely no idea what he was talking about, but I volunteered nonetheless. 'And how long do you need to get hold of them?' he asked me. 'A minimum of one week,' I replied. And that got me the job!" By ducking, diving, sweet-talking, and pilfering, Rabinovich found the tubing and began his career as a *tolkach.* Many of his fellow Jewish entrepreneurs or mafia bosses boasted similar histories. Not only had they developed their entrepreneurial skills in the most trying circumstances, but they were not weighed down, as were their Slav peers, by the torpid traditions of the czarist and Soviet bureaucracies that crushed any hint of personal initiative.

This ability was not restricted to the Jews. It is no coincidence that among organized crime bosses, the other two chronically overrepresented nationalities in Russia were the Chechens and the Georgians, whose talent for overcoming the daily consumer misery of the Soviet Union was similarly the stuff of legend. The criminals and oligarchs emerged from communities who inhabited the twilight periphery of the Soviet Union— although usually denied access to the central institutions, they were not pariahs. Instead they were compelled to seek out the possibilities of social and economic activity that existed in the nooks and cracks of the state. This experience was invaluable for many when negotiating the roller coaster of post-Communist Russia.

For the Jewish oligarchs and gang bosses, Israel was both a retreat and, by dint of its passport, a door to the outside world. They did not wish to draw attention to themselves, nor did they wish to become an embarrassment for the state. This was no mere sentiment—it was a policy, hammered out between the most influential godfathers at a meeting in Tel Aviv's Dan Panorama Hotel in 1995. The biggest names were there, including gentiles such as Sergei Mikhailov, to ensure that they did not alienate the Israeli government. "They decided that Israel is no place for assassinations or settling their difficulties by killing one another," explained Gentelev. "These people did not want to engage in much business here. It was a place where you could launder a bit of money; where you could rest; and where you could find shelter. And receive a passport with which you could travel the whole world."

The new Russians were already well settled in Israel by October 1995 when Bill Clinton's advisers convinced him to sound a warning about the "dark side of globalization." Addressing the Fiftieth Commemorative Assembly of the UN, the president called for a worldwide "assault on terrorism, organized crime, drug trafficking, and nuclear smuggling." Clinton said that "no one is immune," as he listed crimes such as the Aun Shinrikyo "poison gas attacks on the Japanese subway, suitcase bombings in Israel and France, mafia gangs in Russia, and the Oklahoma City bombing" that had shaken America in April that year.

Because of the concentrated Russian presence, Washington turned its gaze to Israel, and by the mid-1990s, the long if arthritic arm of American law enforcement was knocking on Jerusalem's door for information on a number of oligarchs and alleged criminals, such as Mogilevich and Mikhailov. Encouraged by the State Department under Jon Winer, Clinton's undersecretary for drugs and thugs, the Israeli police placed many of the most prominent Russians under surveillance in 1996. "There was suddenly a huge interest in the oligarchs," explained Irit Bouton, now chief of intelligence in the Israeli police Special Operations. "It was like a baby boom in the world of crime."

But huge problems matched the huge interest as the police tried to assess and contain the burgeoning criminality of the new world order. There was the familiar issue of definition: what constituted criminal activity among the oligarchs and what did not? Moreover, the oligarchs and gangsters could draw on effectively limitless financial resources to defend themselves and their image. And they did so assiduously. "Don't worry about these guys shooting you," the Israeli intelligence officer told me when I explained what I was writing about. "They aren't that crude. They'll just sue you to death."

Then there was external political pressure. Iosif Kobzon is renowned as the Frank Sinatra of the new Russia. A tremendously popular performer of schmaltzy songs in Russia, he also enjoys a rich political life, as an MP of the Russian Duma and a backer or friend of many pro-Putin politicians and businessmen, including Solntsevskaya and other organized crime groups. In the early nineties, he received an Israeli passport but was refused entry into the United States. Moshe Shahal, a successful Tel Aviv lawyer, was then the minister for national security who established the anti–Russian organized crime intelligence unit. He sighs when remembering the period. "Both in the Knesset and in government, we came across difficulties in trying to implement the new security policy." On his instructions, for example, Iosif Kobzon was detained at Ben Gurion Airport in January 1996 and refused entry into the country. But Shahal's directive was overridden, the former minister says, by Shimon Peres, then foreign minister. Shahal explains that the then Russian ambassador had called Peres and warned of severe consequences for Israeli-Russian relations if Kobzon were denied entry into Israel. The authorities, seldom susceptible to influence from countries except the United States, allowed him in.

And there was also domestic political pressure. The arrival of one million Russians had a substantial impact on the Israeli electorate, and they represented votes every established politician wanted to win. The central political figure in the Russian community was Natan Sharansky, the former Soviet dissident who was released from prison into exile in the mid-1980s. In the early 1990s, he became the conduit between the oligarchs and the Israeli political establishment, accepting donations from some of the new arrivals from Russia and then establishing his avowedly Zionist political party, Yisra'el Ba'aliyah, in 1995.

Sharansky's was a powerful lobby, as it controlled potentially several hundred thousand votes in a democracy in which small political parties are crucial in forming governments. One should not underestimate how strongly Israel's Russian-speaking community felt about its prominent members being branded criminals, as the ex–Russian media magnate and now owner of the Israeli paper *Ma'ariv*, Vladimir Gusinsky, pointed out: "When we Russian businessmen, Jewish or otherwise, are called mafiosi by American newspapers, it's insulting," he said. "But when Jewish entrepreneurs from Russia are called that in Israel, it's not just insulting, it makes me howl with pain. It's wrong!"

The police had to negotiate all these conundrums and dilemmas in trying to formulate a coherent strategy in dealing with organized crime and trying to understand its relationship to the Russian immigration. But all this took place in the shadow of a very different issue that absorbed not just most of Israel's security budget but much of its political energy as well.

"The whole question of Palestinian terror," said Commander Bouton, "puts a strain on our resources working in the organized crime area—we are always playing catch-up." Marvelous opportunity for criminals, though.

The Palestinian issue is simply overwhelming in Israel. At times, it almost seems that Israelis have willingly diverted all their intellectual faculties into consideration of this one matter. Everything appears illuminated by the torch of the Arab-Israeli conflict, obscuring in the process the fascinating and dynamic nature of Israel's own society, especially since the collapse of the Soviet Union and the advent of globalization.

The existence of an external Arab enemy and, after the Six Days' War in 1967, a Palestinian enemy in the occupied territories, has afforded Israel a powerful domestic legitimacy. But the sacrifices imposed on Israelis by security concerns were only ever one side of the coin: until fifteen years ago, Zionism was underpinned by a remarkably strong sense of collectivism, expressed most obviously in the kibbutzim movement but also in the influence of the trades union movement, the Histadrut. A bitter opponent of the Soviet Union, Natan Sharansky expressed the sentiments of many right-wing Jews when he railed against his new home: "The predominance of the government in Israel's economy makes it the most socialist country outside the Eastern Bloc. . . . It is Israel's fate to suffer the worst from the centrally controlled east and the democratic west."

But for most Israelis the powerful state sector was an important expression of solidarity among Jews, conferring a social and philanthropic substance to the national project. Globalization is chipping away at that relentlessly and in some places driving a wedge between the various parts of a highly differentiated society. "Prime ministers like Menachem Begin and Ben Gurion were public servants, living in small two-bedroom apartments," said Uri Cohen-Aharonov, Israel's leading TV crime reporter. "They got up at six a.m. working for Israel and were still doing so when they went to bed at midnight. Now you say the word *kibbutz* and people laugh. Ariel Sharon has a huge farm a few kilometers from Sderot where the poorest people in the country live. The difference between the rich and ordinary people reminds me more and more of the gap between rich and poor in South America."

After years of modest inflows, direct foreign investment began to swamp the country (rising from $0.2 billion in 1992 to more than $8 billion in 2000) and encouraged by the political stability accompanying the peace process following the Oslo Accords. Exchange controls were relaxed and suddenly billions were moving in and out of Israel every year. Within that context the Russian money flows were seen by Israeli's elite as an indicator of economic success, not of criminality. Even more spectacular was the increase in per capita GDP from $11,000 in 1990 to $18,620 in 2006. Visible wealth was increasing in striking contrast to the stagnation of the surrounding Arab countries. Less visible, however, was the steady rise in unemployment as investors directed their capital into industries with low labor requirements.

The collapse of the dot-com boom resulted in dramatic stories of suicides on Wall Street, but its impact was still harsher on the periphery of the globalizing world. This was especially true in Israel, not just because of the concentration of wealth in the high-tech industries but also because it coincided with the beginning of the Second Palestinian intifada in 2000. Austerity measures replaced the expanding budgets of the mid-1990s. Spending on the Israeli Defense Force (IDF) increased to meet the challenge of the Palestinians, but spending on the police at first remained stagnant and was then cut in real terms. Above all, social programs were trimmed and, in a very short time, the discrepancy between rich and poor that had begun to grow during the 1990s was now very obvious. The change in Israeli society at the turn of the century was rapid and remarkable. As the hangover set in, Israel found itself with high unemployment, a growing budget deficit, a spiraling security budget, and collapsing foreign direct investment. It also had a new subclass of foreign labor (many of them trafficked) to replace the Palestinians now penned into the West Bank and the Gaza Strip; and a culture of avid consumerism that placed individualism firmly above the collectivism of the kibbutzim. Hostility to the Russians started to grow again, especially with regard to perceptions about criminality. When asked in a countrywide survey about attitudes on immigration from the former Soviet Union in 1999 and crime, 24 percent of Israelis had a "very negative view" of the Russian-speaking community. When asked the same question in January 2003, that figure had risen to 38 percent. A month later, however, something happened that led Israelis to abruptly revise their attitude on organized crime. The Russians had agreed at the 1995 El Dan meeting in Tel Aviv to avoid acting in an ostentatious criminal manner within Israel. Now Israelis were about to discover that the years of champagne and excess in the 1990s had spawned a new phenomenon—indigenous Israeli organized crime. And unlike the Russians, these people cared very little about their public image.

Ze'ev Rosenstein's Mercedes pulled over in front of a small currency exchange shop on Yehuda Halevy Street. It was midday in December, with the Eastern Mediterranean's short winter still at bay. "A couple of policemen were arguing with a guy sitting in a red car," Eli, a man in his forties, told the *Jerusalem Post*, "then came the boom. . . . And they all disappeared."

"It was a big, big bang," said Alon, who still works at the Tabul bakery opposite, "and then I see a body flying up into the air. A lot of people came—the police, just like a terror attack. For the first twenty minutes, everyone thought it was a terror attack. We didn't think it had anything to do with Rosenstein; we thought it was Palestinians."

In fact, this was the seventh attempt on the life of Ze'ev Rosenstein, who had for several years been at daggers drawn with the Abergil family. But in contrast to earlier ones, this failed assassination took place in a busy, slightly run-down street in south Tel Aviv. Rosenstein, "the wolf with seven lives," as he is known, drove away with a few bruises and scratches, but three innocent bystanders were dead.

The media outcry was fueled by popular indignation. "It's not like we don't have enough bombs in this country as it is!" said Bilha, who worked at the corner supermarket a few yards from where the bomb went off. "Are they completely insane? What have we come to? Jews blowing up Jews?"

The police blamed the interior minister for starving them of resources. "We don't have the resources to fight a two-front war," said Gil Kleiman after the bomb. Kleiman, who had cut his teeth uncovering criminality in the Russian underground, was now spokesman for the Israeli police and clearly frustrated. "It's a very big bed, and a very small security blanket, and we have to move that blanket around. So if your blanket is covering anti-terror work, those are police officers who can't be working anti-crime work, which is checking and stopping vehicles and doing what proper police criminal procedures are. You can't do both at the same time."

Ariel Sharon called an emergency cabinet meeting and the government promised an extra 500 million shekels ($100 million) in the fight against crime. Newspaper commentators began to compare Rosenstein, the Abergils, and four other families with the Palestinians in terms of threats to the Israeli state. Interestingly, one of those families was a Bedouin clan.

"The indigenous Israeli crime syndicates are different from the Russians," explained Menachem Amir, the country's leading criminologist. "The Russians were very careful. And were able to impose discipline because they were based on an organization. The Israeli crime groups were families." This meant that in structure they were much more like the Sicilian Mafia than the Russians were. "When you have crime based on families, then issues such as honor and vendettas come into play," Professor Amir

continued. The existence of family feuds may result in the occasional innocent victim, as in the Rosenstein case, but in another respect they assist
police. The bloodletting enables intelligence officers to monitor what is
going on in the crime community, "which means that the Russians and
similar organizations are more effective and more dangerous."

Gambling had been the traditional industry around which the Israeli
crime syndicates gathered and thrived. After the Oslo Peace Accords, the
Israelis permitted the Palestinians to open a casino in Jericho to comple-
ment the floating casinos in the Red Sea that hovered just outside Israel's
territorial waters. The Rosensteins and Abergils were alleged to have controlled much of the payoffs from these, as well as the profits from organized gambling trips for Israelis to Turkey.

But in the 1990s, the Israeli syndicates branched out and moved into an
even more lucrative area. The families, "perhaps thanks to their long-
standing ties in Antwerp," the DEA reported, "continue to be the major
elements in the transfer of large shipments of Ecstasy from Belgium [to
the United States]." Those ties referred to one of the five key commodities from which organized crime groups around the world make their
largest profits: diamonds. The other four are arms, narcotics, energy products, and cigarettes.

Ecstasy was one of the few drugs with which the American market was
not yet supersaturated. Europe is the top manufacturing base for this synthetic narcotic that stimulates a feeling of well-being and in particular a
sense of goodwill to one's fellow humans (so clearly there are worse drugs
in terms of social impact). The main West European center is Amsterdam,
although industrial-scale busts have been made since the turn of the millennium in Serbia and Bulgaria as well.

In 2003, the State Department issued a report claiming that Israel is the
hub of global ecstasy trafficking, having branched out from Europe to the
United States. "Israeli drug-trafficking organizations are the main source
of distribution of the drug to groups in the U.S., using express mail services, commercial airlines, and recently also using air cargo services," the
report states. For a country as dependent on American financial, political,
and military support, this was acutely embarrassing to Israel.

The DEA implied in one report that the turf war in New York, Las
Vegas, and Los Angeles over the ecstasy trade may be directly linked to the
open warfare between the families in Israel. It is perhaps appropriate that
Israeli gangsters have such influence in Las Vegas, as this was the old
stomping ground of America's most notorious Jewish criminal, the late
Meyer Lansky, and his protégé, Bugsy Siegel. Lansky was one of the very

few indictees ever to be extradited from Israel to the United States. He sought Israeli citizenship in the early seventies when on the run from American law enforcement. Golda Meir was only convinced to allow the extradition when her aides explained that Lansky was involved with the Mafia. "No. No Mafia! Not here!" she exclaimed.

Ze'ev Rosenstein posed a much greater threat to Israel than Lansky ever could. Both he and his wife were members of Prime Minister Sharon's then political party, the Likud. The Abergils were also members of Likud, and in one famous incident, a Labour member of the Knesset accused a cabinet minister (later assassinated by the Palestinians) of links with Israeli organized crime. Jon Winer, Clinton's anti–organized crime chief, had offered his president serious evidence of the criminal penetration of Likud, a further suggestion of how crime since 1989 was beginning to undermine the country's social fabric.

But in 2004, under pressure from the United States, Israel acted by arresting and extraditing Rosenstein, wanted by America for the sale there of more than 700,000 ecstasy tablets (although Washington agreed that, if found guilty, Rosenstein would be able to serve his sentence back in Israel).

Because of specific political issues, Israel was one of several countries around the globe that was vulnerable to a swift penetration by organized crime in the wake of two epoch-changing events. The first was the collapse of Communism in Eastern Europe and the former Soviet Union, which as we have seen had a unique impact in Israel. But the extent of the internationalization of organized crime and the role Israelis played in it would not have been possible without globalization—and one aspect in particular, the deregulation of international financial markets. The new freedom for capital to travel around the world was not restricted to money from those huge corporations that had slipped the moorings of individual countries and their regulatory systems to assume a global presence. The laundering of profits from illicit activities was also about to enter its golden age. And lest we fall into the error of thinking that Israelis or Jews had a particular penchant and ability for engaging in organized crime, it is worth remembering that the center for the global money-laundering industry was a few hundred miles away in a very different country—the United Arab Emirates.

CHAPTER 6

Xanadu I

And 'mid this tumult Kubla heard from far
Ancestral voices prophesying war!

—Samuel Taylor Coleridge, "Kubla Khan"

On the morning of Friday, March 12, 1993, they emerged after dawn in their millions. From cracked and crumbling Victorian mansions, from spiffing art-deco bungalows, from new high-rises, from tin shacks, from under fraying tarpaulin covers, from gutters and from city sidewalks: the working people of Bombay* launched their chaotic charge on the most besieged and battered but resilient transportation system in the world.

Like deranged wasps, the autorickshaws darted around the streets, stinging any fool in their way. Yet more numerous were the angular black and yellow taxis. Modeled on little Fiat 1100s that even the Italians have forgotten, these beasties scurried and squeaked like motorized rodents, squeezing through gaps in the traffic where none were apparent. By 1993, India's steady liberalization had allowed imperious European, American, and Japanese cars into the market to compete with the domestic Ambassador (né Morris Oxford III Series) and Marutti (né Suzuki Alto).

And, of course, on the dilapidated stations of the Western and Central railway lines, fists were thrown, shirts torn, and saris pulled as the commuters from the northern suburbs engaged in their daily Darwinian scramble to get on the inexplicably reliable urban trains to reach the south of the city.

"I have never quite understood how traffic in Bombay moves and I

---

*The city's name was changed to Mumbai in 1997. References to Bombay denote events before that date.

Dawood Ibrahim's turf: Dubai-Karachi-Mumbai

understand more about this subject than most," mused Rakesh Maria, the charming former deputy commissioner of police (traffic), "but mysteriously it does progress."

Once the frenzied movement of people begins in the morning, it doesn't stop until many hours after sundown. It is accompanied by sticky heat and an incessant din of horns, shouting, begging, squealing, and ranting—on and on until one thinks only of seeking sanctuary from the assault on the senses.

But at 1:28 p.m. on that March 12, a new and most sinister element joined the merry pandemonium: the roar of half a ton of the world's most powerful military explosive, RDX, ripping up from the underground garage of the Bombay Stock Exchange (BSE) and into the pit where traders were just preparing for the lunch bell.

This is always the busiest time of day at the BSE. Traders, hawkers, and food sellers, with their cornucopia of fruit, samosas, curries, lassies, dosas, sweetmeats, and more, descend on the area to assuage the hunger of the businessmen and -women who stream out of the Exchange and its surrounding buildings for their brief half-hour lunch period. But on this day, they didn't scamper out. They were thrown out, dismembered and dead, while the mass of concrete, glass, and metal decapitated and disemboweled the street vendors, their friends, their customers, and their families.

"Four brothers of a migrant family from northern India ran a sugarcane juice stall near the BSE," recalled Hussain Zaidi, author of *Black Friday,* the most detailed history of the bombings that was later made into a riveting documentary movie. "The fifth brother returned shortly after the blast to find his siblings lying dead in a pool of blood. Then there was Gokulchand Gupta, who had run a panipuri stall there for thirteen years. Gupta's head was blown off. His only son, Premchand, who was seventeen, was charred beyond recognition."

Twenty-two-year-old Mukesh Khatri had gone to the Baroda Bank, which had a branch at the BSE. He was queuing outside the building when the bomb went off. "There were pieces of glass flying all around, many were embedded in my body, and my face," he remembered. Drenched in his own and others' blood, he somehow managed to drag himself on foot to a hospital almost one mile away.

The effect of this calamity on the traffic in downtown Bombay was, of course, dramatic. Panic mutated into hysteria to ensure the onset of localized gridlock. Ambulances and police cars were as immobile as the rest, leaving those victims still alive writhing in agony. All told, 84 died and 217 were injured in the BSE blast. This was the beginning.

Over the next two hours, seven more bombs went off at crowded locations throughout the city, while grenades were thrown in another two places by men on motorcycles. The deadliest explosion occurred outside the regional passport office in Worli at 2:50 p.m., when a bomb placed on a double-decker bus lifted the five-ton vehicle off the ground. Not a single body on the bus could be identified, and a merciless shower of burning metal and glass pierced the organs and limbs of hundreds of passersby and residents. The casualties: 113 dead, 227 injured.

Around the same time, Deputy Commander Rakesh Maria was investigating another explosion at the headquarters of Shiv Sena, a young Hindu nationalist party that had its power base in Bombay, the capital of Maharashtra. Hindus were clustering around the Shiv Sena building, chanting anti-Muslim slogans and demanding retribution. "I addressed the leader of the mob and told him that the bombs had nothing to do with religion," Maria said, "but were part of a much bigger conspiracy." This, he added, seemed to disperse the tension. At around the same time, however, he received news over his walkie-talkie that another mob had started attacking Muslims indiscriminately in the district of Mahim.

The unstoppable city had ground to a bloody halt.

Thirteen years later, as the sun sets across Mumbai's police headquarters, an elegant Victorian mansion in khaki and cream, Maria leans back behind his chunky wooden desk. A distinguished-looking Punjabi with an assured military bearing, he recalled: "I had been away from it all on a course in advanced urban traffic management in Tokyo but returned here to some turbulent times. As soon as I got back on January 5, 1993, the chief commissioner put me in charge of the Mahim Chicken's Neck to ensure that the VIPs were able to travel from the airport to the center." Just east of Mahim fort, the Chicken's Neck is a narrow chicane where the city's two main north-south arterial roads merge to form the ninth circle of vehicular hell. Rakesh Maria was charged with securing the passage of VIPs to the city center because Bombay was in crisis: anti-Muslim riots had erupted here in December 1992 and again in January 1993. Many of these riots, indeed, broke out in and around Mahim.

The turbulent times that had greeted Maria on his arrival back in India's commercial capital had commenced even before the riots. Over the previous five years, the BJP, a new political party that espoused an aggressive form of Hindu nationalism, had fostered an obscure religious dispute in another part of India—Ayodhya in the northern province of Uttar Pradesh. Following an ominous pattern, the events around the destruction of the Babri Mosque in Ayodhya, far away from Bombay, had unsettled relations between the majority Hindus and minority Muslims in several parts of India. In Bombay itself, the Hindu mob followed the exhortations of nationalists to attack Muslims indiscriminately. "The day I took over responsibility for the Chicken's Neck was the day the riots broke out again," said Maria. "I was at the junction in Mahim opposite St. Michael's Church, where Muslim workers stored wood, when the Hindus attacked them," he continued. Although he is not a Christian, Commissioner Maria's surname suggests that he is, and he never disabuses people of this assumption, as it affords him a certain neutrality when dealing with tensions between Muslims and Hindus. As the Hindus surrounded the Muslim workers, Maria rushed to the scene and started firing in the air. "I warned them all to disperse, and from that day forth, there was no confrontation in this part of Mahim."

Unfortunately, Maria's courage was not mirrored elsewhere among Bombay's police. Altogether, 900 people, more than two-thirds of them Muslims, the rest Hindus, were slaughtered in those riots as law enforcement officers stood and watched. "We failed the Muslims of Bombay and we failed the people of Bombay during that time," one senior police officer told me. This dereliction of duty was to have severe consequences, most notably the March bombings. "Until 1993," argued Maria, "Bombay's underworld was the most secular part of this city. In other spheres, we saw communal issues having an impact, but we never for a moment imagined that this could affect organized crime."

During the riots, the Hindu mob in Mahim had sought out and destroyed the offices of one Tiger Memon, a mid-level gangster and renowned smuggler who owed allegiance to the most powerful crime organization in Bombay. According to his friends, Tiger Memon was livid when he learned about the attack on his headquarters, and he immediately set about planning his revenge. To do so, however, meant conferring with his boss. But although his boss was a Bombay lad, he no longer lived there. Wanted both by the police and rival gangsters in connection with a string of serious homicide charges, Dawood Ibrahim Kaskar had skipped bail in 1984 and left the city he loved. He moved westward to a place that had long enjoyed a warm, tangled relationship with Bombay but that could hardly be more different.

A few miles east of Heathrow Airport, my cab drives past a billboard the size and shape of a skyscraper. The image of hypermodern buildings stretching toward the heavens beckons drivers on the M4 to leave the light gray chill of London and fall instead into the embrace of a new earthly paradise—Dubai.

Stepping into my air-conditioned cab eight hours later, a peculiar oblong video greets me with an exhortation to visit the Mercato Mall, a deliciously ill-conceived reimagining of Venice; then to buy Gold, Gold, Gold; and finally to invest in an apartment at the Burj Dubai.

The Burj Dubai is one of several pinnacles in the novel architectural movement that I call Emirate futurism, and which ex-pats call the Master Plan of Sheikh Mo (a cheeky if endearing reference to Sheikh Mohammed bin Rashid Al Maktoum, Dubai's enlightened despot). The *burj,* or tower, comprises several clustering metallic sheaves that soar into the air. The bottom thirty-seven floors will become the world's first Armani Hotel, designed by the fashion guru himself. The final height of the core sheaf is being kept a secret. When the developers first announced the Burj in 2003 it was due to reach 500 meters into the sky. Each year, they have enhanced this vertiginous vision—600, 700, and now more than 900 meters. This is partly to keep competitors in Taiwan and Kuwait guessing, lest they trump Burj Dubai's goal to become the tallest building in the world, and partly, I suspect, the result of a keen urge on the part of the Master Planners to clothe any news about the city's development in excited hyperbole. This urge occasionally surfaces as an Orwellian spasm such as the slogan that proclaims the birth of the Burj on huge billboards down the main drag of new Dubai: HISTORY RISING.

This new Dubai hosts glitzy visitors from all over the world—David Beckham, Michael Schumacher, and Tiger Woods are regular visitors. Celebrities and the world's most powerful businessmen and -women are lining up to purchase some of the eye-popping construction projects that are multiplying like a rampant virus down the coast and into the desert. Rod Stewart was quick to purchase the Great Britain island that is an integral part of "The World," man-made islands of luxurious real estate all fashioned to resemble a physical image of the globe when seen from above. Then there is the fabulous complex of Palm Jumeira, Palm Deira, and Palm Jebel Ali, huge tracts of land reclaimed from the sea in the shape of three giant palm trees. Visible from space, this is set to become one of the most sought-after addresses on the planet.

Come one, come all . . . if you have the money. And if you do, then few if any questions are asked about how you came upon it or what you want to do with it. Dubai's discreet attitude to cash has enabled the city to attract leading figures from industries beyond sports and showbiz over the past decade. The Russian arms dealer Viktor Bout, renowned as the Merchant of Death, used to park his planes in Sharjah, Dubai's neighboring emirate ten miles away, while he received his checks for services rendered to warring factions through the Western banks there. The largest cigarette smuggler in the Balkans established his offices in the Burj al-Arab, the sail-shaped Arab Tower, the world's first-ever seven-star hotel (with seven-star prices starting at $1,500 a night).

And for a decade from 1984, Dawood Ibrahim watched as the new Xanadu rose up out of the desert. From his sumptuous residence, the White House (so called because it was in fact about the only building in Dubai to be painted entirely in black), Dawood controlled his empire, with offices in London, Nepal, Pakistan, and Sudan. And although Dawood was unable to travel to Bombay, he succeeded from his base in the Gulf in consolidating and expanding the biggest-ever criminal network Bombay had ever seen.

Dawood was brought up in Dongri, a dirt-poor area of central Bombay with a large but not exclusively Muslim population. His father was a lowly police inspector, but this didn't deter young Dawood from becoming involved in petty street crime. With his friends and brothers, he would go down to the bustling Crawford Market, where he started scamming gullible traders and bargain hunters. "His first trick was to offer a customer an expensive foreign watch," recalled a member of his youthful gang. "After taking the money he would vanish, while the customer would be discovering that Dawood had switched the watch for a stone or some such worthless object during the wrapping."

A natural leader, in his mid-teens Dawood and his elder brother, Sabir, joined—and before long took charge of—a Muslim political movement known as the Young Party. Under its previous leadership, the Young Party had a reputation as a militant Islamic outfit, but once the two Ibrahim brothers had wrested control of the organization, they remolded it into an efficient criminal gang. To fund the party activities, Dawood and his pals robbed a bank, resulting in a first conviction, which was later overturned by the High Court. As a criminal, having a policeman as a father did have a few advantages. D-Company was born.

Since India's independence in 1947, organized crime had troubled the country little, and the four dons who ran Bombay's mafia world were an unobtrusive presence with no great reputation for excessive violence. The economic system that Jawaharlal Nehru had championed after independence saw India erect mighty protectionist barriers to discourage the import of luxury and consumer goods, thereby boosting India's industrial capacity and maximizing the exchequer's income from tariffs. The first illicit trade to emerge was the smuggling and production of liquor, but it was not long before the cash generated from booze was equaled by money earned from another commodity—gold. Gold has always been central to the local culture, and Indians spend a small fortune on the metal at weddings, both in the form of dowries and as jewelry. To circumvent paying the massive tariffs, a substantial smuggling racket evolved in the 1950s and 1960s, which saw tons of gold shipped annually between Dubai and Bombay. This was a stable industry, and the authority of the four dons who controlled it went unchallenged in the underworld for three decades.

By the late seventies, Dawood and Sabir's gang of Konkani Muslims had made a name for itself as the leading incubator of street toughs in Dongri. Emboldened by this reputation, they hired themselves and their subordinates out as muscle to the smuggling operations of the big dons. Sabir had real ambition and began to establish the group's own smuggling network. The Dongri boys began to ruffle a few feathers, notably among the Pathan gang run by the legendary don Karim Lala. Then in the early eighties, two things happened—the first would change Dawood, and the second would change Dawood, Bombay, and India.

The last two or three weeks of February 1984 saw the gentle warmth of Bombay's winter yield to the suffocating humid heat of summer. Although Sabir Ibrahim's wife was carrying the couple's second child, he could not resist the sweet aroma of Bombay jasmine that lured him night after night to the heady atmosphere of Congress House. It was not political idealism that drew Sabir to where the founders of the Congress Party had plotted and planned India's future free from colonialism. In the intervening years, this historic building had degenerated into a brothel, and in this brothel lived Chitra, a pretty prostitute in her late twenties for whom Sabir nurtured a powerful infatuation. It was one o'clock in the morning when Sabir picked up his mistress for a romantic ride in his white Fiat Padmini.

"At some point, Sabir noticed that an Ambassador was following him," said Ishaq Bagwan, a senior police inspector at the Malabar Hill Station. "But it was covered in flowers, and so he must have assumed that it was a couple of newlyweds." Inspector Bagwan cuts a sympathetic figure, sitting taut in his khaki uniform, but he has tired of the world of gangsters, which he first became acquainted with that night. "It was when he stopped at the Prabdhevi petrol station that it happened," the inspector continued. Five men armed to the teeth leapt out of the Ambassador. They were led by Amirzada Pathan, a leading gangster and favorite of Karim Lala's. In a chivalrous gesture, the gunmen pulled Chitra out of the car so that she might be spared the almighty barrage of bullets they then fired at the driver's seat. As Sabir slumped forward onto the steering wheel of the Padmini, one of the assailants came forward and triumphantly slit his wrist.

A couple of bloody incidents had preceded Sabir's murder, but Bombay had never seen a slaying as gruesome as this, or one that would unleash such fury. From the late 1980s, the city was to become much more violent. Inspector Bagwan was not surprised that Dawood would attempt to avenge the death of his brother. "When Amirzada was put on trial the following year," he recalled, "I was in court as a junior officer when another man walked in and without hesitating shot Amirzada dead on the spot. As the killer tried to escape out of the window, I fired my pistol at him and wounded him in the leg—that is how we were able to arrest him. He had been hired by Dawood." There was pandemonium—this was not a country accustomed to exchanges of gunfire inside its courtrooms. Before long, a warrant was issued for Dawood's arrest in connection with the revenge killing.

At the time of Amirzada's trial and murder, trouble of another sort was brewing elsewhere in the city. A charismatic, tough independent trades union leader and former physician, Dr. Dutta Samant, persuaded Bombay's 250,000 textile workers to lay down tools for an indefinite strike. The prime minister, Indira Gandhi, was adamant that the mill owners should not yield to the workers' demands for higher wages and better conditions. Dr. Samant's militancy represented a huge threat to India's postwar tradition of quasi–state socialism in which the government dictated to both management and unions what they could and could not do. The workers stayed away for a year, during which time clothing joined alcohol and gold as the smugglers' stock-in-trade.

The strike ended not with an agreement but with the virtual collapse of Bombay's textile industry. "It rendered nearly 1.5 million workers jobless, causing untold hardships to families," according to a confidential report of the CBI (the Central Bureau of Investigation, India's FBI equivalent) on the growth of organized crime in the city. "The strike forced the mill hands and their children to join the ranks of the *goondas* [mobsters] to make ends meet. . . . Today the vast areas under the textile mills and the chawls around them in Central Bombay have become ideal hide-outs of gangsters."

Few policemen know the world of the gangs as well as Inspector

Pradeep Sharma. The founder of the Special Operations team in 1995 to curb gangster violence, he began his career as a modest subinspector in the Bombay police in 1984 and was posted to the station at Mahim. "There was already a complex and complicated gang equation in Mahim with several different groups. But by then job racketeering had become very important." The gangs were exploiting the high level of unemployment, Inspector Sharma explained, by seizing control of the labor market. "This was very important for their rise at that time."

The collapse of the textile mills was an economic trauma from which India's manufacturing powerhouse never fully recovered—the strikes marked the beginning of the end of Nehru's social capitalism and prepared the ground for the liberalization of the early nineties. And with a sudden huge increase in the number of unemployed in central Bombay, especially in areas close to Dongri, the social conditions were perfect for the rise of a new, more violent generation of organized crime—the time of Dawood had come.

When Dawood skipped India for Dubai in 1984, few Westerners could have located the city-state on a map, let alone talk authoritatively about the place and its people. Arabs, Iranians, Baluchis, East Africans, Pakistanis, and west coast Indians, by contrast, had a deep historical acquaintance with Dubai. At the end of World War II, it was barely more than a coastal village that had survived largely on its wits, since its only indigenous industry, pearl fishing, had been wiped out by the war and by the Japanese development of cultured pearls.

In the barren years between pearls and petrodollars, Dubai quietly resurrected its trading links across the Straits of Hormuz with Iran and across the Arabian Sea to Bombay. Because both Iran and India pursued policies of severe protectionism to build up their domestic industries, Dubai's traders found they could exploit their own light taxation regime by importing all manner of material into Dubai and then exporting it to Iran and the subcontinent. "The bottomless pit that is Indian demand for gold funded many, many people here in those years," explained Francis Matthew, an ex-pat for decades and an editor at Dubai's largest publishing company. "Almost every Indian woman needs it for her trousseau and her dowry; different kinds of gold, different kinds of plate for the various areas of India."

This goes back to Rashid, the legendary founder of modern Dubai, who revived its dormant tradition of trading, including the sector of "independent trading," as it is known in the Emirates, or "smuggling," as the rest of us call it. Sheikh Rashid, the early visionary of Dubai, was on Indira Gandhi's personal list of wanted smugglers for many years. But although he could not step foot in India, he took a cut from the profits of every trinket or gold bar sold into the country. This is when the big trading families in Dubai made friends with the big trading families in Bombay and in Karachi. Those friendships lasted.

In terms of influence, Dubai's ruling al-Maktoum family ranked second only to the al-Nahyans of Abu Dhabi. The discovery of huge oil reserves on Abu Dhabi territory proved a godsend to Dubai and the other five emirates that formed the new state of the United Arab Emirates (UAE) in 1973 after the British decided to withdraw all its forces east of Suez. At present rates of extraction, Abu Dhabi's oil will last for another 200 years. The al-Nahyans' cash makes the fortunes of Roman Abramovich and the other Russian oligarchs look paltry. After less than half a century, the al-Nahyan fortune (which is interchangeable with Abu Dhabi's capital reserves) is estimated to stand at around $500 billion—half a trillion.

Abu Dhabi has been generous in its subsidies to the six other emirates of the UAE, which have no comparable oil fields. But it is a measure of the perceptiveness of the al-Maktoum leadership in Dubai that as early as the 1970s it began preparing for a future when Abu Dhabi would no longer be content to underwrite the federal budget. Dubai itself has modest oil reserves, which even so account for 15 percent of the city-state's income. But these will dry up within the next decade. In the 1980s, the al-Maktoums decided to diversify—probably spurred on by the traditionally competitive relationship with the al-Nahyans. Thus did they conceive the plan to build Jebel Ali port, its sixty-six berths making it the largest marine facility in the Middle East.

While critics scoffed at the grandiose project, the decision to create the new port and trading zone was quickly vindicated. In 1979, Dubai had learned a valuable lesson from the Iranian Revolution and Soviet invasion of Afghanistan: trouble has its bright side. Frightened by the instability in their own countries, Iranian and Afghan traders moved to Dubai, bringing with them their businesses, thereby bolstering the local economy. With neither income nor sales tax, Dubai steadily developed a reputation for being a safe place in the Middle East to stash your money. Since then Dubai has always boomed during a regional crisis.

For Dawood Ibrahim, Dubai was the perfect retreat. The city welcomed the wealthy; it welcomed Muslims; and it was not the least bit interested in how people had acquired their money or what they intended to do with it.

Dubai also had long-standing contacts with Bombay, and a large part of its elite were involved in the trade that Dawood wanted to make his core business activity—gold smuggling. Furthermore, thanks to their strategic vision, the al-Maktoums were making the city-state a very comfortable place to live. Before long, Dawood's house had become a place of pilgrimage for Bollywood celebrities and the stars of Indian and Pakistani cricket, two of Dawood's abiding passions. Still, he had to be circumspect. Dubai has proved to be a civil host to many gangsters in the past two decades, provided they behave with discretion. "The UAE is essentially a state where if they don't like you, they can just simply throw you out," noted *Firoz*, a Mumbai lawyer who has occasionally acted as a messenger between the Ibrahim family and the Indian government. "And the fact that Dawood and his people thrived and prospered in Dubai, well, it could not have happened without the knowledge and—in a sense—with the complicity of the ruling family."

As Bombay's economy began collapsing in the 1980s, dozens of minimafia operations started up across the city. They were small gang-based operations engaged in extortion, gambling, and territorial disputes between and within districts. The traditionally passive city experienced a grim upsurge in violence and murder as the gangs fought for supremacy among themselves and applied ever more ruthless sanctions against those from the business community who refused to pay up for the rackets.

From his distant outpost in Dubai, Dawood set about uniting the various gangs under his leadership. This was a formidable professional achievement. Chief among his lieutenants responsible for recruiting the emerging groups into the D-Company was a young Hindu mobster called Chhota Rajan (Little Rajan) from Chembur in Eastern Bombay.

While still a teenager, Rajendra Nikhalje (who would soon be known as Chhota Rajan) started running a racket in cinema tickets and was swiftly recruited by the local gang leader Bada Rajan (Big Rajan). Together they extended their gang's influence northward, gaining a reputation for violence on the way. When a rival gangster murdered Bada Rajan, Chhota Rajan exacted a daring and swift revenge. Dawood was impressed and recruited him into the D-Company. Before long, Chhota Rajan, the Little Man, had become the key figure inside Bombay, bringing together ten or more disparate gangs and creating one of the world's great mafias. The limbs of this operation stretched north to Gujarat, farther to Uttar Pradesh, and even into Kathmandu, where Dawood's people successfully cultivated members of Nepal's autocratic royal family. Like the new organizations that were emerging elsewhere in the world, the D-Company was made up of cells that paid tribute to Dawood but enjoyed considerable autonomy on their own patch. In the early 1990s, the Criminal Bureau of Investigation (CBI) produced a detailed analysis of how it worked. "His brother Anees Ibrahim controls all the violent characters in the gang who are utilised for running the protection and extortion rackets and for maintaining the gang's supremacy in the terror market," it recorded. "Dawood Ibrahim patronises many small gangs and gets the violent crimes committed through them. While allowing a certain degree of operational freedom to these gangs, he sees to it that they remain totally dependent upon him. If any gangster starts showing the sign of becoming independent, he is ruthlessly eliminated. . . . The smaller gangs are given the contract of eliminating a rival or an intransigent businessman."

In return for their loyalty, the gangs were able to boast the Dawood brand name, which not only afforded them considerable protection from other gangs but might also ensure an easier ride from the police. Dawood and his brothers were major crime figures with an India-wide reputation. They became the target of India's major intelligence and crime agencies, such as the CBI and later India's spy service, the IB (Intelligence Bureau). But in Bombay itself, the police had not sufficient resources to maintain order in their districts without the help of the local gangs.

Chhota Rajan was responsible for supervising the D-Company affiliates, earning him the epithet among police circles of "Dawood's Home Secretary." He was also in charge of the countless murders perpetrated by D-Company. Tiger Memon, meanwhile, coordinated the landing of gold, silver, and other consumer goods in and around Bombay. As India's economy ground to a halt toward the end of the eighties, the Bombay mafia experienced a huge growth and with it competition and intergang violence. Toward the end of the decade, D-Company started to splinter and serious rivals to Dawood's criminal hegemony made themselves felt. The killings escalated and eventually Chhota Rajan felt compelled to flee the city for Dubai. Another "little man," Chhota Shakeel, started to assert himself within the D-Company's Bombay operation, to the chagrin of Chhota Rajan—the two little men did not like each other.

The Bombay textile strike signaled a comprehensive decline in the Indian economy, which reached its nadir in 1991. Globalization saw investment capital sniff out new liberalizing or "emerging" markets while avoiding those such as India's, which were resisting the new codex of deregulation. With imports rising and exports declining, India hit a huge balance of payments crisis—payments on its external debt were now devouring 40 percent of GDP and the country was swaying drunkenly in the throes of an economic infarct. From within the Congress Party a group of influential reformers, led by the finance minister and later prime minister Manmohan Singh, argued that the time had come to break with the sacred tenets of Nehruism.

In effect, Singh and his colleagues announced the consequent, if staggered, dismantling of India's protectionist traditions. A year later, in 1992, Minister Singh looked back on the dramatic changes he had introduced with considerable pride. "When the new government assumed office in June 1991, we inherited an economy on the verge of collapse. Inflation was accelerating rapidly. The balance of payments was in serious trouble. The foreign exchange reserves were barely enough for two weeks of imports. Foreign commercial banks had stopped lending to India. Nonresident Indians were withdrawing their deposits. Shortages of foreign exchange had forced a massive import squeeze, which had halted the rapid industrial growth of earlier years and had produced negative growth rates from May 1991 onward." Singh had indeed stabilized the Indian economy and set it on a radically different path of liberalization, including embracing globalization (newly triumphant over Communism). The end of the Soviet Union, one of India's most important strategic and economic allies, had not gone unnoticed in New Delhi. Among the raft of measures introduced by Singh were the freeing up of foreign currency exchange rules and a plan to gradually lift controls on the import of gold.

By the early 1990s, police estimated that Dawood Ibrahim's annual turnover stood at around a quarter of a billion dollars from his Indian operations alone. By now he had a thriving legitimate construction and property business in Dubai, not to mention business interests in Karachi, Kathmandu, and London. Most of the Indian profits derived from the huge expansion in the gold smuggling trade over which the D-Company had presided. This represented a significant contribution both to India's economic woes and to the gathering strength and accompanying political influence of the shadow economy.

The impact of economic reform on Dawood and other shadow business moguls was dramatic. Before long the staggered relaxation of the gold regime started to inflict real pain on Dawood and D-Company. By allowing the market to determine the price of gold instead of its bureaucrats, the Indian government was steadily draining Dawood's primary source of income. Inevitably people began to ask why they should buy from Dawood when it was possible to purchase gold for virtually the same price on the legal market. Dawood still controlled the perfect infrastructure—he could land any amount of goods in the ports and bays in and around Bombay; he could bribe any number of customs officials and landing agents to ensure a trouble-free passage of his goods to their markets in Bombay and beyond. But the market in smuggled gold was no longer there.

It did not take Dawood long to choose a new product. New markets in other illicit commodities were booming around the world, and many traders from these markets were setting up shop in Dubai, attracted—like Dawood—by the sun, the gold, and the unobtrusive regulatory framework of the place. Russians were arriving in large numbers for the first time to the Gulf paradise; South Africans and South Americans also began showing up; Dubai was beloved of the Balkan mob; and representatives of consumer countries like Great Britain had a historically strong presence there. Dawood took the obvious plunge and started trafficking in drugs, chiefly in heroin bound for the European market and mandrax for South Africa. And in Dawood's part of the world, if you want to guarantee the success of a narcotics business, there is only one organization you need to cozy up to—the Inter-Services Intelligence (ISI), Pakistan's secret service.

At the end of December 1992, Dawood celebrated his birthday with the usual A-list movie and sports stars from the subcontinent. By this time, however, circumstances back in India were beginning to sow discord among the group. The activities of the two Hindu nationalist parties, Shiv Sena (Shiva's Army) in Bombay and the BJP (Indian People's Party) across India, were stirring up frightening memories of the violence that accompanied partition in 1947, when several hundred thousand Muslims and Hindus were slaughtered as millions rushed to the perceived safety of their co-confessionals in Pakistan and India. The BJP and Shiv Sena campaigns, with their demands to fashion India into a Hindu state, were an immense challenge to the secular traditions of the Congress Party, which had dominated the postwar period. I was a reporter in the Balkans at the time, and it was clear that more than any other colleagues, it was the correspondents of the Indian media—all highly educated and secular—who most fervently supported the integrity of the Yugoslav Federation in the face of competing nationalist movements. It is not hard to understand why—on one level, they were writing as much about India as they were Yugoslavia.

In Dubai, Chhota Rajan, hitherto Dawood's most trusted subordinate, grew suspicious of the emergence of a Muslim-only caucus among D-Company's leadership.

At this point, the history of that leadership assumes aspects of an Elizabethan or Jacobean revenge tragedy. It is a sign of profound failure and dysfunction when the politics of revenge begins to consume mafia bosses. In September 1992, Chhota Rajan's rivals in what was effectively

D-Company's supreme council in Dubai ordered a spectacular murder to be carried out in a ward at the JJ Hospital, Bombay's central infirmary—the victim was a close Rajan associate. Rajan realized that Dawood must have approved the murder. Two policemen as well as the intended victim were killed during this operation, which attracted huge publicity around India. A senior officer of the Bombay police takes up the story. Chhota Rajan "burst out in anger against the caucus and Dawood decided he should be killed and buried in Dubai itself. Bhai Thakur brokered for peace and Chhota Rajan was asked to either go on his knees and beg for forgiveness of the caucus or face death. He was given 12 hours to decide."

The next day, Chhota literally genuflected in front of Dawood as the boss demanded and begged to be pardoned. This Dawood duly granted. Chhota Rajan's enemies had whispered into Dawood's ear that Chhota Rajan had designs on the organization. Now he was on the defensive, and to rub salt in the wound, Chhota Shakeel ordered the murder of three Rajan loyalists based in Nepal. Dawood would later have great cause to regret his humiliation of Chhota Rajan, as his erstwhile lieutenant was set to become a bitter enemy.

The communal tensions in Bombay itself were beginning to take their toll on D-Company. According to his friends, the Hindu Chhota Rajan suspected that his nemesis, the Muslim Chhota Shakeel, was encouraging this communal mistrust in order to sideline him.

Dawood was an observant Muslim who regularly undertook the hajj to Mecca, and he was visibly unsettled by the attacks on Muslims in Uttar Pradesh, Gujarat, and Bombay. There is no doubt that Dawood was deeply disturbed by the resurgence of Hindu nationalism and the violence inflicted on the Muslim minority. From his informants in Dubai, Hussain Zaidi, whose knowledge of the Mumbai underworld is unparalleled, has pieced together what happened next at Dawood's office:

> The other phone, whose number was known to barely half a dozen people, rang. Shakeel answered it and, handing the receiver to Dawood, tactfully moved away to the other end of the room.
>
> There was a long muttered conversation.
>
> When Dawood hung up, his demeanor had changed visibly, the earlier dejection replaced by resolution.
>
> Shakeel remained seated quietly.
>
> Dawood walked toward him. "They called," Dawood said. Shakeel had never asked and Dawood had never explained who "they" were. It is believed that the term referred to top officials in Pakistan.

"They say that they want to land some important cargo in Bombay through our landing routes at spots near Shekhadi and Dighi. Tiger and Taufiq will handle the entire operation of landing, paying the doctors, and other such things. In exchange, they will arrange total security for our business." He paused and then continued meditatively, "I think that this cargo will not be ordinary stuff . . . It could be something meant as a retribution for the demolition of the Babri Masjid and the massacre of Muslims. I told them that if it only means using my infrastructure and nothing beyond that then I have no problem. I can seek solace in the fact that the blood of my brothers will be avenged."

Dawood took out a cigar from his pocket and tucked it between his lips, a sign that he was feeling relieved. Shakeel lit the cigar for him. Although the don had not said it in so many words, it was clear that the cargo would be death.

Twenty-seven-year-old *Badshah Khan* admitted to nerves when his Pakistan International Airlines plane touched down in Islamabad, the Pakistani capital, in February 1993. One of his fellow passengers had suffered what was suspected to be a heart attack during the flight from Dubai, compelling the pilots to make an emergency stop in Lahore. This was a bad omen. But Badshah Khan was more worried by the knowledge that he had no visa in his passport—it was, after all, an Indian passport and so bound to attract the careful scrutiny of the Pakistani authorities. Still, at least he was there with several of the lads, and after all, Tiger Memon himself had organized the trip. Even so, he was greatly surprised when he and his friends were escorted off the aircraft and taken to their accommodation without having to prove their identity in any fashion. Clearly, Pakistan was expecting them.

The next day, they were driven a couple of hours outside Islamabad to a deserted forested location. Here they were greeted by an operations team from Pakistan's secret service, the ISI. "I had seen such characters in Hindi movies," Badshah explained, "men who were assigned the task of beating up our thin and short heroes but end up getting beaten themselves. But these two guys looked really dangerous. They could have taken on all our screen heroes together in the blink of an eye!" The raw recruits were streetwise—they had grown up ducking, diving, and thieving on the streets of Bombay—but the most they had ever threatened anyone with was a knife or their bare fists, and they lacked training. Their new mentors were trained to perfection.

"The location of the camp was perfect for our requirements. There were six men to look after the camp: the two Babajis, two servants who served food and cleaned up, and two armed guards. Our meals were delivered by Jeep every day at the same time. I marveled at the excellent organization," recalled Badshah. "One of the Babajis announced that he would now begin training us in the handling of instruments of death. He was carrying an AK-56 rifle. When we came into the field again, we were shown automatic pistols, handguns, light machine guns and Kalashnikovs. . . . For the next two days, we did nothing but target practice. . . . I realized why we had to travel all the way to Pakistan for the camp. There was no other place where we could have received such training; anywhere else the booming shots and loud reports would have attracted too much attention."

I look at the warm and likable face opposite me in a café at the top end of the indefatigably busy district of Bandra. Though it is often referred to as fashionable, Bandra's allure is usually only obvious when you enter smart modern buildings. On my way from the station to the restaurant to meet Badshah Khan, I saw a rabbit-size rat run over a couple of rake-thin heroin addicts lying prone and semiconscious on the sidewalk. Poverty and squalor are ubiquitous in Mumbai, casting a permanent shadow on the attempts by New India, reveling as it does in the unevenly distributed wealth of globalization, to project a shining image of slick success. The gangs of Mumbai have grown out of the slums, acting almost as an organic if malevolent response to the hip bars and conspicuous consumption of the growing, confident middle class. Badshah Khan and his family were evicted from their home when he was just fourteen by a fraudulent land speculator, and the once promising student fell in with a bad crowd around the giant slum of Dharavi.

Away from the crowd in a modest family restaurant that served exquisite spicy prawns, Badshah Khan is dressed in a long white Indian shirt, baggy white cotton trousers, and a small white cotton hat. He is cultured and thoughtful. As he talks about his former life, it is hard to imagine that he played a crucial role in the Bombay bombings of 1993. But then he also voluntarily played a crucial role as state witness in exposing how parts of the operation were planned and executed. "After lunch that day at the camp," he continues the tale of his training in Pakistan, "we were shown some black soaplike lumps. Babaji said, 'This is RDX—research developed explosive.' . . . We began chatting after he set it up. Suddenly an explosion rocked the jungles and mountains. The noise seemed to shatter my eardrums. The sky was raining stones and mud, and the earth beneath my feet was shaking. . . . I think more than ten minutes went by after the explosion before the curtain of smoke gave way and I could see and hear properly. We moved toward the spot where the bomb had been placed. The pit was many feet deep." This was the material that they would be planting across Bombay in one of the most densely populated places on earth less than a month later.

On the evening of March 14, the day after the bombings, the commissioner of Bombay police called in the deputy commissioner (traffic), Rakesh Maria. "Have you rested?" he inquired politely, but well aware that few if any officers had slept the night before (and certainly not DC Maria). The commissioner explained that the prestige of the Bombay police was at stake in the investigation of the attack and that he had selected DC Maria to uphold it by taking over the detection of the case. "I felt numbed by this, of course," Maria said. "This had been thrust on me so that I would have to shoulder responsibility were we to fail. And if I were to fail, what then?"

CHAPTER 7

Xanadu II

The shadow of the dome of pleasure
Floated midway on the waves;
Where was heard the mingled measure
From the fountain and the caves.
It was a miracle of rare device,
A sunny pleasure dome with caves of ice!

—Samuel Taylor Coleridge, "Kubla Khan"

We received a report of one vehicle, a Marutti, abandoned in Worli."
Rakesh Maria leaned back in his chair as he remembered the events.
"I took my team of sixteen officers out there, and it was obvious that
the vehicle had been left in a hurry. There were a lot of roadblocks in that
area designed to hinder the work of the underworld. Being part of
Dawood's D-Company, the bombers would have known that, so they left
the vehicle rather than risk being caught." The car was registered in the
name of Rabiner Memon, Tiger Memon's sister-in-law. DC Maria led his
team to the Al-Hussein building, where most of the Memon family lived.
The police broke down the door to the empty apartment and started looking around for any possible clues. "I noticed a scooter key on the fridge,"
Maria continued, "and I thought we'd better check it and see." Maria had
received a report of an abandoned motor scooter elsewhere in the city—
the traffic police had already taken it in for examination. "I took the key
along and tried it in the scooter—bingo! It fits! And so I turned round to
my men and said, 'We've hit the jackpot!'" There was something else about
that scooter—it still had its cargo of RDX on board.

Maria had uncovered the identity of the chief domestic conspirator,
Tiger Memon, within a matter of hours. It was an astonishing piece of
detective work, even if he and his team were assisted by the lax discipline

of the bombers and a healthy dose of luck. Despite the early break-through, there were still many years of investigation facing the Indian authorities: the bombings were not the work of a small, lean terrorist cell, the type that would proliferate in Europe, Asia, and the Middle East after September 11. The atrocity in Bombay was ambitious in its scope and it required a sprawling organization like Dawood's to make it work, because at its heart lay the import of eight tons of RDX from Pakistan and only Dawood's operation could guarantee this. But because the plan was executed by a criminal syndicate based in Bombay, it meant that dozens of people were involved, wittingly or unwittingly. Most of the landing agents, corrupt customs officials, bent policeman, drivers, fishermen, storage facility owners, vehicle owners, and other accessories to the crime had no idea that they were part of this particular conspiracy: they assumed that, as usual, they were bringing in gold, drugs, consumer goods, or weapons for onward sale. But the D-Company did not lead an exclusively underground existence. On the contrary, its influence extended to Bombay's most famous industry, Bollywood.

Around midnight one mid-April eve in 1993, Rakesh Maria was interviewing yet another suspect in the bombing case. "You police always goes after small fry like me and let off influential people," the man noted bitterly. "I mean, if you are really serious, then why don't you arrest Sanjay?" "Sanjay? Sanjay who?" the policemen demanded to know. "Sanjay Dutt! The film star, son of the MP Sunil Dutt."

Sunil Dutt and his wife, Nargis, were one of the grandest couples in India. He, a Hindu, was a powerful force inside the Congress Party who as a young actor had married his glamorous Muslim paramour. In 1993, their son, the then thirty-four-year-old Sanjay had just broken through into Bollywood superstar status. Like many Bollywood stars and directors, he was cultivated by the Bombay gangsters who indeed continue to finance movie production in the city to this day. Sanjay was on friendly terms with Anees Ibrahim, Dawood's brother, and although his father was a Hindu, the entire Dutt family was sensitive to the fear that had spread among Bombay's Muslims during the riots of December 1992 and January 1993, and had sought to help the community. The nationalists at Shiv Sena had issued veiled threats against the Dutts, which persuaded Sanjay to ask Anees Ibrahim to send weapons so that he might protect himself and his family.

What Dutt did not know was that the AK-47s and grenades he received were of a much larger series of deliveries from Dubai in preparation for the bombings in March. Over the next thirteen years, Dutt served a total of eighteen months in police custody as he awaited his trial and sentencing.

Finally, on a sweltering Tuesday in November 2006, I watched as the bemused Bollywood actor made his way into the old British colonial jail on Arthur Road to hear the verdict in his case, Accused 117. Dutt was found guilty of illegal possession of a weapon but not of conspiracy in the bombings case. Jostling for attention in the scrum stood Deepak Nachnani, a journalist and NGO leader with straggly hair that was tangled and gray. He was holding up a board demanding the extradition of Dawood Ibrahim for his role in the bombings and offering a reward for anybody who assassinated him. "Sanjay Dutt's father was a minister and MP; his sister is an MP; but Sanjay Dutt should face the maximum punishment under Indian law," he exploded with indignation. In the end, Dutt received six years.

But interestingly, Mr. Nachnani appears to be in the minority. Most Mumbaikers still regard Dutt as a hero and a star. Since his arrest in 1993, he has starred in several hit movies, often playing the role of mafia don. There is an affection for Bollywood stars and the Mumbai mob that persists despite the turbulent events of the 1990s. Dutt continues to enjoy cordial relations with Chhota Shakeel, Dawood's right-hand man. But his suspected involvement in the Bombay bombings did mean that over the course of the 1990s some of the links between Bollywood and the mafia were exposed, although there is still much to be unearthed.

Dutt's involvement was one of many surprises that Rakesh Maria's team uncovered during the investigation. Over many months, India's various law enforcement agencies were able to construct a fairly comprehensive picture of Dawood's extraordinary network across Bombay and the planning and execution of the whole operation. Given the hopeless inefficiencies and rivalries that characterize Indian law enforcement, this was a very creditable performance.

Dawood himself remained calm in Dubai, although one person who fled the city-state as soon as news of the bombings filtered through was Chhota Rajan. Convinced quite rightly that Chhota Shakeel now intended to kill him, Chhota Rajan broke with Dawood and disappeared, surfacing occasionally in Kuala Lumpur, Bangkok, and other Asian cities.

Chhota Rajan still commanded a considerable gaggle of gangs in Bombay. He sent messages to the other major Hindu dons in the city, such as Arun Gawli, suggesting that they form a tacit alliance against D-Company. "It was at this point that the IB got in touch with Chhota Rajan," a Mumbai Deep Throat told me. The Intelligence Bureau and its sister agency, the Research and Analysis Wing (RAW), are India's intelligence and counterintelligence services. Normally they are not charged with investigating the activities of organized crime, but if a syndicate has become involved with a major security issue, then the IB and the RAW will assume control of any investigation. "The IB's thinking was that if Dawood was being run by the ISI, Pakistan's secret service, then they should perhaps employ Dawood's enemies to undermine his influence," said the source.

During the Yugoslav wars, organized criminal syndicates throughout the Balkans effectively hijacked most state institutions and subordinated them to their interests. In Pakistan and India at exactly the same time, the opposite was happening: the gang wars of Bombay that exploded with renewed violence in the 1990s were in part a proxy conflict between the intelligence agencies of India and Pakistan, ensuring that they were even more dangerous and unpredictable than hitherto. This ratcheting up of the gang wars, conferring a communal and an intelligence dimension on them, had unhappy consequences for local law enforcement.

By the mid-1990s, the Bombay police were registering a rise in the murder rate that made it comparable with those of Moscow or Johannesburg, confirming the apparent link between drastic economic and political reform on the one hand and gangsterism on the other. The collated police reports detail hundreds upon hundreds of murders of shocking brutality during this period. The majority was committed in the merciless tit-for-tat war that Chhota Rajan and Dawood had launched against each other. Chhota Rajan's capability was based on his comprehensive knowledge of the structures and networks of his former boss's empire. He himself had, after all, spent almost a decade building it on behalf of Dawood. The IB's strategy was working—Chhota Rajan was depleting Dawood's ability to function, and, in the eyes of the IB, that meant that they were limiting the ability of the ISI to carry out its covert activities through D-Company. It also had the side effect of weakening Chhota Rajan's operations, which were themselves under attack from Dawood's operatives.

But for Bombay law enforcement, it was an uncomfortable mess that reinforced its nationwide image as a corrupt and incompetent police force. To combat the violence, the police established three special anti-crime squads in 1995.

Inspector Pradeep Sharma was sitting in his Bandra office one afternoon in late 1996 when there was a knock on his door. "An informant came in and told me that Babloo Srivastava had sent a four-man team into the city from Uttar Pradesh in order to kidnap one of Bombay's wealthiest businessmen." Srivastava was a notorious gangster with links to both Dawood and Chhota Rajan. He had been extradited from Singapore to India on suspicion of having committed about eighty major kidnappings and murders. He was, in fact, organizing the kidnapping of the Bombay businessman from the confines of a Delhi jail. "This was about two in the afternoon," continued Inspector Sharma, "and so I ordered a couple more on my team to come with me to Santa Cruz, just close to Bandra, where the informant had said the gangsters were hiding out." When they arrived at the apartment, one of the policemen knocked on the door. " 'Hello!' he called out. 'It's the milkman. I have your delivery.' " Inspector Sharma pauses for dramatic effect. "As soon as he'd said he was the milkman, the gang just started shooting wildly from inside the apartment. But within a couple of minutes, we'd killed them both. Only then did we discover that the other two gang members were out and had escaped."

The two deceased had fallen victim to what are known throughout India as "encounters"—in effect, shoot-outs between gangsters and police. Inspector Sharma is the encounter king, having killed more than 100 Bombay gangsters in shoot-outs, a bigger tally than that of any other policeman in the city. I cannot recall anyone I met during my journey through the global underworld who displays such a controlled and focused machismo as this scrupulously polite and deeply serious man. Gangsters and some civil liberty groups claim that these "encounters" have in fact transformed the police into extrajudicial execution units, or death squads. The encounter teams forced Arun Gawli, an early ally of Dawood's who later became one of his principal Hindu enemies, to construct an elaborate security mechanism around his headquarters in central Bombay. Numerous armed guards were placed behind four heavily locked gates, all studded with CCTV and state-of-the-art communications. More recently, Gawli has given up his status as don in favor of a seat in the Maharashtra Provincial Assembly, but he still calls encounters "police contract killings," having lost, he claims, sixty friends in the shoot-outs. "Okay," Gawli admits, "there were days a while back when I went astray. But this sort of murder campaign is unacceptable."

Since the formation of these squads, the number of deaths attributed to encounters has been more than 100 a year. "I sometimes take out between six to eight of them in a week," confirms Inspector Sharma, with evident pride.

But he failed to take out Mahmoud, one of Bombay's most successful contract killers, whom I arranged to meet in what turned out to involve an elaborate game of musical cafés. Every time I thought I had arrived at the right tea shop, I received a message to finish my drink and move to another one. At the third one, the sharp, good-looking, if slightly weather-beaten face of Mahmoud smiled benignly at me. "I have to take serious security precautions when I come to Bombay," he explained. "I don't want to come across any police encounters and I certainly don't want to encounter any of my former colleagues." In stark contrast to the other people from this milieu whom I met, Mahmoud spoke refined and sophisticated English. "I studied electronics at college in Pune," he announced, beaming proudly.

In 1989, armed with his degree, Mahmoud made the short seventy-five-mile hop west from Pune to Bombay, India's naked city. Before long he had secured a job fixing photocopying machines. "I was paid about fifty dollars a month for this work, and I was living in a room with ten other men," he continued. "It was really hard." One day Mahmoud intervened when he saw a gang of boys bullying a kid on the streets. A man approached him and congratulated him on his bravery and asked him out for a drink. "For the next eighteen months, this guy showed me a good time—we went to bars, we met women, he gave me money, and I didn't have to do anything. It was great—I was young, fit, good-looking, and this was what I had come to Bombay for!" Mahmoud's benefactor was, in fact, an associate of Chhota Shakeel's, the rising star and future *chef du cabinet* in Dawood's D-Company.

Once the friendship was firmly established, his mentor explained who he was, what he did, and whom he worked for. He offered Mahmoud the chance to join full-time. "The thought of returning to a fifty-dollar job in that hovel meant there was no real choice—I was in."

Mahmoud was taught to use a *kutta*—a pistol manufactured in Uttar Pradesh, with a barrel that has a tendency to blow up. "The first shot is usually safe; after that it's pretty useless. That means that when you're doing a job, you only have one crack at it.

Most of the hitmen were picked up or killed in encounters. But not me. There are two reasons: one is planning. We would monitor a target's route for two to three months. We knew all his habits so there would be no surprises. The second is secrecy—if you or your colleagues blab, you're dead.

My first successful hit took place in Andheri in early 1991. As was often the case, we planned to carry it out at a busy crossroads in the afternoon when the rush hour was in full swing. We would get a car to block the road by the traffic lights. The target was driving a Marutti Esteem—it was a very prestigious car at the time. But he couldn't go forward because we'd blocked the lights and he couldn't go back because of the traffic. There were two teams. The first team approached the car and broke the window glass. Then I went in and boom—straight at the head. It was always straight at the head because you only got one shot at it. I always delivered the goods, which is the message we would send after a job. Once it was done, I disappeared. I never went home after a job and nobody knew where I was.

This warm, urbane man laughed and spoke animatedly in the café, later offering perceptive comments on contemporary social and economic issues facing India, then dropping in to a mosque to say prayers before talking lyrically about Mumbai and its traditions. It was almost impossible to reconcile this with the knowledge that he was a calculating, cold-blooded killer. I felt deeply perplexed—how can I warm to a murderer? I wondered. My experience in the Balkans led me to conclude that most murderers are not congenital psychopaths but people (usually men) whom circumstances and authority encourage, persuade, enable, in short "permit" the violation of the ultimate commandment, Thou shalt not kill. But this man still made a choice. And his choice was all the more shocking precisely because he seemed both normal and intelligent.

In 2002, Mahmoud had negotiated an honorable discharge from D-Company—a very tricky thing to do.

"I was married with kids by then and my wife had no idea what my real job was."

"Has she still had no idea?"

"I told you—secrecy is critical. I was never caught because nobody knew who I was or how I operated. I never made the mistake of relying on anyone else."

I had one final question of Mahmoud. "How did you feel at the moment that you executed a hit?"

Like so many Indians, he chose a cricketing metaphor to answer, referring to the West Indies' magnificent batsman and captain:

"Like Brian Lara when he hits the ball for six!"

As the millennium approached, Dubai had not yet been fully drawn into the deepening mess of Mumbai gangs and international politics even though it was the preferred haven for many of India's leading mobs. During the 1990s, Dubai was primarily interested in attracting as much money into the emirate as possible. As long as Dawood and other gangsters carried out the sordid aspects of their business elsewhere, the authorities in Dubai permitted them to undertake the mundane "administration" of their business in the Emirates.

September 11 proved to be a double-edged sword for Dubai. Its coffers overflowed as the attack on the Twin Towers provoked a spectacular flight of Arab money from the United States to the UAE and Dubai in particular. The estimates range from between several hundred billion to $2 to $3 trillion. At the same time, nobody could escape the fact that eleven out of sixteen 9/11 hijackers had received their cash by wire transfer from Dubai. And it wasn't long before a multiagency posse from Washington saddled up and rode into the desert kingdom. So although Dubai was rolling in repatriated Arab capital from investors worried that the United States might start freezing bank accounts, the emirate also had the feds crawling all over them, demanding greater transparency in the banking system.

By the mid-1990s, 63 percent of the UAE's income was derived from nonpetroleum sources. Dubai itself had become the largest free trade zone in a region stretching from southern Europe to Singapore. It had traditionally attracted large amounts of capital from the subcontinent, central Asia, east Africa, and the Middle East—now Dubai sought to invite Western money to invest. The city-state having no tax, a beautiful coastline, sunshine all year round, no bombs or assassinations (al Qaeda needs its banking and R and R facilities just like everyone else), and enough shopping malls to satisfy a small planet, it did not take long before money was pouring in from every part of Europe.

"In the 1990s, it was a free-for-all in Dubai," explained a European diplomat who worked on Dubai's money-laundering issues. "There were no controls here and the authorities were tenacious in resisting the FATF." Western leaders had established the Financial Action Task Force (FATF) in 1989 because of concern about the laundering of drug money. The Clinton administration elevated its AML (anti-money-laundering) strategy to a list of its most solemn commandments (even if its moral case was badly punctured by the presidential pardon to the fugitive financier Marc Rich in 2000). But progress was patchy. The G7's new compliance vehicle, the FATF, had a tiny staff, which rendered it largely ineffective. Lichtenstein and Switzerland snubbed the whole idea, while the United Arab Emirates, Dubai included, resisted compliance with FATF regulations most vigorously.

But these centers of money laundering found respite in 2000 with the election of George W. Bush, as his team had a very different approach to money laundering from that of his predecessor. Clinton's global AML strategy was ridiculed by the neocons as a dastardly anticompetitive European plot. "Before 9/11 the fundamental concern is to fight what the Bush White House perceives as a European tendency to try to make everybody's regime as business-unfriendly as possible," explained a senior economist who worked under both Clinton and Bush. For Bush and his team, the only good AML strategy was no AML strategy. Then came 9/11.

"There was a 180-degree flip," remembered the economist. "After 9/11 no AML regime is too strong for the U.S. Any kind of concerns about secondary effects go out the window. The brief is, everybody has to have this regime, and the stronger, the more onerous, the better—no cost is too high."

The Patriot Act was designed to put paid to any outlandish notion that President Bush was soft on terrorists and money launderers. But there was a problem: money laundering and terrorist financing are two very different things, as the economist explained: "In money laundering, you are looking for dirty money trying to become clean. In the case of terrorist financing, you are looking at clean money that becomes criminal. The crime is no longer a predicate crime but a subsequent crime, and your whole optic changes as a consequence." A part of the war on terror was the war on worldwide financial transactions—a very blunt and ill-fashioned instrument. "The whole notion that somehow the model for AML can just be translated into terrorist finances is fanciful," the economist continued:

> But if all you have in your tool kit is a hammer, then the whole world looks like a bunch of nails. You get the Office of Foreign Assets Control [OFAC] and stretch still further their original brief, which was to block stuff from Cuba. Take the Balkans: it was hard enough when they had to block Slobodan Milosevic's cash—you know how many Slobodan Milosevices there are in the Paris phone book alone? There are thirteen of them. To shut down an organization like al Qaeda, where the possibilities for false positives on Islamic or Arabic names are staggering, you quickly realize you've got a lousy tool for the job.

Suddenly you are confronted with a mountain of complex and persnickety work—most of it in unregulated overseas banking networks—with barely a clue where to start.

America's new zeal to uncover money-laundering networks was, however, constrained. As Firoz, the lawyer from Mumbai, explains, Dubai posed America with a serious dilemma: "American policy in the Middle East is held hostage to the fear that if you push someone too much, then you might end up with someone a lot worse. The U.S. is not happy with the Emirates because it has attracted a lot of shady companies, but at the same time it is seen as a safe haven for the U.S. in the region. American troops can land there and enjoy R and R—its advantages outweigh its disadvantages. It's one of the few places where Americans feel safe, and they are not keen on seeing change."

Dubai had become so useful for terrorists, the superrich, the United States, dictators, Russian oligarchs, celebrities, Europe, and gangsters that, to paraphrase the nineteenth-century French prime minister Talleyrand's observation about the Habsburg Empire, if it didn't exist, the global elites would have to invent it.

The pursuit of dirty money is a complicated business. Capital springs from human labor to give life to the global economic environment. It emerges from the source before broadening into a fast-flowing river rushing down from the peaks and distributing itself unevenly across the fertile lowlands through channels both organic and man-made. As it cuts unpredictable paths, some drains off unnoticed, perhaps wending through a toxin-infected swamp before seeping back into the main network. Here and there, one may encounter apparently pristine pools that are in fact contaminated with colorless, odorless chemicals. Only the most expert biochemist can tell the good capital from the filthy lucre as it mixes and mingles. Capital itself is neither dirty nor clean—it is human activity and human values that determine the color of money.

The fall of Communism and the deregulation of the international financial markets in the late 1980s triggered a huge injection of cash into the global economy. Traders scanned the globe for the most profitable opportunities. The clients they represented sought out their services for a number of reasons: some were looking for the maximum rates of return, while others were seeking to avoid paying tax; companies were demonstrating their commitment to new markets; and some investors wanted to launder their money and remove the stain of its criminal origins. The sums involved were vast. By the mid-nineties, the foreign exchange markets alone reached a volume of trading that exceeded $1 trillion *every day*. This was more than forty times the value of daily global trade. In the world of licensed financial trading, malfeasance came to light only either when related losses destroyed an institution, as when Nick Leeson's derivatives trading on the Japanese stock market brought down Barings Bank, or when outside regulators were tipped off about malpractice, as happened in the staggering case of the Bank of Credit and Commerce International (BCCI). Several scandals, from BCCI to Enron, have demonstrated that the world's most famous private audit companies cannot be relied upon to alert governments to large-scale malpractice in the banking or corporate sectors.

Money laundering is a predicate crime, one step removed from the criminal deed. The act of transferring a large sum of money is not intrinsically illegal. The illegality lies instead in the association with the criminal act that generated the cash in the first place. Law enforcement has to prove not that money was transferred, but that it was ill gotten.

That is difficult enough. But once international currency controls were relaxed in the late eighties in the name of capital's freedom of movement, it became still more complicated. If it had the evidence, U.S. law enforcement could make a money-laundering charge stick when the offense took place in the United States. If it occurred in a foreign country, then the only way Washington could go after the alleged criminals was by invading said country. In some cases—Panama, for example—that's exactly what it did. But although Washington has traditionally felt less constrained than most governments about invading other countries, it doesn't have the wherewithal to do so every time it hears of something fishy going on in the banking sector. America's own banks were required to assume an ever-greater regulatory burden, summed up by three guidelines—CDD: customer due diligence; KYC: know your customer; and SAR: suspicious activity report. In addition to being an arcane discipline, money laundering is overburdened with acronyms.

The struggle against organized crime had thus created an awkward conundrum for the United States that went to the heart of the still larger issue of the relationship between the liberalization of international capital markets and global governance. "If our banks are required to adhere to a standard, including offshore, and other banks do not and rush for deposits in those U.S. banks," said Senator John Kerry in 1988, "we will have once again taken a step that will have disadvantaged our economic structure and institutions relative to those against whom we must compete in the marketplace." The implication was that a globally level playing field, in the banking sector anyway, would require a worldwide regulatory regime. This was brought home starkly in the wake of the United States' subprime mortgage market collapse in the summer of 2007. Respectable financial warhorses like Parisbas BNP and even Goldman Sachs confessed that the derivatives in which they were investing were so complex that they could not accurately assess the scale of their losses. If they can lose their way in the mist of financial markets, imagine how easy it is for those who do not want to be seen to remain hidden. Globalization needs regulation, but everyone is reluctant to demand it for fear that it may discriminate against them.

In the last decade, Dubai has witnessed a huge growth in investment by

Western companies seeking to get a slice of the market. The authorities could not countenance the imposition of rigorous controls on the import and export of money that the United States was demanding under Clinton and then again post-9/11, as this would have confounded the city's unique selling point (Bring Your Money to Dubai: No Questions Asked!) and undermined the entire strategy of turning the place into the trading and financial pivot between Africa, Europe, and Asia.

In 2002 Sheikh Mohammed went on the offensive by announcing the establishment of the Dubai International Financial Center (DIFC), a bold bid that would transform the city into the largest financial market between Frankfurt and Singapore. Some of the world's biggest banks and financial institutions proclaimed that they would set up their offices in the DIFC. Sheikh Mohammed encouraged everybody by announcing that the accompanying regulatory authority would not be bound by the laws of the UAE but by a new code of governance based on the most progressive and transparent Western principles.

There was no doubt that Dubai was doing everything it could to appear the embodiment of rectitude. But while there was no reason to doubt the city's commitment to an onshore financial center that would stand up to the toughest scrutiny, there was a little catch. In order to accommodate the DIFC and all the new business it would attract, the authorities announced a multibillion-dollar construction plan that envisaged an immense westward expansion of the city along the coast, including such grandiose projects as the Palms and the Burj Dubai.

Within a few years, Dubai became quite literally the biggest building site in the world. During the expansion of the country's airport, when the residential and office construction had already begun, a *third* of the world's cranes were working in Dubai.

Driving down Sheikh Zayed Road is an unnerving experience. Beyond the indoor ski run, skeletons of wire and metal tower menacingly. Vast cinder blocks swing capriciously from the cranes as any sense of human scale is lost and the otherwise ubiquitous sun is here obliterated. You are able to watch a process akin to the whole of downtown Manhattan being built in three years. For the moment, it still looks like an experimental set for the Fritz Lang movie *Metropolis,* as though these dwellings were being prepared to house the subjects of a totalitarian nightmare. The overpowering sense of science fiction is further enhanced by the armies of robotic workers crawling all over the construction sites. They wear standard dungaree uniforms but are differentiated by color—there is a green, a blue, a red, and a yellow army, each tasked with erecting a different building.

Four years after Sheikh Mo's announcement, Dubai and the UAE had yet to pass the legislation permitting foreigners to acquire the freehold in designated areas, let alone define what freehold means Dubai-style. But that did not stop a ferocious rush as foreigners signed up and handed over a 10 percent deposit for the Meadows, South Ridge, the Glades and all the other suburban names culled from America, South Africa, and Australia. The concession for the creation of New Dubai was given to five companies, all owned and run by sheikhs who are close to Sheikh Mohammed. These concessions are worth billions and billions of dollars. Before the first foundations of this project were laid, investors were doubling their money by speculating. With just 10 percent of the price required to reserve a property, once you secured a contract, it was possible to wait a matter of months and then sell on the building for double its original price. Investors began to pay just to get on the waiting list for the most fashionable properties.

"This is the washing machine of the world," an ex-pat property consultant told me after I had turned off my tape recorder. People are reluctant to speak on the record in Dubai for fear of losing their residence status. To uncover how one can bring cash in and out of the country in this post-9/11 world, I turned to one of my old friends from the Balkans. Ranko Lukic is a youthful entrepreneur who was educated both in Serbia and the United States. He hovers in the gray economy like most successful businessmen from Eastern Europe. Having cut their teeth under Communism, they have developed an acute nose for sniffing out how to strike deals with a minimum of fuss. But soon after Ranko first arrived here, he received a shock when he transferred $3,000 to his local lawyer from Citibank Dubai.

> I get a call back and this aggressive guy says, "What is the purpose of this transfer?" So I tell him, it's none of his business, it's between me and my lawyer. But I was absolutely astonished, and I had to fill out some form before they would transfer this lousy three grand! But of course, Citibank is an American firm.
>
> When I had two lots of 2 million euros transferred to the Emirates bank here so I could purchase property on Palm Jumeirah, the bank called me and said, "Tell us, please, the origin of this money." So I tell them that it comes from my tobacco farms in Zimbabwe! And they say "okay" and no more questions asked. Job done! Why would they want to know where my money comes from? If they ask too many questions, they won't get sales!

Once the house or apartment is registered as belonging to an individual, he or she has successfully washed the money and it can be reintroduced into the legitimate financial system anywhere in the world. Gangsters from Mumbai to the Balkans began pouring money into Dubai's property market in an effort to launder their money and, where possible, to launder their reputation as well.

Dubai may be soulless, but a certain honesty underpins the fantasy of a stately pleasure dome for the world's superrich. Only two things rule here—the dollar and Sheikh Mo. Dubai may be a huge, undemocratic money-laundering center in the Middle East, but the country embraces free trade and globalization; it is stable in a region renowned for violence; it has not relied on oil for its wealth but invented itself as a novel force in the Arab world. Furthermore, as long as the United States and Europe permit the existence of offshore banking centers, they remain guilty of hypocrisy. For organized crime, these are equally important instruments, offering a variety of additional services such as flags of convenience, shell companies to disguise illegal activities, and freedom from prying tax authorities. The only credible reason for their growth and success is the fact that many corporations in the licit economy use them for exactly the same reasons (especially tax evasion). The government of the United States could force them to lift their banking secrecy codes overnight if they threatened to apply the same sanctions on offshore centers that they do on the onshore banks. "You could do it quite easily," said a senior NSC official involved in the hunt for drugs and thugs during both the Clinton and Bush administrations. "You go to Lichtenstein, which is one of these places, and you just put a gun to its head and say, 'If you don't put an end to these practices, we're going pull the trigger.' I suggested this under Clinton, but unfortunately the idea was turned down." Without offshore banks it would not be only the mobsters finding it onerous to shuffle their money and companies around. Enron would have found it a lot harder too.

The issue of money laundering will continue to haunt Dubai as it strives to represent itself as a model of transparency. But there is an even higher cost that the city has had to pay for its success—a human cost. For beyond the permanent traffic jam between Dubai and Sharjah lies Ajman, the tiniest of the UAE's seven emirates. Celebrated among the ex-pats as hosting the only liquor store in the country where you can purchase booze without a license, Ajman is also a popular location for the labor camps.

Ajman itself is a featureless city, but as you travel farther east from Dubai, the ubiquitous traffic jams suddenly disappear. Soon almost all vehicles except the one I'm traveling in have evaporated. This is eerie. In the distance, the huge lonely dunes of the desert form an oscillating yet monotonous panorama. It is already dark, and set back ten meters from the road are high, crumbling gray walls surrounded by dust, sand, and scrub. I walk into a yard next to a barracks to find a few plastic chairs occupied by a group of fourteen men. Most look undernourished and aging, but the eldest is thirty-five. They welcome me with bows, smiles, and quiet chatter. For four months their wages have been unpaid by the Saudi-owned business Al Beladi, which contracts these men out to do maintenance work on buildings under construction. Until the wages were stopped, they had been receiving $160 per month. For this they were obliged to leave Ajman in a bus at five-thirty to start work in Jebel Ali forty miles away at seven-thirty. Then followed twelve hours of backbreaking work under a sun that drives most people off the street after half an hour's exposure. Afterward, they are packed back to their barracks in Ajman, where they are expected to provide and cook their own food.

The conditions are subhuman. About sixty men are required to share one stinking toilet that forces an involuntary retch when one stands within five yards of it. Eight to fifteen live in one room—the Nepalis in one, the Bengalis in the next, the Pakistanis in the next, and the Indians in the next. They sleep on thin mattresses spread across the concrete floor or on rickety metal bunk beds. The only other facility is a single gas ring on which they all have to cook.

In a cacophonous Babylonian chorus, they tell how two months ago they downed their tools and actually took their grievance to Dubai's new employment police. The existence of this new office reflects how hundreds of thousands of foreign laborers in the city are showing signs of restlessness, including strikes and protests such as blocking highways. Dubai cannot afford to become synonymous with labor militancy and a strong union presence. But this army of migrant laborers is starting to grow very restive as they contrast the unfathomable opulence of the Dubai that they are building with the aching squalor of the world they inhabit. Their female compatriots, who work as domestic servants, observe the discrepancy close up. In the Emirates these women have no rights, as they are not classed as "workers" but as "family members" of their employers, which leaves them vulnerable to appalling abuse as transnational skivvies. At least the UAE has finally abandoned the import of tiny boys to work as camel jockeys in one of the country's favorite sports. Before the practice was ended, there were countless reports of victims being abused as well as sustaining the severest injuries as they entertained the sheikhs and their guests. At the very bottom of the pile are the women who are trafficked to the Emirates by force. There are no NGOs permitted here to defend these women. In Moldova, La Strada, the NGO that assists trafficked women, despairs of the UAE: "We have one girl who managed to call her mother once," said Alina Budeci. "She is imprisoned in an apartment in Dubai. She is constantly watched and never allowed out. All she does is service clients day in, day out. We get no response from the police in the UAE. If they are trafficked there, the situation is usually hopeless."

Slowly it is dawning on the visionaries of Dubai that they must work more diligently to ward off any eruption of trouble in paradise. And so a few concessions are now being made to these people without rights.

Commendably, the police ordered the Saudi company Al Beladi to pay the back wages (though in the event, they paid only half what they owed). The police also ruled that the men's barracks be supplied with water. "After about two weeks, they turned up with this tanker," Ahmed explained to me as he poured some water from it. "Taste this!" he said, handing me the cup. "Uggh! It's salt!" I said as I spat it out. "Yes," he said. "That is our new drinking water supply."

Hom Bahadur Thapa looks on sadly as I gag from the salt water. He has the gentle good looks common to Nepalis, whose features act as a bridge between India and China. He is one of the 175 million people in the world who have left their homes since the late 1980s, usually to escape poverty, by offering their labor to more dynamic economies. He was also the victim of a duplicitous snakehead—a trafficker of migrant labor. "I paid 100,000 rupees [$2,500] to come here from Kathmandu—it was all our money from the family and I had to borrow some more. My wife and child are back home, relying on me. My wife is now sick and they are receiving nothing from me. I just want the money owed to me so I can get back to Kathmandu."

That's not so easy, because when foreigners go to work in the UAE, their employers take their passport and keep it. These men are indentured to their employers, who may keep them on slave wages for years before letting them go on a whim. But they are also indentured to the snakeheads. The man to whom Hom paid 100,000 rupees to secure a job and passage to Dubai had assured him that he would be earning $550 a month once he arrived in Dubai. But when it transpired he was lying about the wage, Hom was still obliged to pay the remainder of the 100,000 rupees with interest (the collusion between employer and snakehead is transparent). So Hom, like the other men in the barracks, was brought here under false pretenses.

The free movement across borders of capital, goods, and services lies at the heart of globalization as it has emerged in the last twenty years. Until now this has largely been one-way traffic, with developing countries facing demands to open their markets and leave behind the common postwar policies of protectionism. This was a difficult transition for most countries, especially those that, unlike India, Korea, and China, do not enjoy economies of scale. Thus the West began to export its manufactured goods to the developing world, and the West established factories and repatriated the profits while refusing to reciprocate by opening its agricultural market. Equally damaging, however, are the fierce restrictions that the West places on labor migration, or the "missing global flow," as it is sometimes called. Globalization will work only if the free movement of capital, goods, and services is complemented by the free movement of labor, or at the very least, a more generous movement than exists now. We have designed an uneven playing field with at least one major consequence that undermines the progress of globalization and even brings the process into question.

Incalculable numbers cross borders illegally in search of work every year. But while many are willingly smuggled by arrangement, millions are trafficked. This means that force, blackmail, or deception is used in getting them to their destination (if indeed they make it that far—the journey is often extremely hazardous). It is a paradox that as the demand in Western economies for migrant labor has increased during the 1990s, controls on the borders have been tightened almost everywhere. This has created a huge market for the transfer of people, driven by the demand of Western business for cheap, untaxed labor.

Despite Southern Illinois University's large student population, Carbondale was not a happening place in the mid-seventies. But I had ended up there as a visitor because my father had foolishly accepted a guest professorship to translate the works of the great Russian film director Sergei Eisenstein. Fresh out of high school, I needed to earn money, but as a non–U.S. citizen the licit economy was out of bounds (sort of). In the evening, I was a highly lauded pizza deliverer at Mama Gina's (this was a time when an English accent could still add a quarter to the tip). But during the day I worked at the packing plant of Nutrition Headquarters, where I first came across America's profound obsession with vitamins and supplements. For ten hours a day, I had to stand at a desk and pack customers' orders before they were shipped out (the majority, I seem to recall, bound for Florida).

I daresay that these days Nutrition Headquarters is an upstanding employer of legally registered labor—after all, I notice that its headquarters now stands on Nutritional Plaza Drive, doubtless in honor of all the jobs it has created for American laborers! Unfortunately, back in the Victorian days of my youth, Nutritional Headquarters was strictly committed to employing illegals. Not only was I the sole Caucasian among the workforce, but I was the solitary English speaker. The great majority were Vietnamese and, like me, too cowed and frightened to protest against our conditions and pay. The supervisors were uneducated white American females who prowled around the shop floor like wolves, almost salivating at the prospect of a worker found slacking. I was eventually canned when a stomach bug forced me to visit the restroom every hour. I still remember the face of the short curly-haired brunette in her thirties as she proudly announced in nasal tones how my employment was being terminated for unauthorized visits to the washroom. I could scarcely contain my joy, but the other wretches who lost their jobs during my time there trembled and wept before shuffling off to an uncertain and perhaps destitute future.

Since my revealing experience among the migrant laborers of Carbondale, our consumer culture has become yet more bloated with choice and hypermarkets. The need for unskilled labor (especially in the agriculture sector) has reached unprecedented levels, while the indigenous populations in the West now eschew entirely low-paid work in unsafe conditions. The trade in labor is huge, and because it is largely illegal, only criminal entrepreneurs can operate it.

In recent years, there has been a steady downward pressure on the illegal global labor market and the wages itinerant laborers can command in many parts of the world. This is just the very beginning of a phenomenon that will grow ever more influential in the decades to come in all aspects of the global economy. This is China. The sea of cheap surplus labor that waits patiently in the Chinese countryside is seeping out into the wider world. Nobody boasts economies of scale like the Chinese.

Lieutenant General Dahi Khalfan Tamim, head of Dubai's police, was adamant. "We will fight anything that will impact negatively on society," he declared as he set out a new crackdown on prostitution in the city. He certainly had his work cut out. That evening I visited a club called Cyclone in Bur Dubai across the creek from Deira, the heart of Dubai. It is a vast square-set two-story complex with uniformed and plainclothes security guards checking everyone entering. Or rather, every man entering—there are no women seeking admission. Dubai is still mourning the death of Sheikh Rashid al-Maktoum, the man who ruled the city for three decades, reinventing it in the process. His death has led to the cancellation of the Dubai Shopping Festival, the annual consumerist megabinge that witnesses the world's wealthy swooping down on Dubai for even more spectacular tax-free bargains than usual. The lost Shopping Month has cost Dubai an estimated $3 billion in earnings, and the pressure is now mounting on Sheikh Mo to exempt this youthful annual spree from older and inconvenient local traditions.

At Cyclone, the management pays its respects by placing a ban on live DJs for forty days. The club's other core activity, however, continues unimpeded. As I enter the main area, there are two oval bars, one on either side of the entrance. Between the two is an invisible line. The dozens of girls crowded around the left bar never cross over to the right bar and vice versa. I step into the left bar zone to order a drink. Within seconds of stopping at the bar, a hand grabs my wrist and a Chinese woman of about nineteen starts talking. "You like me? No? You want to sleep with me? I am very good at sex. Only 400 dirham [$100]. I am *very* good." I smile and decline politely, provoking a sore look of disappointment—not, of course, because she had been so drawn to my middle-aged jowls but because the longer it takes to find a punter at Cyclone, the less the woman can charge. "By three o'clock in the morning," explains Ted, a twenty-something New Zealander who is, he tells me, broadening his horizons through global travel, "you can pick 'em up for fifty dirham. That's why you see the Africans hanging outside at three, four o'clock, because by then the girls will sleep with anyone for any price." He grins.

The right oval bar is populated by Russian and Ukrainian women. A large blonde in her twenties approaches me and wonders if I would like to sleep with her.

"I am professor of sex," she growls. "I teach you all good things."

I talk to her in pidgin Russian and she to me in pidgin English. We both find the encounter amusing. I turn down the offer but buy her a drink instead, which surprises her. "Why are the Chinese women over there and you over here?"

"We have an agreement," she says. "Nobody breaks it yet. But the Chinese want so much. They want all the business and these girls are younger and they ask for less money. We hate them."

The Russian and Ukrainian prostitutes are being steadily edged out of the market because of the bottomless supply of young Chinese women who are prepared to sleep with men for fewer dollars than the East Europeans.

For those not well versed in this market, the Chinese zone of Cyclone is an intimidating experience. By the time I scurried back to my hotel, I was beginning to wonder who was the predator, so bitter is the competition for the sex dollar among Dubai's foreign prostitutes.

Xanadu II

Dubai's crackdown on the trade is of course pure hot air. The primary class of people that the city wants to attract to live and work here is young single males. Relationships between non-Arabs and Emirati women are very rare and discouraged. Instead, the testosterone-filled newcomers are encouraged to seek other distractions.

There is virtually no petty crime in Dubai. It is one of the safest places to live in the world. So when violence comes calling, it sends shock waves through the place. Late on Sunday, January 19, 2003, Sharad Shetty, a successful hotelier, entered the India Club in Dubai, a grand establishment for Indian ex-pats built on land donated by Sheikh Rashid himself in 1964. Mr. Shetty had come for dinner with friends, but as he strode through the main door and into the hall, two men in their twenties approached and pumped five bullets into him before rushing to their getaway car. Dubai police were quick to link the killers with Chhota Rajan, as Mr. Shetty was one of Dawood Ibrahim's closest advisers. Three years earlier, Dawood's men had attempted but failed to assassinate Chhota Rajan when he was lying in a hospital in Thailand.

Mumbai's gang warfare was now being played out in the exclusive areas of Dubai, and the authorities decided on drastic measures. They swooped against both Chhota Rajan's and Dawood Ibrahim's associates. Two of Dawood's brothers were quickly arrested and eventually deported to India. Dawood himself had started to scale down his Dubai operations as early as 1998, when he sold the fabled White House and spent less time in the city. Instead, he became ever more reliant on Pakistan, eventually moving to Karachi, where he now lives in the opulent hill district of Clifton under the protection of the Pakistani state. He remains an influential figure in the Mumbai mafia, but he is dependent on the goodwill of the ISI. India demands his return to face trial, but the government in Islamabad denies his presence on Pakistani soil—an untruth that was well documented even before the glorious society wedding took place between Dawood's daughter and the son of the much-revered former captain of the Pakistani cricket team, Javed Miandad.

The investigation into the Bombay bombings, which lasted for fourteen years before dozens of suspects came to trial, revealed how deeply gangsterism in Bombay had subverted the city's economic and social life. Above all, the organized crime syndicates that rose from the swamps of chronic unemployment and poverty had absorbed the film industry, Bollywood, one of the world's great cultural icons. Who made films, how much for, who became stars, who distributed the movies—all this was decided by financial patrons such as Chhota Shakeel.

Sharad Shetty's spilled blood at the India Club was reason enough for Dubai to close in and neutralize the more prominent members of Mumbai's mafia. But the constant diplomatic pressure that India had applied on the city-state also played a significant role. India's economic importance to Dubai far outstrips that of Pakistan, even if the latter country is a Muslim state.

Violent crime is very rare in Dubai, and when it reveals itself, swift retribution usually follows. But it does not follow that crime and the shadow economy simply bypass the place. The licit market in goods, services, and capital is as unbridled here as it is anywhere in the world. The shadow economy is similarly unrestricted, and it is in Dubai where the money from the two economic systems converge and where one can begin to perceive just how symbiotic are the relations between the black and the white economies.

Simeon, the boy with everything: the phone, the Merc, the grave.

Bulgaria's nascent capitalist class gathers for its annual general meeting.

The late Ilya Pavlov, the boss of Multigroup.

Top left: Stanko "Cane" Subotic, one of the richest businessmen in the Balkans; top right: The late Vladimir "Vanja" Bokan, the inventor of the Balkan cigarette-smuggling trade; bottom left: Arkan, Milica the cub, and Arkan's Tigers; bottom right: Supporters of Milo Djukanovic, the man who brought Montenegro independence and the cigarette transit tax.

WANTED
BY THE FBI

RACKETEERING; SECURITIES FRAUD; WIRE FRAUD; MAIL FRAUD; MONEY LAUNDERING

SEMION MOGILEVICH

Photographs taken in 2001

Aliases: Seva Mogilevich, Semon Yudkovich Palagnyuk, Semen Yukovich Telesh, Simeon Mogilevich, Semjon Mogilevcs, Shimon Makelwitsh, Shimon Makhelwitsch, "Seva"

DESCRIPTION

Date of Birth Used:	June 30, 1946	Hair:	Gray (Balding)
Place of Birth:	Kiev, Ukraine	Eyes:	Green
Height:	5'6" to 5'7"	Sex:	Male
Weight:	290 pounds	Race:	White
NCIC:	W874119382	Nationality:	Ukrainian
Occupation:	Businessman		
Scars and Marks:	Mogilevich has pockmarks on his face.		
Remarks:	Mogilevich may wear facial hair to include a moustache. He is known to be a heavy smoker. Mogilevich has his primary residence in Moscow, Russia, but also has ties to the United States and England. He utilizes a Russian passport.		

CAUTION

Semion Mogilevich, Igor L'Vovich Fisherman, and Anatoli Tsoura are all wanted for their alleged participation in a multi-million dollar scheme to defraud investors in the stock of YBM Magnex International, Inc. (YBM), a public company incorporated in Canada, but headquartered in Newtown, Bucks County, Pennsylvania. Investors lost more than 150 million dollars through the alleged scheme that included inflating stock values, preparing

Top left: The FBI wants Semion Mogilevich.

Top right: Memorial to the late Viktor Kulivar "Karabas," the gangster beloved of all Odessa.

Right: "Mr. President!" say the mafia. "You are toothless. We are everywhere. Hand over power to us and we will introduce order into Russia and the CIS!"

Left: Sergei Mikhailov, the boss of Solntsevo.

Below top: Ze'ev Rosenstein miraculously survived this assassination attempt on Yehuda Halevy Street in Tel Aviv.

Below bottom: Bedouin youngsters with their contraband having just crossed the Egypt-Israel border in the Negev Desert.

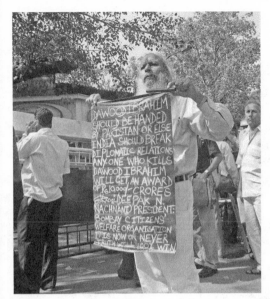

Deepak Nachnani makes his feelings known outside the Arthur Road jail as Sanjay Dutt is convicted of weapons' offenses in the court.

The ever-debonair Commander Rakesh Maria in Mumbai.

Dawood Ibrahim, king of the Mumbai underworld.

Inspector Pradeep Sharma, scourge of the Mumbai underworld.

The murderous Bombay blasts of March 1993.

Merging drugs and guns—the Cape Town gangs.

CHAPTER 8

The Theater of Crime

Jaime Quieroz Lopes had reached the end of his tether. For several days, Nelson Sakaguchi, a fellow director at a leading Brazilian private bank, had been stalling on an urgent request. The board of Banco Noroeste had ordered Sakaguchi to hand over all the documentation relating to the previous three years' business of its overseas operation based in the Cayman Islands. It was another morning in February 1998 as Mr. Sakaguchi started to formulate a new excuse. This time Lopes lost it. Grabbing hold of his terrified colleague's lapels, he screamed, "Look—no more stories! I want to see the figures and I want to see them now!"

It must have been a disorienting moment for Sakaguchi, a supremely successful international banker who had previously run one of Brazil's most influential banks in New York and who felt comfortable at ministerial-level meetings of the World Bank and the International Monetary Fund; a man regarded by all as hyperefficient, with no trace of personal vanity but equally lacking in human warmth; and a man who for fourteen years had enjoyed absolute control of Banco Noroeste's overseas accounts. Now he cowered at the fury of Lopes and muttered quietly, "You know, I have always had gambling in my blood." Then he broke down and was finally compelled to show the figures.

For the first time in anyone's memory, Mr. Sakaguchi was no longer in control.

In reality, matters had slipped out of Sakaguchi's hands three years earlier when his department received a fax from a certain Mr. Tafida Williams, the director for Budget and Planning at Nigeria's Ministry of Aviation. In the fax, Mr. Williams explained that a Nigerian customer of Banco Noroeste had suggested the ministry get in touch. The customer was indeed well known to Mr. Sakaguchi, and so he read the Aviation Ministry's offer with interest. Mr. Williams understood, it said, that the Brazilian bank might be interested in investing in major public works overseas. A unique and very lucrative opportunity had arisen. In 1991, the Nigerian government had moved the country's seat of government from Lagos to Abuja, and the time had come to create a major new airport to service the needs of the fastest-growing city in Africa's most populous country. The Aviation Ministry and the Central Bank of Nigeria, Mr. Williams explained, were now looking for external investors in the airport project. The rates of return, he intimated, would be highly attractive. Shrewd banker that he was, Nelson Sakaguchi replied to the fax saying that his company would like to explore the possibility of cooperation.

Before long, a limousine was whisking Sakaguchi from Heathrow Airport to a swish hotel in central London to discuss the proposal with a heavyweight delegation from Nigeria. As he entered the hotel suite, an elegant, slightly thickset man handed him his card: "Paul Ogwuma, director, Central Bank of Nigeria." Although Sakaguchi had never met Nigeria's most senior banker, Ogwuma's reputation in the world of international finance was solid. And he was there with his deputy, his deputy's wife, and a senior representative of Nigeria's Aviation Ministry. The atmosphere at the meeting was both cordial and businesslike.

Sakaguchi may have seen himself as a risk taker, but he had never played for such high stakes. The Nigerians were seeking about $50 million for the airport, and Banco Noroeste's capital totaled only $500 million. But the potential profits from the deal were enormous. Before long, he had authorized the first transfer of $4 million, and there was more to come.

Mr. Tafida Williams from the ministry's Budget and Planning department was not on the delegation to London. Just as well, really, because Williams, or Bless Okereke, to give him his real name, would never have passed muster as a departmental head. In his early twenties and uneducated, Bless was struggling to fit into his recently acquired role of sophisticated civil servant. Furthermore, he was fatally starstruck. When he started to receive a commission for his role in securing the deal with Noroeste, he could not resist playing the big man by flaunting his newfound wealth. This entailed risks of which Bless was unaware.

By late 1995, young Bless had left his tiny room, known in Nigeria as Boy Scout lodgings, and rented a spacious apartment in his hometown of Enugu, the dusty capital of the eponymous Nigerian province. He had also acquired a brand-new Jeep, and he could not resist showing off his new toy by taking it for a spin around town. His sudden promotion into the monied classes must have astonished his friends and relatives, inviting speculation, jealousy, and admiration in equal measure. "He was just a young boy out of his depth," explained Umar Mamman Sanda, a sober investigator from the EFCC, the Economic and Financial Crimes Commission in the Nigerian capital, Abuja. But his spending spree was not merely due to the joie de vivre that unexpected windfalls engender. Like many young Nigerian men, Bless was proving himself. These days a young man's rite of passage in Nigeria is a peculiar hybrid. To enter manhood, earlier generations had confronted the dangers of the forest and jungle as they engaged in a physical and spiritual battle with the high representatives of the animal kingdom. But the twentieth century had wrought huge changes on Nigeria, and now the smell of Bless and his lucre attracted less noble creatures, wearing Ray-Bans and gold bracelets.

Poor Bless turned out to be cursed. His money had transformed him from hunter into prey. By drawing too much attention to himself, he threatened to jeopardize the safety of his colleagues and the whole operation that had generated such wealth in the first place. That at least is what Inspector Sanda from the EFCC surmises, and he has a deeper understanding of this case than anyone.

That evening in Enugu, Bless noticed that a car following his Jeep was a little too close for comfort. As they gained on him, he leaped out of the Jeep and ran into the courtyard of a hotel, the pack in hot pursuit. He jumped over a fence and into the neighboring courtyard only to find himself cornered. He was dispatched with a few bullets. Many Nigerians will tell you that although their country is riddled with crime, it nonetheless boasts low levels of violence. And they are correct. But there are exceptions. And because Bless Okereke was involved in what became the biggest single advance fee fraud (or 419 scam, as they are also known) in history, he was one of those exceptions—a bit player in a drama that, according to the exuberant description of the EFCC website, "has all the characteristics of a successful movie: thrill, drama, sex, power, greed, suspense, tragedy and you name it [sic]." Oh, and at least two murders, as well.

Bless had been chosen for his role by Chief Emmanuel Nwude, Nigeria's most accomplished scammer. To this day, Nelson Sakaguchi swears he had no idea that his main business partner in the Abuja airport scheme was not Paul Ogwuma, the director of the Central Bank of Nigeria, but Chief Emmanuel Nwude. Although uneducated and described by one lawyer as "a thug," Nwude demonstrated confidence and ability in wriggling around the sewers of Nigeria's corruptocracy. He was a successful businessman, but at the London meeting with Sakaguchi, Chief Nwude had simply impersonated Ogwuma. As he awaited trial on charges of criminal conspiracy in his modest, neat home in Coita just outside São Paulo, Sakaguchi denied that he had noticed anything fishy about the deal or about Nwude. Everyone agrees that Sakaguchi was the victim of the most monumental fraud, but nobody understands why such an experienced banker would fall for the scam, or why he filched his employer's money in the process.

In charge of Noroeste's overseas accounts in the Cayman Islands, Sakaguchi is accused by the bank's lawyers of having skimmed hundreds of millions of dollars from them between 1995 and 1997. Sakaguchi insists he was the victim of a fraudulent scam pure and simple, and he was not stealing from his employees. Each transfer was made in parcels of less than $6 million. Had he gone over that figure, he would have required a higher authorization. Sakaguchi dispatched the money through dizzyingly circuitous routes in the United Kingdom, Switzerland, Hong Kong, and the United States. In Nigeria alone, seventeen different banks were used to shuffle and disguise the money. But despite the huge sums and their unusual passage around the world, nobody thought fit to raise the much-hailed red flags of the Western banking system. "Without any doubt," said Noroeste's asset recovery lawyer in São Paulo, Domingos Refinetti. "The banks just waved it through and shut their eyes."

From the banks, the tens of millions of dollars went into the pockets of Nwude and his main associates, the husband-and-wife team of Christian Ikechukwu Anajemba and Amaka Anajemba. They embarked on a game of global Monopoly, building palaces in Nigeria, buying real estate in Redondo Beach and Huntington Beach, California, and investing in an impressive array of properties in North London. They were good investors. "It made our job easier when it came to getting the money back," noted Keith Oliver, the London assets recovery lawyer. "The houses had increased in value so much that we were able to cover a good deal more than we had at first anticipated."

While the motives of the Nigerian scammers were never in doubt, Sakaguchi's gullibility beggars belief. There is no evidence to suggest that he was in league with the scammers—he was a genuine victim. But he was funding this wild gamble with somebody else's money. Thousands if not millions of man-hours have gone into the Noroeste investigation, which stands as the third-biggest bank theft in history. (Nick Leeson's destruction of Barings Bank and the looting of the Iraqi National Bank after the U.S. invasion of March 2003 take the top two places.) And yet not a single lawyer, judge, policeman, fraudster, or friend or spiritual adviser of Nelson Sakaguchi can answer the two central questions: Why did he do it? And how was he taken in?

"It's hard to see how he was fooled by this," remarked Keith Oliver, holding up a letter from the fraudsters boasting the distinct letterhead: The Federal Reserve Clearing House, Chadwell Heath, Romford, Essex. There are no residential suburbs in northeast London that are more anonymous and bland than Chadwell Heath. Nonetheless, to double-check that overnight the district had not developed into a major center of international finance, Oliver spent a few hours motoring around the Heath "just so [he] could swear in [his] affidavit that there was definitely no Federal Reserve Clearing House there!"

But by this time Sakaguchi was in regular correspondence with Chadwell Heath's Federal Reserve Clearing House and similar institutions as though they were genuine. In all likelihood, he had lost any grasp of the difference between reality and illusion. He was seemingly completely trapped by the addictive fear common to victims of the 419 or advance fee fraud.

The 419 scam comes in many shapes and sizes—it sometimes arrives as an appeal to rich Westerners to come to the aid of an impoverished African child; letters, faxes, and e-mail beseeching Americans in particular for funds to erect a new church or bolster a congregation are frequent—in these cases, the motivation of the victims is well intentioned and charitable. Another lucrative prey of the 419 scammers are the lovelorn, in particular middle-aged widows and divorcées who develop virtual relationships with West African boy toys who slowly leech them of their savings as an advance on a sexual congress that never happens.

But most of all, the 419ers appeal to the basic instinct of greed. Annie McGuire, a Californian victim of the fraudsters, explained that she had a decent education, "a good IQ": "Simultaneously I owned and ran three businesses before retiring in my late forties. My husband and I *had* a very comfortable, growth-oriented retirement fund." And yet, as she confessed, "We wanted more—we wanted to send our grandchildren to private schools; we wanted to set up trust funds for them and hire experts to teach them how to manage their money. We wanted to travel, and have summer and winter homes to save our aching joints from inclement weather. My husband wanted horses, I wanted a drop-dead audio system. I figured I'd been around enough to make a lot of quick money if the opportunity presented itself."

Unfortunately for Annie, she unwittingly hooked up with a high-end Nigerian scammer who allegedly traded in commodities. Before long she discovered that he had channeled close to a million dollars of her own and other investors' money into a fake holding account in the Bahamas. Although she was in deep trouble, Annie was unusual in that she went to the FBI. A majority of scam victims develop a peculiar psychological dependency on the perpetrator—the more money they lose, the more desperate they are to believe the promise of tantalizing riches, and the more prepared they are to throw good money after bad.

Every year countless Europeans and Americans are fleeced of thousands or tens and hundreds of thousands of dollars each. They all believe that they are going to make millions of dollars by hiding and transiting money that purports to originate in the dormant accounts of dodgy Western businessmen or of the widows of former African dictators such as Nigeria's late president Sani Abacha or President Mobuto of Zaire, now the Democratic Republic of the Congo.

The scam is simple—in order for the victims (or *mugus,* as they are known in Nigeria) to get their excited paws on the fabled millions, the scammer will at some point request that they transfer a facilitating fee of several thousand dollars to the bank's "lawyer." This is why the 419 scam (named after the relevant clause in Nigeria's criminal code) is also dubbed the advance fee fraud. Once hooked, the *mugu* is asked for ever greater sums, lured on by the fictive promise of millions just around the corner. "The fraudsters exploit a simple failing in human psychology," said Alhaji Ibrahim Lamorde, head of operations for the EFCC, the Economic and Financial Crimes Commission, in Lagos. "If you have already invested, say, one million in a project and your partner says you need to put in another two hundred thousand for the return to be realized, people think 'Well, compared to the million, two hundred k is not such a big amount.' And so in it goes before the partner comes back two weeks later with a request for a further one-fifty k." It is the same motive that drives an addicted gambler. "They wriggle like a fish on the end of a line," concludes Mr. Lamorde.

Ultrascan Advanced Global Investigations in the Netherlands, which specializes in uncovering 419 frauds, has reported that citizens in thirty-eight developed countries admitted to losses of more than $3 billion in 2005 alone. These estimates are necessarily low because they exclude all those victims who did not confess their gullibility to law enforcement agencies. Most victims report feeling an intense mixture of shame and guilt when suckered by 419ers, and in March 2003, for the first time a 419 victim turned to murder to express his frustration. Jiri Pasovsky, a seventy-two-year-old Czech pensioner, stormed into the Nigerian embassy in Prague and shot dead a secretary after the consul general explained that he could not return the $600,000 Pasovsky had lost to a Nigerian scammer.

Every time Nelson Sakaguchi transferred another $3 to $4 million, he expected the returns to start rolling in. Instead, Chief Nwude and his accomplices requested a further payment in order to pay for fabricated legal fees or bribes. And as his losses mounted, so did the compulsion to pay out more millions in the hope of retrieving the ever-greater sum invested. At some point in any 419 scam, the anxiety must mingle with a thickening despair that leads straight to a living hell. Sakaguchi's response to this descent was to seek advice from macumba, Brazil's syncretic religion that melds West African animism with Christianity. Maria Rodrigues was a macumba priestess whom Sakaguchi was wont to consult.

During the lengthy investigations into the Banco Noroeste affair, Maria Rodrigues introduced some welcome levity for the participants. At one point, the Brazilian government gave exceptional permission for a Swiss judge to hold hearings in Brazil to establish whether Sakaguchi and some of the Nigerian conspirators should face trial for money laundering in Switzerland. (Sakaguchi was eventually convicted and sentenced to thirty months.) The judge heard testimony from Maria Rodrigues. Domingos Refinetti, representing Banco Noroeste, was present and recalled the scene:

"I wanted money from Sakaguchi," she said, "because I needed to buy 120,000 white pigeons for a particular ritual. By having the pigeons," she said, "Sakaguchi would be relieved of his problems. Sakaguchi delivered the pigeons."

"And how might one keep the pigeons?" inquired the judge. "Surely they were flying all over the place?"

At this point, the judge could contain himself no longer and began laughing. Curiously enough Maria Rodrigues then said that she then asked for money for 120,000 black pigeons. The judge, barely able to control his mirth, said, "I suppose if you've bought up 120,000 white pigeons, you will have driven up the price and you need to buy the black pigeons in order to restore the equilibrium of in the pigeon futures market!"

The cost of the pigeons and the advice were no laughing matter, however. Altogether Sakaguchi siphoned $20 million from the Caymans into Brazil and into the coffers of the late Ms. Rodrigues.

Across the Atlantic in Lagos and Enugu, Chief Nwude and his main accomplice, Christian Anajemba, were exploiting the social and business clout that big money brings. Nwude was appointed a director of Union Bank, one of Nigeria's biggest. He put about the story that he was a canny oil trader who had recently joined the big leagues: he began to collect cars both classic and modern, including Mayburys and Rolls-Royces. Anajemba imported millions of dollars' worth of marble for his new mansions while purchasing fabulous jewelery for his wife, Amaka, who would later be dubbed Queen of the 419s by an admiring Nigerian press. And while accounts were hemorrhaging, while huge sums of obscure origin were chugging from bank to bank, and while audits were being merrily signed, nobody noticed a thing—not in Brazil, the Caymans, or the United States; not in the United Kingdom, Switzerland, or Nigeria. Nada.

There are important reasons why Nigeria has become the Broadway of Crime: It is home to the most successful culture of financial fraud in history, which has assumed a global capacity since the early 1990s. As in any good theater, the audience members, or victims, in this case, must be willing to suspend their disbelief for the illusion to work. Nigeria offers the perfect facilities for budding impresarios because it is the world's greatest example of a remarkable hybrid—the Potemkin state in which an elaborate façade of institutions conceals their complete lack of substance.

Dressed in a brightly colored African shirt and tight trousers that hug a sinewy body, Dede Mabiaku forcefully expresses the popular belief that "Europeans" are responsible for Nigeria's ubiquitous corruption and specifically for 419 scams. "They invented the computer!" he explains. Dede is on his way to a party thrown by Hakim Belo Osagie, one of Nigeria's most successful bankers. Dede himself is a popular singer. The nephew and protégé of Fela Kuti, the great musician admired the world over, Dede is adamant that the roots of Nigeria's kleptocracy lie in Western culture. He talks of the tradition of companies exploiting the natural resources of Africa and giving nothing in return, and how corruption was an essential tool in these companies' business practices. "Four-one-nine and the scams are merely the redressing of the global balance," he says. "If Europeans get ripped off they deserve it. They are greedy and trying to make money out of African people."

There is a large element of truth in what Mabiaku says, and the legacy of colonization has been decisive in the fashioning of modern Nigeria. Europe has been cherry-picking Africa's riches for more than two centuries (more recently America and now even China have been feeding at the trough). The European colonists extracted Africa's commodities (whether slaves, palm oil, or diamonds), and in exchange they left borders and bureaucracy, countries and central banks, tariffs and taxes. In short, they left behind the modern state, that intricate web of institutions that over many centuries bound Europe's rulers with her ruled.

Europeans and Americans can scarcely conceive of life without the state. But for many Africans, when the state arrived it was a superfluous imposition that was hard to reconcile with their own traditions. The Africans had not requested this imposition, and neither was there much evidence that they wanted or needed it. But to succeed in their commercial endeavors, the Europeans couldn't do without it. In the late nineteenth and early twentieth centuries, they felt the urge to build railways, cultivate palm, and dig mines across Africa. And in doing so they demanded protection for their contracts, which the word of a chief (the local way of doing business) could no longer guarantee. Such significant investments as the Europeans made required security that would survive the chief's death and override any subsequent dispute about rights to the land or to the commodity in question. And for that they needed borders, banks, taxes, lawyers, and courts. The Europeans erected the façades of their states, but behind them traditional societies remained very different. This was the Potemkin state.

But although Dede Mabiaku's indignation is well founded, it disguises a great chunk of hypocrisy. This is in fearful evidence at the party being held by Mr. Osagie at his villa on Ikoyi Island. Among the wealthiest areas in all Nigeria, Ikoyi is tucked away from the permanent traffic jam on the mainland (residents avoid the hellish drive to the airport by taking the helicopter shuttle). Armed with a Harvard MBA and a reputation of genius in banking, Osagie lives in a vast mansion, where he personally greets each of his 300 guests. Dressed tastefully in well-cut black slacks and shirt, he smiles as the raucous assembly helps itself to champagne on tap. In the garden, the stage is set for stand-up comedians and the cream of Lagos musicians, including Dede, to perform. Blake and Crystal Carrington would be hard pressed to mount a display of such gaudy opulence.

Nigeria's passage into the global market, floating atop the world's sixth-largest oil reserves, has created one of history's most divided societies in terms of income distribution. The razor wire and searchlights protecting the rich in this part of Lagos are sadly reminiscent of the walls behind which most whites in South Africa live. These Nigerian walls have done immense damage to one of the most important African institutions—the responsibility of the *oga* or "big man" in the community to the less well off.

Instead of distributing money, food, clothes, and housing to the village, the big men who have grown fat on oil corruption now hoard their millions in mansions behind elaborate security arrangements.

The Nigerian elite has become rich even beyond many Westerners' imaginations. Since the 1970s, they have been sucking the profits from the country's oil resources almost directly from the wells and into their pockets. Yet this voluminous revenue stream did not dissuade Nigeria from accepting massive Western loans during the 1970s. With Robert McNamara at the helm, the World Bank was working as indefatigably as an insurance salesman on commission, cajoling the developing world into taking out huge sums on tick. During McNamara's tenure from 1968 to 1981, lending rose from just under $1 billion to almost $12.5 billion, and Nigeria was an important client. This was the beginning of the massive global debt scandal in which we are all still embroiled.

Of course, Nigerian oil revenue was not used as repayment for the loans. Instead, the burden was shifted onto Nigeria's poor, for whom the country's rulers made no welfare or development provisions. Nigeria was about to take the Potemkin state to a new level. Its refurbishment lovingly creates all the external attributes of a bureaucratic state—flags, UN speeches, forms to fill out, grand buildings with big golden plaques saying CENTRAL BANK or MINISTRY OF LABOR—but they are mere scenery on a stage. The Central Bank has no money, the Ministry of Labor no jobs. But a small group used the illusion to divert national income into their pockets and those of their families and friends. The state was effectively privatized (which in the 1980s was, of course, in keeping with the zeitgeist of late Reaganite and Thatcherite economics), but the recipients of the money were under no obligation to provide the services that the state might otherwise be expected to deliver.

With the petrodollar rush came huge contracts for public works, which were handed out to Western companies that were colluding in the bribery process. "A government of the contractors, by the contractors, for the contractors," is how Ishola Williams of Transparency International described the notorious rule of General Ibrahim Babangida, known in Nigeria as IBB, from the mid-eighties to the early nineties. A former general in the Nigerian army who resigned his commission, Williams knows whereof he speaks. "The scumbag companies made common cause with Nigerian politicians to rip off the treasury," explained Stephen Ellis, a leading scholar on West Africa, whose indignation provokes his lapse into the vernacular, "and for banks like BCCI this was perfect. Because they could facilitate these deals between Western companies and the Nigerian elite and they don't cry foul because they were corrupt themselves. So BCCI was skimming off everybody and aiding such phenomena as capital flight."

In 1983, the gifted Nigerian writer Chinua Achebe wrote, "Nigerians are corrupt because the system under which they live today makes corruption easy and profitable; they will cease to be corrupt when corruption is difficult and inconvenient. . . . The trouble with Nigeria is simply and squarely a failure of leadership. There is nothing basically wrong with the Nigerian character. I am saying that Nigeria can change today if she discovers leaders who have the will, the ability and the vision."

Ironically, Achebe penned this on the eve of the worst excesses of poor leadership, when a series of military coups allowed the consolidation of corruption as an ideology. It was during the rule of IBB that the U.S. Drug Enforcement Administration (DEA) noticed how Nigeria was becoming the major transshipment center for cocaine destined for Europe and for heroin en route to the United States. Furthermore, it appeared that the organizers of this business enjoyed access to the very highest offices of state.

The Nigerian military effectively announced the start of an unending party of grand theft. And to this day, all who visit the country can see it in full swing, from the minute they attempt (and surely fail) to pass customs without paying a bribe at Lagos's chaotic Murtala Muhammed Airport, to the day they leave when they will have to dispense largesse to a wide variety of airport staff if they are to stand a chance of securing a seat on their flight home. "You go to market, somebody will try to cheat you," says the country's senior anticorruption policeman, Nuhu Ribadu. "You take a taxi, somebody will take something—you must have your eyes open all the time." If you want to fill your car's tank (in a land awash with gasoline there are permanent shortages), you must bribe; get into a decent restaurant, you must bribe; pass through the ubiquitous police checkpoints, you must bribe. Every single economic or social transaction must be refracted through the prism of graft. And all this is decreed by the example set by the oil thieves at the very top.

"Every day the Nigerian economy loses between 150,000 and 320,000 barrels of oil," explained Gary K. Busch, an adventurous American businessman who has worked with mafia-style entrepreneurs in many parts of the developing world, including Nigeria. "These are stolen by 'bunkerers' who have small tanker vessels, which load the oil in the Delta and transship this stolen oil to offshore tankers, which deliver it to other West African states. Further inland illegal tanker trucks load the oil and refined products and drive these into neighboring countries for black market sale. At the current price of around fifty dollars per barrel, this amounts to a 'leakage' of around $7.5 to $16 million a day. On a monthly basis this amounts to around $365 million or $4.4 billion a year."

There is of course no intrinsic moral problem in Nigeria's profiting from its natural resources. But the unwillingness of its small band of hyper-rich to distribute its billions in any equitable manner has very serious implications and unpleasant consequences. While maintaining one of the most venal military establishments in the world, Nigeria does nothing to succor its second army of tens of millions of unemployed and destitute. Sixty percent of the population lives below the poverty line. Equally dis-tressing is the collapse in life expectancy, which, according to the UN, dropped from fifty-four years old for Nigerian males in 1995 to forty-three in 2006. The corruption at the very highest levels sets an example mimicked throughout Nigerian society. If you want to prosper, you have to cheat.

In the late 1980s, the West began to liberalize its financial markets. For some years, large corporations had argued with governments that they needed to move money around the world faster and in much greater quantities in order to take full advantage of its value as they expanded global operations. Their requests were greeted with skepticism until they found steadfast allies in the governments of Ronald Reagan and Margaret Thatcher. By the late 1980s, the most powerful capitalist economies had lifted the bureau-cratic barriers that blocked the free movement of capital between them. The sovereign control of money flowing in and out of individual countries, one of the keystones of the nation-state, was abandoned. Corporations may have retained a symbolic association with a particular country and a residual affection, but they now strove to be present and rooted wherever it was profitable to be so. Globalization had begun in earnest.

Among the global crime fraternity, champagne corks were popping. Western governments were vague about the implications of the liberaliza-tion, and they established only primitive mechanisms to regulate this mas-sive surge in the movement of capital. The exponential growth of organized crime triggered by the collapse of the Soviet Union and the emergence of dozens of transitional and failing states was given a further fillip and indeed became inextricably bound up with globalization—it was here in the huge reservoirs of the international banking system that the liq-uid assets of the corporate and criminal worlds mixed and mingled. Very quickly it became impossible to separate the two. While crime groups big and small took full advantage of the globalization of finance, they were not required to explain their actions before an antitrust commission, nor did they have to abide by the rules of the World Trade Organization and its predecessor.

Something was very new and very different in the world—money was being shifted about with an unimagined ease, and nobody was keeping track of it. Fraud and organized crime were in the vanguard of the brave new world of globalization. Technology and deregulation had changed the global financial markets beyond recognition. Nigerian criminals were masters of both.

In the mid-1980s, the giant investment house Merrill Lynch contracted two different firms to clean and guard overnight their headquarters in New York's financial district. And every night over several months, the cleaners and the night watchmen would make their way to the files storing the details of customers to whom Merrill Lynch had granted "preferential" status. These files held credit card numbers with which a person could enter any financial institution and withdraw $52,000 on any one occasion, no questions asked. The Nigerian cleaners and night watchmen busied themselves for several months photocopying all these details on the company Xerox before transferring the information onto blank credit cards in preparation for one mighty spending spree.

One night the Nigerians let down their guard and left one of the photocopied pages by the machine. Before long, Merrill Lynch had called in the U.S. Secret Service, which, through a quirk of agency history, has responsibility for financial and counterfeiting crimes as well as its more familiar role of presidential guard duty. "That was the first time that we caught on to the Nigerians as scammers," remembers the ex–Secret Service agent Mark Sidbury. "And they were good."

Over the next few years, the Secret Service registered major financial crimes perpetrated by Nigerian gangs in several major U.S. cities, from Atlanta to Chicago to Los Angeles. They involved anything to do with money—insurance scams; checking account scams; credit card fraud; counterfeiting of money and passports; as well as the creation of networks offering U.S. citizenship through marriages of convenience. Above all, the Secret Service observed the speed with which Nigerian fraudsters would adapt technological innovation in the financial sector to their own purposes. A distaste for violence worked in their favor, as they drew much less public attention to their crimes than those working with drug cartels or the more traditional protection rackets of the Cosa Nostra. The amount of money involved, however, was staggering.

The Merrill Lynch case occurred when banking systems were at the very beginning of computerization. What the Nigerian fraudsters demonstrated was a capacity to blend an advanced understanding of mechanical and electronic technology with a convincing theatricality. When surveying the undulating landscape of Nigerian crime, it is hard not to develop a sense of admiration for the loving care and creativity with which it is fashioned.

Most Nigerians involved in crime simply mimic the behavior of their thieving elite. This tiny band of billionaires is drawn mainly from the country's west and north regions. But those who commit crimes overseas are disproportionately drawn from Nigeria's east, as was the case in the New York scam. There are more than 300 ethnic groups in Nigeria, but broadly speaking the country is divided into three main language groups: the Yoruba in the west, including Lagos; the Hausa in the north; and the Igbo in the east. It is too crude to identify these as three separate peoples, as the differentiation within each language group is vast, rather like calling Russians and Poles part of the same tribe.

After almost a century of colonial rule, the three groups embraced independence in 1960 with very different roles in the new state. By 1966, the Muslim Hausa had come to dominate the army; the Christian Yoruba provided much of the civil service and the intellectual elite of the country; and the Igbo in the east continued their role as some of the most effective traders in the world. When oil was discovered, it was mostly in the Niger delta to the east. Igbo leaders felt disinclined to share their wealth either with the north and its unproductive, almost feudal system, or with the Yoruba in the west, whom the Igbo perceived as insufferably arrogant. In 1967, the Igbo announced their secession from the country and the declaration of a new state, Biafra. Not surprisingly, the Hausa and the Yoruba were in no mood to let this precious part of the country slip through their hands. Civil war devastated the east until 1970, when Biafra—broken, battered, and famished—surrendered.

Ever since then, the Igbo have complained that they have been excluded from the riches of Nigeria by the Yoruba and Hausa. The rich of the west and the north became even richer, while the Igbo returned to their old ways. For hundreds of years, the Igbo had forged trading routes along the coast of West Africa as far as South Africa. In collaboration with the emirs of the Hausa and their trading counterparts from Lebanon, they also pioneered a trans-Saharan route that stretched as far as Mecca, Medina, and Jeddah in what is now Saudi Arabia.

Thanks to wars and apartheid, these traditional routes were less easily negotiated in the 1970s than was once the case (although some of the many Nigerians studying in the Soviet Union and its Warsaw Pact allies assisted in the delivery of supplies to the ANC in southern Africa). And so they started looking farther afield—London was a popular destination, as were New York and Washington, D.C., while other Igbo found their way to Thailand, where a proportion soon became involved in the dispatch of heroin to Africa and the West. By 1990, Nigerian nationals (the majority Igbo) made up 30 percent of all people imprisoned at British ports of entry for heroin smuggling, according to the Howard League for Penal Reform. This may be explained in part because Nigerian passport holders are frequent targets of customs officers around the world.

The Igbo entrepreneurs were driven abroad both by the perceived prejudice and greed of the northerners and southerners but also by the consequences of the most appalling mismanagement of the Nigerian economy. By the end of Babangida's rule, the country had ratcheted up almost £30 billion of debt. Large-scale criminal fraud had been a persistent problem since independence, but with rising unemployment, rampant inflation, and a collapse in the value of Nigeria's currency, the naira, defrauding indigenous Nigerians was becoming ever less profitable.

There are two basic types of criminal syndicates—the commodity traders and the protection racketeers. The former is divided into three principal groups: producers, wholesale traders, and retailers. Each sector is usually but not always associated with a specific ethnic group, and the three sectors will establish cooperation across international borders, as production or extraction of a commodity usually takes place a long way from its most lucrative retail markets.

Protection racketeers, such as America's Cosa Nostra, very occasionally develop a transnational operation but are usually contained within a single state's borders; yet, like Tony Soprano and his pals, successful racketeers will also cross over into commodity trading by establishing control over the local retail outlets for whatever the market may demand—drugs, women, and so on.

In the world of illicit commodities, on rare occasions the producer will play an important role as a wholesale trader and even as the final retailer. The most visible example is the Colombian cartels. They are able to use their monopoly position as refiners and wholesalers in order to outsource the cultivation of the coca to the poverty-stricken growers of Peru and Bolivia. And in the case of Amsterdam, the pivot of distribution of coke in

Europe, they use traders in the local Colombian community as the primary importers into Holland.

Turkish syndicates control large parts of the heroin trade's wholesale distribution and in countries such as Germany and Great Britain much of the retail end as well. But they play no role in production, which is highly decentralized over large parts of central Asia (Afghanistan and Burma in particular).

Throughout the world, it is the most adventurous wholesale traders and risk takers in the licit economy who are also most closely associated with criminality in popular perception. Being at the heart of the global economy, trade is a key component in the world of organized crime. On the whole, western and north Europeans are not associated with large-scale criminal activities except in their crucial role as consumers.

This goes back to when Europeans sought to gain a competitive advantage during the mercantilist period of the sixteenth to eighteenth centuries by encouraging the state to back an expansion in foreign trade. Had there been any laws to break, these adventurers would have been the first global organized criminal syndicates. Instead they merely offended moral values by appropriating whatever they came across in exchange for alcohol and the clap. But the early days of high-risk freebooting and pillage became bogged down by colonialist paraphernalia—this was not needed, on the whole, to calm the natives but to secure the advantages of imperial expansion over other European competitors. So European trade was bound intimately with the goals of the state: in the form of the colonialist army, it would protect merchants, and as the state defined what goods were licit and what illicit, its merchants tended to accept that definition in exchange for armed protection that gave them a competitive edge. When Britain decided in the nineteenth century that it was acceptable to sell opium to the Chinese in large quantities, there was no indignant uproar on the part of British merchants. Instead, there was a rush for profits—the state said it was okay and merchants didn't need to be told twice.

Other trading nations did not enjoy such high levels of protection, nor did they have an interest in accepting European state definitions of which goods were permitted and which not. They built their success as traders on other foundations—proximity to the sea; access to valued commodities; exclusion from ruling structures and low economic development; proximity to major geographical and political borders. An inherent aspect of their trading is risk taking and the scavenging of new markets—places that lie on the edge of organized trading networks, of states and of systems of moral values. And on the whole, these traders do not judge a commodity by its social function in its place of origin or consumption. They judge it by its profit margin.

As trade liberalization was hailed in the late 1980s and early 1990s as a cornerstone of the complex new worldwide network of relations known as globalization, traders started traveling farther and in greater numbers than ever before in search of new opportunities to buy and sell. In the forefront were those peoples, often minority communities, who had centuries of tradition in trading and living on their wits along the farthest frontiers of global commerce: the Lebanese, the Chinese of Canton and Fujian provinces, the Balkan peoples, the Jews, the Muslims of India, the Sicilians, the Vietnamese. And it was from a minority of these traders that the pioneers of the new global shadow economy were also drawn.

Of course, crime also relied on producers, such as the Russians and the Colombians. But it is the conveyor of illicit goods and services that plays the most visible part in this global drama. Among the most phlegmatic and inventive of all are the Igbo.

Infected by the corruption of the Nigerian state (itself a cankered product of British colonialism), the Igbo traders of the 1980s and 1990s dealt in those products without regard to any moral considerations save a clear and admirable aversion to violence. But then along came an invention that enabled them to steer financial fraud operations without even crossing the threshold of their front door—the fax machine. And soon the Yoruba, the Hausa, and dozens more of Nigeria's ethnic groups took up the example of the Igbo and began indulging in one of the most exuberantly mischievous examples of crime in history. The possibilities would multiply with the proliferation of the personal computer around the world; cybercrime is a new type of criminal threat that assumes several different forms. But the Igbo can stake a strong claim as trailblazers in this entirely new and lucrative genre—the 419 scam or advance fee fraud.

For many Nigerians the degree to which their country has become associated with and even defined by the 419 culture is both a scandal and a disaster. But according to the musician Dede Mabiaku, the 419 scams were merely the diseased chickens of colonialism coming home to roost in Europe and the United States, like some moral avian flu in the era of globalization. The huge popularity of the 419 anthem, "I Go Chop Your Dollar," suggested that these sentiments are widely held in Nigeria:

419 no be thief, it's just a game
Everybody dey play 'em
if anybody fall mugu,
ha! my brother I go chop 'em

REFRAIN:
National Airport na me get 'em
National Stadium na me build 'em
President na my sister brother
You be the mugu, *I be the master*
Oyinbo man [White man], *I go chop your dollar,*
I go take your money and disappear
419 is just a game, you are the loser I am the winner

The fax machine triggered the advent of global scamming from Nigeria, but it was the proliferation of the Internet that transformed the practice into a gold mine. The scammers put an immense amount of work into their ploys, and again, it is hard not to admire their commitment to theatricality and detail. But ultimately they depend on the victim's greed or gullibility. Police across the Western world have been overwhelmed with pleas for help from victims, but there is very little they can do because the crimes are conceived and executed in areas outside their jurisdiction. "Frustrating and sad" is how Nuhu Ribadu described the ability of criminals to stall trial proceedings literally over decades. "We are yet to record one successful conviction for advance fee fraud [419] in Nigeria. Yet we have over two hundred Nigerians serving jail terms in more than fifteen countries abroad." (The boss of the EFCC, the remarkable Ribadu, has rectified the situation since he made that observation in 2004.)

The fraudsters' ability to evade prosecution is not simply bad luck for the poor suckers who have been fleeced by 419 scammers. Nigeria and its culture of corruption pose two immense challenges: One concerns the stability of Nigeria itself. An increasingly critical energy supplier outside the Middle East and the former Soviet Union, Nigeria is of interest to countries across the world. But kleptocracies are notoriously unstable. This is especially true if such states embrace a large number of ethnic groups with competing elites. In Nigeria's case, the problem is further exacerbated by the economic tensions dividing the Muslim north and the Christian south.

Nigeria's second problem is possibly the largest single difficulty for the successful globalization of commerce—the absence of the rule of law. Nigeria's emergence out of venal military dictatorship has been very difficult.

The Theater of Crime

Unfortunately, although a sine qua non, the regular holding of elections does not guarantee a successful democracy. Political parties often are a vehicle for economic interests to gain access to the state and an unfair or criminal advantage. But equally important in undermining the consolidation of democratic roots is the absence of an impartial judiciary and a disinterested legal system. Business needs to enjoy confidence in the institutions of democracy, known as the rule of law, if it is to risk investing in those markets. For globalization to work, the world needs to be a level playing field: the West has to stop its protectionist practices and it has to reassess its resistance to the free, or at least a freer, movement of labor. The developing world in turn needs to address the issue of corruption and the strengthening of the rule of law. This raises the awkward question of global governance and standards that might be compatible across the world. Nigeria—plagued by the colonialist legacy, the curse of oil, and modern confessional tensions—demonstrates how problematic is the application of universal policies in a world that boasts such diverse local cultures and painful historical experiences. The mixed messages that emanate from America and Europe further exacerbate this: on the one hand, they encourage transparency and good governance in the developing world by applying a system of conditionality that includes both punishment and incentives; on the other hand, they are desperate to secure energy supplies from countries such as Nigeria and are prepared to bend the rules, especially when confronted by the competitive pressure of Chinese and Indian oil requirements. To be blunt, if the Americans and Europeans demand that oil-producing countries adopt higher standards of transparency and anticorruption measures, these countries are increasingly in a position to respond by saying, "Fine—if you don't want our oil, we'll sell it to someone else!" And they have plenty of eager buyers.

It does not follow that the issue of transparent government is doomed. Although not decisive, the external and internal pressures on Nigeria to clean up its act have not proven totally feeble. In the first five years of the millennium, Nihu Ribadu and his team at the EFCC have emerged as the vanguard in the struggle against corruption and organized crime. And their prosecution of the Banco Noroeste case, the largest recorded fraud in history, with the assistance of lawyers and policemen in Brazil, the United States, Britain, and Switzerland, has become a touchstone.

In August 1997, the Spanish Banco Santander made a bid to take over Banco Noroeste and the Brazilian bank accepted it. In December 1997 at a joint board meeting, an official from Santander questioned why half of Noroeste's capital was sitting in the Cayman Islands largely unmonitored. He wanted to examine it to see if returns on this capital gave value for money. The Caymans account amounted in theory to $190 million, almost two-fifths of Noroeste's total value. Nelson Sakaguchi was on vacation at the time, and so it wasn't until two months later that Jaime Quieroz Lopes finally put him up against a wall and extracted the relevant documentation.

The fraud was discovered instantly, but it took some weeks before the auditors were able to ascertain that $242 million had gone missing—$191 million in cash and the remainder as outstanding interest. Sakaguchi was not the only person with a lot of explaining to do. Two subordinates in his department also appear to have colluded in the theft. It was perhaps most embarrassing for the reputation of Price Waterhouse Coopers, who, as external auditors, had given Banco Noroeste six clean bills of health during the period of the fraud. This was unlikely to inspire confidence in a company that was still recovering from its inglorious performance in the BCCI scandal.

The Simonsen and Cochrane families, who owned Banco Noroeste, decided to foot the bill of $242 million themselves to ensure that the sale to Banco Santander went through. Then for six years very little happened. The two families learned the grim news that while the borderless flows of cash through the banking system is hard to stem, it is equally difficult to facilitate cooperation between the criminal justice systems of two states, let alone four of five, as was the case in the world's largest 419 scam. Chief Nwude and Mrs. Anajemba (her husband had been assassinated by now) were free to spend, spend, spend.

"The problem is that nobody was looking for it who knew how to look for the money," explained Bill Richey, a former Florida State DA who was asked by the Simonsens and Cochranes to search for the money across the globe. And so Richey made a smart move—he called a buddy who used to work for the Internal Revenue Service as a criminal investigator. "You know, the IRS are tax people, the American gestapo!" he said. "My guy is a very nice man, but he's a very efficient and effective forensic accountant investigator."

Tracing the money to Switzerland, England, and the United States, Richey assembled the A-team of asset recovery lawyers in London, Kentucky, Los Angeles, New York, Geneva, Hong Kong, Singapore, and Lagos. Slowly but surely, the A-team started to claw back the assets located outside Nigeria. But to get the job done properly, they would need convictions of the criminal group in Nigeria. "And until 2003," one of the lawyers pointed out, "that was a nonstarter."

Chief Nwude and Mrs. Anajemba had already been busy bribing the police, bribing journalists, and bribing the courts. They were untouchable. Until, that is, Nigeria's very own Elliot Ness appeared on the scene.

Nigeria's parliament established the Economic and Financial Crimes Commission at the request of President Olusegun Obasanjo in 2002. The United States, the IMF, and the EU were all pressing Nigeria to tackle the notorious levels of corruption throughout government and society. This had become an urgent issue for the West, as Nigeria's importance as an oil supplier was growing in the wake of turbulence in the Middle East, central Asia, and Venezuela.

What few expected when the EFCC started work properly a few months later was that its director, Nuhu Ribadu, would develop such an unbending devotion to rooting out corruption and crime wherever it might be found. Through a reedy, almost effeminate voice, this thin, bespectacled, and earnest-looking man in his mid-forties expresses his immutable determination to tackle Nigeria's great enemy: "It is corruption that gives Nigeria this terrible image, that drives people from our country; it is corruption that gives rise to these crimes like 419; and because of corruption nobody wants to do business with us. We must bring to justice the powerful, rich, corrupt people who have turned this into a country of fraudsters and cheats."

Ribadu doesn't just talk the talk. In the first three years of its existence, the EFCC recovered more than $1 billion in stolen assets. He put away Nigeria's ex-chief of police and his own mentor, Tafa Balogun, when he suspected him of misappropriating $30 million (it turned out to be $150 million). The EFCC led a successful prosecution against a sitting provincial state president, and, in countering accusations that he is a cat's-paw of President Obasanjo, Ribadu points out that he has taken down the senate president, a key Obasanjo ally. "I am investigating everybody—former heads of state, the president leadership, almost everybody from the president downward."

It would be optimistic to believe that Ribadu and his 500 staff members are going to dig out all the weeds, the roots of which go deep down into the country's social and political fabric. But the EFCC's record of incorruptibility has made a significant difference. Policing global crime is becoming increasingly difficult, but if it is to make headway, then anticorruption strategies in emerging markets such as Brazil and Nigeria are absolutely critical. Corruption is the swamp in which breeds a particularly efficient and heartless species of parasitic criminal.

In 2005, Chief Emmanuel Nwude visited Ribadu at his home and insisted that he accept the gift of two brown paper bags the chief had brought with him. In them were $75,000 in cash. The wealth of the criminals and corrupt officials has been sufficient until now to mold and bend the criminal justice system in their favor. Not only did Ribadu pursue Nwude on charges of attempted bribery, but he pursued him for his attempted kidnap of a key prosecution witness during the chief's first trial.

But the decisive witness in the trial against Nwude in November 2005 was Nelson Sakaguchi. Domingos Refinetti, Banco Noroeste's São Paulo lawyer, finally persuaded Sakaguchi to visit Nigeria and meet his nemesis, the chief. Amaka Anajemba had already started her prison sentence after agreeing to a plea bargain. When Nwude's trial opened, he pleaded not guilty. After Sakaguchi's testimony, the chief changed his plea and is now behind bars with all his money confiscated, in addition to a hefty fine of $10 million.

Nelson Sakaguchi and his motives remain an enigma. After pleading guilty to money laundering in Switzerland and serving time there, he now sits quietly at home in Coita, waiting to hear when the charges of criminal conspiracy will come to trial. He insists on his innocence by arguing that he did not have the authority to transfer the money and that the entire operation was sanctioned by the board.

Whatever Sakaguchi's fate, at least the money is no longer at the disposal of Nwude and his team. Tens of thousands of other victims have been less fortunate than the Cochrane and Simonsen families. "I will not accept a case if it less than $5 million—it's not worth the chase" is the candid admission of Bill Richey, the U.S. lawyer. "I'm not going to tell you what the clients have spent here, but they have spent significantly less than half of what we have frozen all around the world. When we finish dealing with the parties in Nigeria and we find the final recovery and the case is finally over, I think the clients will probably receive a return of about five to one on their investment." But then Richey adds, "It's a sad day that in order to recover, if you are a victim of a crime, you have to be able to afford it."

But that is one of the disheartening lessons of the Banco Noroeste scam. The tens of thousands of other victims of 419 scams have no such recourse to their funds. Global justice doesn't come cheap.

CHAPTER 9

Black and White

Lucy Tshabalala found she could not move. "I couldn't control my body and I was shaking," she said. The customs officer at the Los Angeles Airport, LAX, had told her she could go, but she didn't. "I wanted to move *sooo* badly, but it was like there was a magnet holding me down." Instead, in a near cataleptic panic, she haltingly asked the officer where she could get a bus to Santa Monica. He paused. "Wait here one moment, ma'am."

May 1, 1994, was a joyous day for most South Africans. The country's first free elections three days earlier had given the African National Congress a thumping majority, and Nelson Mandela, the most admired politician in the world, had just become president-elect of his country. "I received my passport on April 18, my birthday," Lucy recalled, "and a week later I went to vote. I told myself I was a lucky person and that this vote was the chance of a lifetime."

"I wanted to see pictures of Nelson Mandela celebrating our victory, but then the customs man came back—with big, big shiny dogs! Big black shiny dogs." Lucy's voice deepens and her hand gestures expand as she draws an imaginary pair of shiny sniffer dogs. They were still sniffing with gusto as customs officers led Tshabalala away for a strip search. But the officers had no need of the shiny dogs to find the 1.5 kilograms of heroin strapped tightly around her stomach. "They were so excited! Bingo!" Lucy recalled. "They told me that this was the biggest haul at LAX for some years. They were thrilled. And all I could think was that I would never see Mandela on television but instead I imagined headlines on CNN— *Sowetan Woman Arrested at LAX!*"

And so at the very moment South Africa took its first steps on the arduous road to recovery from apartheid, one of its young daughters began her own progress through the valley of despair. After being sentenced in Los Angeles to six years' imprisonment for narcotics offenses, Tshabalala was transferred to the Danbury Federal Correctional Institution in Connecticut. Located next to Candlewood Lake, it is a low-security prison whose alumnae now include Martha Stewart.

At first, it was a relief for Lucy. "In some ways, life was better than in South Africa, because I was fed regularly," she said. But a year after her arrival she was raped by one of the warders. "He had befriended me and I thought he cared about my situation," she said. "Instead, he just manipulated me to get sex." It was her word against his, and if she reported it, she said, he would have killed her. Instead, she bottled it up and suffered a nervous breakdown. This led her to the Carswell Federal Medical Center at Fort Worth in Texas, known locally as the Hospital of Horrors. Carswell has an appalling record of mistreatment of prisoners, testified to by the high incidence of warders convicted of sexually abusing the inmates. Lucy's condition deteriorated, but she was sustained by two fellow prisoners. "They looked after me. Perhaps they wanted to make up for what their menfolk had done—you see, they were Nigerians."

Four months before her arrest in L.A., a tall, educated man, Kingsley Noble, introduced himself to Lucy as she trawled the dingy restaurants of Mooi Street at the edge of Johannesburg's business district in search of work. She was desperate to earn money to finance her degree course in economics at the University of South Africa. She was the first girl from her village school in the northeastern province of Mpumalanga to be admitted to college. Her family circumstances were typical. Her father had left her mother with small children to seek work in Jo'burg. He settled in Soweto, the satellite township where black laborers were forced to live and which became a symbol of popular resistance to apartheid. Lucy's father found himself a string of new "wives" there, the last of whom wanted to have nothing to do with Lucy and his other children.

She was young and pretty but itinerant, unemployed, and homeless when Mr. Noble seemed to take pity on her. "I had never met a *kwere kwere** who could speak English like a white person. He said he came from Ghana—he was so educated, and, you know, we think all those *kwere kwere* from places like Ethiopia or Zimbabwe . . . we think that they suffer more than us and that they are all shooting guns," she said, "but he had money and he was smart and then he bought me a meal in the restaurant where I had just failed to get a job! I was so confused."

---

*A derogatory Zulu term for black Africans from outside South Africa.

Lucy followed Kingsley's invitation to live with him at his hotel in Hill-brow, which, although close to a lot of rich white suburbs, was rapidly gaining a reputation in the new South Africa for being a center of drugs and prostitution. And Nigerians.

Within two years of the liberalizing of South Africa's borders in 1993, some 60,000 Nigerians had moved there. At first they received a warm welcome, in part because Nigeria could claim an important place in the anti-apartheid solidarity movement. Nigeria was the other large power on the continent, and many in Mandela's ANC believed that Africa's salvation lay in strategic cooperation between the two countries.

But before long this welcome had fermented into resentment. Xeno-phobia accompanied the sharp pain caused by a sudden rise in unemploy-ment levels as the new government struggled to manage the transition from apartheid to black majority rule. Demands for an end to immigration were heard across the political spectrum from all three communities—black, white, and colored*—while the term "Nigerian" became a generic term of abuse for foreigners in general. This is why Kingsley Noble insisted to Lucy Tshabalala that he originated from Ghana when they first met—even before the elections of 1994, the term "Nigerian" had acquired pejora-tive overtones.

Above all, the Nigerians were branded as criminals in South Africa, where crime had, in a few short months, become the decisive political, social, and economic issue. And Hillbrow, or Little Lagos, in Johannesburg was the center of Nigerian life. Hillbrow became the most feared no-go area in one of the world's most crime-ridden countries.

Yet despite a reputation for ruthlessness, the Nigerians in South Africa (or more accurately the Igbo, who make up between 80 and 90 percent of them) run their criminal gangs, as we've seen, on principles of nonvio-lence. Into Hillbrow and other parts of South Africa, they have imported an egalitarian system of tribal councils stipulating that territories should not be fought over but agreed upon and discussed. "Arbitration, Not Aggravation" could be their slogan.

Nonetheless, South Africans came to perceive Nigerians as the worst criminals because they were highly visible, working tirelessly to expand the consumption of drugs and the use of prostitutes across *all* communities in South Africa, and offering further evidence of their unparalleled ability in devising financial scams and fraud.

---

*Under apartheid, the term "colored" was a racial classification for people of mixed race. It is still commonly used by almost all South Africans.

Under apartheid, the culture of the underworld was affected by separate development as much as everything else—young blacks, coloreds, and whites did not mix, and so there was little or no cultural cross-fertilization. The consumption of narcotics was very clearly defined: blacks smoked *dagga* or *zol*, as the country's homegrown cannabis is known; coloreds smoked "buttons," crushed mandrax tablets, manufactured locally and then mixed with low-grade *zol*; and some young whites used heroin or, very rarely, cocaine—because the apartheid regime controlled its borders very tightly, these drugs were rare, and so usage among whites was also very low.

The Nigerian drug dealers identified early on that the market was ready for diversification, and so they started introducing different communities to new drugs. That meant making *dagga* more easily available to the coloreds and whites while pushing the "buttons" beyond their traditional home of the colored districts and townships. Black, white, and colored youth often came into contact with one another via the good offices of Nigerian suppliers.

By 1994, Nigeria had developed into a new and very significant hub for the distribution of cocaine from west to east and heroin in the opposite direction. And while heroin consumption remains low in South Africa, coke and crack have become very popular in all three communities. And for the Nigerian traffickers to succeed in prying open the South African market, they needed to recruit mules. Mules are people, usually very poor, who wittingly or unwittingly carry the drugs to their retail destination. The Nigerians needed them to bring cocaine into the country, and heroin from South Africa to the United States. Heroin from Afghanistan and the Golden Triangle was transported to neighboring Tanzania and Mozambique by separate networks, usually Pakistanis and East Africans, although some Nigerian teams have been picked up and prosecuted in Thailand.

Lucy Tshabalala had no idea that Kingsley Noble, her "Ghanaian" Igbo sugar daddy, was a coke and heroin dealer until one day there was a knock on their hotel room door. It was a Nigerian signal, one knock followed by a gentle arpeggio of fingers on the door. "Not the loud *Bang! Bang! Bang! Bang!* that is unmistakably South African," Lucy confided while rapping the table demonstratively. And because the knock in the hotel was Nigerian, Kingsley Noble opened the door.

"Two cops, one black and one white, crashed into the room screaming,

'Where's the coke? Where's the fucking coke?' " And, naïve as she was, Lucy wondered why the police had launched an armed raid in search of a soft drink. They locked her in the hotel cupboard. "I was so scared—I thought they were just going to shoot me there in the cupboard." But instead, she heard the screams of Noble as they pistol-whipped and kicked him in an attempt to force him to reveal the whereabouts of his stash. They left empty-handed, but when Lucy managed to get out of the cupboard, Kingsley was quivering in a pool of blood on the floor. To help him out of a mess, Lucy finally agreed that she would accompany a shipment of gold to the United States, but the day her flight left, Kingsley and his boss demanded that she take heroin instead, ensuring that she would greet South Africa's new dawn from the darkness of America's penal system.

And she was not alone. All manner of innocents were ensnared by the engineers of the new illicit economy. Crime sucked the lifeblood from the new South Africa like a deadly leech, leaving it debilitated and wracked by fear and insecurity. Stories of murder, carjacking, extortion, rape, mugging, gang warfare, and more drugs littered the pages of the local and international press.

Most ordinary people lived in fear of random acts of violence or of becoming involved in some nightmare through ignorance or despair as Lucy Tshabalala did. In the 1990s, Colombia was South Africa's only rival in the stakes for the highest murder rate in the world. Jamaica's 30 percent lower homicide rate at the time is another indication of how serious this problem was. In hard figures, it meant that around 20,000 South Africans lost their lives at the hands of their compatriots every single year. (In 2005, almost 52,000 rapes were reported in South Africa, and given the usual ratio of reported to actual rapes, the real figure seems astronomical.)

Not even the most embittered South Africans can blame Nigerians for this level of violent crime. In fact, as we know, the turmoil and terror were generated from within South African society, a profound legacy of apartheid that paved the way for unprecedented domestic violence and criminality that mingled dangerously with mutual suspicion between communities. This neuralgic nexus that has such visible consequences in the area of street crime masked the work of more significant transnational criminal enterprises that were merrily nesting elsewhere in Africa but regarded South Africa as their grandest prize.

There were two separate criminal industries that had designs on South Africa. The first was narcotics, the main players of which hailed from Nigeria, Italy, and South America; the second was the trading of weapons for sub-Saharan Africa's valuable minerals—diamonds, copper, zinc, and a little-known substance called coltan. Primarily involved in this second business were Russians, Belgians, Americans, French, Brits, and Israelis.

South Africa was in a unique position in the 1990s. The fall of apartheid was different from the fall of Communism, because the racist state was already a developed market economy. This meant it bequeathed a rich and advanced infrastructure to a new administration but one whose policing capacity was exceptionally weak. Until 1994, the government had no interest in spending any money on the majority of its population, that is, the blacks and coloreds. The primary concern of the new democratic government was naturally to address that appalling imbalance. But this sudden shift placed a huge strain on South Africa's budget. The new police force faced immense challenges, and so despite South Africa's reputation worldwide as a producer of crime and criminals, the country was in fact one of the most desirable *targets* for transnational criminal syndicates. The fragile new government had to devote the bulk of its resources to domestic policing. Its borders were porous and its transport links open to the highest bidder—drug runners and arms dealers.

Under apartheid, the notorious Group Areas Act, which defined which races could live where, combined with the older practice of using black males as a labor reservoir for work in the mines and heavy industry, leading to an extraordinary concentration of males living in squalid urban conditions, the townships. Many women were left to fend for themselves and their children in the rural areas, ensuring not just that poverty would be handed down to the next generation but that it would worsen.

Replicated over a century, these circumstances engendered two distinct but related gang cultures: One, known as The Number, was found throughout the colored and black inmates of South Africa's prisons. The other lay in the colored and black townships.

The legend of the Number gangs demonstrates a prodigious collective imagination, fusing Zulu lore with the imagery of the colonial British army and the romanticized heroism of the banditry that arose in the wake of South Africa's gold rush of the late-nineteenth century. The three gangs (the 26, the 27, and the 28) trace their heritage back to the 1890s and the memory of Nongoloza, a Zulu who preyed on itinerant workers in Johannesburg at the head of a gang called the Ninevites. From this thin skein successive generations of prisoners wove an elaborate history that contains most elements of religious mythology, including a prophet, arcane rituals, a sacred text (written half on a bull's hide, half on a stone), their own language, *sabela* (a mixture of slang Afrikaans and Zulu with regional dialects), and a priestly hierarchy of incomprehensible complexity.

Number members have claimed, often with good reason, that their association was the rawest form of resistance to apartheid, and certainly the predominantly white prison guards feared its influence (an important initiation of The Number involved stabbing a prison guard). But adherents also launched bloody intra-Number wars (particularly between the traditionally hostile 26s and 28s), which sometimes revolved around the central doctrinal dispute over the admissibility of homosexuality within The Number.

This system belonged inside prison. When members emerged, they were granted respect, but hierarchy in the townships belonged to a different type of organization—the gangs. And nowhere were the gangs more powerful than in the colored townships of Cape Town.

The motorway from Cape Town International Airport into town crosses through a number of townships, such as Mitchell's Plain and Guguletu. Men, women, and children zigzag through the motorway traffic to get from one township to the next. At night, these pedestrians often stagger drunkenly, one reason South Africa boasts one of the worst road death rates in the world. On either side of the highway, the sun bounces off the tiny corrugated tin shacks in which whole families live. Above them stands a dense web of wires that are draining electricity illegally from the main grid. In the luckier districts, European aid programs have erected lines of toilets, offering the inhabitants a minimum of personal dignity. Crammed in like battery chickens, originally by the apartheid regime, they survive to this day on pitiful wages, should they be fortunate enough to find work. The squalor is all the more distressing for being only a few miles from some of the most opulent residential districts in the world, where swimming pools and tennis courts are regarded more as necessities than luxuries.

"Force people to live on top of one another like that," says Al Lovejoy as he describes the townships he knows intimately, "and you are bound to pick up social stress that expresses itself in violence. What I could never understand is why there wasn't *more* violence." His musclebound arms covered in tattoos, Al sits opposite me, drinking South African plonk and rolling a spliff in a student bar in Stellenbosch, the center of the country's wine industry and erstwhile intellectual hub of white racism.

Al was brought up by parents who inflicted unspeakable brutality on him as a child. Packed off to criminal reform school, he was soon using drugs and quickly found his way to prison. As a teen, he swung between prison and the streets. He was accepted as a gang member in Cape Town's District Six, which sits half a mile to the west of the city center. In the late sixties, the government announced its intention to evict all the residents from District Six and to rehouse them in new townships up to twenty-five miles away. The move sparked outrage among the black and colored communities, while some of Cape Town's liberal whites also expressed their disgust at the prospect of wealthy whites taking possession of Zonnenbloem (Sunflower), as the area was to be renamed. The various campaigns led to the postponement of the bulldozing and reconstruction of District Six. And it was here that some of the most famous gangs of the 1970s and 1980s emerged to define Cape Town's violent street culture. Although white, Al Lovejoy was accepted by the local colored population, and before long he joined one of the gangs:

> I became a Mongrel after the most terrible fight I have ever been in. . . . All of a sudden this [knife-wielding man is] looming up in front of me. A huge black square thing rises up, blocking out the starlight behind him, and crashes toward my head. I hurtle sideways and it hits the side of my face, clipping my shoulder and nearly dislocating it. . . . My adrenaline's pumped up to the max and I go for his hair with both hands, ripping his head downward and kneeing him in the face with everything I've got. I hit dead square and he flies back, hitting the wall behind him with one almighty wet crack. I'm not in the mood to stop, so as his legs buckle and he starts sliding down, I grab his hair again, plant his head on the ground, kick the everlasting shit out of him. . . . The fucking fucker's tried to brain me with something made of wood, corrugated iron, and fucking cement.

This was a common experience of adolescence for young blacks and coloreds in the Western Cape and elsewhere. The police under apartheid did little to discourage such aggression—the core of their philosophy celebrated violence against coloreds or black people, regardless of who perpetrated it. If young blacks and coloreds were beating the shit out of one another, it meant they weren't demonstrating against apartheid or taking to the bush with the MK, the ANC's military wing.

Drugs were, of course, woven into the fabric of gang life (another type of social control). And the culture surrounding their sale and distribution magnified the brutal socialization that the township youth went through. Al explained: "Dealers are the first step up from the slime in the food chain, and they almost always work for somebody. . . . Runners are the middle management of the narcotics industry. . . . It is their job to pick up cash and drop off stock and also to report what is happening down on the street to their masters. . . . They need to be clever too. They provide the buffer between the *boere* [cops] and the bosses."

Al talks as we drive into the Stellenbosch township late at night—this is the ultimate nightmare for South African whites and not something I would recommend that anyone try for fun. But as we get out of the car, Al is relaxed. "You don't need to lock it. You can even leave your laptop on the front seat. Nobody will touch it if you're with me." And indeed, when we enter into the warren of shacks we receive a warm, relaxed welcome from all and sundry.

As apartheid began to crumble in the late 1980s and early 1990s, the opportunities for the bosses started to grow rapidly. Two supergangs emerged in the Cape Flats: The Americans, led by Jackie Lonti, and later in opposition to them came The Firm (a carefully planned amalgam of several gangs excluded by The Americans).

According to one of his lieutenants, Lonti was responsible for introducing crack into the Cape Flats:

> He was one of the first guys that went to Brazil—he went over to Latin America to go and negotiate deals and from then onward these mules were coming to SA. These were the kids of rich Muslim Indian families. Many occasions they would get phone calls from Jackie Lonti or his men to demand money from the parents of these kids, whom he held captive at one of his venues and if they didn't pay . . . then he would threaten the families.

The Americans had ambitions that went well beyond Cape Town—South Africa was a huge market. And as another of his collaborators has testified, Jackie had the great idea of appropriating the mystique of The Number in order to spread his operation. "I'm not good with dates, but sometime back then, in the 1980s, Jackie spent a while in jail. When he came out, he brought The Number out onto the street. To deal now, you had to know prison gangs." Lonti proclaimed that The Americans were the external representatives of the 26.

The Number was a countrywide phenomenon. By claiming 26 for The Americans, Lonti was able to expand his dealership among gangs simply by using brand recognition. By dint of its arcane, rigid structure, The Number had no power to prevent the theft of its identity, and before long The Firm had proclaimed itself the 28, which, of course, also accentuated the bloody hostility between the two megagangs. As South Africa's borders effectively dissolved and all manner of new narcotics came into the country, the gangs were able to distribute the new goods faster and more efficiently than in any other country that was opening up to the outside world (such as Russia).

If The Americans created a loose association of gangs across South Africa, The Firm took the idea a step further by establishing a regular cartel with a coherent business strategy. Like the Nigerians, The Firm's leader, Colin Stanfield, understood that there were large gaps in South Africa's shadow economy. So he used The Firm's financial muscle to set up an informal bank. Enterprising members were given start-up capital to set up bases along the Cape Atlantic and Indian coasts with the specific aim of encouraging rich young whites to emulate their peers in Europe and the United States in acquiring a taste for cocaine.

For two hundred meters, wasteland separates a huge police station from Valhalla Park, the colored district with the dark Wagnerian name and a fearsome reputation for its gang and drug culture. The home of Colin Stanfield, it looks too small to be troublesome—just like the Bogside in Derry, Northern Ireland, which looks far too quaint and neat to be the center of such rage and confusion. But Valhalla Park remains to this day one of the most violent and dangerous places in all of South Africa, where anger and crime combine in an explosive mix.

Just as the police stations of the Royal Ulster Constabulary used to be protected by watchtowers and barbed wire, so this police station looks like a fortress under siege. The police, though, must be emboldened by the knowledge that they can call on ADT, an American-owned security company, to dispatch an armed response unit (ARU) should a band of tooled-up Valkyries decide to swoop down from Valhalla.

Where would South Africa be without its ARUs? For every member of the South Africa Police Service, there are four and a half private security personnel in the country. Licensed to use firearms, these men have the primary task of protecting the white middle classes from burglary and assault. The latter live in stupendously affluent districts characterized by high walls, high-voltage electronic fences, and high levels of anxiety.

But in part thanks to the ARUs and in part because life was ever thus, whites are much less likely to be victims of crime than blacks and coloreds, as the townships are the main locus of violent crime. Nonetheless, the ARUs have played a critical, if rather oblique, role in maintaining peace in post-apartheid South Africa. Although the security forces in the Soviet Union and Eastern European countries kept a close eye on their citizens' activities before the collapse of the Berlin Wall, they could all boast a normal police force that was involved in parochial crime-busting, traffic control, and helping old ladies across the road (regardless of nationality or creed).

South Africa's apartheid police force was different—more explicitly political. Their main job was to ensure the functioning of the Group Areas Act and to keep the blacks and coloreds in their allotted districts. You can only enter or exit many of the large townships over road bridges—points that can be easily closed by a few men with guns and vehicles. The South African police had no role to play inside the townships—drunkenness, theft, rape, murder, and their consequences were all problems that the townships had to deal with themselves (unless, of course, the perpetrators had strayed into white areas).

The police were the iron fist of apartheid. The security services (especially those who worked fighting Communists across borders in countries such as Angola and Mozambique) were even worse. Along with their main job of obliterating Angolan or Mozambican villages, they moonlighted by smuggling diamonds and other valuable commodities from neighboring countries into South Africa. They were not so much policemen as proto-organized crime syndicates. These were not nice people. Often trained killers, they were indoctrinated in the belief that black and colored people were lesser human beings. And they demonstrated only the most rudimentary skills of parochial crime-busting, traffic control, and helping old ladies across the road.

When Peter Gastrow was asked by the ANC's first security minister to act as his chief adviser on the issue of police transition, he knew the extent of the problem. "A lot of the police force had been concentrated on white urban areas, and then all of a sudden there were no pass laws and people could go anywhere," he remembered. "These cops could no longer just give a fellow a few whacks to get a confession out of him. They couldn't understand all this new bullshit about serving the people. They had always *told* people what to do and now they had to *serve* them! This created great confusion—you can't imagine . . . you had Swedes and Dutch coming over here and telling them about how policemen had to respect human rights! South African cops! Ha, ha, ha!" Gastrow bursts out laughing at the thought of a shock troop of Scandinavians in woolly sweaters teaching battle-scarred Boer hard nuts how to relate to someone else's pain.

In the first half of the 1990s, Nelson Mandela and the ANC's liberal allies knew that the apartheid police represented a real threat to a peaceful transition. As Gastrow argues, some disgruntled whites were encouraging the incipient civil war among Zulus between ANC supporters and those of the more conservative Inkhata Freedom Party. They were doing so as if, were this conflict among the Zulus to escalate, it could fatally undermine the move to black majority rule. If the whites were to mobilize in response to this war, claiming the need to defend themselves, the South African police looked ominously like a militia-in-waiting.

"So we had to develop a deliberate strategy," explained Gastrow. "You had a powerful security police that was feared by the new government. The first task was to identify the chain or network of the key people who ran the security figures—well-known senior officers—then remove some of them to break up the chain."

It was too risky, however, to throw them out—the last thing you needed was a group of embittered officers with a similarly unhappy loyal following kicking around the streets. Unlike the Russians and East Europeans, or the United States following the 2003 invasion of Iraq, South Africa's new rulers understood that you cannot throw policemen and military personnel onto the streets and expect to maintain a stable society. "So we sat them down and said, 'You and I know that you were involved in some horrible things. And I am not saying as an ANC person that we were all angels, but what about taking a big pension, eh? No big fuss, no big announcements. I don't want to force you—let's negotiate.' And they took it. People took it. But where the leaders were offered these packages, the rank and file were not, and there is still a lot of bitterness among those guys now—they felt abandoned by their leaders, abandoned by the former president de Klerk, and abandoned by the National Party."

The emergence of the armed response units proved to be a blessing in disguise as white police who were unhappy about serving in the new South Africa Police Service flocked to make up the numbers. Furthermore, the costs for the ARUs were borne not by the state but by the white middle classes, who were only too willing to pay a little extra to maintain a comparable standard of protection to that enjoyed under apartheid.

By 1998, the state was spending 22 billion rand ($4 billion) on the entire criminal justice system (including the courts and prisons as well as the police). But the turnover of the private security firms had reached a staggering 50 percent of this sum—11 billion rand. All these funds were channeled into domestic policing as the new government had to ward off the twin evils of social collapse and conflict along racial lines. This left the state exhausted, always playing catch-up with the new democratic reality.

The crime that best represented South Africa's perceived lawlessness during the 1990s was the armed carjacking. Stories of tired commuters being hauled out of the driver's seat at traffic lights and shot before the carjackers sped off laughing were commonplace. To the outside world, it looked like brutal opportunistic theft committed by cynical joyriders taking advantage of the post-apartheid turmoil. In the country itself, it provided a forceful reminder of how the issue of race affected every act. The victims were usually white and the perpetrators black. For many whites, carjacking confirmed their suspicions about blacks. In an atmosphere of fear, accentuated by gruesome media reports, some whites believed every young black male was a gun-toting joyrider waiting to pounce. For their part, blacks would watch well-to-do whites parade along the highways imperiously in their ever-grander luxury cars and 4×4s while they remained mired in poverty. Wasn't this material gulf, they wondered, the very essence of the apartheid that was supposed to have been dismantled?

To this day when street crime is visible in South Africa, it is invariably refracted through the prism of racial politics. This is certainly the case in private conversations, while in public it appears in coded form to prevent accusations of racism. This intense yet covert debate about crime within such a framework is predictable and usually sterile. It certainly does not shed much light on the carjacking industry. In a revealing survey of convicted perpetrators, a researcher at South Africa's Crime Institute discovered that 70 percent of incidents were preordered. Carjackers would look out for specific makes and models of vehicles and move only when one came into view. And although in more than 90 percent of cases the carjackers threatened victims with a firearm, in more than 90 percent of those cases no shots were fired. These were not crimes motivated by racial revenge or violence in the first instance; they were the coal face of a huge and dynamic criminal industry that covered all of southern Africa.

In the late 1990s, some 15,000 cars and 5,000 vans and trucks were carjacked annually in South Africa, while another 100,000 were stolen while unattended. About two-thirds of these crimes took place in a single province—Gauteng—at the heart of which lies Johannesburg, South Africa's pulsating economic engine. Most vehicles were at the high end of the market—Mercedes, BMW, Lexus, and any make of 4×4. Together the total annual value of this theft amounted to *billions* of dollars. As the years went on, the number of temporary kidnappings increased dramatically because the carjackers had to prevent the victim's security firm from switching on the automatic vehicle trackers, which became a common accessory on South African vehicles before they did anywhere else in the world.

Delivery to the buyers took place usually within an hour of the carjacking, and the perpetrator would be rewarded with about $300, which exceeds the monthly income of most blacks. One of the convicted explained that on a good day, he and his accomplices could seize five vehicles. The recipients of the stolen vehicles were syndicates who could immediately respray the vehicle and reengineer the chassis and engine numbers in accordance with the registration documents purchased from corrupt officials at the vehicle licensing center for around $3,000. From here, often with the connivance of corrupt police officials, including many white officers, the cars would be driven to neighboring states—Namibia, Botswana, Zimbabwe, Mozambique, Swaziland, and, farther north, Angola, Zambia, Malawi, and Tanzania. Once they reached their destination, the cars were either sold for cash or, as Jenni Irish, a specialist in South African organized crime, explained, "they become an important form of currency and are regularly used to pay for other goods, such as gold and diamonds."

In order to prosper, most criminal syndicates are obliged to attempt to "capture" or "semi-capture" the state at some level. This embraces a broad range of corrupt activities from paying off the official in the vehicle licensing office to installing your allies in senior cabinet or civil service positions. But much of the tragedy of sub-Saharan Africa in the late-twentieth century lay in the ability of opportunists, dodgy businessmen, mercenaries, and gangsters wresting control of key parts of the communications infrastructure. Cars played an important role as an ersatz currency, but the decisive mode of transport was the airplane, from the light propeller-driven to the cavernous Ilyushin and Antonov transporters. And in that realm, there were many princes but only one king.

Even Chubb and ADT, the top two private security firms in South Africa, would have been impressed by the $3 million mansion in the fashionable Sandhurst district of Johannesburg. But the multimillionaire owner from Russia never thought he would need to call an armed response unit to protect it. He had his own paramilitary team patrolling the perimeter and interior with machine guns and dogs, 24/7. But one afternoon in March 1998, he could have used some backup. Masked gunmen with superior firepower and a boxful of grenades stormed the main gate and the kitchen, where an old Russian woman was chopping vegetables. "She grabbed a large watermelon and smashed it on the head of one of the gunmen before she was knocked unconscious by a rifle butt," as the investigative reporter, Andre Verloy, described the enterprising babushka's response. "The masked men fled with $6 million in cash, but left paintings and expensive artifacts untouched. A message had been sent to Viktor Bout."

Born in Dushanbe, the capital of the Soviet republic of Tajikistan, in 1967, Viktor Bout developed into a gifted linguist with a ferocious intelligence. Graduating from the Military School of Foreign Languages in Moscow, he ended up working in Mozambique and Angola at the time of the collapse of the Soviet Union. Both countries had been the focus of violent proxy conflicts during the cold war.

Although still in his early twenties, Bout succeeded in establishing a number of air cargo services, using old Soviet equipment. His planes were parked in the emirate of Sharjah, his companies registered in another emirate, Ajman, while he used the Standard Charter throughout the UAE for his financial transactions. Slightly rotund, with a clipped mustache, Bout had experienced pilots from the former Soviet Union who developed a reputation for flying into those conflict regions that were so dangerous nobody else would risk it.

By his own admission, he supplied the leader of the anti-Taliban Northern Alliance with weaponry during the mid-1990s before one of his planes was grounded in territory under Taliban control. According to a senior official who served under both Clinton and Bush and was responsible for monitoring Bout's activities, "The UAE was the only country that recognized the Taliban along with Saudi Arabia and Pakistan. This was how Bout established the links with them through his aviation companies. There was a lot of cooperation between Afghanistan's airline, Ariana, and Bout's aircraft." After negotiating the release of his pilots, Bout then started supplying the Taliban with weapons as well.

Bout relocated to South Africa at the same time, doubtless attracted by the climate and lifestyle but also to keep an eye on his burgeoning operation, supplying war materials to the factions in four major wars, one in Angola, the others in Liberia and Sierra Leone, and then finally in the Democratic Republic of Congo.

With his considerable financial clout, Bout bought up Mafeking Airport just south of the Botswana border lock, stock, and barrel, installing his mechanics and administrators there and even paying the salaries of immigration officers. Others were involved in sending weapons to other southern African countries and returning with minerals and even commodities such as rare fish and gladiolus (for sale in the United Arab Emirates).

But Bout obviously made enemies in South Africa. A few days after his house was broken into, more gunmen opened fire at his car in broad daylight as Bout and two assistants were driving through Johannesburg. "Either they were reiterating the warning," a senior operative with the Scorpions, South Africa's elite anti-corruption unit, told me, "or whoever wanted to kill him put our guys onto the job. Because South Africans invariably bugger these things up."

Whatever the truth, the redoubtable Mr. Bout decided the time had come to end his sojourn under South African skies (never underestimate the significance of a good climate in illicit operations). He fled with his family back to Moscow virtually on the first available flight. In Russia, he has since been able to avoid the attentions not only of South African gunmen but of Interpol, whose writ shrivels feebly when it reaches Russia's borders.

But from Moscow, he did at least acquire some new customers. The unparalleled success of his pilots and navigators in delivering weapons to war zones had begun to turn some powerful heads. Nobody else could boast that they had supplied arms to both sides in the Angolan conflict; to the Taliban; to Charles Taylor, the butcher of Liberia; to the limb-severing warriors of Sierra Leone; and to God knows who in the Democratic Republic of Congo.

But the mystery gunmen in Johannesburg were not his only detractors. In 2000, the United Nations published a damning report into Bout's activities, which led Peter Hain, veteran anti-apartheid campaigner who was by now a British foreign office minister, to label him "the leading merchant of death." Hain explained that Western intelligence services had established Bout's companies as "the principal conduit for planes and supply routes that take arms, including heavy military equipment, from East Europe, principally Bulgaria, Moldova, and Ukraine, to Liberia and Angola. The UN has exposed Bout as the center of a spider's web of shady arms dealers, diamond brokers, and other operatives sustaining the wars. Without someone like him we would be much, much closer to ending the conflicts."

From his ministerial seat, Hain explained to me how he decided to go after Bout. "When I was Africa minister," he said,

> I was getting all this intelligence from MI6 and other intelligence services that showed there was a systematic traffic of arms going

into Sierra Leone via Liberia and into Angola in return for alluvial diamonds. I was getting these reports saying that it was Viktor Bout's planes taking this stuff in. And I said, "Well, what are we going to do about this? We know the schedule of the flights. Why don't we just shoot them out of the air?" "Oh," said my civil servants, "you can't do this, Minister, because it's against international law." I said that we must disrupt him, because in the case of Sierra Leone, these very guns and ammo and other military equipment were actually being aimed at our soldiers. On the one hand, we had sent in British soldiers to save Sierra Leone from the insurgents, and on the other hand we knew the very arms supplier who was providing the means to attack our soldiers, and not doing anything about it! In the end, we put some of the arms dealers out of business and severely disrupted Viktor Bout. As a result of lobbying I did there with the emir of Dubai, Sheikh Mohammed, we closed him down there as well and he then retreated back to Russia.

Three years later, Viktor Bout was back in the thick of things. Only this time, he was providing his services to the American war effort in Iraq. Dismissed as an oversight by the UK and U.S. governments, Bout's name had mysteriously slipped off the UN's Most Wanted list at around the same time. Privately, the French government expressed its fury, suggesting that this was Bout's quid pro quo. And although the French had an ax to grind about the war in Iraq, not to mention their own shameful record on the supply of weaponry in exchange for minerals in Africa, it would appear that Bout had pulled off an impressive stunt. In fact, the subsequent outcry gave Treasury officials enough evidence to persuade President Bush to sign an executive order targeting Bout's U.S. assets. Nonetheless, the Iraqi interlude is instructive as it demonstrates how major criminal figures such as Bout can continue to function by existing in that peculiarly opaque netherworld where money, criminals, crises, and security services mix so thoroughly that only the most trained analyst can separate the individual parts.

Viktor Bout is one of the few contemporary criminals who enjoy the distinction of having inspired not one but two Hollywood movies (with a third under consideration), the most recent being the underrated *Blood Diamond,* starring Leonardo DiCaprio as an especially convincing South African mercenary. Andrew Niccol, the New Zealand–born director and writer of the movie *Lord of War,* has said that the lead character, Yuri Orlov, played with real style by Nicolas Cage, was based on about five people, but he admits that one of them was Viktor Bout. The movie captures the essence of much of the ease with which the shadow economy functions on a global scale, and perhaps its biggest flaw is to suggest that Ethan Hawke's American Interpol agent, Jack Valentine, has the resources and the authority to pose a real threat to Orlov. The arms dealer provides a variety of clients with weapons from Ukraine and the former Soviet Union. His main client, André Baptiste, bears an eerie resemblance to the deposed Liberian dictator and mass murderer Charles Taylor, who in one scene offers Orlov a dazzling choice of diamonds in payment for the guns and ammo.

This one episode represents the essence of a remarkable criminal enterprise—the sustained and hideously violent rape of the animal, vegetable, and above all mineral resources of Sierra Leone, Liberia, Angola, and the Democratic Republic of Congo during the 1990s and the early 2000s. The multibillion-dollar enterprise includes politicians, gangsters, businessmen, and large corporations, who all work relentlessly to sate both their unquenchable avarice and the global consumer's equally rapacious demand for mobile phones and things that sparkle.

Nature has endowed Angola with abundant resources. Unfortunately, its leaders have been busy fighting for so long that they neglected to spread the country's natural largesse among the people. Not that Angolans bear exclusive responsibility for the carnage. Even before it declared its independence from Portugal in November 1975, the country had sunk into a fractious civil war that overnight became a four-way proxy war between Soviet military intelligence and Cuba on the side of the governing MPLA, and the CIA and the South African Defence Force (SADF) in similarly inglorious coalition with Jonas Savimbi's UNITA.

That brutal struggle, which saw Cuban and SADF forces assume an ever-greater fighting role, continued until the end of the cold war. It finally petered out in 1991 and, after much cajoling, the two sides agreed to a truce, then a peace agreement, and finally elections. Savimbi was a defeated man. Some of his fighters had given up. Ordinary people were desperate that the tyranny of war be overthrown. And UNITA had no friends anywhere in the world (except for grand mobsters such as President Mobuto Sese Seko of Zaire). Surely the game was up? Only lemmings would have been attracted to another casus belli. And so, instead, Savimbi played on the greed of a handful of rich Angolans and a long chain of foreigners by seizing a majority of the country's most productive diamond mines and alluvial pits.

The *gampieros,* the men who risk their lives digging on the riverbed for diamonds, are cousins of the Ural River fisherman who catch sturgeon—both are involved in dirty, dangerous work to extract a commodity for which they are paid a pittance but which is making others very rich. By 1999, conservative estimates put UNITA's revenue from its diamond operations at $4 billion in less than a decade. The value of the stones when they reach the market is roughly ten times that figure. And during that same period, there was nobody in the diamond industry through whose hands conflict or "blood" diamonds (so called because of the deaths that their passage to market caused) did not pass: from de Beers, the immensely powerful South African conglomerate, through to the workshops of India, where 80 percent of the world's diamonds are polished, and on to the many dealers in Antwerp, Tel Aviv, London, and New York.

It was the perfect trade circle. Weapons manufactured mainly in Eastern Europe and the former Soviet Union (but some from Western Europe, Israel, and the United States) would be flown into the conflict areas of Africa. Russian pilots were especially welcome, as they often knew the terrain well from the cold war period. The weapons were traded for diamonds, which were dispatched to South Africa, Israel, and northern Europe and once sold went through the normal polishing process before arriving at the retail jewelers in perfect shape. The only people who lost out were the dead and maimed Angolans, but everyone else (including the exchequers of Russia, Europe, and America) was making good money.

During the cold war, armed conflict in the developing world was driven by the clash of ideologies—there was no great competition for oil, diamonds, or timber between the United States and the USSR because both superpowers had sufficient access to both. Rebels did not need to fund their operations because they received support from a sponsoring superpower. While millions of Vietnamese, Koreans, Ethiopians, Guatamelans, Afghanis, and indeed Angolans might understandably take issue, this bipolar struggle acted as a partial restraining influence on the practice of extracting and selling resources in order to prosecute civil war.

Once those constraints are lifted, the parties to a civil war seek out the nearest moneymaking opportunity. It is especially easy for African militias in mineral areas where the extraction process is cheap. Almost all the diamond wars have taken place in countries where the diamonds are alluvial, sitting on riverbeds—militias do not have the time or money to invest in deep mines. But Africa is at an especial disadvantage because its commodities are legal on Western markets. Diamond sellers and jewelers may not enjoy enormous social status, but they are certainly a few notches above drug dealers, and few people would argue that their trade is immoral.

And it's not just diamonds. In the mid-1990s, the overthrow of President Mobuto in Zaire (since renamed the Democratic Republic of Congo, or DRC) fused with the aftermath of Rwanda's genocide and the existence of exiled Hutu militiamen in eastern DRC. The country is two-thirds the size of India but with a twentieth of the subcontinent's population. By 1998, a conflict had broken out that in terms of participating armies and numbers killed is comparable to the Great War in Europe—up to 4 million deaths in a five-year period. It has been an immensely complex conflict and one that has drained the blood of not only far too many Congolese but of Africa itself, making an impact far beyond the borders of the DRC.

A map of the main zones of conflict between the various armies and militias coincides with a map of the main concentration of the country's natural resources. They pillaged anything they encountered, be it timber, gorillas (8,000 out of a population of 11,000 were slaughtered, mostly sold as bush meat), copper, diamonds, and a little-known compound called coltan. Eighty percent of coltan's global production is mined in the DRC, and so the deposits became bitter battlegrounds in a four-way struggle (and sometimes more) between the armies of Rwanda and Uganda as well as the Hutu Interahamwe and the Mai-Mai militias in which peasants were forced to mine the material, which at one point reached the staggering price of $300 per kilo.

Coltan's desirability resides in its properties as an efficient conductor that can resist very high temperatures, and it is an essential component in laptops, mobile phones, and video-game consoles. This begs serious questions about organized crime and its relationship to the "legitimate" economy. Ordinary people around the world may think that they have no relationship with transnational criminal syndicates, but anyone who has used a cell phone or computer notebook in the past decade has unwittingly depended on organized crime for his or her convenience.

Until the year 2000, it was possible, if one listened very hard, to hear an occasional "tut-tut" from Western governments about the entanglement of commodities that were sold on Western markets and war in Africa. At the same time, the West Europeans and the United States singled out organized crime as one of the most treacherous craters in globalization's "dark side," as President Clinton dubbed it. And yet Western access to commodities such as coltan depended on the offices of organized crime groups working throughout southern and western Africa, as well as between Africa on the one hand and the former Soviet Union and Europe on the other.

It was certainly possible to identify some of the more prominent players in the chain—such as Viktor Bout. It is another matter trying to gather sufficient evidence to arrest a Bout, let alone find a court with the appropriate jurisdiction. James Bond's nemesis, SPECTRE (the Special Executive for Counterintelligence, Terrorism, Revenge, and Extortion), would have welcomed a character like Bout because he fits the stereotype of a transnational organized criminal—fingers in every pie, prepared to deal with anyone who wants to buy weapons, and an ambition that sometimes smacks of a desire for world domination. But Bout is the exception—most major organized syndicates are made up of clusters of dozens of minor conspiracies that move a product or service a little farther down the chain of distribution. In the end, Bout appeared to overplay his hand by allegedly selling weapons to the FARC in Columbia in what was in fact a DEA sting operation. On a visit to Thailand in March 2008, he was arrested and, at the time of writing, is waiting to see whether he will be extradited for trial on terrorist and gun-running charges to the United States.

Cocaine and heroin are widely defined as illicit and so they remain clandestine from harvest to final sale—but the farther coltan or diamonds are from their place of origin, the quicker the bloodstain fades. Combating organized crime is very difficult in part because in areas such as banking or licit commodity trading, the actors, motives, processes, and objects of commercial exchange move back and forth between the light and the shadow so fast that it renders moral or legal definition impossible.

Until the turn of the century, there was little evidence that the voluminous trade in African blood minerals would be noticed, still less interrupted, notwithstanding the public concern in the Western world about organized crime. But then something rather unlikely happened.

A merrily shabby office in a respectable West London suburb seems an unlikely venue for the throbbing hub of resistance to the trade in blood diamonds. Charmian Gooch was not yet thirty when, in 1995, she and two friends formed an NGO called Global Witness. "We were monitoring the work of a lot of organizations dealing with the environment, and another lot dealing with human rights. And we just kept seeing the bits in between which connected the two areas but which nobody was investigating. We try to look at issues that are being neglected but which urgently need addressing, and then come up with practical ideas for tackling these problems."

With the minimum of resources and at considerable personal risk, Global Witness decided to map every twist and turn in the road that brought diamonds from Angola to London and New York. On field trips to countries, they were shot at and threatened, and at times they felt they were tilting at windmills. "We were very, very small. We had no money, as ever, but it meant we were incredibly focused on achieving change," Charmian continued. "I went to Angola posing as a documentary film researcher. All the diplomats, journalists, and NGOs I spoke to said this was a bad time to work on the role of conflict or 'blood' diamonds in funding conflict because they were trying to cut a big deal with UNITA by turning them into a big diamond company and giving them a stake in the peace progress. We were skeptical that this could work, but out of respect we pulled back for a while. As we predicted, it didn't work and so we started researching."

And in late 1998, they published their report, *A Rough Trade: The Role of Companies and Governments in the Angolan Conflict.* Apart from illustrating who all the bad guys on the ground were, they pointed the finger at the Western corporate world. De Beers was the central target, as it enjoyed a near monopoly on the sale of rough diamonds through its London subsidiary.

The impact of the report was immense, and within two years, with the backing of Congress, several European governments, and—conspicuously—de Beers, the diamond trade moved toward establishing the Kimberley Protocol, named after the historic center of the diamond industry in South Africa. Kimberley signatories obliged themselves to engage only in the purchase and sale of diamonds that had a Country of Origin certificate.

Global Witness followed up their first report with others dealing with West Africa. Before long, the UN published its own report under the chairmanship of the Canadian diplomat Robert Fowler. This document went further than any other in naming Western companies complicit in both the arms trade to Africa and the diamond trade from the continent. Douglas Farah, a talented *Washington Post* reporter, then uncovered an al Qaeda network involved in the West African diamond trade.

These developments confirmed that in order to address a problem of organized crime at its point of origin in Africa, it was necessary to introduce regulation farther down the line on the demand side at a point where criminal influence was no longer felt. Slowly the manufacturers of mobile telephones are adhering to a protocol that prevents the use of "conflict" coltan from Africa.

There is still a long way to go, but Global Witness has successfully highlighted that organized crime is not about sinister corporations planning on taking over the world. It is about a complex interplay between the regulated and unregulated global economy that defies simple solutions but need not be left to fester as it was until Global Witness finally forced Western governments to acknowledge their coresponsibility for the problem. The team also raised the issue of how ordinary citizens in the West are much more closely connected to major criminal industries than they might otherwise realize. If Western governments want to do something about organized crime, they need to give full support to mechanisms such as the Kimberley Protocol and curb the behavior of corporations and the consumer.

President Thabo Mbeki came under considerable pressure to broker a peace deal for the DRC. At the same time, Western governments criticized him for being too indulgent toward Robert Mugabe as Zimbabwe's president started his steady descent into violent senility. "The whole time Mbeki had to be mindful of his need to persuade Zimbabwe's army to get out of the DRC," explained a senior security aide to the South African leader. "But the generals were making huge sums of money from the mineral exploitation in the DRC. Mbeki had to tread with utmost care around Zimbabwe and its president while at the same time trying to come up with some material incentives to persuade the generals to dismantle their operations in the DRC. That's not easy—not easy at all." And he was right.

South Africa finds itself unhappily trapped between the light and the shadow. It is the only country in the world in which the first and the developing worlds exist side by side from one end of the land to the other. The first world provides good roads, 728 airports (according to the CIA's 2004 estimate), the largest cargo port in Africa, and an efficient banking system. By Western standards, property prices are strikingly low, and the lifestyle for wealthy immigrants whose conscience can live with the country's huge social divisions is enviable—great food, great wine, holidays of a lifetime every year, and you still get change out of a twenty-dollar bill.

The developing world accounts for the low tax revenue, overstretched social services, high levels of corruption throughout the administration, and 7,600 kilometers of land and sea borders that have more holes than a secondhand dartboard. "When the transition took place, you could buy your very own airport if you wanted," said Mbeki's security adviser in a resigned tone, "and in fact that's exactly what some people did!"

The combination of first-world discount luxury and the business opportunities that the developing world infrastructure offers has proved irresistible to organized crime, and to major players both in the game for sub-Saharan resources and in the international traffic of narcotics.

Exports of cannabis from southern Africa (chiefly to Europe) are growing faster than from any other producer region in the world, now accounting for about 10 percent of global production. A great deal of dope has traditionally been grown in KwaZulu-Natal and Eastern Cape, but exports were negligible because of the apartheid regime. Within the last five years, however, marijuana from all over southern Africa (notably from Swaziland and Tanzania) is now sent to South Africa for trafficking into Europe. According to the British High Commission in Pretoria, South Africa has become the largest single supplier of cannabis to the United Kingdom, now outstripping Jamaica by a ratio of two to one.

Al Lovejoy described how one smuggled Swazi grass across the border into South Africa, down to Jo'burg, and then on to the Cape for export. He and his accomplices found a squat close to the Swazi border, where they set up "a generator, scales, presses, and a vacuum machine to begin packing." Across the border, "led by the Swazi smuggler, they hefted the bulky bags of *zol* and began walking in the dead of night. The Swazi carrying the handset and counter–night vision goggles, looking out for sloppy Interpol and DEA task agents." Although he had shifted a lot of drugs, Al knew that the key to success was vigilance: "Don't fuck around, china, Interpol and the DEA are active in all the agricultural and manufacturing narcotics hot spots worldwide." Anyway, "the *zol* was taken to base camp and eventually packed into the usual twenty-five-by-twenty-five-centimeter kilo and half-kilo blocks and then vacuum sealed to 98 percent. The rock-solid bricks were then washed, packed into boxes, taped, labeled, and put on the truck. They totaled about 300 kilograms."

On the way to the Cape, the vehicles drove about fifteen kilometers apart as a precaution against being tracked together by police helicopters. At one point, the second vehicle in search of gasoline "drove into town and managed to blow out the right-rear tire against a pavement. Guess who came to his assistance? The *gattas* [cops] of course! The *zol* was in boxes labeled as if he were moving house. . . . The *boere* [cops] helped him change the tire, unpacking the boxes of *zol* to get at the spare wheel, while up on the hill outside of town, Brother E and I sat in cold silence sweating the possible loss of over a million bucks worth of *zol*."

Al got away with it on this occasion and had also undertaken successful runs taking South African dope via Brussels and Paris to Amsterdam. On his return he would bring many hundreds of ecstasy tablets to satisfy the demand of South Africa's growing clubbing culture. His story confirms the thesis advanced by Ted Leggett, an American who has become South Africa's most experienced drugs analyst and now works for the UN Office for Drug Control in Vienna (UNODC). "All this suggests," he writes, "that some sort of international barter is going on, with our *dagga* [cannabis] being traded for more potent drugs overseas. . . . We don't have to trade *dagga* directly with Afghanistan or Burma in order to get heroin back, because international brokers service a complex network of supplies and demands at once. These syndicates may even service demand for non-drug products, such as cell phones and automobiles. Cash is taken from countries with hard currency, and commodities are shuffled between the rest."

Although he insists that in South Africa the drug is not associated with violence and has a benign social impact, he believes its economic function has changed dramatically so that "cannabis is more than a harmless local herb that feeds rural schoolchildren. It may be the lynchpin on which the whole local drug economy is based. With *dagga,* we would have to be paying for our hard drugs with the weak rand, which might price them beyond the reach of any but the most fanatical and criminally inclined addicts."

South Africa has become the new pivot for the international drug trade. Heroin comes in through East Africa and is then shipped to the States; cocaine comes here from South America before being transported to Spain and Amsterdam. But the heart of this problem lies elsewhere—in Washington, D.C.

PART III

Drugs and Cybercrime

CHAPTER 10

Buddies

"Open the back for me, please, Dan." Quiet yet firm—that's how they speak around Metaline Falls. *Dan Wheeler* walked around his pickup truck and unbolted the tray. "Let's clear away all that stuff, please, Dan." Wheeler started hauling the grubby but neatly piled strips of chromium that were lying on the flatbed. The customs officer helped by shifting the snow chains, toolbox, rags, oilcans, and the detritus common to an artisan's vehicle. "I'd like a look at the propane tank, please, Dan." Wheeler skipped under the car to unbolt the steel frame and thick weld mesh that shielded the tank. It was a different officer from the Metaline Falls border crossing in northeastern Washington State who had recommended the protective device to Dan as a means of reducing the chance of an explosion if the truck were back-ended.

Stooping deliberately, the U.S. customs agent positioned his nose just above the propane tank's outlet valve. A jet of noxious gas flew up and the guard straightened smartly. Then he tapped the fuel gauge, which shimmered gently—the normal reaction.

"Thank you, Dan. What fuel is the truck running on right now?"

"I'm not sure. Gasoline, I think."

"Switch it over to the propane, please, Dan, and turn on the engine."

Dan switched the fuel supply and started cranking the engine. Nothing. He tried again. Then again. The third time, the liquid petroleum gas (LPG, or propane) reached the carburetor and the motor burst into life. The officer bent down and breathed in the exhaust pipe—he could tell from the fumes that this was propane; it has a very different odor from gasoline exhaust. He had ascertained what he needed to know—Dan Wheeler was not smuggling BC Bud, one of the most popular and potent brands of cannabis in the world, into the United States. These elaborate tests were necessary—the only other way he could have established Dan's innocence would be by sawing open the LPG tank. And the resulting explosion would have blown him apart and everything else within a 500-yard radius.

"Okay, Dan. Just come on into the office to fill in the forms and you'll be on your way!" Wheeler fumed. "Hey, can you at least give me a hand with reloading the truck?" The officer turned and grimaced before helping reluctantly.

As he headed away from eastern British Columbia through the spectacular evergreen forest of Colville National Park toward the slush and wooden shacks of Metaline Falls itself, Dan's mood darkened. How many times had he been through that damn border? And how many times did he have to take his whole truck apart? And he knew that they liked him. There weren't many of their regulars who could talk with such authority about the things those boys loved—guns, hunting, and fishing. "I guess that's why they're so good at their job," Dan thought. He was sincerely impressed by their thoroughness even though it inconvenienced him most times he traveled.

By the time he arrived at the storage compound in Spokane, Washington, Dan's spirits had brightened, but he was on alert. After entering the PIN code to the main gate, he started unloading the chrome strips into his rental storage locker under the arbitrary gaze of the CCTV cameras. Finally, he drove the truck into the space, closed the door, and hooked up his lamp to the cigarette lighter. "With my tool kit," he explained, "I dove under the truck, careful to place a little blanket underneath so I didn't pick up too much dirt—it's those little touches that make the difference between professionals like me and the amateurs who will at some point get caught." Removing the weld mesh as he had done at the border, Dan then unbolted the propane tank and swung it around 90 degrees so he faced the semi-spherical end.

Telling me the story inside his voluminous garage and workshop, Dan demonstrated the routine with the propane tank. "You can't tell by looking at it, but if you chisel away at the right place with a screwdriver and a hammer, you bust away this glass-fiber body filler, which I used to cover up a socket," Dan explained. He then started to unscrew a small square nut. Pang! "There we go!" he exclaimed with a broad smile. And the end of the tank comes off.

There was no mighty explosion. Instead, I saw small-bore copper tubes inside, which ran from the external sniffer valve, gauges, and fuel pipe to a small cylinder of propane used to fire camping stoves. "The truck actually runs for fifteen clicks on the camping propane, and of course if anyone checks the sniffer valves or the fuel gauge, everything appears to be normal," said Dan proudly.

When he followed the same procedure in the Spokane storage unit, the remainder of the tank was stuffed with fifty pounds of bud from beautiful British Columbia, or God's country, as the locals like to honor its wealth of natural beauty and resources. "That compound was my hot zone," Dan recalled earnestly. "Even when you've taken every precaution imaginable, you can still hear the squeal of the feds' tires in your mind. There was no retreat from the locker and no possibility of talking your way out of fifty pounds and $200,000 in cash."

Fifty pounds of bud is worth $55,000 (U.S.) in British Columbia at wholesale prices. In Spokane, two and a half hours from the border, its value had almost doubled to $100,000. If Dan could be bothered (which he often was), the trip to California added another $50,000 to his haul. If he drove it to Kentucky, he could sell it there for $200,000, almost four times the value in British Columbia. And if he took it as far as Miami . . . well, we'll hear about that later. The turnover of Dan's business was $100,000 a week with minimal capital outlay. As Stephen Easton of the venerable Simon Fraser Institute in Vancouver has noted, the profits from this trade are seductive, even for its most junior participants. "For a modest marijuana-growing operation of 100 plants, harvest revenue is from 13 kilograms of marijuana sold in pound blocks out the back door valued at $2,600 per pound. This amounts to slightly less than $20,000 per harvest. With four harvests per year, gross revenue is nearly $80,000. A conservatively high estimate of production cost is about $25,000. The return on invested money is potentially high: around 55 percent."

For the ordinary folk of western Canada, nothing competes financially. For the pros, such as Dan and his buddies, it comes close to being a license to print money. "I was part of a three-man team," Dan continued. "*Marty* coordinated all the grow ops to deliver the fifty pounds per week—that's no easy job. Much of it came from his own farms, but some smaller ops sold to him, and you have to maintain the quality. This is a highly competitive market, and the guys we sold to, they knew their shit real good." *Michael*, the third partner, coordinated sales in the United States. "Look," said Michael whose laid-back appearance conformed much more to the hippie-ish stereotype than Dan's just-back-from-felling-an-entire-forest look, "there are a lot of problems—not just the question of your clients' reliability but the security issues. God knows how many cell phones we use—we only use 'em for a week or so, then we chuck 'em. There's a real damn problem remembering all the different phone numbers."

Michael conceded that Dan was in many ways the lynchpin of the operation. "The bottleneck has always been in getting the stuff into the U.S. But that's the big market—there's 30 million Canadians but everyone in Canada either grows it themselves or has a buddy who does, even in Vancouver or back east. There's close to 300 million Americans, and that's a massive market. Taking it to market—that's the real pro work, and that was Dan's niche."

Marty, Michael, and Dan are part of an industry that the Organized Crime Agency of British Columbia valued at $4 billion in 2001. Five years later, it is worth a third more according to most estimates, which means that it is responsible for more than 5 percent of British Columbia's GDP. Around 100,000 workers are engaged both full-time and part-time in the cultivation, distribution, smuggling, and retail of marijuana, compared with 55,000 working in the vast traditional sectors of logging, mining, oil, and gas combined. Only manufacturing employs more people—and this is all according to official statistics of Canadian law enforcement. Although weed from British Columbia remains the standard, the farming of marijuana has been spreading steadily eastward over the past ten years, and most provinces now boast a flourishing industry.

The implication of these figures is stark: western Canada is home to the largest per capita concentration of organized criminal syndicates in the world. In turn, Canada has become one of the biggest law enforcement headaches anywhere—organized crime has broken out of the ghetto of marginal communities and conquered the middle classes. "In a town like Nelson," says Dan, "I would estimate that about 30 percent of households are involved in grow ops of some size or other, but in the Slocan Valley, I reckon between half and 70 percent of the households will be involved."

From atop the reassuring slopes of Elephant Mountain (so called as it clearly resembles a dozing pachyderm) I gaze across the western arm of the Kootenay Lake at Nelson's rooftops. As they stack prettily up a steep green incline, they look ripe for transformation into the image on a cheesy jigsaw puzzle. In the background looms the sharp peak of the mountain Silver King, the precious metal deposits of which attracted large numbers of immigrants from southern and eastern Europe at the turn of the nineteenth century. To this day, this twee settlement resembles the idealized images of small-town America before the latter was blighted by unregulated advertising hoardings and fast food joints. Almost every store in Nelson has a picture of its manager or owner with their arms around Steve Martin and Daryl Hannah in commemoration of the time when the town was indeed transformed into America for the filming of *Roxanne,* a feeble update of *Cyrano de Bergerac.* Hollywood likes Nelson: for its unspoiled looks; for the Kootenay's stunning countryside; and because of an evening the crew gets to smoke Cuban cigars and fat joints packed with BC Bud.

But despite these attractions, Nelson and the surrounding area have been in steady economic decline for a couple of decades. Although its tourist and media industries are growing, these have not yet compensated for the slow demise of the traditional mining sector and the crises that have afflicted the logging industry. President George W. Bush dealt the most punishing blow against British Columbia's economy in recent years by bending to pressure from the American lumber industry in his imposition of a 27 percent tax on Canadian softwood sales into the United States. Regulators of the North American Free Trade Agreement (NAFTA) and the World Trade Organization (WTO) subsequently ruled that this was an outright violation of America's free trade responsibilities. The Canadian government has calculated that in three years since the imposition of the tariffs in May 2002, 7,000 jobs were "permanently lost in logging, sawmilling, and remanufacturing across B.C. . . . Including indirect impacts, job losses have risen to a reported 14,000. A common myth assumes that these impacts will disappear with a settlement in the softwood dispute and that jobs will come back to B.C. communities. This is not the case, as our communities continue to witness mill closures." As indeed has been the case.

Many of those who once worked in the traditional industries have moved into marijuana. The trade in weed has attracted large numbers of highly skilled workers who, as I discovered on a trip in the British Columbia interior, have been quick to deploy their skills from other professions into producing vast quantities of marijuana. Three of the four annual harvests are produced exclusively indoors (products of the summer outdoor harvest are often sought after by connoisseurs, but your average consumer can usually be counted on not to give a damn). But "indoors" doesn't quite do justice to the extraordinary installations where some of the plants are grown.

As we embark on the forest road, I am reminded of the train in Friedrich Dürrenmatt's dark surrealist novella "The Tunnel." The passengers descend into hell as the dank bricks wrap themselves ever tighter around the carriages, forcing the travelers to confront their worst nightmares. At first British Columbia's interior is not quite so threatening as

Dürrenmatt's trip through a hellish Swiss tunnel—the leaves are not so dense as to block all the sun as we rush northward for an hour, maybe two, through the towering evergreens. But eventually the sun is bound to set, and there are no cell phone signals here. If the vehicle breaks down, then the living nightmares of British Columbia's infinite interior will appear. Trekking home is out of the question—the terrain is littered with a plant known as the devil's club. These tough, three- to four-foot-tall stalks are topped by a ball covered in vicious spikes. As you walk through them, the club swings back and rips deep into human flesh. But the great fear is the grizzly bear. The world's most powerful natural predator, the grizzly plays cat and mouse with its victim, breaking its bones and its will, then laying it in a shallow grave before returning three days later to munch on the body after it has softened up. Thank God, I've come here with a group of three professionals.

The men look, smell, and move like loggers, their senses finely attuned to the outback. As well as scanning for the telltale signs of grizzlies, they keep their ears open for the distant twittering of helicopter rotors. "Could be game wardens, could be RCMP [Royal Canadian Mounted Police], could be DEA," one mutters. They talk like loggers too, which is to say almost never.

I thought it was a hard ride in the 4×4, but when we finally arrive at the clearing that is our destination, I am rendered speechless by the vision of an idle mustard-colored industrial digger with its bin resting upward triumphantly. How do industrial diggers travel to the middle of nowhere? Sunk into an enormous hole in the forest are two seagoing containers, each forty feet long, which are accessible through a door next to some makeshift stairs carved out of the forest. The containers are humming. Cables lead away into the forest. "Proximity to a power cable is an important factor in the location," said Jim, who had rigged up the electric supply. As an engineer with BC Hydro, Jim had worked on the construction of dams that have helped turn Canada's most westerly province into one of the world's biggest power suppliers. "Basically in order to get the power from the main cables, I have to build a series of substations capable of reducing the voltage until we reach the grow op."

Inside the two sea containers, hundreds upon hundreds of freshly planted cannabis saplings are starting to crane toward the equally numerous halogen lamps. This facility also has a system of CO_2 injections, as one of the horticulturists explained to me. "You are much more in control of the environment by introducing CO_2 at the right time of the day and night. The more CO_2 you give 'em to deal with, the more they like it and they grow into fatter, healthier plants. Increases their potency and you can double the yield and beyond."

At the beginning of the 1990s, the best yield from indoor grow ops was about three-quarters of a pound per one kilowatt lamp. The most recent advance in cultivation techniques has more than doubled this to over two pounds per harvest cycle. Aeroponics is a still more efficient way of channeling nutrients to the plant than hydroponics. "If you circulate the nutrients through liquid, which is what hydroponics is, you lose efficiency, because not all the particles are small enough to enter the roots. But by misting the roots—and it's a very fine mist—the intake of nutrients is still higher. This cultivation method is without peer."

Of the many things British Columbia has in abundance, space and electricity have been decisive in transforming it into one of the world's great marijuana farms. Space, because the RCMP and the U.S. Drug Enforcement Administration (DEA) just cannot find the great majority of the largest grow ops (especially after they are hidden in deep-dig underground sea containers and then covered in earth). "The DEA may have unlimited access to British Columbia," Senator Larry Campbell, former mayor of Vancouver, told me, "but do you know how many logging trails there are in the Kootenays? I mean, you can bring in every Blackhawk helicopter you want—forgot the haystack, you're looking for a needle in a jungle!"

And as for electricity, the lamps feeding the cannabis need huge amounts of power by normal domestic standards, but by the standards of British Columbia's vast hydroelectric capacity, the amount is negligible.

Back home in the Slocan Valley at the end of another tough day, Dan placed one of his favorite tapes in the VCR. "You're going to love this," he said. "This'll show you just how dumb Americans can be!" he added in gleeful anticipation. Presented by Rick Mercer, the CBC TV show is called *Talking with Americans*. The host travels across the length and breadth of the United States and encourages Americans to give their reactions in the spirit of neighborliness to fictitious events in contemporary Canada. "Congratulations, Canada," an attractive New York woman gushes, "on your first one hundred miles of paved highway!" Or "Congratulations, Canada, on opening your first university!" In one show, Mercer persuades an Ivy League English professor to denounce in all sincerity Canada's supposed annual ritual of setting its elderly citizens adrift on ice floes as a method of demographic control. And even the governor of Arkansas (*not* Bill Clinton) is gullible enough to send his best wishes on camera to Canada's prime minister for having constructed the world's first parliament made from ice.

Popular resentment toward America and the intellectual insularity of Americans is part of everyday life in Canada. It is persistent, low level, sometimes dumb, and sometimes funny. It also reflects the inferiority complex tinged uniquely with irritation that characterizes many Canadians' relationship with their southern neighbors. Within a few days of arrival in the country, I, like many foreigners before me, have been invited to play "Name the famous Canadian" before the host reels off a legion of celebrities, from Michael J. Fox through Shania Twain to Glenn Gould and J. K. Galbraith, whom a majority of Americans believe to be as authentic as apple pie but are in fact Canadian, at least by birth.

This social anti-Americanism assumes a more serious form when economic interests are at stake, as demonstrated by the very different attitudes toward the United States in the two neighboring provinces, British Columbia and Alberta. The latter's economy is heavily dependent on investment from American companies, first and foremost because of Alberta's burgeoning oil industry. Already Canada is the largest single supplier of petroleum to the United States, ahead of Mexico, Saudi Arabia, and Venezuela. The province's potential reserves are estimated at a gigantic 175 billion barrels of recoverable petroleum, but this is in the form of so-called oil sands, an intense mix of hydrocarbons, sand, and clay from which it is expensive and polluting to extract oil. For this Alberta needs the cooperation of American oil companies, their most fervent customers. And the benefits are considerable—in 2004, the oil yielded $10 billion (U.S.) in taxes and royalties to the provincial government, contributing to the transformation of Alberta into the fastest-growing economy in the country and the new center of affluence.

Of course, that wealth is the consequence of America's hunger for gasoline, and this has fused with Alberta's traditionally close ties with the United States to confirm the province as the most pro-American in Canada by a long chalk. The quintessential representative of Alberta is Canada's prime minister, Stephen Harper, who built his political career in the provincial business capital, Calgary. In the 2006 general elections, he led the Conservative Party to a clean sweep in Alberta for the first time. A firm friend to President George W. Bush, he is the most vocal supporter of closer ties with the United States in Canadian politics.

Although right next door to Alberta, British Columbia presents a very different political profile. Its main extractive and agricultural industries are logging and marijuana. Here a majority of the seats in 2006 went either to the Liberal Party, the traditional centrist grouping, or the NDP, a left-leaning party. Most strikingly, in the key marijuana-growing areas, parties supporting the decriminalization or legalization of marijuana won huge majorities. In the southern interior of British Columbia, a constituency that includes Nelson and the Slocan Valley, the parties won 80 percent of the vote as opposed to the Conservatives' 20 percent, whereas in neighboring Alberta constituencies, the latter received an average vote of just under 60 percent.

British Columbia, and indeed Ottawa, have locked horns with the United States over the softwood dispute and, equally important, over marijuana. These two issues have contributed decisively to the emergence of a more virulent anti-Americanism in British Columbia than in the rest of Canada. To be sure, British Columbians often appear confused about where their loyalties lie; after all, British Columbia has always nurtured secessionist sentiments that rail against the perceived bureaucratic behemoth in the federal capital, Ottawa. Indeed, in the British Columbia interior there is a strong gun culture that shows affinities with the militia mind-set common in Washington, Montana, and other neighboring American states.

But the issue of cannabis is defining attitudes to the United States in British Columbia and Canada with ever-greater clarity. About 60 percent of Canadians now favor decriminalization or legalization of marijuana possession. British Columbia, however, is way out in front—more than 75 percent of British Columbians want a relaxation in the law relating to cannabis possession. In doing so, British Columbia has entered into a collision course with the United States.

Similarly, cannabis is also influencing attitudes in Washington toward Canada—Vancouver in particular. In 2003, the then Canadian government announced its intention to introduce legislation decriminalizing the possession of less than fifteen grams (about half an ounce) of weed. This would not make possession legal, but the offense would attract a small fine and the recipient would not be encumbered with a criminal record. The U.S. reaction was swift. "You can't wall this off saying, 'We're only talking about a little cannabis,'" exclaimed David Murray, special assistant to Washington's drug czar. He then added an apocalyptic afterthought: "Our experience is they [various narcotics] come together like the Four Horsemen!" And since his appointment in December 2001, Murray's boss, John P. Walters, has placed the issue of British Columbia's cannabis trade close to the top of his agenda. "Canada is at risk, I believe—at a very great risk," Murray told me in his Washington office. "More than they have been willing to acknowledge. The level of crime is in certain provinces really undermining the legitimacy of their own institutions. The issue seems to be a certain Canadian complacency, a sense of self that is disastrously innocent, absolutely unwilling to acknowledge—they find themselves in opposition to us."

As the tension between the United States and Canada over marijuana has surfaced, it has again highlighted one of the most controversial, difficult, and dangerous aspects of global organized crime—the United States' policy on and policing of the international trade in narcotics.

In 1987, the U.S. paratrooper Steve Tuck suffered a serious spinal injury when doing a jump in Central America. Invalided out of the army, he spent a year and a half at the Walter Reed Army Hospital in Washington, D.C. Twenty years and another twelve operations later, he remains in severe pain and on the same dose of morphine he was given at the time of the accident. His body was remolded into a sack full of metal. On medical advice, he turned to marijuana for pain relief and was soon growing the stuff for himself and friends in northern California. In 2001, just as John P. Walters was acquainting himself with his new role as drug czar in Washington, Tuck did a runner from justice after the police came after his cannabis farm—his easiest escape was a hop across the border to Vancouver. The Canadian government welcomed Tuck and even licensed him to sell marijuana seeds to be used in research. At around the same time, the United States began extradition proceedings against Tuck.

In November 2002, the thirty-six-year-old was relaxing by puffing on a large spliff at the New Amsterdam Café in East Vancouver. It had been a tough day—Tuck had been protesting outside the hotel where John Walters himself was staying during his first official visit to Vancouver. Walters intended to acquaint himself with the severity of the narcotics problem in the BC's economic capital. The two men had been sparring in the media. At a press conference Walters described Steve Tuck and his friends as "darker angels of society" for advocating the use of marijuana for medicinal purposes. Tuck had countered in an interview that was broadcast countrywide on the Canadian Broadcasting Corporation by denouncing Walters as a liar.

After the rigors of such a day, the New Amsterdam Café and its gentle clientele provided welcome relief for Tuck. That night was music night, so people had dressed up. "It looked like any yuppie bar in any major city," recalls Steve. "Then several men in black, all with the same standard-issue trench coats, with the earpieces and the high-powered mikes, marched into the café. I knew straightaway they were Secret Service." The visitors were bad karma enough for the café's laid-back customers. But worse was to transpire as the agents fanned out. "I recognized him immediately—John P. Walters, the president's drug czar!" Walters strode up to Tuck as if he knew him. "It was surreal. He obviously knew who I was and just started saying that this was a disgrace and then, pointing right at me, 'Arrest this man!' " Walters stared at the joint and Tuck's stash. *Of all the gin joints in all the towns in all the world, she walks into mine,* Tuck thought. "But he was staring me down and shouting at me and so I just took a toke of my joint and blew the smoke right in his face!"

For a split second, the atmosphere in the café turned nasty—the other customers were rising through the fog of smoke in anger at the presence of this unwanted guest. The bouncers were beginning to wrestle with the Secret Service men, while the chief of Vancouver's police was explaining to Walters that he would not be arresting Tuck, as he was doing nothing illegal.

Tuck tried to calm things down. He announced to the other guests in the café that this was the famous John P. Walters. He advised everyone to sit down and talk. But that didn't prevent the drug czar from continuing to berate his hosts, the guests at the café, and above all Steve Tuck. Finally, the police chief persuaded Walters to leave.

Tuck felt vindicated, but two years later Walters's spirit returned in the form of Canadian police who forcibly removed Tuck from a Vancouver hospital, with a catheter and IV tubes still attached, before bundling him into a car, hooded and manacled, and handing him over to U.S. federal agents a couple of hours later. He was slung into jail and left there, suffering excruciating pain because of the embedded catheter.

Tuck's encounter with Walters was not the only surreal moment of the drug czar's visit. The voters of Vancouver, or Vansterdam, as it had also become known by then, had unexpectedly just elected a mixed bag of environmentalists, leftists, vegetarians, and dope smokers to run the municipality. Standing proud at the head of this woolly sweater invasion was Larry Campbell, the city's coroner, best known for his consulting role on Canada's smash hit cop show, *Da Vinci's Inquest,* the plots of which often unfold in Vancouver's drug-addled quarter of downtown Eastside.

But apart from serving as coroner, Campbell had for many years been a senior officer of the Royal Canadian Mounted Police's Drug Squad. Like a minority of former RCMP officers and DEA agents, he ended up questioning his role in busting addicts come what may. "It wasn't really until I became coroner that my position started to shift," he told me in his parliamentary office in Ottawa, "because in that position you start to worry less about enforcing the law on the users and to worry more about how you keep these damn people alive. Vancouver was always a high-drug-usage area, but in the 1990s there was a glut. Afghanistan was rocking. The Golden Triangle was rocking. In 1976 when I was on the Drug Squad and we took down a pound or a key, it'd have a big effect on the street. They weren't even cutting the stuff then. You had to go hunt the addicts to find 'em. By ninety-six, they were all over the city—everywhere, outside the back door, in the parking lot, in the parks, on the streets. One day we just woke up in Vancouver and said Holy Jesus, this place makes Needle Park look like a children's playground. We gotta do something!"

After his encounter with Tuck, John Walters was heading off to see an even more sordid den of iniquity—Insite, the clinic set up in Vancouver where heroin was administered to addicts under medical supervision. For a while cannabis was the recreational drug of choice for most of British Columbia's users; heroin (which was strictly illegal) had gained a stranglehold over parts of inner-city Vancouver and other urban areas in British Columbia. This was not only a serious law enforcement issue; it was first and foremost a public health issue. And Larry Campbell and the new administration were determined to come up with effective solutions to the problem.

Campbell and his allies visited Europe and acquainted themselves with a system called harm reduction, developed particularly in Holland and Switzerland, which replaced traditional drug programs that sought in the first instance to punish drug users with ones that sought to assist and rehabilitate them. Vancouver went on to deploy their version, known as the Four Pillars. Essentially, this assumes the drug user to be a victim rather than a perpetrator and seeks ways in which the health and social services can embrace the addict as a way of minimizing risk to him or her and to the wider society. A critical element of the program is needle exchange, in which the state provides unused needles to addicts to reduce the infectious spread of HIV, hepatitis C, and other communicable diseases. Similar programs have been hugely successful in Europe, especially in high-drug-usage cities such as Zurich, Amsterdam, and Edinburgh.

But Mayor Campbell went one further than this. In 2003, he sought and received the approval of the federal government to open an injection site at a B.C. medical facility in downtown Eastside where addicts could receive professional help in administering heroin. And if this were not enough, the federal Canadian government announced at the same time its intention to decriminalize possession of cannabis.

For Walters and his Office of National Drug Control in Washington, D.C., Sodom was being built just miles from the U.S. border. It was time to

Chief Emmanuel Nwude, the biggest scammer of them all.

Nuhu Ribadu, head of Nigeria's Economic and Financial Crimes Commission.

Nelson Sakaguchi: Innocent dupe or master criminal?

BC Bud accounts for
6 percent of British
Columbia's GDP.

David Soares, Albany's D.A. with a mission.

Below: The blooming industry in Ottawa,
the capital.

In 1985: Fabio Ochoa *(far left)* of the Medellín cartel and *(far right)* Santiago Uribe, brother of the current president.

The aftermath of *Mia casita* (My Little Home) in Jamundí.

Above: Janneth Pachón, a survivor of terror.

Mr. Pringle, the must-have accessory for cybercriminals.

Below: Commander Protógenes Queiroz, the man who brought down Lao Kin Chong.

The PCC strikes in São Paulo.

Mr. Agata, the deputy boss of the Sumiyoshi-kai in Tokyo.

Pachinko!

Below: LET'S DRIVE THE YAKUZA OUT OF THE NADA-WARD! reads the sign in Kobe. Wolfgang Herbert, professor of German and a onetime *yakuza* associate, remains skeptical.

"Face" houses near Fuqing in Fujian Province.

To you, six dollars the lot!

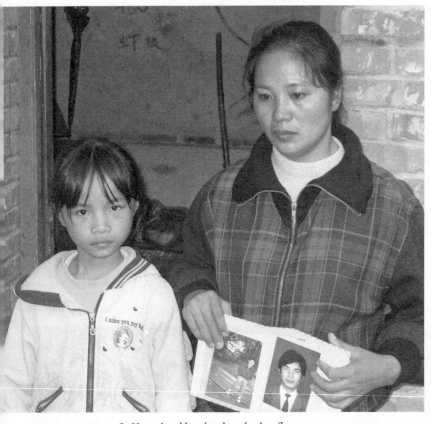

Su Hangqi and her daughter: broken flotsam
on the raging sea of globalization.

issue a warning, so David Murray was dispatched to explain to the Canadian government that the United States "would have to respond" to decriminalization, implying that border traffic between the two countries, which enjoy the most profitable commercial relationship anywhere in the world, may be disrupted. Murray warned that decriminalization would result in "the loss of the mutual cooperative partnership we've had with Canadians regarding our borders, regarding the integrity of the hemisphere, regarding our commerce, regarding the implications of trade and value to ourselves. . . . The loss of that would be something truly to be regretted."

Larry Campbell said he got a still clearer message from a higher authority: "Walters told us that he could shut the border down," he said. "And so I made some offhand comment about it being a shame to see L.A. in the dark." Campbell offers a mischievous smile as he alludes to California's partial dependence on electricity and natural gas from British Columbia.

The debate between Washington and Ottawa and the future course of narcotics policy have enormous implications for the global shadow economy, for transnational organized crime, for international policing, and for domestic policy across the world. It has an impact on economics, on governance, on international relations, and on social and health issues. But for an understanding of organized crime, economics is the heart of the matter, especially if the UN is correct that 70 percent of financial resources available to organized crime derives from the narcotics industry.*

The end of the cold war and the rise of a globalization that has often failed to address the imbalance in wealth between north and south have allowed transnational organized crime to flourish as never before. The trade in the two most lucrative illicit commodities, weapons and drugs, has benefited in a variety of ways from these two developments. The fall of Communism and the end of superpower proxy regimes in hot spots such as Africa, Southeast Asia, and Latin America generated huge instability for criminals to exploit. Furthermore, the states of the former Soviet Union and large parts of the developing world offered new market opportunities

---

*There exists endless academic and policy debates about the absolute and relative size of the markets in illicit commodities and services. But due to the obvious difficulties in gathering this data, this is not a debate I intend to engage in. Where I think it important, I will refer to data published by generally creditable sources (with health warnings attached if necessary).

for the purveyors of illicit goods and services. There was a huge demand for weaponry in the Balkans, the Caucases, central Asia, the Middle East, and Africa.

Some regions also developed into new markets for drugs as cultural globalization advertised the pleasures offered by narcotics. Rave culture, for example, and the accompanying use of drugs such as amphetamines and ecstasy, swept across the world, reaching Japan, Thailand, South America, Israel, Russia, and elsewhere. It was transported effectively by backpackers and the Internet alike. Very soon, chemists from Serbia, Bulgaria, Thailand, and Israel were learning the tricks of the trade from their counterparts in Holland—production of the new generation of drugs was no longer confined to the slopes of the Andes or the remote fields of the Golden Triangle (not that the coke and heroin traffickers didn't benefit from the dozens of new and unmonitored commercial routes springing up around the globe).

The upshot was increased supply and increased competition in the market, which resulted in lower prices and thereby increased demand for virtually every mass-produced recreational drug. There was, however, no comparable increase in the capacity of the world's police forces to deal with this expanded activity in the drug market. Indeed, in some countries, such as Russia, the police's ability to control illicit markets collapsed, especially since the military was frequently involved in the distribution of narcotics from central Asia into Moscow and beyond. And when the drug market expands, so does related criminal activity. In its first major assessment of the global narcotics industry, published in the mid-1990s, the UN pointed out, "In Britain 75% of serious crimes are associated with drugs; that 70% of the income of the criminals who are drug addicts is generated by theft; that a drug addict needs £43,000 a year to support the addiction. In surveys most addicts cite theft, fraud, begging, prostitution, and drug trade as their main sources of income or are prepared to tap such sources." This, of course, puts a huge additional burden not just on the police but the entire criminal justice system.

With support from the great majority of its members, the United Nations Organization for Drug Control advocates a policy of uncompromising prohibition on drugs—a policy that confers the right on the state to deploy its full police resources to intervene and destroy the narcotics market. With a commodity such as fissile material (for which police forces have a fighting chance of tracking regions of production and constituencies of demand), prohibition has a real chance of achieving its stated goals. But with narcotics, for which demand is immense and relentless, prohibition drives the market toward the only place capable of satisfying that demand and regulating the industry—organized crime.

Lev Timofeev, the former Soviet dissident mathematician turned analyst of Russia's shadow economy, has written one of the most comprehensive economic studies of the drug market. His conclusions are stark:

> Prohibiting a market does not mean destroying it. Prohibiting a market means placing a prohibited but dynamically developing market under the total control of criminal corporations. Moreover, prohibiting a market means enriching the criminal world with hundreds of billions of dollars by giving criminals a wide access to public goods which will be routed by addicts into the drug traders' pockets. Prohibiting a market means giving the criminal corporations opportunities and resources for exerting a guiding and controlling influence over whole societies and nations. This is the worst of the negative external effects of the drug market. International public opinion has yet to grasp the challenge to the world civilization posed by it.

From an economic point of view, a person's decision to enter into the drug trade as a producer, distributor, or retailer is entirely rational because the profit margins are so high. This is all the more compelling in countries such as Afghanistan and Colombia where chronic poverty is endemic. Time and again, narcotics traffickers have demonstrated that their financial clout is sufficient to buy off officials even in states with very low levels of corruption, as in Scandinavia. In most countries, traffickers can call on combined resources of billions of dollars where national police forces have access to tens or hundreds of millions (and are further hamstrung by a complex set of regulations constraining their ability to act).

On the whole, governments do not argue that drug prohibition benefits the economy. They base their arguments instead on perceived social damage and on public morality. On the contrary, it distorts the economy because it denies the state revenue from taxes that might accrue from the purchase of a legal commodity (not to mention the immense costs of trying to police the trade and the incarceration of convicted criminals). This huge financial burden is one reason that so many economists, like Timofeev, and indeed one of the great organs of the British establishment, *The Economist* magazine, are adamant in their support of the legalization of drugs. "Ultimately," argues Ted Galen Carpenter, vice president of the venerable American right-wing think tank the Cato Institute, "the prohibitionist approach is an attempt to repeal the economic law of supply and demand, and therefore it is doomed to fail."

Timofeev has identified a further problem. With the manner of a scientist who seems permanently distracted by some knotty intellectual conundrum, Timofeev outlined his findings to me in his wooden dacha just outside Moscow. He is a man as far away from the world of drugs and its related social evil as one may imagine. "The growth of funds available to the drug business," he argues, "along with its enhanced managerial capability, make it possible to diversify their risk assets by transferring capital to other markets. This is precisely what the organized crime groups do when they are shifting their assets from one illicit activity to another. For instance, the Sicilian Mafia invested proceeds from smuggling cigarettes and emeralds into the drug business. In the 'hot spots' across the world (such as Afghanistan or Chechnya) drug dealers invested a considerable proportion of their income into illegal arms shipments."

Prohibition is also a godsend to terrorist networks. Organizations such as the Taliban and al Qaeda fund their activities through the narcotics trade. In this respect, the inability of the NATO-led force in Afghanistan to pacify anything beyond the center of Kabul and the northern provinces since the invasion of 2001 has been a disaster. Cultivation of the opium poppy had skyrocketed by more than 1,000 percent within the first year of Afghanistan's occupation. It was not long before the Taliban was rearming itself by taxing this opium harvest. Attempts by Western governments and agencies to limit the poppy harvests have been an abysmal failure. The only way you can prevent the Taliban and others from sustaining their military capacity through drug sales is to legalize narcotics. When a punter buys some grass, crack, or ecstasy on the streets, only a tiny percentage of his money covers production costs. The great bulk goes toward paying off the distribution network for assuming the risk in bringing an illegal commodity to market. This was demonstrated irrefutably by the economics of alcohol prohibition in the 1920s and 1930s. Then, as now, Canada, which dumped Prohibition a few years before the United States, became a key supplier of the illicit substance. By 1933, the world's largest producer of alcohol was Seagram's, a Canadian company, and its success was not accounted for by Canadian drinkers.

Some argue that there is a difference between today's illegal narcotics and alcohol. There may well be a *cultural* difference, but with regard to the relationship between drugs and organized crime, the economic argument is central—and here there is absolutely no difference between illicit alcohol and illicit drugs. The astronomical profits generated by drugs lie in these commodities' illegality. There is no institutional regulation that might influence the value of the commodity, and so the price comes down purely to what the consumer is prepared to pay. The only indirect involvement of the state lies in its deployment of policing methods to break up the smooth functioning of the market.

In Washington, I asked David Murray, John P. Walters's affable and amusing adviser, if he can counter the argument that prohibition leads to organized crime's violent control of the drug market. "What about Oxy-Contin?" he asked rhetorically about a synthetic opiate that, as with its cousin Vicodin, you can risk buying over the Internet. (But I wouldn't if I were you.) "Well, it's the single most abused drug in America behind marijuana. And it's legal. It's medically produced; it's in a prescription regulatory system. But people are holding up pharmacies with guns to get it. I thought you were going to eliminate the violence and the crime and the profiteering by making it something that the state produces and regulates?" A fair stab by Murray, but by putting OxyContin into a prescription regulatory system, you are blocking the consumer's access to it; that is, to get hold of it you must first convince a doctor that you are ill enough to require the painkiller. That's why people are prepared to use guns—because the market is highly proscribed.

If a country supports prohibition, it is also *guaranteeing* that on the supply side all profits will accrue to underground networks; and on the demand side it is *guaranteeing* that any social or public health problems associated with drug taking will in the great majority of cases only come to light once they are out of control. If the UN is right and drugs account for 70 percent of organized criminal activity, then the legalization of drugs would administer by far the deadliest blow possible against transnational organized criminal networks.

But don't take my word about the inefficacy of narcotics prohibition. Have a look at a report based on access to confidential British intelligence reports. Tony Blair's government had on the whole been a big supporter of the United States' war on drugs. It's no surprise, then, that it tried to suppress its own report, so stark were its findings (see pages 228–30).

Lev Timofeev argues that prohibition tends to distort the market, favoring cartels and monopoly tendencies. This is because, he continues, larger organizations are more efficient at enforcing their monopoly than smaller ones. Translated into the vernacular, this means that big criminal groups can beat the shit out of smaller ones.

In 2005, Dan Wheeler decided to break up his partnership with Michael and Marty. There was no falling out between the three of them, but Dan

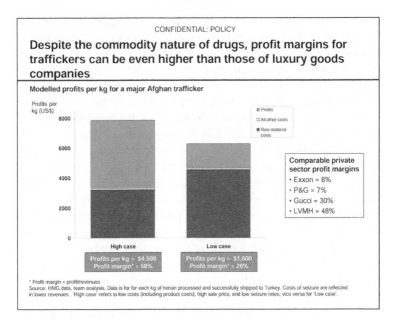

CONFIDENTIAL: POLICY

Despite the commodity nature of drugs, profit margins for traffickers can be even higher than those of luxury goods companies

Modelled profits per kg for a major Afghan trafficker

Profits per kg (US$)

■ Profits
□ All other costs
■ Raw material costs

Comparable private sector profit margins
• Exxon = 8%
• P&G = 7%
• Gucci = 30%
• LVMH = 48%

High case — Profits per kg = $4,500 Profit margin⁺ = 58%

Low case — Profits per kg = $1,600 Profit margin⁺ = 26%

⁺ Profit margin = profit/revenues
Source: HMG data, team analysis. Data is for for each kg of heroin processed and successfully shipped to Turkey. Costs of seizure are reflected in lower revenues . 'High case' refers to low costs (including product costs), high sale price, and low seizure rates; vice versa for 'Low case'.

was unhappy about the direction of the trade. "I was offered the opportunity of doing a trip to Miami," he said. "It was a new kind of deal—for every kilogram of bud I delivered in Florida, I would be paid a kilogram of pure cocaine, the idea being that I'd then bring it back here." Dan was silent for ten seconds. "No way . . . No fucking way. What you have to understand about weed is that it attracts people who have a healthy attitude to life. It never promotes aggression and most of the people I've come across involved in the trade on both sides of the border are thoroughly decent people. The people who handle coke are very different, and in the past few years, I have seen coke and its entourage make ever-deeper inroads into places like the Kootenays." The purveyors of cocaine in British Columbia are also becoming increasingly interested in expanding into rural areas and competing in the profitable British Columbia Bud market. In British Columbia and Vancouver, the most powerful and visible organized crime syndicate (but by no means the only one) is the Hell's Angels.

There are two reasons for the strength of Vancouver's Hell's Angels. The first is common to most chapters of the movement worldwide—organizational discipline. They have a strict hierarchy and place a premium on absolute loyalty. But it takes many years before an aspiring Angel can get

Western government interventions have tended to have a short-lived or negligible impact on retail prices downstream

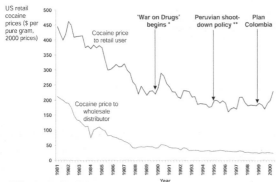

Governmental interventions against the cocaine trade in Colombia

US retail cocaine prices ($ per pure gram, 2000 prices)

'War on Drugs' begins *

Peruvian shoot-down policy **

Plan Colombia

Cocaine price to retail user

Cocaine price to wholesale distributor

Year

- The impact of US & Colombian interventions against the cocaine trade appears to be small and short-lived

- Wholesale price is a better indicator of the impact of upstream intervention than retail price

* US/Colombian campaign against the cartels
** Unidentified light planes flying between Peru & Colombia
Source: ONDCP, 2001, US Institute for Defence Studies

The long term decline in the real price of drugs, against a backdrop of rising consumption, indicates that an ample supply of heroin and cocaine has been reaching the UK market

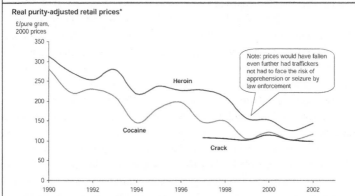

Real purity-adjusted retail prices*

£/pure gram, 2000 prices

Note: prices would have fallen even further had traffickers not had to face the risk of apprehension or seizure by law enforcement

Heroin

Cocaine

Crack

* Real purity adjusted prices show a different trend to nominal unadjusted purity prices. Nominal prices have remained largely stable, while purity has risen over time. This leads to falling real purity adjusted prices
Source: NCIS Streetwise, Forensic Science Service Drug Abuse Trends

---

CONFIDENTIAL: POLICY

Conclusions on the drugs supply market

- Over the past 10-15 years, despite interventions at every point in the supply chain, cocaine and heroin consumption has been rising, prices falling and drugs have continued to reach users
  - government interventions against the drug business are a cost of business, rather than a substantive threat to the industry's viability
  - however, by increasing risk, government interventions are likely to have slowed the decline in prices

---

anywhere close to the center of power. Trainees or "prospects" are expected to carry out any orders handed down from the full-patch members—instructions can range from cleaning up after a meeting to engaging in extortion by the threat or use of physical violence. Because the aspirant must be prepared to accept years of drudgery and hanging around before he (I use the gender advisedly) might be considered a member, Hell's Angels are impossible to infiltrate, sharing a security system as effective as the Chinese Triads. Infiltrating the Mafia, the Colombian cartels, or the Balkan or Russian mafias is, by contrast, like falling off a log.

The second source of the Vancouver Hell's Angels' power is the group's control over the city's port. "The Hell's Angels are involved with bringing in whatever's profitable—marijuana, cocaine, or precursors," said Brian Brennan, chief investigator for the drug squad of the RCMP. "They still have influence in the ports—their influence on cocaine is still strong, and we are now seeing them in synthetic drugs." The Hell's Angels exert that influence through friends, business associates, corrupt officials, and through the Teamsters Union, and control of the port has meant control of cocaine. Vancouver is used both to import cocaine directly from Latin America and from the United States and as a transit point for cocaine going into the United States. "What you've seen in recent times," Brennan continues, "is an increase in violence as the struggle for control of the grow ops heats up."

The Hell's Angels established themselves as a major criminal group decades ago, and in that time, the RCMP can count the number of convictions on the fingers of two hands. "Is the problem big?" asks Brennan rhetorically. "Absolutely—it's huge. The number of grow ops is beyond the capacity of law enforcement as a whole, not just the RCMP. And the money being made by the organized groups, such as the Hell's Angels, means that they can walk away from properties that they own without batting an eyelid. We're talking about a house worth $500,000 [Canadian] on the lower mainland of British Columbia, and if the police go and seize a thousand plants in that house, they'll just walk away. Because they are making so much money they don't care about losing that investment."

The RCMP cooperates closely with the DEA in trying to stem the flow of marijuana to the United States, but as I speak to Brennan, I detect for the first time a note of irritation creeping into his voice—not when talking about the DEA but when talking about Washington politicians and their criticism of Canada's drug policy because this rhetoric implies that the RCMP is doing a poor job in holding back that flow. "The U.S.," continues Inspector Brennan, "has a legitimate concern that the amount of marijuana from north to south is growing—there has been an increase in seizures, so maybe we're getting better at the border—it's hard to measure. But I must stress that only 2 percent of what is domestically consumed in the United States comes from Canada. They make a lot of a fuss about it, but it's down to the fact that the relationship between the two countries is really good, and the border is very long and so it is likely to be porous. It's big news if something like the tunnels are discovered in Canada, but in the last year, they found about twenty-seven tunnels between Mexico and the U.S."

It took me a while to understand the implication of what Brennan was saying. BC Bud is a $6 billion industry. According to the RCMP, between 75 and 90 percent of marijuana produced in British Columbia makes its way onto the American market. But the United States and Canada confirm in their official Drug Threat Assessment that this amounts to a mere 2 *percent* of America's cannabis consumption. Even I can do the math on that one. One might legitimately ask what in God's name are they smoking in the United States? Frankly, there are no accurate figures as to what it is or where it comes from—the only thing we all do know is that there's a hell of a lot of it!

"You know what the figures tell you," a DEA analyst told me in a discussion we had about BC Bud. "They tell you that we have a big problem of civil disobedience in the United States." He wasn't kidding.

Americans who support the spirit of liberalization in Canada are usually people like Steve Tuck who like to use the drug themselves. But in May 2006, Vancouver received an American guest whose visit set the cat among the pigeons back in Albany, New York, whence he came. David Soares was no drug user—indeed, he expends much time and energy trying to get people off drugs. But unlike most of his fellow Americans in law enforcement, he doesn't believe that slinging drug users in jail and throwing away the key (as happens in New York State) improves the lot of the common weal. "My advice to Canada," Soares said in a dramatic speech at a Vancouver conference, "is stay as completely far away from U.S. drug law policy as possible. . . . You, Canada, are headed in the right direction!"

But the biggest surprise of all about David Soares is that he is an elected official, the district attorney, no less, of Albany County in New York State, which means he has legal jurisdiction not just over the city and county but over the whole government of New York State.

"This was the drive-in. People would come off Highway 9, pull in, and shout. And a member of the Robinson family would just throw the drugs down—it was a sort of fast-food outlet for drugs." David Soares gets out of his official car and takes me to the end of the street. Pointing to a row of bollards, he says, "We blocked the street off to prevent direct access from the highway." In front of us, endless traffic zooms along one of America's larger-than-life X-lane superroads. "The white folks from the suburbs would turn in here, buy their drugs from the African Americans, and then shoot back out to the safety of the suburbs."

"About five years ago, there was an article in the paper," Soares continues, "where one of the Robinson family talked about dealing drugs and about there being no consequences, and the police took offense at that. So we got together a multiagency task force to take down the Robinson family. Which we did. What we were not successful at doing was stabilizing the community. And what we didn't know was just how powerful the Robinson family had been in the local market. They kept things more or less under control."

Without the Robinson family, all sorts of new dealers came in to fill the void. The twin problems of drugs and violence got worse. "This community was abandoned," says Soares with a rare tinge of bitterness in his voice. "Until you have a strategy that combines law enforcement with community development and economic development, we're always going to be dogs just chasing our tails. And that's the truth."

At this moment, a battered car drives slowly by and a young man pops his head out of a window. "Hey, man," he calls to Soares, "you like the job I've been doing?"

Soares, whose diction has up to this point been precise and eloquent glides easily into the vernacular. "What job you been doin', brother?"

"I been cleaning up that mansion house."

"Man, I *do* like the job you been doin'!"

Wherever David Soares walks, the people of West Hill come to greet him, to chat about their families and work, to tell him about their drug rehab progress. But above all, the people of West Hill come to thank him. This spontaneous adoration and respect almost has the ring of a corny Hollywood movie from the 1950s. In my walks through the underworld, I rarely encountered anyone who appeared both thoroughly good and thoroughly determined to do good in the face of powerful forces ranged against him or her. This remarkable thirty-six-year-old lawyer has offered the minority communities of inner-city Albany an alternative vision to an existence plagued by the twin cul-de-sacs of drug dependency and prison. But more important for the United States, he has proved that the country's democracy is not entirely hostage to the vested interests of money and established networks who can afford to run for office—and that it is still possible to run for office on a program easily denounced by the vested interests but one that is nonetheless based on unpleasant truths. And most important of all, to run on an awkward but courageous program and win. That's just what Soares did.

When he landed a job as assistant prosecutor in the DA's office in Albany County in the late 1990s, David Soares was thrilled. "I couldn't wait to start this job," he told me, "and for the first year of being a prosecutor, I would say it was one of the greatest of my life." Soares wanted to contribute to the smooth and successful functioning of Albany's law enforcement, and busting drug users and drug dealers was part of that. "But then something happens because you see the same people over and over again. You put people in jail and then they come out and you put them back in. Then you put in their cousins, then you put in their mother and then you put in their father and you start to see a mother/daughter combination. The mother was in jail and the daughter was being arraigned—the mother is released, the daughter goes in. And something clicks and you ask yourself, 'What are you doing?' "

In 1973, inspired by President Nixon's war on drugs, Nelson Rockefeller, governor of New York, introduced a new set of drug laws, which remain in force to this day, continuing to bear his name. For possessing a risible amount of any drugs, New Yorkers risk draconian sentences of between fifteen years and life in a state penitentiary. And New York State pays out more than $500 million every year to keep incarcerated those who have fallen foul of this regime.

When he was six years old, David Soares immigrated to Pawtucket, a small mill town in Rhode Island, three years after Rockefeller had promulgated his New York drug laws. Soares had come from Bravo, the most westerly of the Cape Verde Islands, the Portuguese-Creole-speaking community off Africa's west coast, the most famous inhabitant of which is the singer Cesaria Evoria. Growing up in a poor black neighborhood, he developed an understanding of the mechanisms of deprivation and its consequences. But thanks to his exceptional intelligence, his experience as a second-generation immigrant unfolded as a fairy tale and he ended up winning a scholarship to study law at Cornell.

Soon after he joined the DA's office in Albany, one of President Clinton's initiatives made money available to set up the office of a community prosecutor whose job was to liaise with leaders in those areas of the city where there were high crime rates. Nobody wanted the job, but Soares was the obvious candidate. Although 30 percent of the city's population is African American or Hispanic, he was the first and only assistant prosecutor from the minority communities. "Naturally the melanin content of my skin made me an instant expert in the area of community prosecution," he remarked with a wry smile.

And before long, his experience in working in the inner city challenged his assumptions about law enforcement and about the Rockefeller laws in particular. "I would go to court every morning, prosecuting an individual every day, believing that the job I was doing was going to make that corner a clean corner and a safer corner. But every single day I'm going into the court and I'm prosecuting this kid that I saw arrested on the block and I'm coming back and there's a new kid, same age, same complexion, doing the same thing. And it was just incredible that here we were doing the same thing every day—locking up and destroying entire communities. Meanwhile on the other side, I'm watching law enforcement and they're coming in saying here's a twenty-dollar street rip—what we call a twenty-buck control buy. We were shooting fish in a barrel. This was supposed to be good law enforcement work? Resolving problems? Cleaning up communities? No—this was a factory! This was a moneymaking operation—a collars for dollars scheme that I was not going to be part of anymore. I made my stand because I was tired of watching people on the corners getting pummeled. It's the same feeling, I imagine, as grabbing slaves and putting them on a ship."

Perhaps the most terrifying statistic of all that Soares uncovered was that in Albany County (minority population 13 percent) more than *95 percent* of imprisoned drug law offenders were black or Hispanic. Whichever way you look at the figure, it can mean only one thing—something is rotten in the state.

Buddies

. . .

Special Agent Matthew Fogg knew that he had to be careful but found it difficult holding his tongue. Ever since he testified in Congress in 1989 that his boss, Ronald Hein, was a racist and should not be appointed to the prestigious position of U.S. Marshal for the D.C. Superior Court, he had encountered difficulties in his career. Despite his being an outcast among his fellow police officers, Fogg's courage in speaking out as a whistle-blower was eventually vindicated in 1998 when a jury awarded him $4 million plus full back pay in his suit against Janet Reno, then U.S. attorney general, and the Department of Justice. The court concluded that not only had Fogg been the victim of racial discrimination at the hands of his bosses but that the U.S. Marshals Service was institutionally racist.

The landmark ruling was neither the beginning nor the end of Fogg's determination to highlight corruption and racial discrimination both within the ranks of America's law enforcement agencies and in their application of the law in various communities. Fogg made a lot of enemies. On one occasion, he was set up by his own colleagues during an operation to arrest a fugitive in Baltimore and was almost killed. That was during the early nineties when he had been seconded to the DEA from the U.S. Marshals Service, where he served as a deputy. His job at the DEA was to supervise a metropolitan task force that would carry out drug sweeps in the largest cities across the country.

Fogg is a tall, tough-looking guy, but his speech is modest and gentle even when his anger quickens. Even now that he is in his fifties and despite a life of hard knocks, he still seems bewildered at how unfair and unjust the world can be. "Over the course of my career, I've been responsible for locking up somewhere in the region of 2,000 fugitives," he told me at an office in Washington. "'Cause I was involved in dragnets—we swept everything moving in all the major cities around the country. At the task force, we'd fix the operation with the local police department and supply them with federal funds for it, give 'em overtime and everything. We'd give the dragnets fancy names like Operation Gunsmoke or Operation Sunrise and it was a ninety days deal. In that ninety days you go hog wild on locking up as many folk on anything you could get. But of course we would concentrate on the urban areas mainly where African Americans and people of color were. Eighty-five percent and more of the folk we arrested were black or Hispanic."

Dispirited at hauling in hundreds of men and women from his own community, Fogg came up with a new proposal for his boss at the DEA. "I suggested we go out to Potomac, Maryland, and to Springfield, to places where whites live, and out to Alexandria, because our job was to find the drugs and white folk do drugs too. The DEA ASAC, the [assistant] special agent in charge, got hold of me and said, 'We gotta talk about this.' He said, 'Fogg, you're right. People do drugs everywhere. White folks do drugs too. But, buddy—we start going out into those areas with the task force, those people know judges, lawyers, politicians, and let me tell you something, they'll shut us down and there goes your overtime. We'll go after the weakest link instead."

The discussion degenerated into an argument. " 'This is selective enforcement,' I told him. 'Man,' I said, 'we even got white guys in the force coming up to us saying we're doing too many black guys.' Me and the other black guys on the force, we'd talk about this all the time, but we never did anything about it. And then I realized. Here we are, part of the plantation, doing the massa's bidding."

Because of the system of financial incentives that is built into the war on drugs, and because of the protection from prosecution, as described by Fogg, that white communities enjoy, this war in the United States is waged against blacks and Hispanics. In light of his experiences, Matthew Fogg is now convinced that the strategy is designed as an institutional tool that is used to control African American communities and limit their economic and social opportunities. This is taking conspiracy too far, but there should be no doubt that the war on drugs inflicts massively disproportionate damage on America's underprivileged minority communities. The ability of the criminal justice system to levy crushing penalties of imprisonment and for law enforcement officers to be rewarded for the numbers charged and convicted is an open invitation for corruption.

Fogg concluded that the harm done to African Americans by the policing of drugs far outweighed the harm caused by the drugs themselves. There is now a growing number of former law enforcement officers from federal and state agencies, including the DEA, who like Matthew Fogg speak out in favor of the decriminalization or legalization of narcotics in the United States. And like most of these men and women, Matthew Fogg does not use drugs. He discourages their use among his community. But although in the late 1990s he represented a growing constituency that has support among members of both Democratic and Republican parties, no single politician seeking office ever dared challenge the orthodoxy of the war on drugs in public. However compelling the arguments for a liberalization of America's drug wars might be, in the hothouse of Washington and state politics, it is a third-rail issue—touch it and you're dead.

That was until David Soares came along.

In the late 1990s, working as an assistant DA and using his office of community prosecutor, Soares embarked on projects to try to clean up the West Hill inner-city area, the focus of Albany's narcotics trade. His first focus was on the environment. "There's a reason people don't deal drugs in the suburbs in front of nice fresh-cut grass. It's because there's something about the environment that sends out a signal to the offender that says, 'This type of behavior is not acceptable here.' But when you have boarded-up buildings, when you have overgrown bushes and cars abandoned in lots, it sends a message that says, 'Anything is tolerated here.' We set about removing some of those obstacles—trimming the trees, cutting the grass, and we were using offenders in bringing that about, while also instilling in them the idea that this is their neighborhood. They began to see that they were not cleaning the broken glass and syringes off a basketball court as punishment but because their little brothers and little sisters would be playing here later on. In less than a year, we were able to drive down the emergency calls without increasing the number of arrests."

Soares's success didn't just interfere with the drug-dealing network; it started to irritate a political network—a very powerful network indeed. "This became an issue for my boss at the time, who would sit in his office and talk for hours about what I'm doing wrong. I was, for example, getting trash cans for people who wanted trash cans. What they were concerned about was that I was attempting to destroy a system. If you were a resident and you wanted a trash can in front of your house, you would call the committee men, who would then contact the deputy ward leader, who would then contact the ward leader, who would then let the mayor know that there was a trash can needed. They would inform you who got you the trash can and they would inform you about what you needed to do to repay this. That's been the political culture—it's called The Machine."

The Machine reacts poorly to those who challenge its authority. Soares's bosses started withdrawing resources and support staff. Before long, Soares found he was no longer able to do his job. He was treading water with no prospect of advancement in Albany. Once he had disturbed The Machine, he could expect no mercy, especially not from his boss, the DA Paul Clyne, member of one of the most influential Democratic families in the city and an unbending supporter of the Rockefeller drug laws.

Soares decided to sell up and move to Atlanta, a magnet for thousands of middle-class blacks from the Northeast. " 'Do you really want to move?' my wife asked me. And I said, 'Yes.' She accused me of running away like some kid from school. 'If these guys had been at school in Pawtucket, you would have punched 'em.' She brought back my little Pawtucket spirit."

The next day, Soares gave the train to Georgia a miss and walked into Paul Clyne's office to inform the DA that he intended to run against him in the forthcoming Democratic primary. "The meeting lasted seven minutes," Soares recalls. "He laughed the first five and he then fired me in the next two."

The Machine, a corrupt Democratic Party operation similar to the Daley dynasty's fiefdom in Chicago, has always governed Albany, and there was one community who had never been granted membership. "The party appoints the judges; the party appoints the chief of police, the mayors, everyone here—the legislators all come out of the same institution. But there's only one African American judge and then there's me—only two in any policy-making positions in this county. But the issue of race has never been dealt with here—they live there and we live here. They'll tell you that they employ a lot of African Americans in the city. What they don't tell you is that they're all picking up trash!"

In the autumn of 2004, Soares stood against Clyne in the Democratic primary and then again in the election to the DA's office, as Clyne stood against him as an independent. Soares had been out on the stump, holding rallies and knocking on doors in all communities throughout Albany County, although whites made up more than 80 percent of the electorate. Soares placed reform of the Rockefeller drug laws at the center of his campaign. "The Rockefeller drug laws smack of everything that is offensive," he said at the time. "The image of the criminal justice system is Themis, and she has a scale, a blindfold, and a sword. It is supposed to be just. If we lose faith in the criminal justice system, then what do we have? We have chaos. The Rockefeller drug laws are offensive to the image of Themis. We know that the drug law acts negatively on African Americans and Hispanics so disproportionately that the fact that it is still on the books today makes you wonder. I don't like to look at this in terms of race so much, but to say here is an issue that is important to everyone. Addiction is something that affects everyone, whether it is crack cocaine or alcohol. Most people, whether it be immediate family or a cousin, have that experience; they know what damage addiction does to families. So to have a system that treats addiction in the way that it does, so disproportionately, is wrong."

In both the primary and in the main election, Soares whipped Clyne and all other opponents. His election destroyed the political consensus in New York State. On the eve of his election victory in November 2004, Soares said, "It is unquestionable that . . . the days of this antiquated statute are numbered. The fact that the most vociferous, inflexible member of the New York State DAs Association is in jeopardy of losing his position and primarily on the issue of the Rockefeller drug laws is a moment for pause for every single elected official in the state of New York."

It is also a message to Congress and the presidency—slowly the American people may be realizing that after almost four decades of the war on drugs, dependency levels and usage are higher than ever before; that the prices of all major recreational drugs have been declining resolutely over that period; and that the state has wasted hundreds of billions of dollars in a criminal justice system that delivers a lot of crime but very little justice. The funds used to sustain bureaucracies such as the DEA that prosecute the war on drugs are a drop in the ocean when compared with the gazillions that organized crime syndicates have earned because Washington is determined to drive the market underground. The social and criminal problems related to drug abuse will never go away until the state can exercise control over the industry as a whole.

And that is just in the United States. Pity those less affluent countries who fall victim to America's war on drugs. Above all, pity Colombia.

CHAPTER 11

March of Fear

Soldiers

The road to Jamundí, fifteen miles south of Cali, is quite a tour. First I drive past the training ground of Cali America Soccer Club, owned by the Rodríguez-Orejuela clan, a.k.a. the Cali cartel. A few miles farther on, I am astonished to see a full-size bull ring belonging to the Ochoa brothers, erstwhile partners of the late Pablo Escobar in the Medellín cartel. Jamundí is a favored recreational destination for narco-traffickers (as they are universally known in Colombia), where they have built grand *fincas,* complete with lakes, full-size floodlit soccer pitches, indoor and outdoor pools—all on the same property. Right at the far end, the *fincas* stop abruptly and the modest dwellings of the impecunious Indians begin.

As the little town tails off, there is a welcoming sign at the beginning of a drive lined by tall green hedges. Underneath the words MY LITTLE HOME: PSYCHIATRIC HOSTEL there is a phone number and an arrow pointing down the drive. Two hundred yards farther on around a couple of bends is the Little Home itself, set in delightful grounds—although the rusty green and red iron gates and the barbed-wire fencing are less welcoming.

At five-thirty on May 22, 2006, the commander of one of Colombia's crack Special Forces units stopped his convoy of three cars at just this spot. Accompanied by nine men and a civilian informer, he emerged from his car and strolled toward the gates—the informant had assured him that there was more to My Little Home than meets the eye.

Without warning a group of uniformed men who had been lying in wait opened fire on the police unit, killing its commander instantly. Twenty-eight gunmen were hidden among the unkempt undergrowth adjacent to the drive. "We were just preparing supper at the time," said a member of the staff at the hostel, "when all of a sudden there was this tremendous noise of gunfire from the gate." A couple of the police officers had thrown themselves into the open drains for protection. "We heard these men screaming, saying, 'Stop, please don't shoot! We're police!' And then, 'We have wives and children.' "

But the shooting went on for a full twenty minutes until every last policeman was dead. When a regular police team came to clean up the mess, they found that one of the attackers had made a point of placing a bullet in the back of the head of the civilian—as a message, perhaps?

Unnatural deaths like those at Jamundí are always a shock in this country but never a surprise. There is a bewildering number of potential perpetrators—a whole book's worth of murdering acronyms has been stalking this country for thirty years, each staking its claim to political and moral superiority by means of massacre, torture, and bombings. And that's just the freelancers. The police and the military have frequently acted as unaccountably as the traffickers, the paramilitaries, and the guerrillas.

Colombia's powerful Marxist guerrillas, the FARC, are often mentioned first as possible culprits in attacks on the military or the police such as the one in Jamundí. They certainly operate quite close to the town; they derive a large part of their income from cocaine; and they have never shied away from mounting armed assaults on government agents. As if to emphasize this, while I was visiting Jamundí, a FARC unit was busy killing six policemen on the other side of Cali with pipe bombs that they had been taught to build by members of the provisional IRA. But these days their military units rarely penetrate this far into urban areas, and the attack did not fit the profile of a FARC operation.

Then there were the local paramilitaries (known as the AUC) who often fight alongside the regular army against the FARC. Claiming to be upholders of the right to private property (especially property they have seized by intimidation and murder), many members of the AUC had disarmed in a deal brokered with the government earlier in the year, only to emerge as new organized criminal gangs in the lawless barrios that grow, tumor-like, from the nether regions of all major Colombian cities.

And finally, there was the Cartel del Norte, successors to the even more infamous Cali cartel. Although the Cartel del Norte had lost its leader, Fernando Henao, a year earlier after a New York court had sentenced him to nineteen and a half years in jail, the business was still functioning smoothly under his partner, Diego Montoya. The cartel was sure to be a prime suspect.

Whoever pulled the trigger, it was not difficult to guess the motive—cocaine.

Indeed, it quickly emerged that cocaine was indeed at the heart of this case, but the identity of the Jamundí killers still took everyone by surprise. It was not the FARC, the AUC, the ELN, MAS, the PEPES, or any other self-appointed law enforcers who perpetrated this crime. The Special Forces team was executed by none other than a twenty-eight-strong platoon from the Twenty-third Mountain Brigade of the regular army. The Colombian military has, of course, never been retiring in its use of force; and it boasts one of the worst human rights records in the world. But it is highly unusual for the military to murder their colleagues from the Special Forces. This came as a real shock to everyone—to the Colombian people; to its president, Alvaro Uribe; and to his government; and it came as a big and unpleasant shock to members of the U.S. Congress and President George W. Bush.

The platoon commander, the square-jawed Colonel Bayron Carvajal, at first issued a statement describing the incident as a tragic case of "friendly fire." It had happened at night, he claimed, and the soldiers had mistaken the unit for FARC guerrillas. The eyewitnesses from My Little Home and the neighboring Indian houses were baffled—they knew the attack took place in broad daylight and that the distinctive uniforms of the Special Forces would have been instantly recognized by the army.

Far from being friendly fire, this bore the hallmarks of a calculated execution. Furthermore, as the attorney general Mario Iguarán investigated the matter a little closer, it seemed suspiciously as though the soldiers had been acting to protect whoever owned the drugs. "This was not a mistake; this was a crime," he proclaimed after a preliminary investigation. "They were doing the bidding of a drug trafficker."

There was good reason for the long faces in Washington when this news hit D.C. The United States had recently handed over the last wedge of the $4 billion it had donated to Bogotá under the auspices of Plan Colombia. This five-year plan, introduced by the Clinton administration and expanded by President Bush, had been designed to save the world from the joint scourge of cocaine and the FARC. Eighty percent of these funds was earmarked for upgrading the military. With the exceptions of Egypt and Israel, Washington lavished more hardware and cash on the Colombian armed forces in the first years of this century than on any other in the world. The dual aim was to eradicate coca plantations, the cocaine business, and the left-wing guerrillas. But in Jamundí, those selfsame recipients of military aid were working on behalf of narco-traffickers and murdering policemen! What had gone wrong?

As well as having a reputation as the most violent, Colombia is one of the most richly endowed Latin American countries, with fertile plains that produce the finest coffee in the world; gorgeous Atlantic and Pacific coastlines; jungles stuffed with exotic wildlife; mineral resources from emeralds to coal and oil; the majesty of the Andes; part of the Amazon basin; and even a city, Medellín, with a climate that is rightly described as "eternal spring." On my first day in the capital, Bogotá, a Colombian wit explained that when God made the earth, he decided to give this one country every form of munificence he could muster. "When all the other countries complained that this amounted to discrimination against them," my friend continued, "the Lord turned to them and said, 'Just wait till you see some of the people I'm going to give Colombia. Then you'll be happy with your lot!' "

This idea of a paradise stained by a satanic, venal minority is a common theme in Colombia. Behind the seductive power of magical realism in the Nobel laureate Gabriel García Márquez's *One Hundred Years of Solitude* lies an intense consideration of the role violence has played in Colombian history, where a sincere struggle in the name of a cause or ideology is repeatedly eclipsed by and subordinated to the violence it begets:

"Tell me something, old friend: why are you fighting?"

"What other reason could there be?" Colonel Gerineldo Márquez answered. "For the great Liberal party."

"You're lucky because you know why," he answered. "As far as I'm concerned, I've come to realize only just now that I'm fighting because of pride."

"That's bad," Colonel Gerineldo Márquez said.

Colonel Aureliano Buendía was amused at his alarm. "Naturally," he said. "But in any case, it's better than not knowing why you're fighting." He looked him in the eyes and added with a smile:

"Or fighting, like you, for something that doesn't have any meaning for anyone."

As a BBC correspondent, I had seen a good deal of butchery in the Balkans and in the Caucasus, but Colombia's reputation for violence unsettled me. When I left London for Bogotá, it was the only time during my investigations that I was distinctly worried that I was taking an unnecessary risk. My fear was, of course, an exaggeration and a deeply unfair criticism of many of this country's warm and outgoing people. An exaggeration, yes. A fantasy, no. Just over a week before my departure, I had enjoyed dinner in Washington with a friend, a most gentle man, who said as we parted, "This is not a joke, you know. It really can be a very dangerous place." He knew better than most. Six years earlier, his wife had stopped at traffic lights in Pereira, a town 100 miles west of Bogotá, when a motorcycle pulled up beside her car. The pillion rider then took out a gun and shot her dead in front of the nanny and her four-year-old daughter. My friend fled to Washington and is unable to return to his home country to this day. And while in Colombia I met an inordinate number of people forced to bear the murder of a family member or of close friends.

Even by Colombia's standards, the mayhem of the past twenty-five years takes the breath away. The violence of the nineteenth and twentieth centuries came in many shapes and sizes—full-scale rebellions or armed uprisings, arbitrary government incursions to intimidate or cleanse an area in preparation for its seizure, individual terror, or fearful massacres. The rivalry between the Conservative and Liberal parties fashioned the political framework, while the issue of land ownership provided the economic motivation. One of its many high points, sparked by the assassination of the presidential candidate Jorge Eliécer Gaitán in April 1948, is known simply as *La Violencia,* a decade-long festival of bloodletting that was eventually brought to an end by a reconciliation between the Liberals and the Conservatives, the two parties that had dominated both the country and the bloodshed for more than a century.

Until this point, violence in Colombia had been largely a domestic affair. And indeed, during the 1960s, Colombia's people dared to imagine a future of greater civil harmony, of slow but steady prosperity, and of growing influence in the north of South America. Not only did an internal consensus appear to develop, but there was none of the overt political manipulation by American companies, politicians, or mobsters that was so visible in Central America and the Caribbean.

Then three things happened in just more than a decade to force this country down every circle of Dante's hell. And there it remains to this day—the greatest victim of the most relentless organized crime networks in the Western Hemisphere—networks that in the process have become hideously intertwined with an entirely different form of politically motivated armed conflict.

First, in 1968, in an attempt to bolster its domestic economic performance, Colombia proudly established the Institute of Advanced Chemical Research as part of the Universidad Nacional de Colombia in Bogotá, which started to train top-class chemists, who were later to find lucrative work in the employ of the Medellín and Cali cartels.

Second, at around the same time, American horticulturalists began to grow marijuana in sufficient quantities to meet most needs of the United States' domestic weed market. This led to a depression in the healthy cannabis trade that had sprouted around Colombia's northern coast. Those traffickers who had made an impressive living in the north looked to diversify their agro portfolios to reverse their declining fortunes in marijuana futures.

This search coincided with the third development—a dramatic return to fashion of cocaine among the thirty- and forty-somethings in Florida and the Northeast. As America's baby boomers turned from protesting to making money, they sought a champagne-style narcotic that represented this shift in their lives from philosophical introspection to brash acquisitiveness. Cocaine had none of the mess associated with shooting up—just a quick snort and then head out to Studio 54. It wasn't long before everyone wanted a piece. "No longer is it a sinful secret of the moneyed elite," reported *Time* in a July 1981 edition featuring a cocktail glass full of coke on the cover, "nor merely an elusive glitter of decadence in raffish society circles, as it seemed in decades past. No longer is it primarily an exotic and ballyhooed indulgence of high-gloss entrepreneurs, Hollywood types and high rollers, as it was only three or four years ago—the most conspicuous of consumptions, to be sniffed from the most chic of coffee tables through crisp, rolled-up $100 bills. Today, in part precisely because it is such an emblem of wealth and status, coke is the drug of choice for perhaps millions of solid, conventional, and often upwardly mobile citizens—lawyers, businessmen, students, government bureaucrats, politicians, policemen, secretaries, bankers, mechanics, real estate brokers, waitresses."

There had been little research into the drug since it had been pilloried and then banned by the American government during the 1920s. Most people thought erroneously that it was not very addictive and that it had no serious side effects. And if that wasn't enough, it was rumored to enhance sexual performance.

Demand was going through the roof, and the plodding rural economies of Peru and Bolivia couldn't keep pace. This conjuncture convinced a group of Colombians—the narco-traffickers—that there was money in them there Andes.

Narco-traffickers

To discover how they got their hands on this source of cash, I visited a downtown Bogotá nightclub to meet a man nicknamed "The Demon" but whom everybody addressed as "Nixon," perhaps a playful reference to the late U.S. president.

After walking through a harmless bar area peopled by men in their mid-thirties to late forties and women in their early twenties, my friends and I walked into a hall containing a large indoor swimming pool in the shape of a figure eight. Across the middle was a gaudy Rialto-style bridge, while around the walls there were little enclaves surrounded by the most tasteless red drapes. In each enclave was a group of four to six men drinking while naked young women thrust their crotch into the face of one man at a time to the rhythm of the accompanying Latino Euro pop, played at thunderous volume. Each to his own, I suppose, but not really my cup of tea.

Fortunately, Nixon took us to a floor overlooking this bacchanalian parody where we could at least hear ourselves talk. Nonetheless, he insisted on bringing two young prostitutes with him, one of whom sported the largest bosom I have ever seen (Colombia prides itself as the world leader in breast enhancement). By now Nixon was so coked up that he was talking like a machine gun. To kick off, he produced a handkerchief with the flourish of a stage magician for his audience to examine and then carefully drew it through the hole that years of cocaine usage had burnt through his septum.

"I was a young teenager, completely normal, from Boyacá, about two hours from Bogotá. I had no idea about drugs when one of my cousins turned up from New York." The 1960s and seventies witnessed a significant exodus of Colombians seeking work in the States after the country's textile industry collapsed, and among the emigrants were the first cocaine traffickers, including Nixon's cousin. The two men would purchase coca paste from the growers in Bolivia and Peru, processing it into cocaine hydrochloride themselves and then sending it up to relatives who had nested in the burgeoning Colombian communities of New York and Miami. "My job was to transport the stuff within Colombia, usually by car or truck," Nixon explained, "then from the coast or the airfield it would go either directly to New York or to Mexico or the Caribbean."

Nixon was swept up by drugs and the surreal experience of becoming very rich very suddenly while still young. He snorted, screwed, and shot his way across Colombia. Until January 1994. "My boss was driving down one of the main streets in Bogotá and I was in the passenger seat," he recalled. "And then it happened just like people have always described it. Two guys on a motorbike stop by us at the lights and the pillion rider pulls out a gun and starts shooting my boss. I ducked under the dashboard, looking for my gun, but I couldn't reach it. But my boss managed to get the car out of the line of fire and he survived despite taking three bullets." That was when Nixon got out of the high end of the business. "We soon found out that the hit had been ordered by my boss's partner, and I thought, This is too much. My girlfriend and I now had a little daughter and I didn't want her to end up fatherless." Nixon managed to downgrade his status—instead of shifting kilos, he started dealing in grams to Bogotá's emerging yuppies.

In his heyday, Nixon belonged to a respectably sized wholesale operation. But this had been a mere tributary that trickled into the raging river of cocaine flowing to New York from its source in Cali, about 200 miles southwest of Bogotá. The Cali cartel was one of the top three cocaine clans to emerge in Colombia during the 1970s and 1980s. In an agreement with the other two clans, who were based in Medellín, the Cali cartel had carved up the U.S. export market with precision—New York belonged to Cali. Anyone exporting there would have to link up with their operation.

In 1981 and 1982, the Ochoa clan, partners in crime with Pablo Escobar in the Medellín cartel, convened a series of meetings at their ranch, Las Margaritas, to which the major cartel bosses from around Colombia were invited. The most senior delegation to join Escobar and the Ochoas were the Rodríguez-Orejuela brothers, Gilberto and Miguel, who controlled the Cali cartel.

These high-level summits were prompted initially by the abduction of the Ochoa brothers' sister, Martha, who was snatched for ransom by left-wing guerrillas. But the gatherings became much more—indeed, despite the mutual suspicion that later decayed into deadly hostility, this was the foundation not so much of empires but an industry that thrives to this day and continues to shrug off all attempts to sabotage it.

The individuals at Las Margaritas were all eventually killed or imprisoned. Nonetheless, for almost twenty years, the Escobar, Ochoa, and Rodríguez-Orejuela groups were the most important figures in the global shadow economy that grew up alongside the licit economy as the United States and Europe pushed through the liberalization of financial and commodity markets—the economic cornerstone of globalization in the 1980s. In key respects, the Medellín and Cali cartels succeeded in anticipating the mechanisms of globalization, and for many years they were also able to merge their illicit operations with licit ones.

The three clans made strange bedfellows. The Ochoas were from a smart and wealthy middle-class family with a passion for horse breeding, while Escobar grew up in the slums of Medellín, ducking and diving through the trigger-happy world of Colombia's petty criminals. In Cali, the Rodríguez-Orejuelas were more familiar with Escobar's lifestyle, but it was the Ochoa family that made the introductions between Escobar and the Rodríguez-Orejuelas and succeeded in maintaining the peace between them before the two groups' mutual loathing led to a bitter struggle between them.

During the discussions at Las Margaritas, two momentous decisions were made. First, they agreed to fund a clandestine organization, MAS, Muertes a Secuestradores (Death to the Kidnappers), a private militia that would later blossom into the more powerful and organized right-wing paramilitary the AUC. Second, they agreed to carve up the North American cocaine market—Escobar was awarded the color code yellow for Miami, the Ochoas were blue for Los Angeles, and the Cali cartel was red for New York.

Although he enjoyed a reputation as the most notorious narco-trafficker, Pablo Escobar was not in fact as successful as the Rodríguez-Orejuela brothers. These two had first come to the attention of the police for their role in a series of high-profile kidnappings in the late 1960s. By the mid-seventies, the elder brother, Gilberto, had gathered sufficient funds to buy a light aircraft with which he ferried the semi-refined coca paste from Peru to Cali. Here he would arrange the final stage of processing into cocaine hydrochloride before shipping it off to the States.

Within a few years, the Cali cartel's fleet numbered more than 700 aircraft, which were dispensing drugs all over North America. In a country where geography usually makes transport a nightmare, Cali's location is perfect. To the east and south lie coca and opium poppy cultivation areas, while to the west Buenaventura's deep harbor is only a short drive away. Upon this geographical serendipity, the cartel built a superbly efficient corporation. Even the Drug Enforcement Administration (DEA) could not entirely disguise its admiration for the cartel's business acumen (admittedly after the gang leaders were arrested in 1995):

> The Cali mafia's annual profits were estimated at between $4 and $8 billion a year, and the organization operated like a well-run multinational business with Cali mafia leaders micro-managing business decisions in Colombia and in the United States. They were able to

run their global enterprise through a sophisticated system of telephones, faxes, pagers and computers, and employed an intelligence network that rivaled those of most developing nations. The Cali drug lords controlled the Cali airport, the taxi system and the phone company. They knew who came and went in Cali, who talked to the police, and who was cooperating with U.S. law enforcement agencies.

The DEA was right to identify the cartel's intelligence-gathering capacity as the key to its success. "They knew who we all were and who our informants were—they had phone numbers, movements—completely ahead of the game," remembered Jim Milford, who headed up the DEA's team responsible for hunting down the Rodríguez clan. The DEA understood the extent of the cartel's surveillance capacity only after it seized an IBM mainframe computer, comparable to systems used by major banks, from a building in Cali in 1996. Here they found telephone logs that had been leaked by insiders from the municipal telephone exchange that detailed all calls from U.S. agents in Colombia to their contacts in Cali.

This was typical of the operation, which was always looking to maximize its competitive advantages. Gilberto, who took pride in his nom de plume, the Chess Master, conceived three masterstrokes.

At home in Colombia, he eschewed the flamboyant violence with which Escobar turned Medellín and Bogotá into abattoirs. Instead, he preferred to exploit the chronic weakness of the Colombian state by subverting virtually every public or private institution that might assist his business, up to and including the presidency. Banks were an early investment target of the Cali team. Having created its own in 1974, El Banco de los Trabajadores, the cartel bought into banks elsewhere in Central and South America that had close ties to banks in Miami and New York, including Manufacturers Hanover and Chase Manhattan.

Equally important, Gilberto developed the policy of "state capture." Less prosaically, he bought protection from the entire government by corrupting presidents. His influence reached its apogee after the election of President Ernesto Samper in 1994. "He gave a bunch of money to Samper," a senior former government official told me, "and everyone in Samper's gang ended up jumping cartwheels to accommodate the Cali cartel."

Finally, to produce 100 tons of cocaine, you need millions of liters of precursor chemicals. The great bulk of those chemicals are produced in the United States and the European Union. Some, such as potassium permanganate, are easy to bring in because they are used for the manufacture of food like pizza crust. But for others you need a license. The Cali cartel's answer to this problem? Simple—use some of your spare cash to establish Rebaja Las Drogas and build it up into the largest drugstore chain in the country, and you can import anything you want with no questions asked!

Money laundering in those days was still a simple affair, with neither banks nor governments giving two hoots as to the origin of large amounts of cash. As the noose tightened a little on the financial system during the 1980s, the Medellín and Cali cartels perfected the black market peso exchange system whereby dollars earned in the United States would purchase fridges, TVs, cars, and other consumer durables, which were then smuggled into Colombia and resold for pesos. "Since the early 1970s, Colombians have purchased contraband goods, knowing that they are part of the illicit drug money-laundering chain," explained Francisco Thoumi, Bogotá's leading authority on organized crime. "They have sold real estate, art objects, fancy cars, and jewelry at inflated prices to mysterious individuals who paid in cash without questioning the origin of the funds involved. From their point of view, the responsibility to control those actions was the state's, not personal or social." Just as the state is indifferent or unable to police large tracts of Colombia, Thoumi argues, so people feel no reciprocal responsibility to the state and are instead happy to ignore its judicial and policing systems. "Why are those constraints weaker in Colombia than in other societies?" he asks rhetorically. "In Colombia everything is allowed; there are no personal or social sanctions. Every illicit act is tolerated and even approved as something brilliant, heroic, clever, and cunning, but if the responsible person gets caught, he is left to hang out by himself. In other words, there is great social tolerance to anyone who obtains results, independent of the means used, but at the same time there is no trust or solidarity."

Overseas, Gilberto pioneered the strategic commercial alliance with counterparts in Mexico, Spain, Italy, Brazil, Nigeria, and finally Russia. His decision in the early eighties to divert the bulk of exports to narco-traffickers in Mexico demonstrated the depth of his vision. The overwhelming business risk for Colombian narco-traffickers lies in delivering the merchandise across the U.S. border and to a "legitimate" client; that is, one who is not working for law enforcement. By establishing agreements with the Mexicans, Rodríguez was unloading that risk onto them (and condemning northern Mexico to the same miserable fate as Colombia suffered). At around the same time, he established links with organized crime groups in Spain, as well as with the Mafia in Italy via Brazil. Most dramatic were the meetings between the Rodríguez brothers' representatives and members of Moscow's Solntsevo Brotherhood on the thoroughly sinful Caribbean island of Aruba in the early nineties. As the market for cocaine in the United States had reached the point of supersaturation, the collapse of Communism was a gift from above for the Colombian cartels. Both the European market and the routes thereto could suddenly flourish.

The cartels are the nearest phenomenon to have emerged in the past thirty years that correspond to the popular image of the organized criminal syndicate; that is, a vast, ruthless organization that is bent on destroying Western civilization. Once the sophisticated networks of Colombia appropriated the processing and distribution of cocaine from more modest industries in Peru and Bolivia, then cocaine did become a commodity that was handled by some of the largest criminal networks in the world. But contrary to popular perceptions, the Cali cartel, like the other major cocaine corporations, was in fact highly decentralized. The cartel is a holding company, an agglomeration of small, flexible mafia groups that have differing stakes in the overall industry. The Rodríguez brothers were unquestionably the most senior managers of this group who conferred stability on the overall business environment and derived huge profits from its activities. The impact of their arrest and consequent removal from the trade had only a brief knock-on effect on the price of cocaine in the United States. This was occasioned by the struggle in the Cali region following the arrests, as the smaller mafias making up the cartel jostled to seize the top spots the Rodríguezes had vacated. Taking down an Escobar or a Rodríguez is the stuff of law enforcement legend, and rightly so. But in the case of cocaine, these spectacular operations do nothing to disrupt supply or demand.

It is now more than a quarter of a century after Ronald Reagan announced the Colombian cartels to be the prime target in a war on drugs that the president redefined as a central national security issue for the United States. And yet cocaine from Colombia is cheaper and easier to acquire in the United States than ever before. Billions upon billions of dollars have been spent in an attempt to root out an industry that has merely grown in size, in scope, in profits, and in human sacrifices—tens of thousands of people have lost their lives; millions more lives have been shattered.

"By all empirical standards," argued Alvaro Camacho, Colombia's leading academic researcher into U.S. narcotics policy in South America, "the war on drugs has been a complete failure." The execution of this ill-

conceived policy, he and others claim, has frequently been exposed as farci-
cal by the competing and contradictory interests of the CIA, the DEA, and
state, whose squabbles have often made life for the narco-traffickers even
easier than it otherwise might have been.

But Professor Camacho's most disturbing observation is that at most
the cocaine industry accounts for just 3 percent of Colombia's GDP. (Later
the UN anti-narcotics chief assures me it is even lower, just 0.8 percent). In
Afghanistan, since the fall of the Taliban, the United Nations estimates,
opium amounts to a staggering 57 percent of GDP, rendering it impossible
for the central government in Kabul to impose any effective control on the
country outside the capital and the north. And that is despite the assistance
of 19,000 heavily armed NATO-led troops. Far from cleaning up the
scourge of cheap heroin on Britain's streets, as Tony Blair promised in 2001,
the intervention has caused Afghanistan to become an epicenter of organized crime, insurgency, and terrorism. The country now nourishes all
manner of organizations, from the Turkish smack cartels through the
despotic leaders of Turkmenistan and Uzbekistan, not forgetting al Qaeda,
whose prime source of income in the region is the Afghan opium trade.

Colombia's economy is more sophisticated and much richer than
Afghanistan's. "So that although the drugs make up only 3 percent of the
GDP," Professor Camacho points out, "that is more than enough to sustain
at least two private armies—the paramilitaries and narco-traffickers on the
one hand, the guerrillas on the other." Armies who for several years could
keep 70,000 fighters permanently under arms.

The havoc that the cocaine trade wreaks on Colombian society is wildly
disproportionate to coca's economic value. Bombings, massacres, and
motiveless killings perpetrated by all sides are well documented and frequently define foreign perceptions of the country (as I discovered when I
tried in vain to insure myself before traveling there). But it is yet another
army that inflicts the greatest damage on Colombia's moral capacity to
emerge from the morass—an army of refugees. In 2004, Jan Egeland, head
of humanitarian affairs at the UN, explained that Colombia's drug wars
had resulted in "the biggest number of killings; the biggest humanitarian
problem; the biggest human rights problem; the biggest conflict in the
Western Hemisphere." He also warned that the government in Bogotá had
run out of funds to deal with the most dramatic expression of that crisis,
the 3 million refugees driven out of their homes since the mid-1990s—the
largest refugee population in the hemisphere and the third largest anywhere in the world.

March of Fear

Guerrillas

In 1980, Susanna Castillo and her husband, Ephraim, used the few hundred dollars she had inherited from her father to buy a farmhouse with several hectares of land in the Colombian province of Meta. The tiny village of San José lies to the north of the broad, meandering river Guejar. Beyond its banks, the serrated mountain range of La Macarena rises, while jostling with jungle that thickens southward, home to thousands of unique plant and animal species. "At the time there was no electricity, no roads to San José. There was nothing except malaria," remembers Susanna, "but we found the land was very fertile and we grew bananas and corn." There she and her husband raised seven children, modestly prosperous in an unpredictable environment. Then in the space of two days, through no fault of her own, she lost her home and her livelihood and embarked on a wretched life as a refugee.

Mrs. Castillo answers my questions patiently and precisely but with no emotion, and I suspect the previous twelve months have drained most hope or expectation from her. We are sitting in the office of Roberto Sicar, the ombudsman for Tres Esquinas (Three Corners), an unmappable agglomeration of shacks, huts, and makeshift houses that accommodates an estimated 155,000 people, 80 percent of whom are refugees. In a community the size of Cambridge, England, or Bonn, there is no electricity and just a few punctured hoses that supply water.

Tres Esquinas is itself just a small part of Ciudad Bolívar, Bogotá's rambling barrio that spreads across the hills rising to the south of the Colombian capital. Sicar recognizes that his job is quixotic. "As far as the people here are concerned, I am the Colombian state," he says with a gentle smile, "even though I am actually funded by the United Nations. But there is little or nothing I can do for them."

During the day, the economy in Ciudad Bolívar revolves around the construction of shacks for the newcomers. As dusk falls, women, children, and the elderly hurry into their shelters as the nocturnal creatures emerge. "We have identified three paramilitary groups and eight crime syndicates in Tres Esquinas," Sicar says calmly. "If I come here at night, I need an army escort. The syndicates are subordinate to the paramilitaries—they are the ones who really run the economy here, through cocaine and guns. They control everything and are an ersatz state. All I can do is help the refugees to fill out forms and write letters. And they draw their own conclusions about the capacity of the Colombian state and the capacity of the ersatz state." The people of Tres Esquinas know full well where power lies in these dusty, ugly streets.

Opposite the ombudsman's building, there is an office of the United Nations Development Program. It is padlocked shut and looks as though it has been so for some time. The only other building is a spanking new library courtesy of Plan Colombia, the $4.7 billions' worth of assistance that the United States gave to Colombia over the first half decade of the new century. Of those funds, 98 percent were devoted to beefing up the Colombian armed forces' assault on coca plantations and left-wing guerrillas. I feel rather pleased for having uncovered one of its few civilian outlets. All the library needs now is to open (padlocked like the UNDP), a few books (there were none), and, most important, some people who can read (a rare species in Ciudad Bolívar).

Susanna Castillo does not need a library right now. As a recent recruit to Colombia's 3 million–strong army of refugees, she needs money, more space to live, and access to water and electricity. She has bright blue European eyes set behind sharp indigenous Indian cheekbones—like the majority of Colombians, she is of mixed race, a mestizo. Although she is forty-seven years old, the lines dug into her face add a good ten years to her age. "When we first arrived there, we were able to survive off the income from the bananas and corn," she continues. The Castillos were not obliged to pay taxes. The state simply didn't penetrate that far into Colombia's interior. "No tax collectors, no policemen, and no post office unless you walked to Vista Hermosa, which was two hours away on foot." And even in Vista Hermosa, the local town where the Castillo family sold their crops, the pace of life was glacial.

This experience of living in a country without ever encountering its official representatives is common in underdeveloped countries. But Colombia is not underdeveloped. Rather, it is the country's geography that militates against the consolidation of state power in the countryside. Bogotá is a good example: pitched high in the mountains, with poor transport links to the rest of the country, it is becalmed. Traditionally, power resided in the urban and coastal areas or the neighboring rural lands—the economic centers have no access to Bogotá. Elsewhere, the interior remained untouched by the state, and these boundless tracts of jungle often remain a mystery to this day. According to Sandro Calvani, the Italian who heads the UN anti-narcotics program in Colombia, the effect of "a large territory over which there was no state control at all for many decades has been profound. People have become accustomed to this and still now there is a large part of the territory where there is no rule of law. So people have grown up here, knowing that they are Colombian but without ever having come across the state in the form of police or justice."

At first, this indifference to their existence didn't bother the Castillos—quite the contrary. Their income proved sufficient to raise a family of seven children, five boys and two girls. The latter eventually left the village to marry, while the five boys remained, working the land for their parents. But as the 1980s turned into the 1990s, it was not the Colombian government that began to interfere with their lives but the impact of shifts in the global agricultural markets, of which the family had no notion. Technological innovation and the "banana wars" between the EU and America's fruit corporations were pushing down prices. Producers in areas such as the Macarena were among the first to feel the effects, baffled as to why nobody was willing to pay the same prices as in the past.

Something else was happening in the Macarena at the same time. The government's indifference was being steadily exploited by one of its fiercest competitors, the Fuerzas Armadas Revolucionarias de Colombia, or FARC.

The FARC is not just any old ragtag guerrilla operation conducting the occasional hit-and-run attack or the bombing of shopping malls. With anything between 15,000 and 20,000 combatants, it is an organized military force that has attracted into its ranks men, women, and children (with the emphasis often on the two latter categories) across large swaths of Colombian territory. Since Manuel "Sureshot" Marulanda founded the insurgent army in 1964, it has recruited members with ease from a large peasantry that has suffered systematic abuse by the more exploitative landowners and fruit companies controlling the agro-economy. Many landowners have never hesitated in employing thugs to assassinate those peasants who evinced even a passing interest in political activity. Colombia is the least safe country in the world to indulge in trade union work.

So for two decades, the FARC grew impressively in size and influence, living off the produce from countless towns and villages where they operated; and where they didn't enjoy that support, they had the weapons and the ruthlessness to persuade the peasants otherwise. The FARC has successfully inured itself to human pain and misery, an entry requirement for any organization (whether state agency, rebel, drug trafficker, or freelancer) aspiring to take part in Colombia's tragedy. When you introduce the cocaine industry as a catalyst to 150 years of bloody political struggle, this is hardly a surprise.

Powerful as the FARC became in the 1960s and 1970s, it was not able to halt the unstoppable tide of migration from the countryside into the cities.

Like their counterparts everywhere else in the globe, Colombia's peasants were desperate to escape the poverty and violence of the countryside. The FARC's ideological appeal, stirring though it may have sounded to the dispossessed, could not compete with even a dim prospect of casual work in the barrios of Cali, Medellín, or Bogotá. By the beginning of the 1990s, only 30 percent of the population remained in the countryside.

Hemorrhaging its raw recruits and producers in this way, the FARC had to rethink its economic policy. So it decided to renounce its traditional indifference to Colombia's most notorious product and started encouraging the cultivation of the coca plant on the territory under its control. The logic was simple—a kilo of bananas during the 1990s would fetch $2 on average; a kilo of coca base (before the most expensive part of the refining process) was worth between $750 and $1,000.

At an anonymous shopping mall in Cali, I sit down for a beer with two senior members of the clandestine Movimiento Bolivariano, the FARC's urban wing. They are an elegant, educated, and articulate couple, both doctors, but quite frank about their activities. "We became engaged in kidnapping in the early 1990s soon after we had set up the cells here in Cali," they explained. "At first the FARC leadership was reluctant to allow us to become involved in this, but we were able to convince them that there was a war going on in the cities as well as the countryside."

Like the other side, the FARC and the MB take the conflict very seriously but are impervious to the consequences. "We are not particularly interested in supplying people with drugs," Lola explained, "but the movement decided to engage with the *cocaleros* for financial reasons. But we do *not* process cocaine. The leadership merely taxes the peasants ten percent for its crop and in return provides a social security network." Police and military intelligence reports tell a very different story. They suggest that FARC's military bases are frequently situated close to the kitchens that process the coke and are more deeply involved in the trafficking than their supporters maintain. A dispassionate observer with access to this material but nonetheless deeply skeptical of American policy in his country described the FARC as "organized crime in fatigues."

It is difficult to verify the precise function of the FARC in the coke industry beyond the fact that it protects and encourages cultivation of the plant. That was certainly Susanna Castillo's experience. "We did what everybody did then—we switched from bananas and corn to coca," she explained. "Actually, we did not grow the coca ourselves but we rented out our land to a *cocalero* and he grew the crop. He paid tax to the FARC and we paid tax to the FARC on the rental he paid us." Rather touchingly, the 10 percent that the FARC charges for every harvest consciously builds on the church's tradition of collecting the *diesmo,* or tithe.

This arrangement earned the seven-strong Castillo family about $2,000 a month—not a fortune inasmuch that six family members were of working age, but given that more than 50 percent of Colombia's population live on just two dollars a day, it was a respectable figure.

In November 1998, President Andrés Pastrana took an extraordinary step. In the hope of resuscitating Colombia's moribund peace negotiations with the guerrillas, he ordered the army and police to clear a vast area of territory, roughly the size of Switzerland, in Meta and Caqueta provinces. This left the FARC in complete control of what became known as the *despeje* (cleansed area), which included most of the Macarena as well as the land of the Castillo family.

Many Colombians have excoriated Pastrana retrospectively for establishing the *despeje.* They argue, not unreasonably, that this allowed the FARC to consolidate its military base. They also point out that the ceasefire did not dissuade the FARC from indulging in one of its major pastimes of kidnapping people either for fiscal or for political ends. In 2002, as he was preparing to cede the presidency to Álvaro Uribe, Pastrana announced the end of the deal and warned the FARC that the government intended to restore its sovereignty over the region by force.

This was bad news for the Castillo family. While the *despeje* had been in force, their business had flourished—the FARC left them alone except when collecting taxes, and there was no prospect of the bottom falling out of the coca market. But after President Uribe was sworn into office, the government announced its determination to confront the FARC militarily and claw back the Macarena. Susanna Castillo suddenly found herself on the front line of a merciless conflict.

"The FARC became much more aggressive when manual eradication was embarked upon," explains the UN's Sandro Calvani. "It was the first time that we saw the FARC defend the crop as its safe-deposit box was being attacked. If someone were to attack my pension fund, I would also be aggressive. The crops in Macarena is where all the funding for their operations comes from."

"Things were getting worse through 2005," Susanna recalled. "In February three children playing on a field were killed by a land mine." The FARC had started to lay quite a few mines in the region as the Colombian army appeared to be preparing a serious offensive—the U.S. government wanted to see some results for the billions of bucks it had been pouring into the eradication program and the war against the FARC. There was no lack of political will to prosecute the war, but there was a legal problem: La Macarena was a national park and therefore strictly exempt from Washington's favored method of coca eradication—the spraying of plantations with glyphosphate, a killer cocktail supplied by Dow Chemicals and delivered in the field by the U.S. company DynCorp International. How much of La Macarena's unique flora and fauna would be eliminated along with the coca?

Instead, President Uribe announced a new plan, Green Colombia, which would see the military protect hundreds of peasants sent into Meta to pull up the coca by its roots (in any case a more effective method of eradication than fumigation). This was a huge challenge to the FARC—not only was the government intending to move into its area, but it was also bent on literally ripping up its source of income.

"It was about five-thirty in the morning, just as we were getting up, when there was a huge burst of gunfire like thunder right on top of us." Susanna was describing the morning of December 27, 2005, when a 400-strong detachment of FARC guerrillas ambushed soldiers who were protecting the eradication operation. "We just hit the floor and hid under the beds. The fighting continued for two hours and we just remained still." Trapped in their village, the Castillo family sought refuge with a neighbor a little farther from the battle, and here they spent three days. From there they went to join the stream of the dispossessed in Ciudad Bolívar. Susanna admits that her chances of returning to the farm, if it still exists, are now minimal—instead, she, her husband, and five adult sons live in two cramped rooms while during the day she learns to fill out forms.

At least Susanna and her family escaped with their lives. The soldiers of the Colombian army were less fortunate—twenty-nine were killed that day, the bloodiest attack by the FARC in 2005 and further proof that for all the military beef served up by the U.S. Congress in the shape of Plan Colombia, the government of President Uribe does not have the wherewithal to defeat the guerrillas.

Paramilitaries

Massacres such as the one in La Macarena leave a dangerous legacy for local inhabitants. The FARC follows predictable guerrilla tactics: once it has mounted a successful attack such as the one on December 27, they then withdraw and begin preparations for their next surprise attack, allowing the armed forces to assume again their precarious control over a specified territory.

All too often, however, threatening bands of armed masked men follow in the wake of the military. These are the paramilitaries, or *autodefensas*. Like the FARC, they are not nice people. Within days of the Macarena massacre, the paramilitaries had assumed the vanguard role in sniffing out anyone among the civilian population in the area whom they suspected of being FARC collaborators.

In early April 2006, twenty-six-year-old Eliades Pachón, his wife, and their two young children were traveling by bus from Vista Hermosa south to Puerto Rico on the very edge of the Macarena National Park, where he worked as a mechanic. A couple of kilometers before the village of Mattu Bambú, the bus was waved through one of the military checkpoints that had multiplied in the area since the December 27 murders. But in the village itself, the bus was again halted, this time by men wearing undefined fatigues. After ordering everyone off the bus, a masked man read out a list of names, including Pachón's. "They had a list of people, a physical list, and they appeared to be sorting out the passengers according to that list," said Eliades's sister, Janneth. "They called up another couple of people, including the guy next to my brother, who was also wearing a blue jersey, and then the guy with the covered face shouted, 'No—not him. Take the guy with the baby.' He gave the baby to his wife and went with the guy who picked him out. They didn't take him where they had taken the first group but down toward the river instead."

At this point, Janneth's pretty, bright young face began to cloud over. I assumed that she, as a newly recruited NGO worker, was going to outline the general situation facing refugees. Her own story not only took me by complete surprise but did the same for my Colombian friends listening with me as well. As the horror of her narrative unfolded, the entire company bit its collective lip in an effort to hold back the tears. "My brother said, 'Don't kill me—I'll give you anything you want, but please don't kill me!' As he was begging for his life, the man ordering him about took a machine gun from another paramilitary and shot him four times in the face."

As the shots rang out, Janneth's sister-in-law begged the paramilitary leader to allow her to see her husband's body. "If you want to die," the *jefe* answered, "you can go and join your husband. So if I were you I'd stay here and look after your children." Eliades was one of four murdered that day in Mattu Bambú—one of several attacks on civilians in the area that followed the FARC murders in December.

Both Eliades and Janneth were members of the local committees that ran the towns and villages in the absence of any other authority. This is why they were listed as potential FARC sympathizers. This area is on the front line between the FARC's *despeje* and government-controlled territory. Janneth insists that the committees existed purely to ensure that minimal services functioned in what was essentially a lawless area. The twenty-eight-year-old seems an unlikely revolutionary. A single mother of two children, she worked in Puerto Rico as the manager of a liquor store and a waitress at a billiards café. "You have so many groups in the region, so many battles, so many confrontations with the civilians. Three doors down from where we lived, a soldier was killed in a clash with FARC people. The civilians just take their children and hide under a bed. We have nowhere to go, we have no support from anyone—we are entirely unprotected."

She was able to escape the paramilitaries who hunted down her brother and take her two children to Bogotá, where she now works voluntarily assisting other refugees from La Macarena to find somewhere to live in the capital. She is also involved in what appears to be a doomed battle to identify her brother's murderers.

When President Uribe promised President George W. Bush that he would redouble efforts to rein in the cocaine traffic, he faced one problem that towered above all others—the paramilitaries. This loose association of armed killers, infused with extreme right-wing views, act principally as the militia of the drug cartels. But given their close personal and ideological ties to important parts of the Colombian military and their significant fighting role in the war against the FARC, they have long enjoyed both impunity and immunity for their role in the narcotics trade.

"*Autodefensas* is not an enemy of the government," said Sandro Calvani, the chief of the UN anti-drugs office in Bogotá. "They never attacked the government. Instead they are fighting the terrorists; they are protecting people. They are enforcing the law. You'll find many places where police officers are enjoying beers with *autodefensas* all over the country—there is no enmity between them."

In areas like Chocó in the northwest of Colombia, the paramilitaries have "cleansed" entire villages and towns in their efforts to secure cheap land where they can grow not only coca but also large-scale palm plantations to cash in on the growing worldwide market for palm oil around the world and notably in the United States. These villages are as miserable as anything I witnessed during the Yugoslav wars: the peasants have had to leave in a hurry, sometimes in the middle of a meal, and some of the buildings have been leveled by the paramilitaries to force the villagers to join Colombia's army of refugees.

The depth of the difficulties facing President Uribe became apparent in the fall of 2005 when secret tapes revealed that the boss of Colombia's secret police, the DAS, had been trading and selling information to some of the most notorious paramilitary groups. The DAS chief and his deputy were forced to resign, but the president vigorously denied any involvement. Just as well, as the DAS stands accused of having handed out slush funds (provided by the U.S. taxpayer through Plan Colombia) to armed groups who were not only responsible for killing civilians and trades union activists but who were also cultivating and producing cocaine before selling it to the United States.

Since money from Plan Colombia started flowing to the military, the DEA and some Republican members of Congress have been applying pressure on President Uribe to arrest the leaders of the paramilitaries and then to extradite them to the United States. Already embattled in his war with the FARC, the president recognized that he simply didn't have the resources to take on another enemy—armed, motivated, and 30,000 strong—especially as this enemy was inextricably entwined with the military.

Uribe's solution to the paramilitary problem was the Law on Justice and Peace. By this, in short, the paramilitaries agreed to disarm and their leaders would hand themselves over to Colombian justice but they would be exempt from extradition to America. Several thousands of paramilitaries have indeed disarmed and left the countryside, but only, according to UN officials in the barrios of Bogotá, to set up new criminal organizations in the slums of the major cities, where they have quickly established large networks to traffic narcotics.

Gringos

Like the FARC, like corrupt elements in the military, like the narco-trafficking bosses, the paramilitaries in Colombia seem unwilling and unlikely to atone for their devastating impact on society. The country registered a dip in the number of cocaine war–related deaths in the two years after 2002, but at the beginning of 2005, they started creeping up again.

Since the advent of Plan Colombia, the number of hectares of land under the cultivation of coca was down by a few thousand. But thanks to improved techniques, the yield was up year after year. Having started Plan Colombia operating in just six provinces, the FARC finished the four-year period with active units in all but two. The evidence since the early 1970s is overwhelming: the combined policies of the U.S. and Colombian governments fail in what they set out to do—they neither erode the power of the FARC nor stop supersaturation of America and Europe with cocaine.

Since 9/11, the war on terror has been the overriding priority of American foreign policy. The war on drugs, by nurturing a huge and unmanageable criminal swamp in which all manner of undesirables roam freely, almost guarantees that the war on terror can never be won. Those involved in the war on drugs develop an extraordinary zeal and determination to prosecute it whatever the cost. I was shocked when the UN's Sandro Calvani, a biologist by background, confessed, "If somebody should tell me that they have found a new Agent Orange gas that kills all coca but damages the environment very heavily, I would consider it."

Not only does the war on drugs turn biologists into advocates of toxic defoliation programs, but over the decades it has also absorbed trillions of dollars—not just in the obscene profits it generates for the cartels in Colombia and Mexico or the Taliban and the warlords in Afghanistan, but in the incalculable sums spent on offenders around the world. These offenders are usually from underprivileged classes (and in the United States that means that more than 80 percent are drawn from the black or Hispanic minorities). But they languish in jail in the prime of their productive capacity just when the Western economies are suffering a severe long-term shortage of labor.

If the consumption of narcotics in the Western world (the originator and prosecutor of the global model) had dropped by an appreciable amount (after almost half a century), then the supporters of the war on drugs would have a credible argument for staying the course with this policy. But consumption has gone up and up and up. Production has kept pace and the price has gone down and down and down. If, however, the aim is to nurture the gangs, the hoodlums, the terrorists, the insurgents, and the drug billionaires who can corrupt entire countries, then we must carry on regardless.

Ironically, it is Signor Calvani who offers Colombia a chink of hope for the future. Not because of anything concocted by the UN, the United States, the Colombian government, the FARC, or anyone else but because of the shifting drug culture:

Cocaine has no future. Wherever amphetamines and synthetic drugs have arrived onto the market, such as China, Southeast Asia, Mexico, then there is always a big boom and it replaces everything, cocaine, heroin, the lot. It is a pill that looks like an aspirin and is much more user-friendly, it works fast and doesn't involve the paraphernalia of injecting or sniffing, a much better kind of drug— more dangerous, but it works. Here it has already started in Medellín. So the future is in the new drugs. The market will change and determine this. They don't need the narco-traffickers. The future will be completely different.

If it rescues Colombia from purgatory, then there are real benefits to this future.

CHAPTER 12

Code Orange

A s I hand over my laptop to SuperGeek in an anonymous hotel room in downtown São Paulo, I ask him with as much authority as I can muster whether he wishes to use Internet Explorer or Mozilla Firefox. A polite smile is accompanied by a tone usually reserved for those with extreme learning difficulties:

"I'LL BE USING SOMETHING CALLED C-Y-B-E-R-S-C-R-I-P-T."

And then.

"IT'S LIKE . . . mIRC."

You may well ask . . .

I now know that CyberScript enables you to enter IRC (Internet Relay Chat). For some people, this system is as mundane as cornflakes, but for cyber toddlers like myself, IRC is an unknown, unexplored parallel world—a silent cacophony of virtual chatter inhabited by hackers, crackers, geeks, terrorists, and security agents (among others). They communicate in languages that are recognizable on the page, as it were—English, Portuguese, Russian, or Spanish, perhaps. But syntax and vocabulary render the contents of these exchanges unrecognizable. Every step of the way, SuperGeek has to explain a term or an idiom, and still I must strain to get my head around the new concept.

SuperGeek is everything you might imagine. Fresh out of nappies to my aged eyes, he with his fingers on the keyboard recalls the virtuosity of the concert pianist, whereby hands, arms, and mind meld together, enabling human and instrument to act as one. It is only minutes before others are attracted by his siren skills.

At my request, SuperGeek has sent a message over mIRC seeking a *laranja*, or "orange." For reasons neither the crackers nor the police are able to explain, an "orange" is a go-between, a medium who can put living people in touch with their alter egos in the cyberworld. More parochially, the orange's job is to turn stolen virtual money into hard cash. As such, these characters are pivotal figures in the world of cybercrime. A successful orange should move effortlessly in the esoteric world of the hacker while demonstrating the old-fashioned ability to bully, bribe, bamboozle, or blackmail bankers and retailers into accepting ill-gotten credit card and bank account funds.

And we don't have to wait long before an experienced orange with the unusually simple handle, "Bob," is offering his services. "Portuguese isn't his mother tongue," SuperGeek notes. "Could be Spanish, could be English," he adds. "Could he be a copper?" I ask. "Could be," warns my friend. "You never know."

We explain to Bob that we have siphoned several thousand reals from a Banco do Brasil account and we need it in cash. "No problem," messages Bob. "I can deposit it for you in a bank account. Or you can have it by DHL inside some magazines. Or I can transfer it abroad and you can retrieve it as remittances."

Bob further tells us that he has contacts inside a couple of branches of Banco Bradesco (one of Brazil's biggest) and they can disguise any incoming transfers from credit cards or other accounts, no questions asked. He charges 50 percent for the service but will undertake the first transaction free as a gesture of goodwill.

On this occasion, our several thousand reals from Banco do Brasil are not virtual but imaginary. But they needn't have been. SuperGeek knows very well how you go about extracting millions upon millions of dollars from ordinary bank accounts because he was an intimate witness to one of the biggest heists in the short but lucrative history of Brazilian cybercrime, which culminated in a huge police sweep dubbed Operation Pegasus.

In late August 2005, a young man answered the doorbell to a small flat in São Paulo. Standing in front of him was the postman. "I have a book to deliver for Max," he said. The young man hesitated—this was not the same postman who had delivered letters to his address for years.

"There's nobody called Max living here," he lied, thinking on his feet. "You must have the wrong address."

"But I have a parcel for him. It's very urgent."

As Max closed the door, the postman tried one more time.

"It's from The Apprentice," he called in vain.

"If I'd have accepted that parcel, I would have been arrested," Max said later. On that day and the next, 114 people were arrested in seven different provinces of Brazil and in the capital, Brasilia. All were taken for questioning on suspicion of involvement in the theft of around $33 million from bank accounts in Brazil, Venezuela, the United Kingdom, and the United States. The investigation by the newly formed Federal Division of Cybercrime police had been running for several months, having evolved out of two earlier cases—Operation Cash Net and Operation Trojan Horse.

Back in the São Paulo hotel, SuperGeek recalled the events that led up to the arrests. "It all started when I was chatting with a few friends online about tech stuff," he said. His two closest cyberpals in the IRC chat room were young Brazilians, KG and Max, with whom he would exchange all manner of information about computers but also about games and music. They were teenagers having fun.

"Every so often, this stranger called The Apprentice would enter the chat room and ask the same question: "Does anyone have any shells?" At first, SuperGeek, KG, and Max told The Apprentice to get lost. They were a touch mystified as to why anybody would persist in trying to collect shells—programs that enable people to interact with operating systems (the building blocks of most computers).

But The Apprentice was persistent, returning each time with the same question: "Does anyone have any shells?" Finally, KG decided to investigate and agreed to enter into a private chat with The Apprentice.

For a month or so, KG disappeared. Max and SuperGeek attempted to contact him over Microsoft Messenger or IRC, but in vain. This loss of contact is common in a culture that prizes anonymity above all else. Like most such online relationships, the friendship between the three cyberpals was fragmented and based on a minimal yet intense intimacy. They did not know where one another lived, what their socioeconomic backgrounds were, or what they looked like. When somebody just disappears off the screen with no apparent explanation, you can't drop in on them at home to find out what's going on. And it is axiomatic that any virtual partner may be lying. Calibrating trust on the Internet is even more difficult than doing so in the real world. This uncertainty is both the sword of Ajax and the Achilles' heel of cybercriminals.

A month after vanishing, KG returned to the chat room with a virtual swagger. "The Apprentice and I have been working on something real big," he told his two friends. "And very worthwhile." Despite their irritation at both his disappearing act and his sudden reappearance, Max and SuperGeek were curious to hear KG's story.

The shells that The Apprentice so prized, KG explained, were needed to send e-mails. Lots of them—50,000 in each batch. In order to stop e-mail servers from recognizing these e-mails as spam, it is necessary to hijack the shells from other people's computers so the e-mail server cannot tell that the same source is generating them all.

KG revealed that The Apprentice would pay him fifty dollars for every 1 million e-mails he dispatched to unsuspecting PC users. That amounted to a few evenings' work, and for a young unemployed Brazilian such as KG, this wage was a small fortune. KG now wanted Max and SuperGeek to join in.

To speed up their work, they developed their own computer program called GetMail, which was able to scan particular countries and servers and download millions of e-mail addresses. They then wrote a second program called Remover, which canceled any duplicate addresses, and, finally, using the shells they had collected beachcombing the Internet, they put together the lists of 50,000 e-mails a shot.

KG had already been doing this work for a month, and evidently he had performed his tasks well. In consequence, The Apprentice had promoted him to the position of recruiter (cutting out the arduous task of spam-list building), for which he earned a basic wage of $1,500 per calendar month plus commission. So KG was on the second rung of a hierarchy that is almost impossible to map—learning from insurgency and terrorist networks in particular, cybercriminals operate in cell form and so each player interacts with only two or three colleagues. The rest of the conspiracy is as obscure to them as it was initially to the police.

Although only 14 percent of Brazil's 188 million people are regular Internet users (or *internauts,* as they are known there), almost three-quarters of these carry out the bulk of their financial transactions online, which along with South Korea is thought to be the highest ratio of users to Internet banking in the world. Ninety percent file their internal revenue returns online as well. Compared with those in the United States and Western Europe, Brazilian banks offer much wider services with correspondingly more sophisticated security arrangements. For some years, bank customers in Brazil have enjoyed real-time transfer of money throughout the system. Clients have to overcome up to five different security hurdles in order to access their accounts. They have become used, for example, to onscreen keyboards activated by mouse clicks to circumvent Trojan spyware that monitors the strikes of physical keyboards. The banks were also the pioneers of dynamic fobs on which users receive constantly changing passwords. "When you arrive in America from Brazil," chuckles Rogeriot Morais, head of the Brazil operation of the global cybersecurity firm ISS, "and you see them still fiddling around with checks, it looks very quaint."

For the customer, Internet banking is seductively convenient. For the banks, it is a monumental money saver, as their labor costs have plummeted since its inception. For the light-fingered, it is an irresistible source of revenue. And for law enforcement, it presents a taxing challenge. Essentially, the Net cannot be policed without massive assistance from the private sector—even then, as a member of the cybercrime unit in Brasilia remarked, law enforcement is "always running behind these people." "They get round new security blocks within hours of their insertion into a network," he continued.

The Apprentice and his regiment of Pegasus spammers sent out a variety of e-mails to the addresses they had culled, containing one of two types of messages. The first, for domestic consumption, purported to come from one of the big Brazilian banks or from the Inland Revenue. These were simple "phishing" e-mails, requesting that the customer fill in his or her details and return the e-mail. The details, of course, would go to the scammers, who would then roam around the "phished" bank accounts at will.

Still more insidious is the type designed for international consumption. E-mails carrying messages like "Someone loves you! Find out who!" encouraged the recipient to click on a hyperlink to a website. "As soon as that screen came up, you had a key logger on your computer," said SuperGeek. "You were finished."

A key logger monitors every stroke of your keyboard and sends back the information to whoever placed it there. Using that information, the cybercriminal is then in a position to extract your passwords and enter your bank account and clean it of funds. SuperGeek tells me that each batch of about 50,000 e-mails would guarantee The Apprentice about 200 infections—that is 200 computers that the criminals could effectively control. Although a mere 0.4 percent of the e-mails sent, this take-up allows the theft of phenomenal sums and explains the attractiveness of cybercrime. According to the federal police, The Apprentice and his dozens of co-conspirators got away with $33 million before Operation Pegasus put an end to it. The scam had been running only a few months, and an even larger conspiracy from the previous year, 2004, had netted the criminals $125 million.

The era of the malicious virus that chewed up computer screens, destroyed your hard disk, or directed you to vile pornographic websites is fast coming to a close. These attacks were the work of so-called ego hackers. They were designed to make the computer users' life a misery as projects that had taken months or years were destroyed for the sake of an adolescent giggle. Now viruses, Trojan horses, worms, and other malware go largely unnoticed because the sun has set on the age of the ego hacker and the dawn is rising on the era of the criminal hacker, or cracker. In 2003, "90 percent of attacks were still the work of ego hackers," reported Peter Allor, the head of X-Force, the intelligence division of ISS, one of the world's biggest Internet security companies. "Now that is reversed—90 percent of attacks are criminal and therefore much more difficult to detect. They want to disguise the fact that they are out there. So when the Zotob virus provoked the crash of CNN's system in 2005," he continued, "we knew that the virus's designers had made a mistake—they had failed to update their virus to take into account a Microsoft update. That's a good thing—the criminals make mistakes too." But not often enough.

With stealth becoming a guiding principle of malware, the ordinary computer user has become yet more vulnerable than before. "The only safe computer is one that is switched off," I am assured by Kau, a Brazilian of Lithuanian parentage who specializes in testing computer security. "Maybe you can check what's on at the local movies on the Internet, but any more than that and it is only a matter of time before you are infected, even if you are assiduous at keeping your antivirus updated." Standing proud next to Kau is a pack of sour-cream-'n'-onion-flavored Pringles. When he pops open the plastic top, instead of those annoyingly addictive chips he pulls out a copper wire with a series of silver disks placed at regular intervals. "If we attach Mr. Pringle to the laptop," demonstrates Kau, "then we immediately have a live directional antenna that can home in on any local wireless system." For his research work, he has already hacked into the systems of several major companies in the center of São Paulo (he is *not* a criminal). If that's what you can do with a tube of chips and a bit of metal, just imagine what is possible with some really fancy gear!

But interestingly, it is not technology that inflicts the greatest damage in the cyberworld. "You tell me that the only safe computer is the one that is turned off," retorts Marcos Flávio Assunção, a demigod among the white hats (noncriminal good hackers) of Belo Horizonte. "But what if I can persuade somebody to turn that computer on? Not so safe after all!" He beams. Marcos is explaining to me about what the cybercriminal and security worlds refer to as "social engineering"; that is, the ability to influence people's actions. The most popular method of invading computers is through downloads and websites that many users find irresistible—music and pornography.

And here, dear reader (especially the men among you), is an important lesson—if you indulge in either of those two habits, stop it now if you value your privacy. Lesson two of Glenny's cyber gospel concerns e-mails—if you are not convinced by both the sender and the subject of an e-mail (the computers of your closest friends can be invaded and transformed into part of a "botnet" that sends out illicit e-mails at the will of the criminal), then don't open it—just delete it. Among the most successful e-mail-borne viruses of all time was the I Love You virus, an assertion that brings out the irrational in even the most urbane among us. I was extremely fortunate, as the first person to send me this e-mail was an ex-girlfriend who nursed all sorts of feelings about me, but love was decidedly not among them. I deleted the e-mail without further ado and spared myself a nasty infection.

It is not just your bank account that is at risk: your entire "identity" can be seized, whereby somebody else rifles through not just your credit cards and bank accounts but your social security number, your passport, and so on to the point at which if the person commits a crime, a warrant may be put out for your arrest. "In 2005, global losses attributable to identity theft stood at $52.6 billion," Peter Allor of ISS told me. But, as he explained, although the spectacular identity thefts make the headlines, they are sometimes inadvertent. If you have a big "data breach," as he terms it, "then you get the Secret Service and the feds on your back." Much cybercriminal activity is aimed at filching small amounts of money from large numbers of people. "If I can get one credit card from you and I do a twenty-five-buck transaction, will you notice? Will you report it? Will they do anything with it? Twenty-five dollars—no police force in the world is going to chase twenty-five dollars." But if you take twenty-five dollars from a million people, you will become rich.

Allor believes a Manichaean, even apocalyptic, struggle drives his industry of cybersecurity. "This is an arms race. I call it a sword-and-shield issue. In the underworld, they have an ever-sharper sword, the malcoders, and you have to research it all to have a shield that can cover every thrust of that sword. If you can determine that something is not working properly, a vulnerability in your system, then you know you've got a big problem, because if you've found it, you can bet the underworld will know about it soon—if they don't already. It now takes the underworld about forty-eight hours to sniff out a vulnerability. How long does it take a corporation to be made aware of that and find an update? The fast ones are about thirty days. The majority are running thirty to sixty days. And the home user? Are they even aware?"

ISS's Cyber Control Center in Atlanta, Georgia, is so reminiscent of The

Code Orange

Bridge on the USS *Enterprise* from *Star Trek* that I almost expect a Klingon commander to appear on one of the vast screens dominating the end of the room and issue a sinister threat. In fact, the screens are reporting all manner of security alerts, attempted attacks, and a frenetic blizzard of data, all of which means nothing to me. The nearest we get to a Klingon is the giant image of a CNN anchor, as ISS has a constant news feed in case a relevant story crops up. In front of this spectacular control panel sit maybe a dozen computer operators with the appropriate sprinkling of pimply adolescents, ponytails, and Asian Americans who are silently warding off attempted attacks on ISS's corporate clients around the world by spotting and then shoring up vulnerabilities in their computer systems.

ISS is one of the leaders in the multibillion-dollar Internet security industry, which has flourished in the wake of the viruses and Trojans. The company helped to reformulate the entire concept of computer protection—instead of going after specific viruses and spyware (which is how programs such as Norton AntiVirus function), they started examining the defense capability of individual programs or systems. In fact, they ape the hackers and crackers by sniffing out vulnerabilities in anything from Windows to entire banking networks. And X-Force is the virtual equivalent of the CIA, trying to penetrate the mind-set and logic of the enemy. At times, Peter Allor's explanations of what X-Force actually does sound as mind-bending as the most impenetrable passages from Stephen Hawking's *A Brief History of Time.* "You're familiar with darknet, right?" he asks me. I shuffle and cough a little, not wanting to appear stupid. "Errm . . . not terribly familiar, no."

> Okay. Darknet is a set of IPs [Internet protocols, for the uninitiated] that have never been addressed—they were never assigned anywhere . . . they're dark, so nothing should ever come out of them and nothing should ever be addressed to them. Well, we run a darknet and we have a nice set of contiguous IPs there and so we see a lot of back scatter from across the Internet, which is scanning, and it shouldn't be there. So we take the information from gray nets and honey nets, which are waiting for things to come out, and we also crawl the Internet. Are you familiar with drive-by browsing?

You know what? I think to myself. *I'll save drive-by browsing for another day.*

Obscure though their work might be, X-Force, ISS, and similar organizations form an absolutely critical barrier, preventing the world from being swamped by viral infections, Trojans, and spyware. But the shift from ego hacking to cybercrime contains huge dangers.

Computer technology is advancing into every sphere of Western homes and businesses. No longer restricted to obvious gadgets like printers, scanners, and ATMs, it is being built into telephones, televisions, cars, washing machines, vending machines, and more. "If you find yourself in a hotel where hackers are holding a conference, stay clear of the elevators," warns Allor, smiling. "You'll never make it to the right floor—believe me, it's happened." There is nothing that a mischievous hacker enjoys more than telling a lift to go to the seventeenth floor when someone presses on the button for the thirty-third floor. Each of these peripherals (the gadgets hooked up to the central computer) has an IP address; that is, it has a separate cyber identity, which is then linked to other machines with IP addresses through a network. In a medium-size business, there will be hundreds of these units—and each of them is a separate portal through which an attack can take place.

Already businesses store data of incalculable value on their systems, but soon most people will be using voice-over Internet Protocol telephone systems for the bulk of their verbal communications. VoIP networks such as Skype are increasingly attractive for offices, as they reduce costs so dramatically. But what would happen if your business depended on telephone sales and somebody inserted a virus into the system to block the phones?

"Today antivirus programs are becoming ever less important because they can't protect you," Amrit Williams pointed out. The thoughtful chief of security analysis at America's leading tech consultant, Gartner, Williams is concerned about the potential for destruction now that organized crime has lured the hackers away from mischief and into the underworld. "Virus companies can detect only things that have signatures. Now cybercriminals are writing specific malware designed to attack a single company—be it Morgan Stanley, be it Visa, or be it the BBC," Williams continued. "We recently came across a worrisome case in which the Russian mafia was producing perfect copies of Windows with the plastic wrapping and everything. They looked perfect—but of course they had the spyware already loaded on them." As Williams pointed out, it is not difficult for organized crime to insert such software into the licit market, as syndicates are especially practiced at controlling distribution and retail markets.

It is not a coincidence that Russia and Brazil are world beaters in electronic crime. Along with China, they form the top tier. The only country missing is India.

> With loads of money, the world is your oyster, you can do whatever
> you want whenever you want, all women are the same to a man with
> money, and the next day will dawn even better. The thing to do was
> to buy heaps of coke and go round chopping out lines for his
> friends . . . buy a flat in Copacabana, screw doctors' daughters, have
> a phone and TV and hop over to the States from time to time like his
> aunt's employer. One day he'd hit the jackpot.
>
> —Paulo Lins, *City of God*

It was soon after the millennium that Brazil started creeping onto the
radar of cybersecurity firms. With Russia and China, it now forms a
mighty triumvirate of the virtual underworld. It has earned its place for
several reasons, a curious confluence of social and economic factors. Even
if these were to change in the near future, Brazil will remain a key center of
cybercrime simply because the profit levels are astronomical. No other sector of organized crime can match the growth rates of cybercrime, which
are currently running in the region of 25 percent annually. Furthermore,
the industry is multifaceted, accommodating old and new crimes. Policing
it is a nightmare, even though in its mass form, it is still extremely young.

In the legitimate world of computer technology, particular branches
"cluster" in certain geographical regions. Scandinavia has long been at the
forefront of cell or mobile phone technology, for example, while California, Toulouse, and Munich are leading biotechnology centers. A variety
of circumstances may contribute to the emergence of such clusters—
proximity to cutting-edge research institutes; tax incentive schemes and
other government policies, local and national; significant financial and
lifestyle benefits for employees; and even serendipity.

The clustering of cybercrime is the result of an equally complex mix.
There are several prerequisites, but three are paramount: steep levels of
poverty and unemployment; a high standard of basic education for a
majority of the population; and a strong presence of more traditional
organized crime forms. Nobody fits the bill better than the so-called BRIC
nations—Brazil, Russia, India, and China. These are the leading countries
among the emerging markets, the second tier of global power after the G8
(though politically Russia straddles the two). South Africa is regarded as a
reserve player in the BRIC grouping because although a regional giant like
the others, it cannot compete economically. It also fails as a cybercrime
center because its standards of education have yet to recover from the
damage inflicted by apartheid (see page 274).

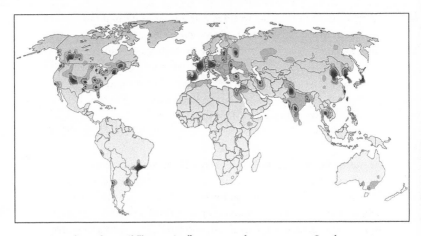

Snapshot of e-mail "harvesting" centers and spam targets, October 2006. São Paulo, Beijing, and Moscow are the chief farmers; Western Europe and the United States are the main targets. South Korea and Bangalore (India's main techno-cluster) are also important.

Brazil, by contrast, fits the bill almost perfectly. Even in the *favelas*, various government and NGO schemes are steadily improving access to computers and the Internet. With social disparities and tensions akin to those in South Africa and Colombia, Brazil is well known for its high level of crime. Foreigners are warned to keep wallets well guarded and told not to resist when confronted by a knife- or gun-wielding assailant. The *favelas* of Rio and other major cities mix extreme poverty with drugs, guns, and violence—sometimes less than a mile from the most fabulous dwellings overlooking the beaches of Ipanema or Copacabana. It is this profound division that lies at the heart of Brazil's hugely powerful criminal culture, described with such biting accuracy by Paulo Lins. In his novel *City of God*, he details life in the eponymous grim estate in western Rio, which in the 1960s drew its inhabitants, including Lins, from the inner city of South America's funkiest city with the false promise of improved living standards. Fernando Mereilles's Oscar-winning film of the same name freezes the blood with its evocation of violence and despair fueled by the *favelas*' tribal rivalries and drug trade.

Rio's *favelas* produce some of the finest documentary films in the world, a testimony to the openness of the culture. This was the only country I encountered in which not a single person asked me to turn off my tape recorder when I spoke to him or her. Brazilians are fanatical communicators (witness the huge success of Orkut, an equivalent of MySpace in Brazil), and so it is easy to learn a great deal about the country (the dark and light sides) in a short space of time, especially in Rio.

But in the past decade, São Paulo has eclipsed Rio, becoming the great epicenter of both Brazil's crazed spurt of economic growth and the uncontrollable rise of its organized crime. Flying into São Paulo from the Atlantic toward its airport lying in the west is an unbelievable experience. No longer a city but a megalopolis of 20 million people, from above it looks like an entire civilization built from tons of Lego bricks and stretching beyond the horizon. But it is not like Chicago, Jo'burg, or even London, where huge skyscrapers gather tightly in a center surrounded by sprawl. The skyscrapers appear on the outskirts and never stop, the *favelas* almost having to fight for their place in between them.

The economic force pulls in migrants not just from Brazil's poverty-stricken northeast and west-center but from all over South America and beyond, pumping out goods and services with a frenetic energy at which the *cariocas* in Rio sneer (just as the *paulistas* sneer at the *cariocas* for believing that the main aim of life is the pursuit of pleasure and not the pursuit of money).

Despite the dire warnings regarding street crime, the center of São Paulo, serviced by an excellent metro system, feels as secure and as modern as the center of Madrid. It certainly doesn't feel like Crime Central.

But surrounding this urban vortex lies a network of prisons that are among the most overcrowded in the world. The conditions for the prisoners are atrocious, and there exists a permanent state of low-level warfare among inmates and between the inmates and the warders. Two days after I had set foot in South America for the first time in May 2006, these prisons exploded in violence—right on cue. The uprising of the Primeiro Comando da Capital (PCC, the First Capital Command) was shocking in the bitterness of the violence it spawned.

Founded in 1993 by a hulk called Geleãio (Big Jelly), the PCC is one of the largest, most unpredictable, and most dangerous organized crime syndicates in the world. It can mobilize many thousands of members, who are recruited while stagnating in Brazil's crumbling jails. The money available to the leading prisoners enables them to corrupt and subvert the warders, allowing them all manner of privileges, most critically mobile phones, which prison officers will permit inside the jails for a consideration of $300.

Its pampered, violent leaders can direct the tentacles of the PCC deep into the *favelas,* transforming the slums into training grounds for deadly drug warriors. In contrast to other major organized crime groups around the world, it does not seek to expand abroad, and neither does it assiduously avoid law enforcement and detection. Instead, it occasionally and viciously confronts it. Its most determined and sustained attempt began in mid-May 2006.

At first, the *paulistas* appeared to dismiss the May events as an insignificant eruption of lumpen aggression. But on the first night of the unrest, the PCC demonstrated how powerful it had become in the thirteen years of its existence. Members tore through the streets of São Paulo, slaughtering policemen and their civilian relations. Patrol cars, off-duty coppers sitting down to dinner, senior officers having a drink in bar—all were targeted. Clearly, the PCC possessed significant intelligence, which they deployed ruthlessly as they ranged around the city on bloody parade, wielding machetes, machine guns, and hammers. They set fire to dozens of buses and cars and threw up roadblocks. The marauding criminals moved around many areas, rich and poor, delivering an especial fright to the former, who are not used to the quotidian violence experienced by the latter.

The following day saw the zinging megalopolis stilled as the industrious population cowered inside their homes. Workers were too frightened to risk traveling on the city's vulnerable public transport network.

Soon spokesmen for the PCC started cropping up regularly in the media, couching their reasons for rebellion within the cliché-ridden language of universal human rights, saying that they needed to draw attention to their plight. Their pleas were rather undermined by the brutality of their methods, and over the next few days, the many public prosecutors and detectives whom I met all said the same thing: "This is a challenge to the police—they want to show us how powerful they are and that we must negotiate with them at all times." Elizeu Eclair Teixeira Borges, the state military police commander, was more forthright at a news conference: "This is war and we are not going to retreat. There will be more death," he said.

What he didn't say was that it was the police's turn to do the killing. After the initial mayhem resulted in almost 100 deaths, the police responded in the next two months by killing almost five times as many—and just as the prisoners were not too choosy about whom they wasted, neither were the coppers. It almost began to look as though the kumbaya human rights rhetoric that the PCC spokesmen had been using might not be so spurious after all.

Latent mob violence in Brazil lies nearer the surface than in its counterparts in Europe and Asia. This degree of paramilitary organization among criminals, with the will and ability to confront the authorities, would be unthinkable in Moscow or Beijing.

My guide to the peculiarities of Brazil's extensive criminal landscape could not have been better informed. A judge and former chief of the National Drug Office in Brasilia, Walter Maierovitch is the most respected voice on organized crime in Brazil. In clipped, detail-laden sentences, he outlined to me the various factors that in his opinion have allowed the country to become the great center of transnational criminal operations, in particular linking the markets and production regions of southern Europe, West Africa, and North and South America. He regarded the events of May 2006 as nothing less than a declaration "of war on the state of São Paulo . . . Like fundamentalist terrorist organizations and the mafia, the PCC uses attacks and then goes into hiding, lulling authorities into a false sense of security." The origins of the crisis lie in what Maierovitch calls the "inhuman conditions" that pertain in Brazil's prisons, but he is nonetheless perturbed at the state's inability to counter the cancerous growth of the PCC.

The political response to the challenge of the PCC in May 2006 highlights a profound weakness in Brazil's system, which helps to explain why the country became a refuge for transnational crime organizations during the 1990s. As soon as the PCC took to the streets, the government of President Lula offered to send in the army to quell the troops. The governor of São Paulo province, who was from the opposition, rejected the offer as a provocation, saying that forces under his control were perfectly capable of dealing with the issue. It was hard to avoid the impression that both the federal and provincial governments were more interested in scoring political points than in dealing with the crisis.

As Walter Maierovitch pointed out to me, Brazil also suffers acutely from a problem that often dogs federal systems—dueling policemen. The animosity and jealousies that inform relations between the state police, the federal police, the military police (which have civilian jurisdiction), and the special forces are crippling. "In the United States, you have regular difficulties between federal agencies such as the DEA, the CIA, and the FBI," Maierovitch explained, "but at least it demonstrates that they talk to each other on some level. With our federal system in Brazil, there is no conflict because the provincial and the federal agencies have no contact whatsoever with one another. And they certainly don't do anything radical like share information," he added with an ironic shrug.

He ascribes the growth of the PCC and their equivalents, such as the

Red Command in Rio, in the first place to the profits they have made from the drug trade. Maierovitch was a scourge of the huge multisyndicates who made Brazil their home base in the 1980s and 1990s. Nonetheless, he insists, "The war on drugs is a farce. . . . And it looks as though Lula, our president, will continue to bend to America's prohibitionist policy. However, there are signs that Europe is continuing to distance itself from the UN Conventions, which follow the American line. As the market leader, the United States' strategy of consumer reduction is a dead end."

While the Colombians sent most of their cocaine to the United States through Mexico and the Caribbean, the supplies for Europe (via West Africa and later South Africa) were processed through Brazil. The presence of Latin America's largest chemical industry in Brazil encouraged this growth, as Brazilian narcotics traffickers did not have to import precursor chemicals to the turn the paste into powder (unlike their counterparts in Colombia, Peru, and Bolivia). But Maierovitch says they have been greatly helped by the specific weaknesses of the Brazilian system of policing and the profound levels of corruption met throughout the judicial and political system.

Soft-spoken, with owlish features, Maierovitch first came to prominence in the early 1980s when he assisted Giovanni Falcone in his successful efforts to track down Mafia fugitives from Italian justice. Together the two men persuaded Tommaso Buscetta to return to Italy and become a state witness in the so-called Maxi Trial of the Sicilian Mafia's *cupola,* its secretive board of directors. This evidence eventually led to the conviction of some 350 senior Mafia operatives in January 1992.

Falcone and his fellow magistrate, Paolo Borsellino, are the titans of anti-mafia law enforcers the world over. When they were murdered in Sicily within two months of each other, soon after the Maxi Trial sentence had been confirmed in 1992, their deaths shook and finally toppled the old political establishment in Italy. Both men had worked on the assumption (quite correctly) that the major figures of the Sicilian Mafia enjoyed protection among the highest political echelons of Rome.

Maierovitch reminisces about his dinners with Falcone and how they sought to protect the great *pentito* (informer) Buscetta from either assassination or suicide. (He very nearly succeeded in killing himself on the Brazilian judge's watch.) At first Maierovitch smiles when describing his late Italian friend, but before long he starts shedding quiet tears—a fitting tribute to Falcone (after whom Maierovitch named his Institute on Organized Crime), whose charisma and commitment to justice in the face of resistance from Rome's corrupt elite has made him a folk hero throughout Italy and among crime fighters everywhere.

The crimes of the Mafia and the two deaths led to a popular revulsion, which ensured that the Sicilian Mafia has been in full retreat ever since. (Unfortunately, the same doesn't apply to their cousins in crime, the 'ndrangheta, the Camorra, and the Sacra Corona Unità.) But although Maierovitch helped to inflict a devastating blow on the Mafia inside Italy, Buscetta's arrest had little impact on the transnational activity of the Mafia's overseas diaspora, not least in Brazil. Along with Montreal, Canada, Rio and São Paulo had become home to the mightiest export and money-laundering syndicate in the world, devised and run by two families, closely related through marriage, the Cuntrera-Cuarana clans, known collectively as the Rothschilds of the Mafia.

Ironically, the two families had fled from Sicily in the early 1960s to escape a fratricidal Mafia war to a Brazil under military dictatorship, where they found the perfect environment to set up in business.

But their masterstroke involved moving into Aruba, the semi-independent Dutch colonial possession off the coast of Venezuela, during the 1980s. Aruba became renowned as the Mafia's very own island. "A magnificent washing machine is sold here, its trademark is Aruba," a despairing minister of Aruba's government warned in parliament. "The machine is an Aruban-Colombian product, its model called Cartel. The brand is well known for its good performance in the United States and Europe. It is recommended by former ministers, members of parliament, owners of casinos, supermarkets, cosmetics manufacturers, and importers of cars and batteries. The washing machine fits everybody who has become inexplicably rich from one day to another."

It was here, through the good offices of the Cuntrera-Cuarana families, that the Medellín and Cali cartels opened negotiations with Solntsevo representatives from Moscow; with Bulgarian traffickers; and, of course, with countless Caribbean and Central American traffickers about the global expansion of cocaine that took place during the 1990s.

Some senior family members were arrested in Canada, some in Venezuela, resulting in deportations to Italy. But the grand old octogenarian founder of the whole scheme still lives unmolested a stone's throw from the Copacabana beach in Rio.

It is an epic tale that Maierovitch tells. And implicit at every stage of his narrative lies the struggle between Brazil's astonishing exuberance and dynamism and its befouled institutions; a tale of a country of people who are deeply proud of their achievements and viscerally angry about the injustice and corruption encountered daily. Never underestimate, for example, the social cohesion that Brazil's status as the world's most gifted soccer nation confers on them. For many years, this was an important compensation for having to live in the shadow of Argentina. But now Brazil has eclipsed their southern neighbor as the decisive economy in Latin America. But for all its growing wealth, the great heart of its economy, São Paulo, can be brought to its knees in a matter of hours by one of the most powerful and unaccountable criminal networks in the world. Dealing with the PCC and its associates would probably be more than a match for most police forces (even properly organized ones). In São Paulo, Rio, and elsewhere in Brazil, the police and prosecutors I talked to were committed, smart, and very hardworking. But deeply ingrained traditions of hierarchy and authoritarianism restrict their capacity to act. There are signs that this may be beginning to change, but when it comes to policing the transnational threats that coalesce in and around the country's borders, the Brazilian police simply do not have the resources to manage. As Maierovitch is detailing the permanent sense of crisis among Brazil's police and judiciary, he talks of crime in Brazil as a hydra—cut off one head and another two appear. I ask him for an example. He is quiet for a moment and then says just three words. "Lao Kin Chong."

Commander Protógenes Queiroz was going to take no chances this time. In late May, he flew his special unit into São Paulo incognito. The director general of the federal police (FP) in Brasilia had chosen him personally to carry out the climax of Operation Shogun (or Operation Gatinho [Kitten], as the FP team referred to it among themselves). The easiest way to blow months of careful planning was to give the police in São Paulo advance warning of the impending raids.

"The first five officers arrived early, part of the Federal Police Tactical Operations unit, which is a special force we have," recalled the urbane but determined police chief. "Any incoming aircraft would have aroused the suspicions of the São Paulo police. So my officers had a cover story: one of them came in handcuffs so it looked like a straightforward prisoner transfer." To make sure that the real purpose of the mission remained secret, Commander Queiroz was also monitoring the São Paulo force. "The head of the airport called the police superintendent, informing him: 'An aircraft from Brasilia is arriving, with federal police officers.' 'How many are they?' 'Four, bringing a prisoner.' " Success—the ruse had worked.

Code Orange

Earlier that year, a commercial agent from São Paulo approached the head of a parliamentary inquiry examining Brazil's rampant culture of piracy. The agent explained that his associate, Lao Kin Chong, a naturalized Brazilian from China in his early forties, was interested in assisting the senator in his efforts to address this troubling issue. This was not wholly surprising, as Lao's activities were at the center of the inquiry. And the assistance the agent was offering was not designed to clear up these circumstances—it was in fact a very large bribe. The senator agreed to meet Lao, but he also informed the federal police.

The main street in the São Paulo district, Iphigenia, reveals the extent to which counterfeit goods are available to the consumer. Outside the shops, young men stand in front of boards pinned with CD-ROM covers—there is not a computer program in the world not sold here, all of them pirated, and I am able to buy for two dollars a copy of the forthcoming Windows OS, Vista, long before it is available on the licit market. Delighted by my interest, the vendor starts chanting in Portuguese, "Don't be an American slave, be a patriot and buy fake goods!" This commercial anti-Americanism helps to sustain popular support for the trade in illicit goods in Brazil and, indeed, throughout South America. Other than the police and lawyers involved in the struggle against piracy, not a single Brazilian to whom I spoke considered the trade immoral. Minutes after my purchase, the street vendors' efficient system of lookouts has signaled that two policemen are scouring the streets. Within seconds, the stalls are packed up and the salesmen have been soaked up by the viscous sea of shoppers trying to crowd into the malls. Inside you can buy any type of electronic goods imaginable—cameras, iPods, laptops, real Sonys, fake Samsungs, all piled higgledy-piggledy on top of one another. "My friend, my friend," they shout, "please buy, very cheap." They specialize in the generic fakes—a Microsoft keyboard that is in fact proudly produced by Krown Electronics; or a flat-screen TV by Semsing. But they all share one characteristic—Made in China.

Ismael, a seller of Lebanese descent (of whom there are many in South America), explains that they come in through three entry points: through the Bolivian border into the central province of Matto Grosso; via the northeast port of Natal; and above all through the legendary Ciudad del Este, the Paraguayan gangster capital suspected by American intelligence as a center of al Qaeda activity. It sits next to Brazil and Argentina in the so-called tri-border region. "The bulk of Lao's goods arrived in São Paulo through Ciudad," explained Pedro Barbosa, the prosecutor for the São Paulo state with responsibility for the Lao case. "And there was a lot of it."

Working with the Paraguayan authorities has its challenges. "You must remember that 60 percent of Ciudad's annual income is derived from smuggling," Barbosa continued. "We have one reliable contact with whom we liaise, but generally Paraguay is not a reliable channel."

Barbosa explained that there had been several attempts to arrest Lao in the past, but all of them failed—"that's why Protógenes Queiroz didn't tell anybody what he was doing that morning." Lao Kin Chong began building his enormous empire, based around his shopping malls on the Avenue of March 25, in the early 1990s. He would import anything into Brazil, paying minimal, if any, taxes and flagrantly ignoring any rules of international copyright. Most of the patents and rights to this intellectual property reside with Americans and American companies, and the U.S. government takes its role seriously, pressing Brazil and similar recalcitrant nations to do something about piracy. Days after Lao's arrest, Jack Valenti, CEO of The Motion Picture Association of America, excoriated Brazil's record on piracy as "abysmal." Describing the end of Lao Kin Chong's activities as the "one bright spot" to a Senate hearing in Washington, he also claimed that in Brazil "one out of every three tapes or DVDs is pirated. Our member companies lose an estimated $120 million every year in Brazil to piracy. . . . Even in those jurisdictions where police have conducted raids, less than 1 percent of all raids result in convictions."

Lao himself has always kept his counsel, denying any wrongdoing and restricting his comments to one sentence on his arrest: "This is a bad joke." But he could not get around the fact that his commercial agent had offered the senator $1.5 million. Nor could he deny the videotaped evidence of the agent turning up with the first $75,000 in cash as a down payment for the senator's help in influencing the appointment of a new São Paulo police chief. Once Lao was remanded in custody on charges of bribery and obstructing the course of justice, the federal police had a free hand to investigate his entire business dealings. Several of his relatives, including his wife, were arrested, and before long new charges of piracy and smuggling were preferred against him, ensuring that he will remain in jail for a long time.

When he was sentenced in July 2005 for bribery, the federal police and Queiroz in particular rightly patted themselves on the back for the success of an arduous operation fraught with risks. Lao was the most powerful and successful criminal businessman ever arrested in Brazil. But within a few months of his initial incarceration, Roberto Porto, investigator at the Chinese organized crime unit of the São Paulo police, noticed something happening. "Most of the Chinese working in the markets of São Paulo are illegal immigrants. They are unprotected, and the last thing on their mind is to go to the police—they think as soon as they do, they'll be deported," he said. "So Lao Kin Chong gave them protection." In São Paulo's Chinese community, Lao was the state and the police. "When Lao was arrested two years ago," Porto continued, "everyone lost their protection." And that is when things for the Chinese of São Paulo started to get nasty.

Porto's office noticed that two groups were vying for supremacy. "There is the Hong Kong triad, Sun Yee On, and their competitors are from Fujian Province on the mainland," he revealed. Both use much more direct methods to consolidate their influence. "Both appear to send teams from China as enforcers. They arrive through Ciudad but remain here only for a few months." During this time, these SWAT teams of organized crime will intimidate, threaten, assault, and if necessary murder anyone who fails to pay protection or who tries to shop them. "Then, having done their job, they return to China or, who knows, somewhere else. We simply don't have time or resources to keep track of them." Porto described what happened to one of his few informers who was watched by the extortionists—the details are too vile to reproduce here, but the informant did not survive the ordeal. "We don't have any Chinese-speaking officers, only interpreting services," he lamented. As I looked around his spartan office with its dowdy sofa, fraying carpets, and peeling paint, the enormity of the problems facing law enforcement in a globalized world was all too obvious. Even if Brazil's police forces were rationally organized, this country cannot afford the facilities and equipment needed to even monitor with any accuracy what people and goods are entering and exiting its borders. The rapacious desire to trade, to buy, to sell, to make money, long overtook any capacity of either the developed or the developing world to regulate how one trades and how one might ensure similar ethical standards across the world. One may denounce corruption in the developing world and the developed world alike, but in the age when billionaires stalk a globe on which 50 percent of its people live on less than two dollars a day, can one really be surprised that customs officers, policemen, judges, politicians, and bureaucrats are often tempted?

Roberto Porto faces an even bigger problem, as I learned when I asked him whether he is able to cooperate with the Chinese police. "I have no authority to deal directly with the Chinese police," he explained, "so I can only talk to the consulate here in São Paulo." "And are the diplomats there helpful?" I wondered aloud. "They help the criminals we are trying to arrest," he added in a deadpan voice. "We ask for help in dealing with a particular case and they promptly hire lawyers on behalf of the people we are investigating."

Wherever one looks in the world, Chinese citizens are soaking up the slack in labor markets. In my travels, I have noticed that their ability to undercut the wages and the capacity for work in the licit sectors is mirrored very precisely in the illicit world. I have also noticed that the Chinese state, which clearly encourages the global wanderings of its labor force, does not differentiate between these two sectors. Whether in the overworld or the underworld, Chinese influence is growing at a remarkable pace. Early on, I had concluded that the future of the global shadow economy will be decided by the direction that China's engagement with the outside world will take. So now I had to travel west from Brazil in order to arrive in the East, where a new era of organized crime is dawning.

PART IV

The Future of Organized Crime

CHAPTER 13

The Overunderworld

Early one Wednesday morning in the warm September of 1994, fifty-four-year-old Kazafumi Hatanaka opened the door to his apartment while still in his pajamas. Very little is known about his visitor that morning, except that he was unusually tall. Police deduced this because the single shot he fired entered the front right temple of Mr. Hatanaka (who was himself of above-average height) at a downward angle. It then exited at the lower left back of the skull, pausing but for a nanosecond to cause a massive cerebral contusion. Because the bullet had gone right through the head, the police report recorded a huge amount of blood surrounding Hatanaka's corpse when a neighbor discovered it at 7:20 a.m.

There were no obvious leads. Investigators found no evidence of a struggle inside the apartment, which suggests that Hatanaka might perhaps have known his assassin. Notwithstanding the mess, it looked to be a professional job. But there were neither eyewitnesses nor, at first, any apparent motive for the killing.

Two months later, it seemed the police's luck had turned. They arrested Tadao Kondo, a man with so rich a criminal pedigree, he would have done time for jaywalking. Apparently seized by a fit of conscience, Kondo had given himself up and handed over a .38 pistol to investigators. Ballistics then confirmed that this was the very murder weapon sought in the Hatanaka case. Kondo, a seventy-three-year-old serial extortionist and thief, described how Mr. Hatanaka had surprised him as he was carrying out an opportunistic burglary.

The police's initial delight at the ballistics report and confession soon turned sour. "An opportunistic burglary?" the chief investigator asked rhetorically. "On the tenth floor?" Surely if he was breaking and entering an apartment, Kondo would have chosen the ground floor precisely to avoid someone such as Mr. Hatanaka catching him in flagrante, and to ensure a quick getaway? Then there was Kondo's height—the position of the body indicated that Hatanaka was standing when shot. But Kondo was ten centimeters *shorter* than his supposed victim, which meant that he could not have fired the bullet down into the skull unless he was standing on a chair. All agreed that this was a cumbersome way to commit either a robbery or a murder. As the police questioned the suspect more closely, they concluded that the only details he knew of the case could have been gleaned from newspaper reports. He had no idea of evidence that they had held back from the media but which the killer must have known.

After some weeks, Kondo admitted to having lied about the murder. In a revised, rambling confession he spoke of a group of men at an illegal gambling event who had promised to resolve his debt problems if he were to take the rap for the hit on Hatanaka.

Gambling debts and the well-established practice of going to prison for a crime somebody else committed could only mean one thing—the killing was ordered by the *yakuza,* the largest and most meticulously organized protection racket in the world.

Hatanaka's murder sent a cold, cold shiver down the spine of the financial and corporate elites to which the dead man had belonged. And with good reason: since the early 1980s, *yakuza* groups had become very circumspect about resorting to violence. Even if they did, their targets were almost always competitors from their own milieu. But Hatanaka was not some lowlife thug made good. He was a major figure in national and international finance, the boss of one of the key regional branches of Sumitomo Bank. As a board member, he was involved in the strategic decision making of one of the world's three biggest banks. (The other two leading banks were also Japanese.) He had developed an unparalleled reputation in the company for managing large and difficult projects with a high rate of return. Why would the *yakuza* commission such a high-profile assassination as this and risk a huge crackdown on their activities?

To start uncovering the answer, first take a ride on the *Shinkansen,* the Bullet Train. As it travels west from Tokyo, this magnificent engineering achievement passes through a visual cacophony of concrete, metal, and other man-made detritus. For hundreds upon hundreds of kilometers, the Japanese construction industry has squeezed houses and apartment buildings into unfeasibly small plots, sheltered under a hideous web of thick, disorganized electric cabling. For the most part, it is impossible to identify where one city ends and the next begins. Indeed, I arrived in Kobe from

Tokyo, having traveled at over 200 miles per hour for almost three hours with the slightly unreal sense of never having left the Japanese capital.

This strip of land running from Tokyo to the Kobe/Osaka agglomeration is the most densely populated area of the world, cramming more than 1,000 people into every square kilometer. Postwar Japan was seized by a construction mania that saw anything old uprooted to prepare the ground for the planting of the world's most extensive concrete jungle. This reached its apotheosis in the late 1980s and early 1990s, during the period known as *baburu*—the bubble—a phenomenon that eventually changed the essence of Japanese society and its self-perception. It certainly turned the center of the country into the most unrelenting urban landscape.

Two-thirds into my trip through this Eternal City of the East, my bullet train pulls into Nagoya, renowned as "the sprawliest of the sprawl." In the middle of this sprawliest bit, there is a rare stretch of lush parkland at the heart of which sit two imposing mansions—Tsukimigaoka Sections A and B—which, if one leaves out the sections A and B, translates poetically, if disingenuously, as "The Hill from Where One Contemplates the Moonlight." And it was on the tenth floor of Section B that Mr. Hatanaka was murdered.

Not only did he live in the center of the sprawl, but he had made a significant contribution to its development—indeed, it was his role in handing out huge loans that fed the construction frenzy in the bubble that led to his murder. Or rather, it was his role in trying to call in the bad loans after the bubble burst.

While losing patience with Mr. Kondo and his false confession, the Nagoya police had started looking into Mr. Hatanaka's business dealings to discover that he had been close to some notorious exponents of land sharking—the most ruthless business practice to emerge during the *baburu,* and one that quickly inspired a dizzy mixing of Japan's mighty corporate world with the proud *yakuza* underworld.

The chain of events leading up to Hatanaka's death in 1994 began nine years earlier, halfway around the world at the Plaza Hotel in New York. Ronald Reagan, under pressure from Congress but emboldened by his ideological partner and friend Margaret Thatcher, was now convinced that the world of international finance needed a big shake-up in order to usher in the regime of free trade that became known as globalization.

Reagan's vision of free trade and of the liberalization of international financial markets was coming under intense pressure from the Democrat-controlled Congress. The dollar was dangerously overvalued, especially against the yen and the mark, and this had enabled Japan and Germany to flood the American market with cheap imports. Above all, the U.S. auto-mobile industry was in serious trouble, incapable of competing with the smaller, cheaper, and more reliable vehicles produced by their Asian and European competitors. By September 1985, Japan posted a record trade surplus with the United States of $50 billion. Along with Congress's rowdy demands for restrictions to be imposed on Japanese goods, U.S. authors published a spate of books warning how Japan was poised to take over as the world's number one economy. One advertising campaign showed a compact vehicle above the rather ominous slogan "Made in Japan—You're Not Laughing Anymore."

President Reagan's insistence that Tokyo do something about its currency and its trade surplus came toward the end of a bad year for Japan. It had begun in late January with the sensational murder of Masahisa Takenaka, the fourth-generation *oyabun* (godfather) of the Yamaguchi-gumi, the Kobe-based *yakuza* group. Takenaka had only been recently elevated to the most senior position in the largest and most powerful organized crime syndicate in Japan. Controlling more than 100,000 members, Takenaka could claim the title *capo di tutti capi nel mondo.* But unfortunately for him the claim was contested by a significant minority of his followers, a disgruntled faction known as the Ichiwa-kai. And late one January evening in northern Osaka, the Ichiwa hitmen murdered the *oyabun* in his mistress's apartment along with one of his chief lieutenants. In the long modern history of the *yakuza,* such a provocative attack was unprecedented.

Over the next two years, large parts of Kansai (western Japan) were rocked by the bloodiest *yakuza* war on record. Hundreds of members and associates of the Yamaguchi-gumi and the Ichiwa-kai fell victim to carefully coordinated hits.

Manabu Miyazaki was on the run from the police during the Ichiwa wars. As his portly frame settled into an armchair at one of Tokyo's poshest hotels, he told me in vivid terms how nerve-racking life as a fugitive had been at that time. "Yakuza guys I met in Osaka right after Takenaka was killed were all thirsting for blood. 'It's different this time,' many told me. 'I'll either get killed or end up in jail.' " Miyazaki, known by the title of his riveting biography as Toppamono (Wide Boy or Wiseguy, freely translated), continued with a broad, warm smile. "Local tabloids splashed big reports under headlines like 'Yamaguchi-gumi Determined to Exterminate Ichiwa-kai.' Underneath would be a little box near the bottom of the page labeled 'Today's Yama-Ichi War Scorecard,' with a daily tally of deaths, serious injuries, and light injuries, broken down by category."

The public despaired both of the *yakuza* behavior and the apparent inability of the police to do anything about the violence (in fact, the police had an interest in seeing the Yamaguchi-gumi eviscerate itself and were happy to stand back and watch the spectacle). Japanese culture, which so prided itself on social concord, was being publicly humiliated by thugs and an incompetent police force.

At home the *yakuza* were running amok, and abroad anti-Japanese sentiment was growing in the United States. A malaise descended over Japan. Tokyo resented Washington's insistence that it open its domestic market to American goods while reining in exports to the United States. But it reasoned that if it did not cooperate, the backlash against Japanese interests in America would be even more damaging. The coincidence of the *yakuza* civil war and sustained American economic and political pressure on the Tokyo government convinced many Japanese that the harmonious age accompanying the country's remarkable postwar ascent was coming to a close. They were right. It was. But not quite in the manner that most imagined.

On September 22, 1985, together with the governors of their respective central banks, the finance ministers of the G5 gathered in the banqueting rooms of the Plaza Hotel on New York's Fifth Avenue under conditions of strict secrecy. In order to bring down the dollar against the yen, James Baker, the new Treasury secretary, realized that there would have to be a massive sale of dollars on the currency markets by central banks. This flew in the face of Reagan's "the market regulates everything" approach, but everyone buckled to the demand. (There is much more that is managed in globalization than its authors and advocates care to admit.) In the final communiqué, Japan agreed to resist protectionism and begin the "steady implementation of the Action Program announced on July 30 for the further opening up of Japan's domestic market to foreign goods and services," as well as the "intensified implementation of financial market liberalization and of the yen, so that the yen fully reflects the underlying strength of the Japanese economy."

In Tokyo, the view prevailed that as America emerged from its recession with the aid of a weakened dollar, Japanese growth would slow down. Within twelve months, the yen had indeed strengthened and a deep gloom spread across the boardrooms of Japan. Resentment toward the United States continued to grow, along with the perception that Tokyo had been bullied into sacrificing a successful economic policy. The government felt compelled to act to combat this perception, and so it lowered interest rates and eased open the money supply.

Business started to borrow money. Lots and lots of it.

The unexpected consequences of this move included the unlikely marriage between the *zaibatsu* (Japan's Godzilla-like corporations—Mitsubishi, Mitsui, Hitachi, et al.) and the *yakuza*, pulling them both out of the doldrums of the mid-eighties into one of history's greatest and most destructive moneymaking ventures.

"Around the end of 1987, we noticed something odd was going on," explained Raisuke Miyawaki, the founder of Japan's anti-organized crime squad. "At the time, I was working as a special adviser to Prime Minister Nakasone, and the economic figures we received from the Central Bank didn't seem to add up. Something strange was happening with the money supply, but we weren't quite sure what!" Nobody from the PM down had anticipated the sensational outcome of the government's monetary policy—the stock market shot into the stratosphere like a rogue firework, fizzing, sparkling, and mesmerizing on its unpredictable path to the heavens.

The boom in Japan's financial markets was of such intensity that, as one economist noticed, "every investment seemed to make money, and speculators were quick to jump on any new development. When American physicists announced that they had achieved cold fusion in the laboratory (a claim later shown to be unproved), eager Japanese investors ran up the share prices of firms that had any sort of relationship with potential cold fusion processes. In retrospect, it appears that by year-end 1988 the Japanese stock market was in the midst of a full-fledged bubble."

It was not long before the extraordinary speculation on the Nikkei stock exchange found its way into the property market. Financial corporations and banks wanted to transfer the notional money of the stock market bubble into hard assets, and property was the best bet.

It did not take long for the vortex of speculation to consume the existing housing stock, and so the banks and big corporations started looking for new land to develop. But the postwar construction mania had ensured there were no empty spaces on which to build. To make way for the glistening new bubbly buildings, existing owners or tenants would have to move. And if they didn't want to, someone would have to persuade them: Enter the Sharks.

"It was also around then that I remember seeing for the first time the big burly men in black suits hanging around Tokyo's fanciest hotels," remembered Miyawaki. He is an unusual man. Even by Japanese standards, he comes across as exceptionally polite and respectful. But most strikingly, Mr. Miyawaki talks and talks frankly, unlike the majority of cops and ex-cops in this country. Most prefer to sweep the presence and role of the *yakuza* under the carpet. Miyawaki believes they represented and still represent a serious threat to social stability. In the late 1980s, he was among the few to alert Japan to the implications of the burgeoning friendships between gangsters and businessmen. "What worried me was that I could see these men were lunching with the most unlikely business and finance leaders. The corporations wanted to buy land in clusters, big plots," continued Miyawaki, "but things didn't always go that smoothly. A lot of people didn't want to sell, and so the companies and banks turned to muscle—the *yakuza*."

First, the *yakuza* would offer financial inducements for tenants to leave their apartments while negotiating with the owner to buy the land. And if either the tenant or the owner refused to budge, then the *yakuza* would issue verbal threats or a physical warning. (One of the most common and tasteless entailed spreading human feces in and around the desired property.) Those who remained stubborn then ran the gauntlet of *yakuza* intimidation. In its mild form, this might involve the notorious sound trucks (audible to this day in Tokyo), which would park outside a property and blast frenetic political rhetoric from huge loudspeakers, rendering life impossible for the targets. The final stage of intimidation was of course physical assault and murder.

Toppamono, or Manabu Miyazaki, the Wide Boy, was never actually a member of the *yakuza* despite growing up as the son of an *oyabun*. But in his colorful life, he has been involved in all manner of *yakuza*-style activity, including land sharking, and he makes no bones about it. With a mischievous grin across his broad face, he shakes his head as he relives those heady times:

> With hundreds of millions of yen flying around, each day passed in a haze of Dom Pérignon and Rémy Martin. . . . During a land speculation I helped out with in Tokyo's Kanda district, where an elderly couple lived in a shabby house, the old woman we negotiated with on behalf of her sick husband stubbornly refused to pursue the matter, leaving us nothing to go on.
>
> "The old bitch is making things difficult because she wants more money," we naturally concluded. "Okay, let's double the offer!"
>
> Twice the original amount was stuffed down her throat.
>
> As it turned out, the old woman wasn't holding out for more. She only wanted to let her husband, who had terminal cancer, die in the house.

The banks, the corporations, the politicians (who were soon in the thick of it), were making tens of billions of dollars in speculative deals. At first, the jamboree seemed to confirm that a superior form of capitalism had evolved from Japan's peculiar culture. With the price of land doubling every month, nobody seemed to notice the wholesale removal of thousands of unwilling, disenfranchised residents from their apartments and houses. This could only happen because the core institutions of the Japanese state and economy were content to work hand in glove with organized crime at the expense of ordinary citizens.

It did not take the *yakuza* long to figure out that their role as policemen to this shameful larceny was a modest ambition. If the big corporations and their political cronies were making money hand over fist by speculating on land, why shouldn't the *yakuza*? Japan's legal and illegal worlds were steadily becoming indistinguishable, and nowhere was that distinction fuzzier and more impenetrable than at the Sumitomo Bank.

Sumitomo was Japan's second-oldest corporation, tracing its beginnings as a purveyor of medicines and books back to the early-seventeenth century. Its banking division was established in the late-nineteenth century, and by the mid-1970s, it had developed a reputation for turning around the fortunes of declining corporate dinosaurs such as Toyo Kogyo, the truck manufacturer, or Asahi Breweries. In 1984, it sought to expand beyond its main base in the industrial heartland of Kansai—Osaka, Kobe, and Kyoto—by purchasing Heiwa Sogo, a relatively small bank but one with a high concentration of branches in Tokyo, where Sumitomo had a relatively weak presence. Heiwa Sogo also carried a lot of bad debts—*yakuza* debts, many of them from the senior members of the Yamaguchi-gumi.

But it was the takeover of Heiwa Sogo, masterminded by the Sumitomo president Ichiro Isoda, that catapulted the bank into the world's top three. The international banking community and the Japanese government showered Isoda with awards for his achievements, and Sumitomo reveled in the speculation of the late 1980s.

One of the bank's subordinate companies, Nagoya Itoman Real Estate Corporation, became a vehicle for Sumitomo's strategic land purchases in Tokyo, and Mr. Hatanaka of Sumitomo Nagoya became ever more closely involved with this operation. What Hatanaka may not have known is that a fellow Itoman board member enjoyed a close business relationship with Takumi Masaru, the *wakagashira,* or deputy godfather, of the Yamaguchi-gumi. As the champagne flowed, Itoman's board lost its head, embarking on a shopping spree for artworks as collateral for dubious loans. Paying vastly inflated prices, often directly to the *yakuza,* Itoman squandered about half a billion dollars of its capital, and police estimated that about half of this ended up in the coffers of the Yamaguchi-gumi.

The exposure of Itoman in July 1991 led to the disgrace and resignation of Ichiro Isoda, perhaps Japan's most respected international banker until this point. Sumitomo's headquarters gradually put the screws on Hatanaka to call in some of the horrifically bad loans he had sanctioned. But, as many corporate figures discovered after the bubble had burst, a lot of their most eager customers had no intention of paying up, least of all the *yakuza*. By now Hatanaka was hopelessly compromised—many of his Nagoya associates were also associates of the mafia, and the Nagoya police finally concluded that he had pressed one of them too vigorously to make good on a loan.

Not surprisingly, the police were never able to clear up exactly which of his clients Hatanaka had upset so grievously. But his murder, along with several other attacks on prominent corporate executives (including the murder of Fuji Film Corporation's managing director) provoked Japan's cowed government into taking the unprecedented step of writing off the bulk of the major banks' and mortgage companies' bad debts. In effect, Japanese taxpayers underwrote the excesses of the bubble period, subsidizing the obscene money-grabbing in which both the *zaibatsu* and the *yakuza* had indulged. The post-bubble period was soon known as the Heisei recession in Japan, referring to the age that had begun with Emperor Akihito's accession in 1989. Abroad, it was more usually dubbed the *yakuza* recession. This was unfair—the *yakuza* was the junior partner in this venal cavalcade, albeit a truculent and dangerous one. But it certainly highlighted how profoundly well rooted the *yakuza* are: they are not an ephemeral force but an institutionalized element of Japanese society.

It was appropriate that the underworld and surface world should find their common interest in real estate speculation—the corporations are inveterate speculators. And construction, if not the heart of *yakuza* business, then certainly is its lungs.

"All these guys here in Kama are dependent on the *yakuza*," says Django, my guide around Kamagasaki, where the poorest and most desperate people in Osaka seek jobs as day laborers. In front of us stands a line of poor, huddled masses—some of them certainly Chinese and Korean, undoubtedly a few *burakumin* (Japan's underclass, born into caste discrimination), and others whose lives at some point took a downward spin. Unshaven, sometimes toothless, acquiescent, they are lining up in front of the Kamagasaki Labor Exchange, a bleak gray monument to bureaucratic function-alism. Gone are the endless flashing lights, the digital advertising, and the incessant electronic noise that characterize so many urban areas in Japan—this long line of the dispossessed hardly makes a sound in the twi-light. "We are waiting for the buses to take us to the homeless hostels, where we can sleep," one exhausted man explains. "Not everyone gets a place," he adds, which means those who don't will have to chance their luck sleeping underneath the railway arches next to Kama.

"Eighty-five percent of the labor agents here are *yakuza*," my friend Django continues. "You have to arrive at about five-thirty in the morning, when they come around and pick out the best." Django started here as a laborer at the end of the eighties, when the bubble was ratcheting up demand for new buildings. "It was easier at that time, of course, because there was such a demand for construction workers," he recalls. "The only criterion you had to fulfill was a working knowledge of Japanese." We walk down the dingy streets of Kama, past the tiny hotels where the more suc-cessful laborers find a bed for ten to fifteen dollars a night. Past the new police station, which looks like a fortress—all part of the post-bubble image that the police are now doing something about the *yakuza*. That particular illusion is quickly shattered when, in this otherwise dingy area, we chance upon two immaculate, grand redbrick buildings with blacked-out limos parked outside. "The only change is that since the 1992 anti–organized crime law, the *yakuza* aren't allowed to mount plaques out-side the buildings with their names and symbols." Django stops briefly. "See that guy at the crossroads? Careful how you look at him. He's *yakuza*—acting as lookout for a gambling den." And as we walk by, a little door opens to reveal a dark circle of mah-jong players.

We stroll into the bar on the corner. On seeing us, the clientele—a smoky mixture of workers, drunks, and outcasts—lets out a huge cheer. Behind the narrow bar, the landlady has hung pictures from a calendar depicting famous tourist destinations: London, New York, Prague, Cairo, and other places a few light-years away from Kama. In place of the usual plasma HD screen is a cumbersome old TV from the 1970s on its last legs but still pumping out Japanese music videos. In general, the stereotype holds that the Japanese maintain a stark social reserve, but such considera-tions are brushed aside as the landlady beams excitedly at Django while placing some raw fish and tofu in front of us. She grabs the telephone and calls her friends. "Django's here. Come on down!"

Django hasn't stepped into this bar for five years, but he is greeted like a soccer star returning to his childhood home. The assembly becomes riotous when he picks up the microphone and sings along to an all-time *yakuza* karaoke favorite about two "brothers" and the inevitable themes of trust, loyalty, and death. As his sonorous bass growls out the tale in Osaka working-class dialect, his shirt rides up his forearm to reveal the tail of a blue dragon tattoo—that forked tip is enough to warn people.

Over a couple of suckers of raw octopus, Django told me of his first encounter with his old *yakuza* mentor, Ken-chan. "I walked in and he was staring at me. This is very important in that scene—it is very macho. They are always checking out how much of a man you are. It's done in subtle ways as well as in more obvious physical ways. I had no problem about people staring at me because I knew how to calibrate the return stare."

Although slight in build, at eighteen years old Django was a national junior karate champion. "People involved in martial arts probably don't like to hear it, but the way the martial arts business here in Japan is organized, it is like the *yakuza*: the dojos, the training, how the sensei relates to his students. The sensei has the complete say and the students are supposed to be enormously deferential. In Japan when the sensei steps out of the dojo, he will have the same way of swaggering with the students. They must carry his bag and so he makes his position very obvious and public. Even the way they greet and the way they talk is very close to *yakuza* language." Django's facility with the habits of the martial arts world was decisive in persuading the *yakuza* to trust him.

Ken-chan befriended Django and showed him around the food stalls of Kama. "I control all of these," Ken-chan explained as the mama-sans who ran the joints handed over their cash. "I never once saw one of them do this unwillingly," Django insisted. "While this was a protection racket, it was also a protection service. Nobody would ever touch one of Ken-chan's stalls without the most severe consequences. And when the police are unable or unwilling to do their job, you need somebody like Ken-chan looking after you. If there was the slightest hint of trouble—unruly customers, unpaid debts, brawls, harassment of waitresses—the mama-sans would call Ken-chan and his boys would be down like a shot to sort it out. They all insisted that the police are absolutely useless. Ken delivers what he promises—this is a real service."

Before long, Ken-chan was taking Django on his collection rounds around a much more significant revenue source—Namba, one of the biggest entertainment districts in Osaka:

> We'd go in, he'd call the mama. We'd have a drink. We would sing a
> song or two on the karaoke and while I was sitting chatting to the

waitresses, he would go behind the counter and the payment was made. It was done on an amicable basis—there was no tension, no reluctance, it looked to me like business as usual. Of course, we weren't on our own; he would have his young goons with him, rather bulky guys, two or three of them. Some had shaven heads, missing pinkies, or gold chains, so it was absolutely clear who was visiting.

On one occasion Django left a bar in Kama with two drinking buddies to take the subway home. His friends were jumped on by two others from the bar who claimed they were owed money. As the fists were swinging, Django's two friends screamed for help: "Come on, karate boy! Help us! Use your strength!" Django didn't move. If he failed to come to his friends' aid, it would mean breaking the bonds of loyalty—they would never speak to him again. But Django had no choice—he could not get involved, as it would have threatened his entire livelihood and existence in Japan.

This was because Django was not Japanese but a university professor, born and raised in the most unlikely *yakuza* recruiting ground of Bregenz, capital of Austria's most westerly and chintziest Alpine province, Voralberg, which sits on Lake Constance close to the German and Swiss borders.

Leading a double life, Django, or Wolfgang, to give his real name, was lecturing at the Goethe Institute in Osaka by day while at night he hung out with Ken-chan, who liked to introduce him as his international associate. "I have to say what was revealing and shocking is that I felt a real affinity to this world," explained Wolfgang, who is exceptionally honest about his life with the *yakuza*. "And maybe it was due to karate and this swagger, this feeling like a real man. But the greatest shock to me was when I realized that we were walking down the street, four, five of us maybe, and of course I was in the middle and I saw how ordinary people on the street perceived us. They averted their gaze and many had real fear in their eyes. And I have to say that, yes, in some sense I felt comfortable with this proud walking, with everybody showing respect. And one evening, I saw in myself how corrupt and corrupting this feeling can be."

One of Austria's leading sociologists and Japanologists, Dr. Wolfgang Herbert researched his doctorate by immersing himself in Osaka's underworld. He belongs to a new breed of researchers who in the past fifteen years have completely transformed academia's understanding and approach to organized crime. Along with colleagues in Russia, Western Europe, South Africa, and the United States (and doubtless elsewhere),

Wolfgang has revealed a huge amount about the culture, ambition, and economic motivation of major criminal structures.

These young researchers also have one other thing in common—they have a bible to which they invariably refer: *The Sicilian Mafia: The Business of Private Protection*. Written by Diego Gambetta, a professor of sociology at Oxford University, the book condensed several key ideas about organized crime that had been floating aimlessly about academia for many decades into an utterly convincing theory about the Mafia. Instead of regarding the Mafia as bullies for whom violence is the be-all and end-all, Gambetta argues that the Mafia is involved in the business of protection. "To define the Mafia as 'the industry of violence' is open to misunderstanding. Violence is a means, not an end; a resource, not the final product. The commodity that is really at stake is *protection*. It may be argued that ultimately protection rests on the ability to use force, but it does not follow that it coincides with it. . . . There are people who find it in their individual interest to buy Mafia protection. While some may be victims of extortion, many others are willing customers."

Gambetta has also separated the core Mafia activity—protection—from those criminals involved in trading. The Mafia can operate in legal markets, as Ken-chan does, offering protection to legal businessmen and -women such as bar owners in Kama and Namba, but they also operate in illegal markets: a drug dealer will require some protection in order to ensure that his buyers or sellers do not renege on a deal. In order to understand and hence combat organized crime, it is important recognize the distinct activities involved.

Gambetta highlights the extreme difficulties involved in carrying out fieldwork in this area. "Scholars," he notes drily, "do not like to waste time with uncooperative sources who refuse to talk and, alternatively, they do not like to be shot." But several acolytes around the world, such as Wolfgang in Osaka, have taken up the challenge. Not only has this work begun to locate the economic and social role of the mafia in societies across the globe, but their work is teeming with observations that have rarely been included in classical criminology studies.

At the moment when Wolfgang suddenly realized that he was *enjoying* being a *yakuza* associate, something else dawned on him: "It was instantly clear to me why young Japanese guys who do not have any other means of making a career get hooked by this lifestyle. They will do everything for their *yakuza* mentors because their ego has been bloated in a unique way. All of a sudden they are somebody big and powerful, just by walking in a group of *yakuza*. If we think about, say, Koreans or people without any education, society has been shitting upon them for a long time and suddenly they ain't being shat on. And they need no qualifications—it is almost effortless. So emotionally for them it is not only this feeling of being something important but having found a group where they are at home. I felt the psychodynamics of it quite intensely."

The good doctor could feel himself being overcome by the intoxicating aura of power that surrounds the *yakuza*. He found the tension of leading a dual life ever harder to bear and eventually he concluded that he must kill off "Django," his own Mr. Hyde.

The Namba is a rather tired arcade with little shops squeezed between the pachinko parlors, the giant temples to Japan's collective commitment to compulsive gambling. Just a decade ago the teenagers drifting through the Namba with red- and blond-dyed hair and gothic clothing were both exotic and provocative, a challenge to Japan's carefully calibrated social sensibilities. Now ubiquitous and mundane, they nonetheless act as an important reminder of the changes triggered by the collapse of the bubble and the cultural impact of globalization.

At the far end of the arcade, the teenagers thin out and the noise from the pachinko halls recedes. In the corner of yet another bar with the standard attributes of karaoke, cuts of primeval sea-dwellers, and alcohol, a quiet man sits hunched in the corner. He could be an aging hippie. In fact, he is one of the most senior tattooists to—among others—the Yamaguchi-gumi.

Like most established organized criminal communities, the *yakuza* has a complex mythology about its origins, its founding purpose, and how this has developed and modernized. The *yakuza* cultivate an ur-image of the samurai, going back to the Tokugawa shogunate of the early modern period. In fact, their genesis was messy and on the whole less romantic, drawing on, among others, traditions of the itinerant trader and the gambler. The very meaning of the word *yakuza* is revealing. A composite of the slang for eight, nine, and three, it refers to a set of mah-jong tiles that at first sight looks like a winner because it adds up to twenty but under specific rules is in fact worth zero. The *yakuza* have traditionally drawn a large number of recruits from those on the margin by dint of their birth, in particular Koreans and the *burakumin*. The latter is an underclass whose status was defined centuries ago by their professions: those who worked in abattoirs or in some capacity with "feces and flesh." It is a prejudice that infects Japanese society to this day. "On the surface," Wolfgang interpreted this for me, "the *yakuza* are ostentatious, dramatic, and recognizable like the winning card hand, but underneath they feel shunned, like zeros."

Apart from those who have lost their little fingers, the most ostentatious mark of *yakuza* membership is the tattoo. Nothing so cheap as I ♥ YAMAGUCHI-GUMI across the biceps, these tattoos are breathtaking full-body representations of gods, animals, warriors, mythological creatures, or women, often intertwined in dramatic pose, imprinted on the body through millions of tiny pinpricks. Aside from the considerable physical pain, a *yakuza* tattoo has significant social and psychological implications. And of course the tattooist has to make sure that the customer walks away content—the last thing he needs is an unhappy *yakuza* on his books. "The skin has several layers," explained Horitsune II, the master tatooist, "but in order for the image to be retained and reproduced by the body, the ink must reach about the third or fourth layer. The problem is that the thickness of the dermis varies at different parts of the body—you have to know every inch of the body if you want to do a proper job." Sipping a beer, Horitsune II exudes the quiet concentration of a watchmaker. He clearly regards his work not as a profession but as a higher craft. "I don't tattoo just anyone who walks in here," he continued. "Taking on a tattoo is a serious business and so I spend a lot of time in consultation with the client to ascertain whether they are ready for it."

The painting of a full-body tattoo takes between one and two years (or several years, as Horitsune jokes, if the *yakuza* recipient is in and out of prison), and it can cost more than $10,000. In a society in which procedure and hierarchy are pervasive, the *yakuza* "families" invest their rituals with greater importance than any comparable organizations in the world. Loyalty to a "family" should be lifelong (although one may on request negotiate an honorable discharge, albeit for the possible sacrifice of a little finger), and, as with the Mafia, the commitment supersedes one's obligations to blood relatives. Betrayal or gross insubordination are capital offenses. The tattoos are a physical reminder of one's vows. They also serve as an effective warning to outsiders and competitors. Of course, this extreme loyalty can have horrific consequences if the family structure breaks down, as its logic requires a fight to the death. The Yamaguchi-Ichiwa war of the 1980s was an internal family matter, hence the intensity of its violence.

Ten to fifteen years ago, 90 percent of Hortisune II's clients, he explained, were *yakuza*. "Nowadays, it is 50 percent civilians and 50 percent *yakuza*. And of course most of the civilians are young adults who see tattoos as a fashion accessory rather than as a sign of loyalty and commitment." Certainly the cultural breakout of the younger generation in the 1990s and its sudden experiment with individualism represents a huge change for the country that until the 1980s clothed its citizens in the uninspiring uniforms of school and work from birth till death. But that statistic also reveals something about the *yakuza* and their current situation. "The bosses would always pay for their soldiers to be tattooed," sighed Horitsune, "but frankly it has become too great an expense for many of them—that's why my *yakuza* trade is going down." Things aren't quite so rosy these days for the *yakuza*. They remain a core element of Japanese society, but since the collapse of the bubble, they have faced unprecedented challenges to their authority both from their enemies at home and, increasingly, from foreign rivals who are beginning to squeeze their economic base. Like the rest of Japan, the *yakuza* are encountering some difficulty in adapting to a globalizing world.

Through much of the twentieth century, the *yakuza* may not have been as popular as their members like to believe, but they have been influential. Their status as outsiders was always paradoxical. While the *yakuza* "families" emerged in large degree from lumpen classes, they were often attracted to and supported extreme right-wing nationalist ideologies, and in the interwar years, they were used by both government and business as effective strike breakers. When the United States occupied a devastated Japan at the end of World War II, it was the *yakuza* who within days of surrender were resurrecting the country's economy with the establishment of a vibrant black market. The Americans tolerated and often collaborated with the *yakuza*, just as they accepted the assistance of the Sicilian Mafia in establishing order throughout southern Italy after the 1943 Sicily landings. The Mafia developed decisively corrupt connections with the Christian Democratic Party, which dominated Italian politics during the cold war. Similarly, the *yakuza* struck up an intimate relationship with the key factions of the LDP, the Liberal Democratic Party, which dominated Japanese politics during the same period but unlike the Christian Democrats survived the fall of Communism and, despite some hiccups, still runs the country today.

The bubble—when the *zaibatsu*, the LDP, and the *yakuza* all joined forces to realize what one commentator dubbed "the great transfer of wealth"—was no aberration. It was merely the country's crony capitalism assuming its highest form for a blowout that lasted five years. This begs the question as to how the *yakuza* was ever able to occupy such an exalted position in Japanese society. Contrary to popular assumptions, they did not shoot, extort, or bribe their way to the top: they are, bizarrely, a product of Japan's legal system.

"Traditionally, of course, the *yakuza* has always been involved in prostitution and gambling. Everyone more or less accepted this state of affairs, and that accounted for the bulk of its income," says Yukio Yamanouchi. "But in the 1960s, it started getting involved in civilian affairs, and this soon grew to be one of its greatest revenue sources." The chirpy Mr. Yamanouchi is in an excellent mood. After a number of years in the wilderness, he was recently welcomed back as the chief lawyer to the Yamaguchi-gumi after his old friend Shinobu Tsukasa was chosen as the sixth-generation *oyabun* of Japan's largest crime syndicate. This is like having a lawyer in the United States who introduces himself breezily as lawyer to Don Anthony Soprano of the New Jersey Mafia Corporation. "This move into civilian affairs began with the collection of outstanding debts—this is all because if anybody went to court in order to get a debt paid, it would take an eternity and if judgment was finally passed down in a case, it often resulted in nothing. The *yakuza* are able to offer a much quicker solution to the problem."

This "move into civilian affairs" (i.e., resolving disputes) in the 1960s came about because of a law passed in 1949. In order to discourage the use of litigation, which was felt to be divisive and contrary to the spirit of *wa* (harmony) that underpins Japanese society, the postwar government ruled that only 5,000 lawyers would be permitted to graduate from the Legal Research and Training Institute in Tokyo each year. The great majority registered in Tokyo and Osaka and sought comfortable and lucrative positions working on behalf of one of the *zaibatsu*. Few were interested in representing members of the public, and before long the entire judicial system was clogged up with civil cases that made the deliberations in Dickens's *Bleak House* reasoned and swift by comparison.

"It was only a short step before people realized that they could use the *yakuza* for resolving a host of things—they have since developed a close involvement with all manner of transactions in the property business of course; but they also act as bankruptcy assessors; in anything, really, where the courts ought to be responsible, such as insurance claims after car accidents," outlined Yamanouchi. By the late 1990s, the consequences of Japan's policy on legal training were jaw-dropping by international comparison: Germany had 1 lawyer for every 724 heads of population, Britain 1 for every 656, and the United States 1 for every 285 citizens. In Japan, there was one lawyer for every 5,995 people. Basically, the mafia occupies a huge segment of Japan's de facto legal system, which is, of course, what some people observe about lawyers in the United States.

In its core activity, the *yakuza* is not only a privatized police force; it is a self-contained judicial system as well—criminal syndicates as cops, attorneys, judges, and juries.

Two interest groups are if not entirely unhappy with this situation then at least ambivalent. The first is the general public—their demand for law enforcement and conflict resolution is what keeps the *yakuza* in business. And although in many cases the *yakuza* will provide a good and efficient service, they are accountable to nobody if they don't. Yamanouchi is very frank about his clients' impact: "You know they have become so closely involved in civilian affairs that for some ordinary people their presence and behavior have become a real burden. That's why the 1992 law was so well received in public."

The government felt able to pass the Law Regarding the Prevention of Unjust Acts by Organized Criminal Syndicate Members in May 1991 because public disquiet about the *yakuza*'s involvement in the bubble had led to a real slump in the *yakuza*'s image. The law's focus also enabled the government to shift responsibility for the bubble away from the primary culprits, the *zaibatsu* and the LDP, and onto the *yakuza*.

Although designed to clip the *yakuza*'s wings, the law contained some astonishing features that illuminate how the Japanese mafia is in fact an institutionalized element of this democracy. It stipulates that all the families or associations must annually submit their membership lists to the police, both full members and candidates. When I asked the lawyer Yamanouchi whether this confers legal status on members of the organized criminal syndicates, he leaned back in his chair, pondered the question, and then averred, "Yes, it does." So the *yakuza* enjoy the unique status of being a legal and an illegal entity simultaneously.

Every year, the police White Book informs the public on the fluctuation in *yakuza* membership and what type of activities particular families indulge in. The law also forbids the *yakuza* for the first time from displaying their symbols on the doors to their office, although it is still perfectly legal for them to have offices. "After the law was passed," said Mr. Yamanouchi, "the police told the Osaka Bar Association that I was no longer permitted to print the phrase 'Legal Counselor to the Yamaguchi-gumi' on my business card. But apart from that, it hasn't affected me too much!"

The gold standard of anti–organized crime legislation is the RICO Act (Racketeer Influenced and Corrupt Organizations Act), passed by the U.S. Congress in 1970 and thought (apocryphally, some say) to be named in honor of Edward G. Robinson's character in *Little Caesar* ("Is this the end of Rico?" he asks rhetorically while breathing his last in the 1930s classic). It took ten years before a mafia boss was actually convicted under RICO. But since then, it has proved more effective than any other policing tool against organized criminal syndicates. Using RICO, prosecutors don't have to prove specific crimes, merely that individuals are involved with groups that follow a criminal pattern. This breaks the defensive wall erected by criminal bosses whereby foot soldiers take the rap for their superiors' crimes, enabling the feds and district attorneys to smash much of Cosa Nostra in the United States during the 1980s and 1990s.

The Japanese borrowed from RICO but then diluted it. *Yakuza* bosses can now be held accountable for the sins of their subordinates, but the police will use this only in order to exercise a measure of control over *yakuza* affairs—they are not out to destroy them. "The earlier economic relationship, when the *yakuza* could bribe the police—that is now unthinkable," explained Yamanouchi. "Furthermore, the police are much more confident about moving against the higher instances of the families. My chief client, Mr. Tsukasa, for example, is in custody at the moment for a trivial matter. The reason behind this is because the Yamaguchi-gumi is moving into the east which, if successful, would greatly increase its power. The police are trying to clip its wings, not destroy it."

It is hard to underestimate the influence and standing of the Yamaguchi-gumi. At the top of a quiet residential street in Kobe's fashionable Nada district, a wooden sign stands proud: WE WILL KEEP ORGANIZED CRIME GANGS OUT OF NADA! A few yards farther down, past houses that are uncharacteristically spacious by urban standards, there stands a cutesy gray and white hexagonal building at the top of a side street—the local police station. Grrrr! the mouse roars. Fifty meters down the street from the mouse hole, there are fortress walls around a garage door of gray corrugated metal. Cameras and security lights are dotted everywhere, and should anyone succeed in scaling the wall, he would also need to contend with a roll of matted barbed wire. As I walk past the headquarters of the Yamaguchi-gumi, my luck is in and, as if reproducing a scene from *Thunderball,* the metal starts to roll slowly upward, revealing a line of five men in light green uniforms and sunglasses standing ramrod straight. Behind them is an elegantly manicured lawn and in the distance a passable imitation of a renaissance Italian courtyard. As I stand gaping, their eyes settle on me, and having no letter of introduction, I move slowly on. One Yamaguchi soldier ushers a big man with even bigger sunglasses into the driver's seat of one of several limos parked in the drive and it screeches out before the gray metal drops again, locking away the secrets of the Yamaguchi-gumi once more. Good luck, Nada-ku police—you've got your work cut out.

Since 1991 the police have registered a significant consolidation of *yakuza* power into just three families—the Yamaguchi-gumi and two Tokyo-based groups, the Sumiyoshi-kai and the Inagawa-kai. The 1991 law enabled police to weaken or eliminate many of the smaller *yakuza* associations, and so to protect themselves several have affiliated with the Big Three. Since the millennium, the Yamaguchi-gumi has been extending its influence ever deeper into Tokyo, taking advantage of a simmering feud between subgroups of the Sumiyoshi and Inagawa, which sporadically breaks out into murderous violence. By 2005, Yamaguchi-gumi accounted for 45 percent of Japan's "designated" gangsters according to the police White Book, and when Shinobu Tsukasa was named the sixth-generation *oyabun* in July that year, police began warning of the possibility of a major gang war breaking out.

Yakuza leaders themselves downplay the prospect of a war between the Big Three. "We have cordial relations with the Yamaguchi-gumi," says Mitsunori Agata, deputy chairman of the Sumiyoshi-kai, Tokyo's largest criminal syndicate. "We have great respect for them and we think they are an effective operation."

The slight reserve I detected in Agata-san's response was explained three months later in February 2007 when a leading young Sumiyoshi-kai man was gunned down by members of a Yamaguchi-gumi affiliate in Tokyo. For several days, Japanese newspapers speculated furiously that the country was on the brink of the mother of all gang wars between Yamaguchi-gumi and Sumiyoshi-kai. Then news leaked that the Yamaguchi affiliate had paid a substantial sum (estimated at around $1.3 million) to the Sumiyoshi-kai group as blood money. Behind the drama, however, is the economic reality that Kansai (western Japan), the Yamaguchi-gumi's base and traditional hunting ground, is lagging behind eastern Japan economically. This is what lies behind the Yamaguchi-gumi's eastward drive into the capital. Contracting markets still have the potential to trigger a major conflagration between the two big groups.

In public, all the major *yakuza* figures remain admirably circumspect in their pronouncements, not wishing to provoke unnecessary bloodshed. In his late sixties, Agata has been through a lot in the *yakuza* world: rebellion against a stern middle-class father in postwar Japan; doing time for a murder he didn't commit; a ruthless streak that propelled him to the leadership of his gang, the Blue Dragons, around Shinjuku metro station in Tokyo; his recruitment by a Sumiyoshi-kai operative; and then building a protection racket around Kabuki-cho, one of the toughest and most contested turfs in Tokyo.

Now in his cozy, cluttered room where no more than three people can sit cross-legged, Agata-san insists to me that his methods have changed—the *yakuza* now stress the importance of diplomacy, and violence is a final and always undesirable resort. "We hold a meeting on the twentieth of every month with all the families and associations in eastern Japan and we resolve our differences through dialogue," he continues. "The Sumiyoshi-kai does not seek conflict but of course if anybody attempts to encroach on our territory, then problems will ensue. . . ."

There is no question that since the Yamaguchi-Ichiwa war in the 1980s and the collapse of the bubble in the early 1990s, there has been a significant reduction in *yakuza* violence. The key to an effective protection racket as run by the *yakuza* is less the actual deployment of violence as a sanction than the credible *threat* of violence. Too much violence is bad for business—it draws heat from the police and opprobrium from the public and the media, and it can lead to retaliation. All these take a heavy toll on the *yakuza*'s raison d'être: making money.

On the edge of Kabuki-cho, Tokyo's main red-light and gambling district, lies the highest concentration of *yakuza* offices anywhere in the country. As one of Tokyo's most important bosses, Agata has two offices and he still observes the *yakuza*'s traditional symbolism: he reveals a magnificent dragon tattoo across his chest and proudly shows me the DVD of the ceremony (theoretically illegal) at which he was elevated to deputy chair. These days, however, *yakuza* bosses such as Agata are as much harassed senior managers as they are traditional gangsters. When he speaks of the recruitment crisis facing the *yakuza*, we drift surreally into the discourse of human resources wonkery. "Like all organizations we are facing problems encouraging young people to join," Agata said, explaining the impact of Japan's fabled aging society on the *yakuza*. The country currently registers the lowest birth rate in the world, so the *yakuza* are competing with all legitimate businesses for members. "For young people there are many more attractive and lucrative trades to go into nowadays," he continues, "so we as an organization are now aging—too many chiefs, not enough Indians, frankly. The most effective way for us to respond to this is to point out that we are a family and this is very attractive for young lads who maybe don't spend as much time with their own family. This is something that is lacking in society."

But for Agata as for many of *yakuza*'s management class, their main headache recently has been the police—not in the shape of any crackdown on the families but because of pachinko, Japan's national sport.

Just around the corner from Agata's office is a five-story pachinko building. A visit allows you to revel in the profound otherness of Japan. On every floor row upon row of bright blue, red, yellow, or green pachinko machines splutter, crackle, zing, and trill as an army of seemingly brainwashed people, of both genders and from all classes and age groups, send dozens, hundreds, thousands of little balls into an upright slot machine. These contraptions gobble up most of the balls (2.5 yen each), but some fall into special holes. These trigger three revolving wheels in the center, and if when they stop the symbols match, then the machine pays out more balls. Neatly stacked around the more successful players are baskets full of little balls representing winnings that sometimes run into thousands of dollars. Hyperpolite young men and women in Disney-esque uniforms smile and provide the addicts with more balls to feed the machines and their habit.

The sheer size of this industry and the fanaticism of its devotees are hard to comprehend. Pachinko machines colonize whole high-rise buildings like mechanical spores, and players remain anatomically attached to their machines for hours on end. Having accumulated a treasure chest of little balls, the player is permitted to exchange them for goods—insignificant gifts, dolls, cigarettes, and the like. The player is then permitted to exchange these goods for cash at a separate kiosk, which must be out of sight of the main pachinko hall. This bizarre accounting ritual, known as *santen hoshiki,* emerged in order to circumvent Japan's laws on gambling, which is itself strictly illegal. But while pachinko *is* gambling, it is in fact strictly legal and has an annual turnover estimated at about $300 billion, twice the value of the entire Japanese automobile industry, and somewhere in the region of the total global narcotics market!

Until the 1991 law, it wasn't only the *yakuza* that was making money out of pachinko: traditionally Korean businessmen and their syndicates controlled large parts of the trade, while Chinese gangs also took a cut from the *santen hoshiki* kiosks. There was so much money that all three were able to help themselves to a piece of the action without getting in one another's way. But after the 1991 law, the police themselves started muscling in on the *santen hoshiki* system—often retired policemen backed by their working colleagues. And so by bureaucratic fiat, the police have largely requisitioned the *yakuza*'s most important legal business for their own ends. It's an unorthodox crime-fighting strategy but an effective one. *Yakuza* bosses such as Agata-san can barely contain their indignation: "They are trying to take over a business that generates enormous amounts of money, so suddenly we have been deprived of these huge revenue streams. All these retired policemen came in and robbed from our banks, so all this black market money is now going into their fat pension funds!"

In Kabuki-cho, snapping turtles and puffer fish (the ones with fatally toxic organs) compete with misty-eyed prostitutes and escort boys for the punters' attention. In Tokyo's most famous entertainment district, there are four activities—eating, drinking, fucking, and pachinko. Occasionally, there is a murder or two.

On my stroll around the district, it looked like business as usual. Soliciting clients for sex has never been easier or more clinical for the workers and procurers of Kabuki-cho. The client has merely to walk into a small room. In the middle stands a single table and telephone; on the walls, illuminated posters advising of establishments offering a variety of ethnicities. After selecting a favorite, the client calls on the special phone and before long a courteous guide leads him off to his chosen fantasy. Japanese men are keen on Caucasian women, which explains perhaps why 70 percent of Japanese visas issued to Russian women in the past ten years have been "entertainment" visas, and why Japan receives more trafficked Colombian women than any other country. Foreigners are unlikely to be offered Japanese women, as it is widely held that "Westerners are hung like horses and disease-ridden." But there are plenty of Chinese, Burmese, and other Asian women on offer to satisfy the seedy curiosity of the Western male.

Kabuki-cho's best restaurants are hidden down impossibly narrow side streets, up rickety wooden stairs, and then through low doorways into a small room. Gangsters seem to colonize at least one table in each joint. Everyone understands the rules—no staring and no loud talking.

The Parisienne, slightly gaudy but somehow endearing, was a favored hangout for the foot soldiers of the mob. All kinds—Korean, Taiwanese Chinese, or Shanghainese and Japanese. Early on Friday evening, September 27, 2002, two heavies from the Sumiyoshi-kai swaggered down the stairs and into the bar area. They closed in on a group of mobsters from the Chinese mainland and demanded money. The rent for that area had gone up. As the discussion became heated, one of the Chinese unexpectedly pulled a gun and fired. The first *yakuza* fell dead on the spot; the second was badly wounded and losing consciousness as the Chinese fled.

Two and a half years earlier, the governor of Tokyo, a right-wing rabble-rouser, Shintaro Ishihara, had issued a chilling warning to the capital's residents. "Crimes in Tokyo are getting more violent," he thundered. "If you ask who is committing them, they are all *sangokujin* [derived from the derogatory wartime term for Koreans and Chinese]. In other words, foreigners . . . who have entered illegally and remain in Japan are the criminals, is that not so? Are the snakeheads [Chinese people-smugglers] any different?"

Statistics clearly refuted Ishihara's hysterical claims. But opinion polls suggested that many in Tokyo agreed with him. And that was the point—he intended to tap into a suppressed fear that has started to erupt sporadically through the skin of the Japanese psyche.

Japan has largely recovered from the bubble and the devastation it wrought. But for the first time since Hiroshima and Nagasaki, many Japanese feel uneasy about an external power—not the United States this time, but China. Visiting Tokyo, one can almost feel the deep pulsing boom of economic growth from across the East China Sea, like the approaching footsteps of a new Godzilla. Is this adolescent giant benign or malignant? Until this is answered, Godzilla excites and terrifies in equal measure. Both Japan and Taiwan benefit substantially from being nested so close to the twenty-first century's new economic superpower. But the political implications of change remain opaque. Speaking at a closed session of the World Economic Forum in Davos in 2007, a senior Korean corporate leader articulated the fears of all China's neighbors. "I am very impressed with Hu Jintao and the current Chinese leadership," he said. "They are good and honest partners and I like doing business with them. But what happens if we get a different, more nationalist leadership in China—we will all be worried and afraid." Being close to the outer edges of the economy, the *yakuza* have sensitive antennae that are often able to pick up changes in the environment earlier than others.

Yet in contrast to most major national criminal operations, the *yakuza* do not travel well. When they venture abroad it is not to make money but to have fun. Prevented from gambling at home, the *yakuza* started traveling in the 1960s, looking for casinos and cheap sex. Their quest coincided with a huge influx into East Asia of American men involved in the Vietnam War. But this group too, when they left the battlefields of 'Nam, went looking for the brothels of Korea, the Philippines, Thailand, Taiwan, Hong Kong, and Macau. The regional criminal economy the Americans and Japanese fostered has since expanded hugely, embracing consumers (almost exclusively men) from the subcontinent, Europe, the Middle East, and parts of Africa. But the *yakuza* did not seek to establish overall control of this trade. They certainly invested heavily in the legitimate tourist trade, purchasing hotels, restaurants, and other facilities, but the selling of protection and the use of violence was left to the Chinese, the Thais, or the Filipinos.

When *yakuza* pockets started bulging during the bubble, they looked farther afield for businesses that would provide high returns, turning their attention to the United States. Laundering vast amounts of money accrued from the bubble and the more traditional criminal activities of gambling, prostitution, and trafficking in methamphetamine (East Asia's drug of choice long before it hit the States), the *yakuza* bought into leisure facilities across the western United States, but especially in Hawaii and Las Vegas.

Nobody would admit this publicly, but many Japanese derive some satisfaction from the knowledge that the *yakuza* is eating into the licit economy of Pacific America. While the two countries proclaim their dependency on each other in economic and security matters, U.S.-Japanese relations are misted by an unspoken mutual cultural suspicion. Congress has expressed this most forcefully in a report on Asian organized crime activity in the United States after the FBI had indicated its difficulty in combating the *yakuza* because Japan's police were dragging their feet: "Anemic Japanese law enforcement efforts against Boryokudan gangs have had an adverse impact on the United States," according to the report. "The executive branch should negotiate formal and informal agreements with Japan to improve law enforcement cooperation and intelligence sharing. In addition, the State Department should amend current visa regulations to make Boryokudan membership an independent basis for denying a visa."

To this day, the *yakuza* enjoys laundering its cash through the United States. But its business remains concentrated inside Japan. In contrast to the Sicilian Mafia, which has taken some heavy blows in the last fifteen years, the *yakuza* continue to enjoy a powerful and lucrative position at home, so there is less incentive to expand abroad.

But as more mainland Chinese enter Japan as legal and illegal labor migrants, so do the Triads and other organized crime operations expand their influence in the country. In 2003, a senior official at the National Police Agency in Tokyo told a researcher that clashes between the *yakuza* and the Chinese gangs were proliferating. He explained this as the conse-quence of a "conflict over turf and the low price that Chinese assassins charge for the job. A Chinese gangster will do three jobs for the price a *yakuza* will charge for one." Just like everyone else, the *yakuza* are worried about the influence and strength of Chinese organized crime in Japan.

The notorious murder at the Parisienne brought swift retribution from the *yakuza*. "After the two Japanese were killed, Chinese clubs were fire-bombed," recalled Agata-san, whose patch as a senior Sumiyoshi-kai boss includes part of Kabuki-cho. "Fecal matter was spread all over them and I think some dead Chinese were found lying on the rail tracks. That's the last we heard of them. . . . Nobody has been arrested yet and we don't know who the Chinese were. Nonetheless, the *yakuza* sent a clear message that if you mess with the mafia, then this is what you get. I think the message was well communicated."

What is less well advertised is the symbiotic relationship between the *yakuza* and Chinese gangs in cities such as Tokyo, Yokohama, and Osaka. Increasingly, the *yakuza* outsource the punitive deployment of violence to Chinese gangs. "The mainland Chinese don't care about this," a Taiwanese businessman who travels low under the radar as he moves between China, Taiwan, and Japan explained. "If they are caught, they face a short spell in jail and then deportation. Then the snakeheads bring them right back here. And the *yakuza* will go out and commission them again." The implication of this truth is extraordinary—the *yakuza* are combating their recruitment difficulties provoked by the aging society and the declining prestige of their organization by subcontracting Chinese groups to carry out the least attractive and riskiest part of their business.

When I ask the old *yakuza* hand Toppamono whether he thinks Chinese organized crime has come to represent a long-term threat to the *yakuza,* his smile broadens into a smirk. "Let me put it like this," he says. "If I were a broker I'd be telling my clients now to move out of *yakuza* stocks and start investing in the Triads!"

CHAPTER 14

The Future of Organized Crime

nother sip of delicate green tea. Another pause. Then another whispered explanation. "Behind Chen Kai there was a shadow. A dark shadow. This is an invisible force, a dark force here in Fuzhou, and it did not operate behind Chen Kai alone. You only see the shadow when it strikes—then it is too late."

Talking in metaphors is central to the experience of China. The invisible shadow conjured up by a cautious businessman in Fuzhou catches the sense of unease that is common to all police states. Unlike most police states, however, China has made room for a rampant culture of conspicuous consumption that obscures the presence of the shadow. As "the richest man in Fuzhou," Chen Kai had sophisticated instruments for tracking the capricious moods of the shadow, and so perhaps he had less to fear than most.

Until his arrest on May 16, 2003, he was on top of the world. Good-looking, tall, and in his early forties, he sported a diamond-encrusted watch. And Chen could survey the capital of Fujian Province from atop his glitzy Music Plaza, or from the penthouse suite at his luxury apartment development, Triumphant Garden, the most expensive real estate in the city. Or indeed from any one of the other hotels, restaurants, and housing estates he owned.

A few months earlier, Chen had welcomed Song Zuying in person when she performed at the Plaza. China's most glamorous singing star and a Grammy nominee, Song had followed the path already traveled by many of the country's glitterati to the Plaza's stage door. Chen's generosity was fabled—he was happy to shell out up to 200,000 renminbi ($26,000) for a half-hour performance. And the Music Plaza was the place to be seen.

As in many parts of China, the money and celebrity also attracted the distinctive blacked-out cars with a "K" or an "O" registration, denoting senior party and security officials, respectively. The chief of police and other big shots would regularly join in an evening of gambling, supplemented by bottles of vintage mao-tai liquor and Hennessy XO champagne cognac, served by some of the joint's 200 hostesses.

Nobody from Chen's village in nearby Minhou County could have dreamed that his career might develop so spectacularly. Born just after the Great Leap Forward, Mao Zedong's murderous program of agricultural reform, Chen grew up during the Cultural Revolution, a living nightmare for most of China, characterized by fear, intimidation, starvation, and butchery. From 1959 to 1976, hundreds of millions of Chinese shared a single goal—survival. Tens of millions didn't make it or were so damaged by the state-inflicted violence that their lives were barely worth living. This was especially so in Chen's poor community in Fujian. Mao Zedong suspected this backward province of harboring all manner of class traitors and counterrevolutionaries, and so for two decades he neglected the region as a punishment for suspected thought crimes and recidivist bourgeois habits. Perhaps it was to compensate for Mao's vindictive behavior that China's great reformer, Deng Xiaoping, chose the city of Xiamen in southern Fujian as one of the first special economic zones (SEZs) in the early 1980s to inspire local entrepreneurs in thawing out the economy that had been frozen solid by the Maoist ice age. Agog at the success of the Xiamen experiment, it wasn't long before Fuzhou's local bosses opened up the provincial capital as well. Deng did not confer the honor on Fujian by chance—80 percent of Taiwan's people trace their roots back to Fujian. By opening up this province, Deng hoped to attract huge investment from Taiwan to the mainland. And he was proved right.

Chen's peasant father took advantage of the new opportunities. "He started his own business, transporting goods into Fuzhou from the surrounding countryside with a hand-pulled cart," said *Mr. Jiang* as he took a tea break at a small tile shop, Wild Goose Ceramics. By the standards of the time, Mr. Jiang observed with a smile, this made him a master entrepreneur, the equivalent of a Harvard MBA. We drank our tea in small gulps and stared at the huge blue mansion, now empty, that Chen had built for his mother and father. Although he's still alive—probably—Chen's ghost already stalks all Fuzhou.

Chen graduated from his father's laborious trade of hauling vegetables and such to selling carpets door to door. He accumulated enough capital to rent a shop, where he sold electronic goods. This was in itself revolutionary. In the early eighties, the state still told most Chinese what profession they would pursue and at what location. Choice was both precious and rare. Generally life was unutterably boring. "There was nothing—nothing to buy, nothing to do at the time," said the photographer and businessman *Wan Sui*. "Shops selling anything but the most basic goods barely existed, and so Chen stood out." Traditionally, Fuzhou boasted a bigger selection of consumer goods than almost any other part of China. In the 1980s, it was the only place you could buy blue jeans, for example, and people would come to this province from all over the country for a pair. The reason for Fuzhou's relative diversity was one of the many reasons Chairman Mao so despised its people. A hundred miles from the port of Fuzhou lies Taiwan, the Nationalist thorn in Communist China's flesh. If Taiwanese smugglers made it across the small stretch of water to the mainland, they landed in Fujian. Apart from proximity, Fujian Province and Taiwan are linked by language—they speak the same dialect, and even those who hail from Shanghai or Beijing must strain to understand a single word the Fujianese are saying.

Days after Deng announced his cautious economic reforms twenty-five years ago, dozens of fishing boats from Taiwan and Fujian were meeting in the sea halfway between the territories to exchange money for cassette recorders, which were then sold by men such as Chen. And his experience in electronic goods led to his first big break—securing the exclusive concession to sell Hitachi color televisions in Fuzhou. These were the first color TVs to hit China, and the concession opened the door to considerable wealth.

In the early 1990s, a shy young man, Xu Li, took a shine to one of Chen's girlfriends. Despite his charisma, Chen was rarely seen with a trophy on his arm, and he magnanimously acceded to Li's request to start dating the girl. Soon after, Li introduced Chen to his father—Xu Congrong. Xu grew very fond of Chen and before long he had pronounced himself Chen's godfather. A blessed embrace for Chen, it turned out, as Xu Congrong was the chief of Fuzhou's Public Security Bureau. The marriage of Chen's restless entrepreneurial spirit to Xu's power as the province's most senior law enforcement officer was happy and fruitful. It spawned one of a new breed—the Political Criminal Nexus (PCN), a profoundly corrupt relationship between the local tycoons and party leaders. The Chinese government has watched perplexed as these mischievous offspring grow across the country. Beijing feels threatened by the PCN, "mainly because it is eroding the authority of the Chinese Communist Party," as Ko-lin Chin, America's foremost expert on Chinese organized crime, has argued. "In other words, for the Chinese government, the PCN is first a political issue and second a criminal justice issue."

But it is also a matter of economics—the PCNs create a lot of wealth, and in Fuzhou the golden years began. Under Xu's protection, Chen Kai started importing slot machines into his clubs. Gambling is strictly illegal in China (with the jaw-dropping exception of the former Portuguese colony of Macao). Except under Mao, however, that has never stopped most Chinese from indulging in the habit with an industrial zeal. As the gamblers of Fuzhou fed the machines, the coins fell out the other end into Chen's pockets. In November 1997, Gu Wei, a reporter with the newspaper *Fuzhou Evening,* published the only story ever written on the trade. It was intended as the first in a series, but after a gunman fired shots into Mr. Gu's front room, he chose discretion over valor and dropped his interest in the subject. Meanwhile, Chen kept on making money and shrewdly investing the profits in the Chinese businessman's most important commodity—influence in the Communist Party of China (CPC).

This arrangement is not peculiar to Fuzhou. "The only people you are afraid of in this country are the Party or the police—nobody else. So you *have* to keep them onside," explained Paul French, a British businessman living in Shanghai. "Nobody gets rich here by being 100 percent clean," he continued. "I'm not 100 percent clean and nobody else is. If we did everything by the book, nothing would ever get done. But of course these guys who are getting megarich know that the government has stuff on them."

The government, or more precisely the Party, maintains this close control over its citizens because it is frightened. Like its imperialist predecessors in power, the CPC nurses a visceral fear of the chaos that could ensue if its authority was undermined. The anarchic collapse of the Soviet Union struck terror into the hearts of China's bureaucrats, and a possible repetition in the Middle Kingdom keeps them awake at night. They have located multiple sources whence this chaos might burst forth: the PCNs, peasant unrest, fragmentation along provincial and regional lines, mass social and religious movements such as the Falun Gong cult, excessive foreign influence in the economy, democratization, or a significant economic downturn. While all these threats to the Party's authority are real, some are more remote than others. The Party's ability to assess and handle potential disruption lies at the core of the debate among China's elite and sinologists worldwide as to where China is heading and what its impact on the rest of the globe will be. Yet frequently the Party discovers that in capping one source of disruption, it simply diverts the flow of latent chaos to a second, adding to its force in the process.

The Future of Organized Crime

The futurology of China is hence an uncertain science. As perhaps its primary concern, however, the Communist Party monitors social unrest in the impoverished countryside. If the CPC fails to provide sufficient new jobs every year for the rural masses streaming into the coastal cities in search of work, or if the staggering gap in wealth between town and country continues to widen, then the disappointed peasants are perfectly capable of shaking the foundations of regional Party power. In the last five years, the number of peasant riots has risen spectacularly to roughly 80,000 per year, and they continue to proliferate. These outbursts of discontent can be serious, involving the wrecking of local government offices and the lynching of officials. In spring 2007, the BBC's James Reynolds visited Zhushan deep in central China after news had filtered through of one such riot. Twenty thousand protestors had taken to the streets after the local privately owned bus company exploited its monopoly by doubling the fares. Buses were overturned and burned before the authorities mobilized the military and riot police. On arrival, Reynolds described a town under martial law. A few weeks before this, the government in Beijing had relaxed restrictions on foreign journalists, allowing them to travel anywhere in the country without prior permission. Nonetheless, within a matter of hours of his arrival in Zhushan, Reynolds was detained, interrogated, and then expelled from the town.

Anything is possible in the Chinese strategy of creating jobs. "It doesn't matter whether the cat is black or white," mused Deng Xiaoping when he was explaining the need to introduce economic reforms in the 1980s. "It only matters if it catches mice." It doesn't matter how China runs the economy, as long as it makes money.

Deng realized that for the Chinese to make money, the traditions of central economic planning had to be dumped, and so for twenty-five years (and especially since the early 1990s) the government has afforded the provinces considerable autonomy in their economic policy. Their confidence in exploiting this exposes an important myth—China is not a huge monolith moving inexorably toward global domination. Indeed, economic change is fragmenting the country, highlighting its tremendous cultural diversity; reinventing rivalries and alliances; and heightening the tension between "the center" (Beijing) and "the periphery" (everywhere else).

Having established their independence from Beijing, provincial government and businesses devote much energy to warding off the capital's interfering ways. They are much more comfortable than Beijing with the Political Criminal Nexus as both a system of governance and an economic strategy: the local elites can feather their nests and deliver the requisite job quota demanded by the center year after year. "It doesn't matter whether the mice are black or white," as Deng's saying has now been paraphrased, "as long as they avoid the cat." The provinces may be as corrupt as they wish in making their money, as long as Beijing doesn't catch them red-handed.

Once Deng Xiaoping had given his blessing to economic experiment, a truly wild version of capitalism quickly swept away decades of stagnant socialist planning in the SEZs (special economic zones), especially in the south of the country. Entrepreneurs could manufacture and sell anything they wished if there was a market. All they needed was to find their *baohu san*, or "protective umbrella," the spokes of which were local Party bureaucrats able to reduce business risks by signing licenses or stifling the curiosity of regulatory bodies. The cost of the umbrella was high but could be paid in a variety of currencies. "If we ran into a senior CP official," explained a European businessman in Fuzhou, "we might have bought him an apartment; we might have bought him a car; we might have arranged a scholarship for his son or daughter to go to the Sorbonne, Heidelberg, or perhaps Oxford."

Mysterious events can curtail the careers of Communist Party officials without warning or explanation. Once expelled, they must survive on a measly pension that cannot keep pace with inflation. In his perceptive novel *A Case of Two Cities*, Qiu Xiaolong relates the gripping fictional tale of a PCN that straddles Fuzhou and Shanghai. Contemplating a difficult interview with a powerful Party official, Qiu's hero, Chief Inspector Chen (no relation to Chen Kai!) reflects on the pressure of public service and money in China:

> Chen understood why a large number of Party cadres were unable to resist the materialistic temptation. As Dong had implied, the system was far from fair. As a hardworking chief inspector, Chen earned about the same state-specified salary that a janitor in the bureau did. . . . Once he had seen a Ming-style mahogany desk in a furniture store. It took him five or six months to save enough money for it. When he finally went there with the sum, the desk was long gone.

The logic for both bureaucrats and policemen is inexorable—they have to leverage the moneymakers, be they businessmen, criminals, or both, while they are able. And even if they are not inclined to corruption, pressure from their peers will usually change their minds—a single mouse cannot survive in a house of cats. Chinese officials invest billions of dollars every year across the globe as personal guarantees against enforced retirement or, worse, a political purge. The latest vogue for both businessmen and Party officials is for their children to be born abroad, preferably in the United States, so that the youngsters are eligible for American citizenship. Because the relationship between the bureaucracy and business is corrupt and not accountable to an independent judiciary, the Political Criminal Nexus creates an environment in which weeds and flowers alike can bloom. The more poisonous varieties draw the immediate attention of the head gardener: criminal groups prone to violence or fomenting public disorder usually attract swift police intervention. In stark contrast to Russia in the 1990s, the Chinese state has fiercely resisted ceding its monopoly on violence to private organizations.

Until 2003, Fuzhou's PCN was rampant—Chen Kai's friends in high places included the mayor and deputy party secretary of Fuzhou and the most senior members of the Party Consultative Committee. Even when Chen's main protector, Xu Congrong, retired, he was able to appoint his successor as police chief to ensure that Chen's economic dominance was not interrupted. Over a ten-year period, Chen paid out tens of millions of dollars in bribes, securing influence throughout the entire administration.

Fuzhou is no ordinary provincial capital—it is the center of one of the globe's biggest illegal operations—the trade in Chinese migrant labor. Squeezed by a rapidly growing population and high rural unemployment, more than half a million Fujianese were smuggled abroad between 1985 and 1995. Around a fifth of these landed on America's eastern seaboard and headed for New York, including most of the 286 souls who swam to New York's shore from the *Golden Venture,* run aground in 1993 after its human cargo finally mutinied after months of mistreatment. In São Paulo, in Belgrade, in Berlin, in Dubai, and in South Africa, the Fujianese have either established or come to dominate the Chinese communities. The province's distinct dialect is steadily eroding Cantonese as the lingua franca in many Chinatowns around the world. Brooklyn's Eighth Avenue began as a Cantonese settlement but in just six years since the millennium, immigrants from Fujian have come to make up almost 50 percent of the population.

The snakeheads of Fujian pump these people relentlessly into boats, planes, and trains to replenish what has now become the biggest retail trading and migrant labor network in the world. And in return the migrants pump remittances and capital back into Fujian. They also reduce the unemployment rate in the province. Let there be no doubt: the snakeheads enjoy the tacit backing of the authorities both thanks to the rules of the PCN and because at an even higher level, it is not in Beijing's interests to disrupt the trade. The local authorities are brazen in their support for emigration, some styling themselves as part of a "New Overseas Chinese Area." They even organize classes instructing aspiring migrants in "general knowledge about foreign countries (legal affairs, customs, local conditions abroad) and training in sewing, cooking, and trading," as Frank Pieke, a leading Oxford scholar on Chinese migration, has observed.

The government in Beijing completes the virtuous circle of profit by placing all manner of taxes and financial incentives for overseas Chinese to invest back in the mainland. There are no awkward questions asked about its origin, which goes some way in explaining why the two biggest sources of capital invested in China are Hong Kong and the British Virgin Islands!

Fuqing, fifty miles southeast of Fuzhou, is just another million-strong city that has sprung up in a decade unbeknownst to the rest of China, let alone the outside world. Fuqing exports two main commodities—car windshields (it supplies 90 percent of China's needs) and labor migrants. In the city center, preposterously garish skyscrapers overwhelm the unprepossessing residential blocks of the Communist period. The showpiece is the enigmatically titled Surefar Enjoy Hotel, adorned by hundreds of reflective copper windows, a reminder of how post-Communist arriviste chic always has a surprise in store. The more outrageous the architecture, the more prosperous the city, and there is a lot of cash in Fuqing. The snakeheads, conveyors of men and women to their Yankee dream, generate much of it.

But it is the rural settlements around the major cities such as Fuqing that offer the most astonishing testimony to the adventurous spirit of the Fujianese. In place of rice and tea, the Fujianese peasant has planted houses. Not shacks or cutesy cottages but five- and six-story neoclassical monsters financed by their earnings overseas. Hundreds upon hundreds are dotted around the Fujianese countryside—the majority contain just one family, who occupy only a single floor. Many are completely empty. These are the most ubiquitous and grand manifestations of "face" in Fujian. Regardless of one's personal woes, "face" dictates that one must project one's achievements in as ostentatious a manner as possible. As a foreigner, it is nigh impossible to pay a restaurant bill if dining with an indigent in China, as all would regard this an unacceptable loss of "face." And so to show their "face" to the outside world in all its pomp, the labor migrant of Fujian cultivates houses.

The seeds of this strange fruit are scattered by the snakehead. It is the snakehead who enables the unemployed to escape rural poverty and have a shot at making it big somewhere in the world. Whole villages or communities club together to pay for the trip. It costs between $20,000 and $70,000 (depending on the émigré's location) to send a single person abroad. Once the nominated worker has arrived at a foreign destination, he or she is expected to work all hours for the benefit of those who have pooled their savings to pay the snakehead.

In the West, the moniker "snakehead" has a pejorative ring to it—they are portrayed popularly as evil, manipulative crime bosses, exploiting the misery of China's despairing poor by sending them to a labor hellhole in some godforsaken part of the world. Cases that conform to this image— the *Golden Venture* in New York, the Dutch truck in Dover with its payload of dead men, and the Morecambe Bay cockle pickers tragedy—are in fact the exception that prove the rule. Snakeheads are not Triads, the criminal outfits based in Hong Kong that are classic mafia protection and extortion rackets as well as traders in illegal goods. Nor are they linked organizationally with the syndicates that dominate Taiwanese politics, such as the United Bamboo Gang. Rather, they are effectively travel agents who include illegal entry to a third country in their service remit.

In the United States, the Department of Justice floated an idea of offering an amnesty to illegal Chinese immigrants who would testify against the snakeheads. "When the DOJ came to me with this idea," explained Professor Ko-lin Chin in New Jersey, "I said, 'You've gotta be crazy!' These snakeheads are regarded as heroes by the illegal immigrants. They pay the fee quite happily—there is no coercion. The snakeheads are heroes, not villains. The last thing the migrants want to do is turn these people in—they want to thank them!"

We will never know what Lin Guohua thought of the snakehead who flew him to Belgrade. The Serbian capital witnessed the fastest growth of any Chinatown in the world during the late 1990s, despite Serbia's status at the time as an international pariah. Slobodan Milosevic had cultivated the Chinese leadership after the imposition of economic sanctions on the former Yugoslavia in 1993. This included lifting Serbia's visa requirement for Chinese citizens: the snakeheads could now fly planeloads of would-be migrants close to the heart of Europe. No more dodgy boat trips; no more expensive negotiations with Russian and Ukrainian policemen. No more setting up safe houses in Bucharest or dodging police in Budapest. Wham! Fly to within 250 miles of the European Union's borders and receive a friendly welcome. The infrastructure was up and running within weeks—

at Belgrade's administrative offices, bilingual signs went up in an attempt to assist the Chinese seeking to smuggle themselves into the EU. A bubbling Chinatown sprang up among the tower blocks at the end of Yuri Gagarin Street in New Belgrade. As I wandered around this cacophonous retail madhouse, it was clear that unlike in most Chinatowns, the traders had no interest in penetrating the local Serbian market (ridden by hyperinflation, gangsterism, and poverty): they were servicing the itinerant Chinese with final provisions for their journey north and west. This is where many of the fifty-eight men who suffocated in the Dutch truck at Dover in the summer of 2000 first touched European soil before being taken across Slovenia into Austria and then up to Rotterdam.

Milosevic, of course, knew perfectly well why the Chinese were arriving every day in the hundreds. It was his way of sticking two fingers up at the EU for Brussels's hostility toward him. The Chinese government knew this as well. Because it doesn't view the snakeheads as criminal, either. By exporting labor, the snakeheads extend China's influence around the world and contribute to the economy hugely by alleviating unemployment. Moreover, those workers abroad send back remittances to bolster the Chinese economy further. Others who celebrate the snakeheads (often tacitly) include the European, American, and Middle Eastern businessmen and -women who revel in the Chinese's unstinting work ethic that comes at a bargain price. The consumer also benefits (albeit unwittingly) because the cost of labor drives down prices and extends choice.

So if all parties involved profit from the work of the snakeheads, should they not, perhaps, be legalized? And why are they so excoriated in the West?

The snakeheads are smugglers, not traffickers. They do not, on the whole, fix up jobs in the country of destination—they get you there and then it is up to you. Victims of labor trafficking are kidnapped or duped by traffickers in league with employers who intend to enslave or coerce the migrant laborers. The snakeheads who arranged the travel plans for the ill-fated cockle pickers who were swept out to sea from the beach at Morecambe Bay in Lancashire had nothing to do with their employment. They conveyed them to the United Kingdom as they had agreed—no more and no less. And few Chinese are forced into overseas labor contracts—they enter into them willingly. The illegality of labor smuggling lies in the illogicality of globalization. The EU (the United Kingdom, Ireland, Spain, and Italy in particular) is desperately short of labor. By 2050, Europe's median age will have risen to fifty—only Japan is aging faster. As Europeans get older, they place an ever-greater strain on the generous welfare state systems that became the Continent's hallmark after the Second World War.

But because they are also having ever-fewer children, the workforce able to sustain the welfare system through taxes is shrinking.

And so Europe is faced with a choice: either its citizens rediscover the joy of reproductive sex, or they allow more people from outside into the labor market. Few Europeans objected to the opening of markets in far-flung places to allow the export of their goods, services, and capital as globalization took hold. But they have proved stubbornly reluctant to accept the quid pro quo of labor movement *into* Europe. The governments of the EU find themselves trying to balance the disparate interests of two powerful forces—the populist media that warn against the "swamping" of indigenous culture by immigrants, and the urgent entreaties of business, which needs cheap labor to survive in a ferociously competitive global market. At a European summit in Helsinki in 1999, prime ministers from across the continent pledged to cooperate in developing a managed immigration policy to introduce some order into this unholy mess. Eight years later, even the most experienced observers of Brussels's arcane bureaucracy have yet to register any verifiable sightings of the policy in action—and so for shrewd entrepreneurs such as the snakeheads, opportunity continues to knock.

Because of its very nature, the level of illegal migration is impossible to ascertain, but Britain is generally regarded as the favorite destination for migrants seeking work. Throughout the 1990s and the first decade of the millennium, the long-term impact of Margaret Thatcher's economic reforms ensured that there were plenty of low-paid jobs available in Britain as the service and construction sectors boomed. In the retail sector, supermarkets demanded produce in much larger quantities than before as Britain aped the megastore patterns familiar in the United States (but rare elsewhere in Europe). Farmers and food-processing companies looked abroad for the army of laborers prepared to undertake the miserably repetitive and physically shattering work of picking and sorting produce for low pay. The decline of trades unions and the rise in affluence of the indigenous population enabled employers to drive down wages in these industries for the predominantly immigrant workforce. Outside of Starbucks and McDonald's, the only time immigrant workers came to public attention was either when they committed a crime or when they died in gruesome circumstances.

Although the Fujianese dominate the Chinese communities in south Asia and helped to establish new Chinatowns in places like Budapest and São Paulo, in Britain they came up against one of the most entrenched communities, the Cantonese from Hong Kong, whose pedigree stretches back to the nineteenth century. Unable to assimilate into this community, the Fujianese were pushed to the margins, where they became prey to some of the most unscrupulous employers in the country—the gangmasters. And this was the misfortune of the cockle pickers in Morecambe Bay. Of the nineteen who drowned there in February 2004, sixteen came from Fuqing and surrounding villages.

"He called me just a few hours before he drowned," sobs Su Hangqi quietly. "He told me about the cockle picking and how he hated the job and that it was badly paid. He said he received five pounds for one bag of cockles but that he would have to carry on if he were to receive his back pay. One fellow called his wife, my friend," Su continues, "from the beach as they were drowning. 'The water is up to my chest,' he told her. 'The bosses got the time wrong. I can't get back in time!' " He was still talking as the water engulfed them.

In her early thirties, Su now brings up her daughters in two rooms of a rundown cottage twenty minutes from Fuqing. She has no electricity and one gas ring, and she occasionally secures work at a local restaurant, washing up. "I still owe 300,000 renmibi [$40,000] to the cosponsors and I am paying interest on this," she continues. Her nine-year-old clings to her side, looking frightened and sorrowful. On her fleece is written a message in English. I MISS YOU, MY FRIEND.

Su and Mrs. Lin, whose husband, Lin Guohua, also drowned, are quick to exonerate the snakehead who transported their menfolk. "This is simply supply and demand," Mrs. Lin says briskly. "Our husbands and cousins wanted to travel to England, and they provided that service." They insist that the snakehead (or "the boss," as they call him) demanded the money only once their husbands had confirmed arrival in Europe and the UK. But I sense they protest too much when I inquire whether they had been in touch with the boss since the accident. "I never met him. I never saw him," says Su nervously. "I only know his bank account and after I paid him— I didn't have any contact." I am still convinced the two women were holding back, frightened of retribution should details about the snakehead leak out.

It is only by accident that Mrs. Lin reveals how the smugglers had threatened her husband with violence if he complained about his treatment. Snakeheads regularly use violence against clients who don't pay up. Most have associates living in Chinatowns the world over to enforce the pay schedule if necessary. The journeys are uncomfortable, uncertain, and frightening at best. At worst, they are fatal. They are not nice people and they are involved in organized criminal activities. Nonetheless, the migrants whom they smuggle are clients more often than victims.

They are not disposed, of course, to hand out compensation to their clients if things go wrong, as at Morecambe Bay. The two widows, Mrs. Su and Mrs. Lin, cling desperately to the fanciful notion that the British government will compensate them so that they can escape the misery of a hand-to-mouth existence defined by huge debt. Their creditors refuse to believe that London has not granted them compensation. In reality, they have abandoned hope—they are flotsam on the turbulent seas of globalization and crime.

> JAMES B. COMEY, the United States Attorney for the Southern District of New York, and DUAN DAQI, Police Liaison Officer for the Ministry of Public Security for the People's Republic of China, announced today that 25 defendants have been indicted in Manhattan federal court for being members of a massive heroin-trafficking organization that smuggled more than $100 million worth of Southeast Asian heroin into the United States from 2000 to the present. At present, 20 people have been arrested, both here and overseas.

The joint statement by Comey and Daqi in May 2003 was triumphant. They had arrested the 125 Gang's four top leaders, known in the heroin-smuggling trade as "The Untouchables." The quartet's nickname was not just an ironic homage to Eliot Ness, the purported nemesis of Al Capone. The number one Untouchable, Wong Kin Cheung, had boasted that they would never be caught. The Untouchables were the masterminds of the 125 Gang, named after stubby Mr. Wong's great weight, 125 kilograms (275 pounds). Wong had first come to the attention of U.S. law enforcement in 1989 for his role in a drug network run out of Manhattan's Chinatown. Arrested and convicted, he was sentenced to four years in jail followed by deportation to China after he had completed his sentence in 1994.

Back in Asia, Wong secured Hong Kong citizenship for himself but commuted between Britain's colonial territory (until it came back under the jurisdiction of the mainland in 1997) and Fuzhou. In Fuzhou, Wong set up his own nightclub, the Huamei Entertainment Co., which is located a few hundred meters from Chen Kai's Music Plaza. According to Chen's business partners, the relationship between the two men was cordial. Using Fuzhou and Hong Kong as his two headquarters, Wong established links with heroin wholesalers among the rebel Shan tribes in eastern Burma, the world's second-largest opium-growing region after Afghanistan. A significant part of the resistance to Burma's foul military junta is based on two less than salubrious trades—trafficking in heroin and trafficking in women, the former servicing addicts throughout the world, the latter servicing primarily the tens of thousands of Western men visiting Thailand every year for cheap sex. The opium is grown in the Golden Triangle, much of which is in Shan-held territory. The failure of Western policy in Afghanistan since the intervention of 2001 has ensured that the central Asian country has outstripped all other poppy-growing regions in the world. But thanks to the liberalization of trade between Burma and China, the Golden Triangle has also experienced a revival of its opium tradition.

Until 1949, China had been a major grower, consumer, and exporter of opium. But after Mao Zedong's Communist takeover in 1949, the industry was eradicated as the Party constructed an effective and ruthless police state. Opiates disappeared from China for forty years, but as Deng Xiaoping's economic reforms accelerated in the early 1990s, the drug in its modern form, heroin, began creeping back. By 1998, the Shanghai Annual Police Review reported that drug-related crime was up 250 percent over the previous year. This increase reflected a trend visible across the country, but it was especially resonant in Shanghai, China's first port and second city, because of its pre-war history. Shanghai in the 1920s and 1930s was an international treaty city that was used by imperial powers to manage trade in and out of China. It was divided up into different zones, or concessions, each run by a European power and the United States. Along with Chicago, it was also the largest center of criminal activity in the world. Thanks to the organizational genius of Du Yuehsheng, known by all as Big-eared Du, the Shanghai Triads were consolidated under his group, the Green Gang, whose history became intimately linked to the rise of Chiang Kai-shek as the head of China's nationalist movement. Just as political parties in Eastern Europe and the Soviet Union fused with crime groups to finance themselves after the fall of Communism, so did China's political movements (including the Communist Party) fund themselves through crime in the 1920s and thirties.

Where Al Capone rose on a tidal wave of illegal liquor, Big-eared Du developed Shanghai as the largest center for the sale and global distribution of opium from the Golden Triangle. Even more than gambling and prostitution, opium was Shanghai's trademark, reinforcing the port's separateness from the rest of China, and notably from its great rival, Beijing. Although the Green Gang opened tentative negotiations with Mao and the Communist Party in the late forties in anticipation of the coming political earthquake, no agreement was reached. Once the revolution triumphed in 1949, Mao succeeded in destroying the influence of the Shanghai Triads. Organized crime, which had exerted such a profound influence on Chinese history in the nineteenth and twentieth centuries, was obliterated as a social and economic force for three decades. The Triads, the entrepreneurs of rebellion and collaboration in the name of profit, and whose name implied the harmonious balance between Heaven, Earth, and Man, were eradicated. The traditions and structures survived in the colonial remnants, Hong Kong and Macao, but also in Chiang Kai-shek's Taiwan and the Chinatowns of Southeast Asia and Europe. Some have argued that the destruction of Shanghai's Triads was one of Mao's monumental achievements. Others have countered that in dismantling them he turned the Chinese state into one of the most powerful criminal instruments ever devised, a killing machine that has the blood of 40 million people on its hands.

Mao's legacy remains palpable in Shanghai: the Triads have not returned since the liberalization of the country's economy. But heroin has made a forceful comeback. It did so with the millions of migrant workers that Shanghai needed to construct its hypermodernist skyline. From their cramped, miserable quarters in squalid districts such as Xuhui, the peasantry, often illiterate and already with a heroin habit picked up in the villages, have been building the new Shanghai's skyscrapers at frenetic speed. Thanks to his astonishing documentary series *Shanghai Vice,* the British director Phil Agland has given an excellent insight into how seriously Shanghai's police forces now view the issue of the heroin trade and what an immense challenge it presents. The chief of the criminal investigation unit, Li Ruiping, reported that by 1999 hundreds of kilos per month were entering Shanghai to supply local addicts. This estimate suggests ferocious rates of drug dependency. "There are two networks that supply heroin to Shanghai," he continued. "We haven't penetrated them yet, but these rings are very sophisticated." One network transports heroin from the far west, Xinjiang Province, which borders Kyrgyzstan and receives its heroin from Afghanistan. The other comes up through the Burmese border into southern China. Both pass through the central distribution center of Guangdong, Canton Province. Here not only are prices low but levels of police corruption are high. In one dramatic sequence of *Shanghai Vice,* the Shanghai police mount an undercover sting in Guangdong without alerting the local police because—as they openly admit—their Cantonese colleagues are so corrupt that they would tip off the heroin wholesalers immediately.

The Shanghai police are frank that with these levels of corruption and limited financial resources, it has been extremely difficult to infiltrate the new decentralized crime networks that have spread across the country. In the drug trade, they wield one very blunt but intimidating instrument—the death penalty. The courts can order the execution of anyone found with just fifty grams (1.75 ounce) of heroin, or long periods of imprisonment for possession of less. "China has plenty of state-run rehabilitation centers," as one commentator noted, "but they function more like prisons and treat drug users like criminals. Some addicts even find it easier to buy drugs from crooked guards inside the detox centers than on the streets. Not surprisingly, the failure rate at these facilities is alarmingly high: relapses are estimated at between seventy percent and ninety percent."

Chinese jails are now being clogged up by vulnerable users. The big dealing syndicates who have sufficient cash not just to bribe police forces but to establish their own intelligence and countersurveillance operations are netted less often. The Intelligence Division of the U.S. drug-busting agency, the DEA, has now reported that "many individuals and criminal organizations involved in drug trafficking are increasingly arming themselves with automatic weapons and grenades to protect their drug shipments from theft by rival organizations. Many firefights occur along the Burma-China border, where larger drug shipments are more prevalent. Traffickers also arm themselves to avoid being captured by the police, and some smugglers are better armed than the local police forces. Furthermore, many traffickers believe they have a better chance of surviving a firefight than the outcome of any legal proceedings."

The emergence of armed groups inside China and around its borders threatens, of course, to undermine the state's monopoly on violence and is therefore regarded with utmost seriousness by the authorities. This may have influenced Beijing's deliberations when it agreed in 2000 to permit the creation of the first-ever joint DEA–China Public Security Bureau operation. The Chinese have a long history of suspicion of outside powers that was heavily reinforced by their experience as major victims of imperialism and colonialism in the nineteenth and twentieth centuries. For Beijing to sanction a joint police task force that saw DEA agents operate on Chinese soil was a hugely telling decision that symbolized China's deepening relationship with the outside world. Operation City Lights was set up after a DEA informer working in Manhattan's Chinatown told his handler that the 125 Gang was exporting heroin to the eastern seaboard from Fuzhou. After an operation that lasted a full two years and encompassed not just China, Hong Kong, and the United States but India as well, the federal government was understandably pleased that the arrests of The Untouchables and the 125 Gang, led by Wong Kin Cheung, involved "unprecedented cooperation between the DEA, FBI, Bureau of Immigration and Customs Enforcement, the New York City Police Department, together with the People's Republic of China, and the Hong Kong Special Administrative Region. This represents the first coordinated dismantling of a narcotics-trafficking organization by the United States, the People's Republic of China ('PRC'), and Hong Kong in history."

One of those picked up in the Fuzhou swoop on May 16, 2003, was none other than Chen Kai, "the richest man in Fuzhou." He was arrested on suspicion of having laundered drug money on behalf of Wong. To the outside world, Chen's arrest was largely meaningless—he was an unknown accessory of the 125 Gang. But in Fuzhou itself, the news provoked panic among the local administration. Xu Congrong, the former chief of police and Chen's main protector, fled the country for the United States, where he quickly lost himself among the Fujianese of New York.

It was not long before the focus of the investigation into Chen Kai switched from narcotics to corruption. The leading figures from a Political Criminal Nexus in China always attract jealousy and hostility, especially from those bureaucrats who are excluded from their network. But whistleblowers are few and far between in China—exposing corruption is a very risky undertaking. Unless they gain the confidence and ear of an official with more clout than the one they are trying to nail (and that means finding someone influential in Beijing), campaigners against corruption have in the past usually found themselves demoted, publicly humiliated, and even imprisoned. The trick is to wait until the PCN is genuinely vulnerable. When Chen Kai was arrested, some fast-thinking official got the message to Beijing that this went even deeper than money laundering. "Once Chen Kai was arrested," the tea-sipping Fuzhou businessman explained, "then his enemies in Fuzhou moved very quickly to alert the Party Disciplinary Committee."

The purge began with eight senior officials being placed under house arrest, including Song Licheng, the deputy party boss in Fuzhou. By the end of December another seventeen were taken in for questioning and charged with corruption. Two years later on and "we still hear of people being arrested," said the businessman. "So many have been arrested that we stopped counting and barely notice it anymore."

The rot ran so deep that President Hu Jintao, the most powerful man in the country, personally ordered the dispatch of thirty investigators to Fuzhou in April 2004. The president also requested that he be informed of all developments in the Chen Kai case. The team from Beijing started their work by dismissing the most senior anti-corruption official in the city (who had allegedly secured an apartment in Chen's luxury Triumphant Gardens complex).

Eighteen months after his arrest, Chen Kai was finally tried at the Intermediary Court in Nanping, a provincial town in Fuzhou. (It was reasoned that there was a high chance of any proceedings in Fuzhou being nobbled either by Chen's allies or by his enemies.) But there was a surprise in store when the charges were read out. There was no mention of the laundered drug money. The accusations of bribing officials were relatively minor. Instead, Chen's main crime was the running of a brothel.

Nobody in Fuzhou disputes that prostitution rackets were part of Chen's empire. Indeed, at the Baihe Hot Springs Hotel, where I stayed and which was part of Chen's operation, there was no question that the massage and hot springs parlor on the fourth floor was nothing other than a knocking shop. Chen's guilty verdict shocked nobody, but the city was stunned to hear that he was sentenced to death for the crime. "If you execute everyone in Fuzhou involved in running brothels," said a friend of Chen's who, like everyone else, was insistent on remaining anonymous, "then you'd wipe out half the city."

Chen protested the sentence and by law his appeal should have been heard within two months of the original sentencing. "But we have heard nothing since then," said the friend. "We don't even know if he is alive or dead. But there are a lot of people in the city administration who will be relieved if he is dead." Chen Kai was no angel, but his conviction and death sentence for running a brothel looks suspiciously like a state-sponsored murder, designed to keep the details of the PCN firmly beyond the public domain.

The case of Chen Kai does not suggest that China is an especially dangerous or crime-ridden place. Prostitutes, for example, rarely have to pay off a pimp. In Shanghai sex workers openly negotiate their own price with Westerners in bars that are well known to the authorities as pickup joints. As long as there is no violence, nobody interferes. Street crime is very low by comparison with Taiwan or Hong Kong. But Chen's case does highlight that in the absence of the rule of law, corruption renders the distinction between legitimate and criminal business opaque and sometimes completely obscure. Within China itself, this has developed into a political problem for the party, the authority of which is threatened by the political criminal nexuses that rule most cities.

But this blurring of the line between the licit and illicit becomes an even greater headache when projected onto the international stage because of the most widespread crime in new China—counterfeiting—and America's determination to enforce intellectual property law or copyright. Of course, counterfeiting in China is not about currency (that is the specialty of North Korea) but goods. If it is popular anywhere else in the world, you can bet that within months somebody will be producing a counterfeit version in China. No one fakes it like the Chinese.

Most megalopolises such as São Paulo, Mexico City, Istanbul, and Cairo have a history stretching back hundreds if not thousands of years. Twenty years ago, Shenzhen had a population of several thousand and was no more than a few scattered villages. From the gentle agricultural pastures of northern Hong Kong, you can now cross into a 12 million–strong giant of hypermalls, factories, tower blocks, and work, work, work. Shenzhen on the Pearl River Delta is the gateway to the new China, having formed a profoundly dynamic symbiotic relationship with Hong Kong. One of the original special economic zones, not only has Shenzhen become the blazing vanguard of China's future, but it has even rescued the former British colony from decline by throwing it a lifeline of economic opportunity. If there is a market niche, the entrepreneurs of Shenzhen will sniff it out and fill it. Mo Bangfu, a Chinese journalist who has traveled to Chinatowns throughout the world, explained how it works. "I went to Dubai recently," he said. "There is a river and there are all these little boats heading for Africa packed with mountains of products. All the products are made in China. They are like little capillaries coming off the veins, feeding places like Sudan, feeding places like Iran despite the American embargo, feeding places like the DRC, feeding Zimbabwe—feeding places with goods from China that other people don't go to, as well as the ones they do go to. They ship very cheap things to Dubai and to Africa—there is very little added value. Maybe it's a bra; maybe it's little plastic things for the kitchen. So to bring it from China to Dubai and then Dubai into Africa, how could you make a profit once you take the shipping costs into account?"

The goods are shipped from the world's cheapest miscellany goods markets, such as Yei Wu near Shanghai or Shenzhen. Mo explained how China's economies of scale allow their traders to produce goods at a tenth of the price found elsewhere. "And they will push down the price to a point where nobody else can be bothered to compete," he concluded. That same day, I watched a report on BBC World Television demonstrating how manufacturers in Egypt had given up producing the souvenirs sold in Cairo and at the pyramids—they are now almost all shipped from China.

The world economy has never experienced a change comparable to the release of energy of 1.25 billion people that followed China's renewed reforms in 1991. From accounting for less than 1 percent of global trade in 1990, China had become the world's third-largest trader by 2004, outstripping Japan and lagging behind only the entire European Union and the United States. Analysts at the World Trade Organization predicted that its 6.7 percent of global trade in that year would top 10 percent within a decade. In its 2007 Trade Policy Review of China, the WTO also pointed out that in the course of this ten-year expansion the country would need to create yet another 100 million jobs. China's economies of scale mean that China can already compete in any industrial sector and before long in most service sectors too.

But with China, there is one major problem, which is visible more or less wherever you travel in the country. As I prepared to cross the border from Shenzhen to Hong Kong, I was funneled through a long marketplace selling all manner of knickknacks. I could not judge many of the Asian products on display, but the Rolexes and the DVDs were as bent as a three-dollar bill. Even so, the fake DVD market has now attained such levels of sophistication that some fake brands advertise themselves as "genuine fakes"; that is, 100 percent reliable copies made from master tapes. They have developed this branding to ward off competition from even cheaper DVDs. As a consumer, the reason is soon apparent. In Shanghai, the traders I bought from would slip the DVD into a player in the store to prove before I purchased it that the DVD was studio quality with English dialogue or subtitles. Such a facility was not available in Fuzhou, and as a consequence I picked up a copy of *Night at the Museum* with dialogue only in Russian or Ukrainian (good practice for me, but a huge disappointment to my nine-year-old son), and *Volver*, the English subtitles of which bore no relation to Pedro Almodóvar's heartwarming story about a single mother but instead a preposterous B-movie spy story.

But the DVD store that fascinated me most was on the border between Shenzhen and Hong Kong—not because of the quality of the fakes but because the goods were laid out in one of the country's most heavily policed customs zones. Customs officers were indeed strolling by unconcerned as I was purchasing counterfeit DVDs for less than a dollar apiece (all for the purposes of research, of course). Being offered a fake DVD by a Chinese trader is an everyday experience in many parts of the world. But in

China, if you want to show "face" to the outside world, you can be much more ambitious. Why bother buying a Mercedes-Benz when you could buy a Geely! A quarter of the price of a Merc but physically almost identical. And the fervor for faking it doesn't even stop there.

In January 2004, the two German engineering and electrical giants, Siemens and ThyssenKrupp, watched proudly as their Maglev train, the Transrapid, left Shanghai's Long Yang Station for its inaugural commercial journey to Pudong International Airport. The Transrapid's electromagnetic technology enabled this remarkable train to complete the twenty-mile journey in just under eight minutes, traveling at a top speed of 270 miles an hour. It is the fastest ground transportation system in the world. But it was expensive. When the Chinese announced a possible eighty-five-mile extension to the tourist destination Hangzhou, they received a shock when the German consortium put a $6 billion price tag on its construction.

One December evening in 2004, CCTV cameras were monitoring the maintenance depot of the Transrapid in Shanghai when they recorded the unexpected arrival of a team of Chinese engineers. They began measuring, weighing, and testing the entire train. Within a year, China announced it would be building its own high-speed Maglev train. Before long, the German foreign minister, Frank-Walter Steinmeier, had become involved in the row and the German press accused China of having stolen the technology and pirated German know-how on an unbelievable scale. Siemens and ThyssenKrupp were faced with a dilemma. Although the Transrapid was a huge project, they were bidding for other major investments in China as well and opted to tread very cautiously. Furthermore, Shanghai is the only world showcase for the Transrapid, and the consortium needs cordial relations with the Chinese to demonstrate the achievement to other prospective customers. Eventually, a compromise was reached whereby 90 percent of the new trains would be manufactured in China under German supervision, which still represents a huge loss to the consortium.

There is nothing the Chinese will not copy. Whether it is Harry Potter involved in entirely new adventures such as *Harry Potter and the Crystal Turtle;* Swedish bathroom fittings; spare parts for aircraft; furniture; non-toxic paints (the fakes made, of course, with highly toxic materials); food-stuffs; clothes—anything that is produced is fair game for the Chinese counterfeiters. The European Union Commission estimates that fake goods around the world are worth between $250 and $500 *billion* a year. Of these about 60 percent originate in the People's Republic of China—between 20 and 25 percent of exports from China are counterfeits, while between 85 and 90 percent of products sold in the domestic Chinese market are fake.

Intellectual property theft has assumed center stage in the relationship between China on one side and the world's other three main trading powers—the EU, the United States, and Japan—on the other. The latter (the United States in particular) advance two arguments in demanding that the Chinese government do something about the problem. First, they insist it is unfair for counterfeit manufacturers to derive profit from goods into which they have invested no development or marketing capital. Second is the issue of safety. This began to exercise the government in Berlin after German customs confiscated $200 millions' worth of counterfeit goods in 2003, among which they discovered spare brake pads for Volkswagen vehicles. Though the spares look authentic, they are invariably cobbled together in a hurry—safety is not a primary concern of the counterfeit manufacturers, and the brake pads have the potential for transforming their host vehicles into death traps. Although refreshingly entrepreneurial, the producers and retailers of these goods are organized criminal syndicates.

Since being admitted to the World Trade Organization in 2001, the government of China has rapidly introduced the core legislation required to combat intellectual property theft. Three serious issues, however, ensure that implementation is a different matter. First, although China is a one-party police state, its various police forces suffer from shortfalls in funding as well as from huge inefficiencies and corruption. Second, the government is reluctant to launch a concerted campaign against counterfeiting companies that employ an incalculable number of workers who might otherwise be on the streets. And finally, the Political Criminal Nexuses that run the provincial economies are even less interested than the central government in playing by the book, even if it means alienating Western partners.

The expansion of global trade that has accompanied China's rise in the past two decades has undoubtedly assisted in lifting tens of millions out of poverty—this is a monumental step forward for China and other emerging economies. But the rush to trade has left the world's ability to police and monitor trade flows in a mess. The World Trade Organization is supposed to ensure fair play and as free an exchange of goods around the world as possible within existing rules. But noble though its aims are, in practice the WTO just holds the ring as a group of prizefighting countries use their muscle and guile to secure as great an advantage as possible at the expense of others. In the blue corner, a tag team defending unfair subsidies shapes up to the producers of counterfeit goods in the red corner. Naturally, the weak and defenseless take quite a bruising in this arena.

The Future of Organized Crime

In 2007, the despairing failure of the Doha round of world trade negotiations, the aim of which was to smooth out such conflicts and contradictions, suggests that trade disputes will become ever bitterer in the coming years. China's imperative to create jobs through exporting goods means that the temptation not to clamp down on fake products will remain high, especially as its ability to police the trade is limited.

Individual Western companies have found that China's Public Security Bureau is a weak, inefficient, corrupt, and unwilling partner. So increasingly they are turning instead to the many foreign and domestic business consultants now found throughout the country. Companies engage these consultants for all manner of services, chiefly to negotiate a passage through the Scylla and Charybdis of the national and local bureaucracies. But frequently they charge them with the task of tracking down clandestine operations that are aping Western brands. By painstakingly building up local contacts in the Communist Party (not to mention investing in their futures), in the police, and in Western trade missions, some consultants such as Paul French and Matthew Crabbe's Access Asia in Shanghai can arrange for raids to be mounted with the collaboration of local law enforcement agencies. "We have to find the factory," explained French.

> We have to do the due diligence. Then we get the court to issue the raid order and then we get the cops—we get on well with the Shanghai police. The problem is they have to tell the local police, who may or may not inform the people we want to raid. So we send an advance guard to the factory and then go to the police. If you work with an American brand, the consulate will send somebody to the courts and on the raid. Then we go in, Rambo-style, kick down the doors and seize the goods. But piracy is only a civil offence in this country. We can fine them but we can't put them in prison, and in a couple of days, they've opened up somewhere else.

China allows these private law enforcement agencies to operate, but under strict supervision—and the muscle work is usually left to the police. Cracking down on opportunist enterprises churning out Louis Vuitton bags for the tourist market is enervating work, as they seem to breed like rabbits. Still, they are vulnerable to rough policing if the local authorities are genuinely committed. But bigger and more troublesome enterprises are now springing up in several parts of China that are not so easily cowed. The Empire of Counterfeiters is beginning to strike back, and the strength of the Dark Side is gathering at an alarming rate.

Traveling inland southwest from Xiamen in southern Fujian Province, the road begins to rise. As one climbs ever higher, the vegetation becomes less verdant, the trees craggier. The constant business of China's cities recedes in favor of a Confucian quietude. In November 2006, a young officer from the TMAD (Tobacco Monopoly Administration Department) was on roadblock duty when he spotted a motorcycle with a driver and pillion passenger heading in his direction at speed. The TMAD, which is a crack law enforcement unit, spends much of its time in these mountains, which are notorious for hosting huge factories that are buried underground (literally and metaphorically), producing counterfeit cigarettes. The young officer, tough and fit, put out his hand, gesturing the bikers to slow down. As he did so, the pillion rider took out a machete from under his jacket and brought it down with immense force on the officer's arm, severing the limb completely. Although his colleagues rushed him to the nearest hospital an hour away in Xiamen, surgeons were unable to reattach his arm.

The TMAD established which village the attackers came from and approached its elders with the request to hand them over. The elders refused to cooperate with the investigation and in consequence of the attack, the TMAD has dismantled the roadblock program, which had been hailed as a major initiative in the plan to neutralize some of the most powerful gangsters in China. The aim had been to identify the whereabouts of a large underground factory that had been producing American and Japanese brand cigarettes.

The region in southern Fujian is called Da Shan (Big Mountain), and it is home to some of the biggest and most lucrative counterfeit factories in the world. These facilities, built deep into the mountain, produce millions of cigarettes a day, which are then either introduced onto the huge Chinese domestic market or taken by containers around Asia, over to the United States, and elsewhere. Health concerns and legislation aimed at reducing smoking in the United States and Europe may have dented tobacco companies' profits in the West, but in China and Asia, it's party time! As Asians sample smooth Virginian blends in ever-greater numbers, these exceptionally lucrative cowboy operations of Da Shan employ whole villages and communities in this remote region of Fujian to undercut the market with their inexpensive and ever-improving fakes. In doing so, of course, they also undercut the Chinese government's income from sales tax on tobacco, and it is a measure of how seriously Beijing takes the problem that in the

China State Tobacco Monopoly (CSTM), it has created probably the most effective police force in the country.

This is not quite war but something close—the illegal tobacco producers have developed their own intelligence networks, which monitor the activity of the CSTM and customs officials. Law enforcement loses several officers or private sector workers a year to the illegal cigarette producers, and when the CSTM launches a raid, it does so with a mighty paramilitary force. "What if I were to take a drive around Da Shan as a tourist to see what I could find there?" I asked one operative involved in battling the 'baccy mafia. "You can go there," he replied, "but you won't be coming back."

One man well known both to the 'baccy mafia and the Chinese police was Tung Yan Yuk, a.k.a. Tony Tung, who had started his life as a fishmonger north of Xiamen in Fujian. In the late 1990s, Chinese police issued a warrant for his arrest and for that of his two younger brothers. They were charged in connection with tax evasion and cigarette smuggling to the tune of 600 million renminbi ($78 million). One of the brothers was caught and imprisoned indefinitely in 2001, but Tony and the second brother got away. According to a confidential intelligence report on Tung, he no longer visits either Hong Kong or mainland China for fear of arrest. But he is happily ensconced now in Singapore, from where he controls one of the biggest counterfeiting and container empires in Asia. According to police:

> Tung's cigarette smuggling enterprise alone ships between 20 and 50 40-foot container loads of international brand-name cigarettes each month. The cigarettes generally are collected and consolidated in Singapore and then shipped through Manila and Subic Bay to the port of Currimao, Ilocos Norte, in the Philippines bound for China either directly or via Vietnam. Tung owns or controls three container ships, as many as seven oceangoing tankers, and an unknown number of other vessels that he employs to smuggle cigarettes and fuel oil from/to Taiwan, China, the Philippines, and possibly elsewhere in East Asia.

Many of the details of Tung's operation came to light when the Philippines National Police organized a raid against his Forietrans factory, where hundreds of millions of cigarettes were being manufactured illegally. This was a tough job: "Tung's factory—where he made the half a billion sticks of counterfeit Mild Seven—was in Pampanga, north of Manila," reported one operative involved in the raid. "This town is part of the legislative district represented by Congressman Mikey Arroyo, the son of President Arroyo."

Investigators discovered what they had long suspected: evidence showed that Tung was paying off legislators in Taiwan and that he had established links with a factory in North Korea's miserable little free trade zone, Raijin, that was also feeding counterfeit cigarettes into the retail chain.

In criminal terms, these links to North Korea are disturbing. This tawdry state has almost realized the totalitarian dystopia imagined in George Orwell's classic novel 1984. Stalin himself might have blushed at the cult fashioned by the Kim dynasty, whose self-regard grows in inverse proportion to the misery it has spread among the people. Millions face a daily battle against starvation as their leaders gorge themselves on a surfeit of imported luxury foods. To fund their lascivious lifestyle, Kim Jong-il and his acolytes have turned North Korea into a major hub of the shadow and criminal economies in Asia. Renowned as the world's largest producer of virtually undetectable counterfeit $100 bills (the so-called supernotes), North Korea also has a pharmaceutical industry that is primarily devoted to the manufacture of methamphetamines to keep up with demand in Japan. According to sources in the CIA, a major Russian criminal oligarch developed a healthy trade in fissile material with North Korea during the 1990s.

More recently, North Korea has discovered the profits to be made in counterfeiting goods. Like the Chinese, they are willing to turn their hand to anything, although they have proved particularly adept at producing fake cigarettes.

North Korea's emerging reputation as a counterfeiter is grist to the shadow economy's mill because it brings the country ever closer to China's gray zone. Yet North Korea's engagement with the global criminal economy has an unexpected positive side effect. It paradoxically makes Asia a more stable place: the deeper North Korea is sucked into China's economic orbit, the greater the influence Beijing exerts over Pyongyang. Beijing is not interested in a rogue nuclear neighbor acting unpredictably in a region where things are changing very quickly.

China's emergence as a regional superpower with aspirations to reprise this role on a global stage has shuffled the security pack vigorously in Asia. Tensions between China, the two Koreas, Japan, Taiwan, and Russia that until recently appeared abstract are taking on more concrete forms. The most immediate concern both to the United States and to the big regional players—China, Japan, and South Korea—is North Korea's emerging identity as a dysfunctional nuclear power. Japan and the United States have also expressed disquiet about China's growing impact on the security of the entire Asia-Pacific region. Essentially, the days of the United States overwhelmingly defining the security parameters of Pacific Asia are coming to a close.

This has already led to nervousness borne of uncertainty, but China's rise and its hunger for economic growth also demonstrates a profoundly stabilizing effect on many of its smaller, volatile neighbors.

China's economic drive, both as a producer and as a market, is spilling over into transitional neighbors such as Vietnam and the Philippines but also to more settled countries such as Thailand. It is encouraging growth throughout the region. Even the once isolated economies of countries such as North Korea and Burma are beginning to mingle in an ever-more-intimate manner with China's. In the critical case of North Korea, the United States' policy of confronting the government in Pyongyang with angry rhetoric and implicit threats may prove much less effective than the slow, steady absorption of North Korea's economy by Beijing. (The Middle East, where two other members of the Bush-appointed "Axis of Evil" are located, signally lacks a stabilizing power like China.)

China can muster immense influence in North Korea if it feels so inclined. But investigations into sprawling criminal organizations such as the Tung empire reveal that the primary mechanism with which China pacifies the lunatic tendencies of Kim Jong-il's regime in North Korea is through economic integration. The outsourcing of production to North Korea is not restricted to fake cigarettes, counterfeit $100 bills, and methamphetamines. North Korea produces goods even more cheaply than China, and some of the wares we find in Western stores marked "Made in China" are in fact made in North Korea. Rather than threatening to bomb North Korea, the Chinese are very sensibly slowly transforming it into an economic vassal.

And thanks to perhaps the most egregiously silly program instigated by the Bush administration's war on terror (although there is stiff competition for this award), those goods made in North Korea often have a swift and untroubled passage straight to Los Angeles or New York.

After 9/11, Washington decided it would have to beef up its port security. Ninety percent of the world's commercial traffic is transported in containers on the high seas. "In 2001, U.S. Customs processed more than 214,000 vessels and 5.7 million sea containers," according to a U.S. Customs statement. The four largest foreign ports of departure for the United States were 1. Hong Kong, 2. Shanghai, 3. Singapore, and 4. Kaohsiung in Taiwan. And so it was decided by Commissioner Robert C. Bonner that "a proactive stance by Customs in screening sea containers will significantly contribute to the agency's overall efforts to secure the borders against dangers that might be introduced through commercial traffic." The Container Security Initiative (CSI) was born.

Testifying to Congress a few months later, Bonner outlined that "the specific purpose of CSI is to prevent terrorists from using cargo containers to conceal nuclear weapons or radiological materials. With CSI, we are partnering with foreign governments to target and screen high-risk containers for nuclear and radiological materials using technology before the cargo is shipped to U.S. ports. The targeting aspect of CSI involves using sophisticated automated targeting technology to identify high-risk containers, those that may contain terrorist weapons or even terrorists."

All very exciting. And so Bonner dispatched teams of U.S. Customs officers all over the world to the ports that signed up to the CSI—those ports that refused, of course, would lose out to competitors also trading with the United States, and so most were prepared to join in this global extension of U.S. power. Once the containers have been screened in Shanghai or Kaohsiung, they have gone through the Green Channel and are effectively already in the United States.

The great majority of customs officers dispatched around the world have never worked abroad, and only very few speak foreign languages. In Kaohsiung, Taiwan, one of the biggest foci of the CSI, not a single customs officer speaks Mandarin, let alone the Fujianese dialect of Taiwan. And so in order to ascertain which containers might be containing nuclear material or not, they depend upon customs officials from the local port. "These people are the most susceptible of all to bribery and corruption," explained a senior Hong Kong police officer. "And so far as we understand, if you are not carrying nuclear material, if you can succeed in getting your container selected for examination in Kaohsiung or Hong Kong, then you are home free! It is an ideal way to smuggle any manner of goods into the United States." And any number of those goods originate in North Korea.

I asked Mo Bangfu whether the corruption and deceit inherent in China's political and economic life were not in danger of corrupting the world trading system. "Two hundred years ago, people from England came to Shanghai," he began to admonish me. "They were not your fabled 'English gentlemen'! They were pirates! Just as the British pirates came and raped our shores, so there may be pirates out there with the Chinese traders of the present day. But when the market reaches a certain scale, the worst practices will fall away and something that *demands* regulation and an adequate regulatory mechanism will emerge."

If Mo Bangfu is correct in his assumption, then governments around the world may be able to stem the growth of the global shadow economy and the powerful dose of instability that it injects into our lives. But if we fail to construct an adequate regulatory mechanism—that is, some form of global governance—then organized crime and corruption will combine with protectionism and chauvinism to engender a very unstable and very dangerous world.

EPILOGUE

As consumers, we are all involved—often unwittingly—in the shadowy world of transnational organized crime. Food prices have plummeted as a proportion of household income in the past fifteen years. Illegal and trafficked labor has driven down costs in the agricultural industry, and, in Britain, inflation has been kept at acceptable levels in part because of the low wages paid to migrant workers.

In 2005, Italian scientists measured the River Po for a chemical derivative found in urine only after cocaine usage. The highly accurate procedure recorded that the 5 million people in the Po Valley were consuming 1.5 metric tons of the drug every year. This is *twenty* times previous estimates that were based on a haphazard collation of statistics from sociological studies (as with smoking and drinking, users usually underestimate the amount of cocaine they consume, if they are prepared to admit to the habit at all). The white powder still regularly graces the tables of white middle-class professionals at dinner parties in Berlin, London, and New York. By using prohibited narcotics, consumers are not only contributing to huge criminal profits, they bear indirect responsibility for the trail of blood that marks every stage of the drugs' journey.

When I was a student in the 1970s, it was considered completely unacceptable among my peer group to visit a prostitute. Yet today, educated young European men think nothing of flying to Estonia or similar East European destinations on stag weekends where hiring prostitutes is all part of the fun. The profits from these activities derive from the willingness of individuals to break the law or cross social taboos to satisfy their own desires.

But what the ordinary citizen may gain from organized crime in terms of lower food prices or indulgence in recreational drugs, they are at risk of losing in other areas of criminal activity. A huge second revenue source for criminal syndicates is theft, either straightforward larceny or through deception. Cybercrime now threatens all of us and thanks to the ever-greater use of computers in every area of our lives, this even includes people who do not go online. Cybercrime has witnessed an astonishing growth since the millennium and represents perhaps the greatest challenge for public law enforcement worldwide. Cyberpolice suffer from both poor funding and a lack of qualified personnel.

But perhaps the most attractive profession for modern transnational criminals involves taking money from governments. Smuggling goods with high rates of tax is the oldest form of organized crime and remains popular today in industries such as the illegal cigarette trade. But the ability to move money and goods in huge quantities at great speed has also encouraged new forms of crime, especially those that exploit discrepancies in tax regimes around the world. The profits offered by taking advantage of these loopholes are staggering. Europe's most vigorous criminal industry between 2002 and 2007 was "carousel fraud." This involved gangs importing goods into the European Union or between EU countries and illegally claiming the VAT, or sales tax, on these items before reexporting them. The EU reported in 2006 that it could not put an exact figure on the fraud but estimated that the exchequers were losing at least $100 *billion* dollars a year to these fraudulent schemes. The arcane nature of fraud and its status as a "victimless" crime (nobody suffers direct personal injury by the theft of taxpayers' money) boosts its popularity, along with the extraordinary sums it can earn.

The move into large-scale financial crime has been assisted by what has happened to the global financial markets since their liberalization in the past two decades. In 2007, with GDP at around $50 trillion, the consulting firm McKinsey estimated that the world's financial assets were now three times that figure. Even more dizzying and frightening is the figure of $300 trillion that is accounted for by "derivative" securities. In lay terms, the vast sums accruing to the world's largest banks, hedge funds, and private equity firms are the result of ever more arcane speculation on the performance of markets around the world. Successive financial meltdowns have demonstrated that the level of risk associated with these activities is much greater than was predicted.

In the summer of 2007, the collapse of the so-called U.S. subprime mortgage market gave the world a hint of how closely this structure resembles a house of cards. When tens of thousands of Americans with low credit ratings could no longer keep up with the rising interest payments on their homes, financial institutions around the world showed signs of buckling. Central banks in the EU, Japan and Australia, the Federal Reserve in the United States, and Japan's Central Bank pumped more than $150 billion of taxpayers' money into global markets to ward off a greater collapse (roughly the same amount that the beleaguered taxpayers of the EU shell out annually to carousel fraud criminals). BNP Parisbas was among the world's grandest institutions to confess that they were unable to calculate exactly how many hundreds of millions of dollars they had lost in consequence.

This last admission reinforces the urgent need for greater regulation in the financial markets: in a world where legitimate institutions are unable to account properly for their dealings, the ability of criminals to launder their money through this merry-go-round of speculation is greatly increased. The Caymans, British Virgin Islands, and all the other offshore banking centers are the back door through which criminal money can enter into the legitimate, if increasingly opaque, money markets. Western governments could close this anomaly overnight if they took decisive action, making money laundering a significantly trickier prospect. But they don't. And the deeper the involvement of shadow funds with the licit money markets, the harder it becomes to follow the cash that is the key to the successful policing of international organized crime.

Politicians are fond of talking tough on law and order. In June 2005, Prime Minister Tony Blair urged the European parliament to focus on

cross-border intelligence and policing on organized crime; developing proposals to hit the people and drug traffickers hard, in opening up their bank accounts, harassing their activities, arresting their leading members and bringing them to justice; getting returns agreements for failed asylum seekers and illegal immigrants from neighboring countries and others; developing biometric technology to make Europe's borders secure.

The need for strong, well-equipped law enforcement agencies to combat organized crime is axiomatic. But appeals like Blair's that offer solutions based on the greater engagement of the police or military alone betray a profound abdication of political responsibility. They are the product of unimaginative politicians who lack either the vision or the interest to address the great structural inequities in the global economy upon which crime and instability thrive.

It is not globalization in itself that has spurred the spectacular growth of organized crime in recent years but global markets that are either insufficiently regulated, especially in the financial sector, or markets that are too closely regulated, as in the labor and agricultural sectors. In the 1990s, we witnessed the beginnings of a global regulatory regime of the financial markets that held out hope: there was a chance that we might establish a grip both on the partially regulated licit economy and the entirely unregulated shadow economy. Since the millennium, however, a hostile United States, an incompetent European Union, a cynical Russia, and an indifferent Japan have combined with the unstoppable ambition of China and India to usher in a vigorous springtime for both global corporations and transnational organized crime.

ACKNOWLEDGMENTS

The research and writing of this book have occasionally presented me with daunting challenges. I could not have overcome these without considerable help. This book has thus enabled me to work with some wonderful people around the world. I cannot acknowledge them all here and a significant number have asked me not to mention them. They know who they are and many thanks to them.

Over the past several years, I have been privileged to participate in annual discussions hosted in Greece by the leader of Pasok and the former foreign minister of Greece George Papandreou and Ada Papandreou at the Symi symposia of the Andreas Papandreou Foundation. My most sincere thanks to both of them, and to George's vision.

Many participants at the symposia have been generous with their time and knowledge in helping me frame this project, but I must single out four in particular whose friendship has sustained me through thick and thin. Alex Rondos was the inspiration behind an initiative to promote reconciliation between the peoples of Eastern Kosovo, South Serbia, and northern Macedonia, in which I learned for the first time in detail about the overwhelming social and economic importance of organized crime in the region. Richard Parker has always been patient in answering queries on the political economy of the post-Communist era, and the banking industry in particular. Ivan Vejvoda is a masterful observer of the Balkans and one of the region's most distinguished representatives. Mark Medish not only willingly shared his knowledge and experience but also assisted me in reaching several people and places that would otherwise have been impossible, not to mention providing accommodation in Washington, D.C. His influence on this book is considerable.

Juliana Ruhfus researched much of the Nigeria chapter for me in situ. Her reporting was tenacious and illuminating, and she deserves great thanks. Vesna Vucenovic has combined tireless backup support with welcome optimism. Ted Braun and Melissa Llewelyn-Davies were honest and encouraging critics of the text. Thanks also to Chris Harrison for his help. Juliet Sydenham, Tamara Glenny, and Paddy Glenny assisted as usual, in a variety of ways. Thanks also to Ralph Glenny for the photo. Neil Belton and Colin Robinson have provided friendship, advice, and laughter over many years.

In Bulgaria, Ivan Krastev and Ognyan Zlatev were unfailingly cheerful in the face of my numerous demands on their time, knowledge, and contacts. I would also like to thank Boyko Borrisov, Jeremy and Katy Hill, Iain Stewart, Dessislava Gavrilova, Vessela Tcherneva, and give a special thanks to Yovo Nikolov. In Serbia, Braca Grubacic has been a great friend and ever-willing source. I also wish to thank Dejan Atanasijevic, Milos Vasic, and Spomenka Vejvoda. In Macedonia, thanks, as always, to Saso Ordanoski and Güner Ismael, whose knowledge of corrupt networks is almost unparalleled. Roman Kupchinsky in Prague was most generous in sharing his expertise on Ukrainian and Russian matters. The John Smith Fellowship Program and several of their fellows provided me with invaluable help in several parts of the Soviet Union. In Moscow, my particular gratitude is reserved for Tessa Szyszkowitz and her family for putting me up and for providing me with many insights. I also wish to thank Yelena Rubin, James Hill, and Alexei Mukhin. In Ukraine, Olga Bondaruk was forever willing to undertake great challenges. I also wish to thank Alexander Radovic, Roman Olearchuk, Helen Fawkes, and Alexei Stepura. In the Czech Republic, I wish to thank my old friend Oldrich Cerny and Jan Zvelebil. In Moldova, thank-you to Eugen Burdeliini, Stella Mocan, and Alina Budeci. In Kazakhstan, I could not have got anywhere without the support and assistance of Shannon Crownover and Christopher Pala in Almaty. I also wish to thank Artur Shakhnazarian and Oksana Martinuk in Atyrau.

In Israel, my particular thanks go to Alon Farago. I wish further to thank Professor Menachem Amir and Alexander Gentelev, as well as Orla Guerin and everybody at the BBC offices in Jerusalem and Gaza City. In Dubai, Julie Studer provided sterling support, as did Ashfaq Ahmed. I also wish to thank Driss Mekkaoui and Ron Bagnulo.

It was my greatest fortune that Vikram Chandra kindly introduced me to Hussain Zaidi in Mumbai. Hussain is without peer as a student of Mumbai's and India's organized crime groups, and he opened all the crucial doors to his knowledge. I would also like to thank Mrinmayee Ranade.

Justice Malala was an exemplary mentor in South Africa. Special thanks to Suzanne Lang, who introduced me to the work of Al Lovejoy. I was then privileged to meet Al himself, whose wit and intelligence I greatly admire. Thanks also to Nick Dawes, Jonathan Lang, and Justine Lang.

Acknowledgments

Special thanks go to my Canadian publisher in Toronto, Sarah MacLachlan of Anansi Press, as well as to Noah Richler, and also thanks to Merita Ilo.

In Washington, D.C., my thanks to Robert Gelbard and Jaime Jaramillo-Vallejo, as well to as several others who prefer to remain nameless. In Colombia, my sincere thanks to Juan Pablo Morris, and in London, to Landa Acevedo. In Brazil, I owe a great debt to Emily Sasson Cohen, Ana de Andrada, and not forgetting Caboclo Sonhador. I would further like to thank Tony Smith, Marcos Flávio Araujo Assunção, Fabricio, and my publisher in Brazil, Luis Schwarcz.

In Japan, I was very lucky to work with David d'heilly and Shizu Yuasa. Before I left Britain, I received important guidance from Peter Hill. In Tokyo, Velisarios Kattoulas was a lifesaver, while in Osaka, Wolfgang Herbert offered me profound insights as well as a great night out.

Thanks in China go in the first place to Rui Huang. I could not have managed without the friendship of Lindsey Hilsum, as well as Betty Du and Max in the Channel 4 office. Thanks also to James Kynge and Paul French in Shanghai. Ko-lin Chin at Rutgers University gave me an essential grounding in the subject before I visited China.

My thanks as well to the remarkable team at Global Witness, in particular Charmian Gooch and Alex Yearsley. And thanks to Alex for putting me in touch with Gary Busch, who has been most generous in sharing his experience and material. The European Stability Initiative team, led by the indefatigable and disarmingly intelligent Gerald Knaus, has been consistently ahead of the field in explaining the rational relationship between society on the one hand and organized crime and related phenomena on the other. I also wish to express my gratitude to Federico Varese for sharing his knowledge and material.

In London and New York, I would like to thank my editors, Will Sulkin and Dan Frank, whose enthusiasm and belief in the project have sustained me throughout. Their editorial comments and guidance have had a significant impact on the final version of the book. I would also like to thank the staff at Bodley Head and Knopf, particularly Dan Hind, Fran Bigman, Rebecca Carter, Drummond Moir, and Lily Richards.

Clare Conville, my London agent, has been a close friend for thirty years. Her input into the genesis of this book was uniquely important, and she proved a wonderful calming influence, particularly when the going got tough. I cannot thank her enough. Much gratitude also to my New York agent, Michael Carlisle, for his drive and commitment.

Acknowledgments

My greatest debt goes to my wife, Kirsty Lang, to whom this book is dedicated. She assisted me in every aspect of researching and writing this book and kept me afloat when I was in danger of sinking. She is an exceptional woman in every respect, and I am very fortunate.

And finally, my love and thanks go to my three children, Miljan, Alexandra, and Callum.

A NOTE ON SOURCES

T he primary source material for this book emerged from nearly three hundred interviews that I undertook between May 2004 and April 2007. Many are quoted here, but those that are not still contributed vitally to the text. In addition to these interviews, I have referred to countless articles, studies, and a number of important books.

The key criminological study informing this work is Diego Gambetta's *The Sicilian Mafia: The Business of Private Protection,* which, I believe, has transformed our understanding of organized crime. On the Sicilian Mafia, I would also recommend Peter Robb's stunning *Midnight in Sicily* and the partial autobiography of the former mayor of Palermo Leoluca Orlando, *Fighting the Mafia and Renewing Sicilian Culture. The Shadow Economy: An International Survey* by Professor Friedrich Schneider and Dominik H. Enste has laid the groundwork for our growing ability to quantify the shadow economy.

There are also several valuable general studies on the rise in organized crime and the shadow economy. Moises Naim was the first to identify the true significance of transnational organized crime in our globalizing world. Jeffrey Robinson's *The Merger* contains fascinating details on some of the global crime networks. See also *Gangster Capitalism: The United States and the Global Rise of Organized Crime* by Michael Woodiwiss, and in German, *Die Barbaren kommen: Kapitalismus und organisiertes Verbrechen* by Jean Ziegler.

Foreword

For how recent banking failures have promoted—and will continue to promote—global crime, I referred to the report entitled "Undue Diligence: How Banks do Business with Corrupt Regimes," published by the British NGO Global Witness in March of 2009.

Chapter 1: Death of an American

The work of Yovo Nikolov and other journalists from the Sofia newspaper *Capital* has been especially helpful in this chapter, as have several monographs produced by the Center for the Study of Democracy in the Bulgarian capital. I have also drawn on the memoirs of Dimitur Ivanov, *Sesti Odel* (Sixth Department) and *Afera* by Bogdana Lazarova.

Chapter 2: Bloody Lucre

There has been a great deal published in the former Yugoslavia on this subject both in books and magazines, as well as in some academic studies. The only material in English is the important series by *Nacional,* a Croatian magazine, on the cigarette trade, published in 2002. This was based partly on interviews with some of the players but also on Croat secret police sources (so it comes with attendant health warnings). In German, see Norbert Mappes-Niediek's *Balkan-Mafia: Staaten in der Hand des Verbrechens—Eine Gefahr für Europa.* The most interesting book in Serbia is Milos Vasic's *Atentat na Zorana,* which looks at the background to Djindjic's assassination. There is important material in all major Serbian news magazines and in Montenegro's *Monitor.*

Chapter 3: The Mafiya and
Chapter 4: Spreading the Word

There are two crucial English texts dealing with the Russian mafia: Vadim Volkov's *Violent Entrepreneurs: The Use of Force in the Making of Russian Capitalism* and Federico Varese's *The Russian Mafia: Private Protection in a New Market Economy. The Oligarchs: Wealth and Power in the New Russia* by David Hoffman is a masterful account of the power behind Yeltsin's throne. Stephen Handelman's *Comrade Criminal: Russia's New Mafia* was an early recognition of what was happening in Russia. Olga Kryshtanovskaya's research was indispensable to me. In Germany, the works of Jürgen Roth are probably the best introduction to the narrative of the Russian mafia. *Der Oligarch*, Roth's biography of Vladimir Rabinovich, is one of the most useful and detailed explanations of the social psychology of this rare but hugely influential breed. Much of Rabinovich's quotes in my book are from this text, although I also interviewed Rabinovich myself. See also Roth's *Die Gangster aus dem Osten.* In Russian, I have used Artyom Tarasov's *Millioner,* the story of Russia's first millionaire, as well as an interview with him. Alexei Mukhin's various books are vital chronicles of the emergence of individuals and groupings, especially *Rossiskaya organizovanaya prestupnost i vlast.* Also see *Tenevaya Rossiya* by Lef Timofeev and Igor Klyamkin. The only book in English dedicated to the murder of Gongadze is *Beheaded: The Killing of a Journalist* by J. V. Koshiw. See also Global Witness's report *It's a Gas.*

Chapter 5: Aliyah

The late Robert I. Friedman's *Red Mafiya: How the Russian Mob Invaded America* details how some of the links between the Russian mafia and Israel developed. It is

A Note on Sources

a rip-roaring read but needs to be taken with a pinch of salt in parts. There is no comprehensive study of the growth of organized crime in Israel, although Mark Galeotti, the British scholar, has written about it in various publications. *The Global Political Economy of Israel* by Jonathan Nitzan and Shimshon Bichler is a very useful introduction to the shifts in Israel's economy over the last two decades.

Chapter 6: Xanadu I and Chapter 7: Xanadu II

Material on Dubai beyond the journalistic is scarce, but *From Trucial States to United Arab Emirates* by Frauke Heard-Bey is a superb introduction to the modern history of the UAE. On money laundering, John Kerry's report into the BCCI scandal is a seminal text (chiefly penned by Jon Winer), but see also *The Outlaw Bank: BCCI* by Jonathan Beaty and S. C. Gwynne, as well as Nick Kochan's *The Washing Machine: How Money Laundering and Terrorist Financing Soils Us,* and the more academic *Chasing Dirty Money* by Peter Reuter and Edwin M. Truman. On the relationship to terrorism see *Terror Inc.: Tracing the Money Behind Global Terrorism* by Loretta Napoleoni and the National Commission on Terrorist Attacks upon the United States's *9/11 Report. The Journal of Financial Crime* and the *Journal of Money Laundering Control,* published in the United Kingdom, are also very useful.

On Bombay and the bombings of 1993, by far the best source is Hussain Zaidi's *Black Friday: The True Story of the Bombay Bomb Blasts.* There are countless articles and studies published in India and elsewhere on Dawood Ibrahim and his network. It is also worth checking the several Bollywood movies that take the Mumbai underworld as their theme.

Chapter 8: The Theater of Crime

The two most useful books for understanding crime and corruption in Nigeria are Karl Maier's *This House Has Fallen: Nigeria in Crisis,* and *A Culture of Corruption: Everyday Deception and Popular Discontent in Nigeria* by Daniel Jordan Smith. Equally valuable are the writings of Chinua Achebe and Wole Soyinka.

Chapter 9: Black and White

The best resource for anyone trying to understand crime in South Africa is the Institute for Security Studies (www.iss.co.za), which has superb intellectual resources. The most riveting and illuminating book is Al Lovejoy's *Acid Alex,* while Ted Legget's *Rainbow Vice* and Jonny Steinberg's *The Number* are also very important. See also *Crime Wave: The South African Underworld and Its Foes,* edited by Steinberg. For the diamond and coltan trades, the most important source is Global Witness and their pathbreaking reports, as well as Douglas Farah's *Blood from Stones: The*

A Note on Sources

Secret Financial Network of Terror and, on Viktor Bout, *Merchant of Death: Money, Guns, Planes, and the Man Who Makes War Possible* by Farah and Stephen Braun.

Chapter 10: Buddies

Two books are very revealing about British Columbia, Canada, and the politics of crime: *Bud Inc.: Inside Canada's Marijuana Industry* by Ian Mulgrew is the first, and *Angels of Death: Inside the Bikers' Empire of Crime* by William Marsden and Julian Sher is the second.

Chapter 11: March of Fear

There are three highly readable texts on the cocaine industry of the past two decades. The first is Dominic Streatfeild's excellent *Cocaine: An Unauthorized Biography,* the second is *Killing Pablo* by Mark Bowden. The third is Ron Chepesiuk's *Drug Lords*. Finally, in Spanish there is the masterful *Los jinetes de la cocaína* by Fabio Castillo, a copy of which is hard to obtain, but it is easily available in various forms on the Internet.

Chapter 13: The Overunderworld

On the modern *yakuza*, start with the classic *Tokyo Underworld* by Robert Whiting, but don't miss *Dogs and Demons: The Fall of Modern Japan* by Alex Kerr and *Yakuza: Japan's Criminal Underworld* by David E. Kaplan and Alec Dubro. Peter Hill's *The Japanese Mafia: Yakuza, Law, and the State* is essential reading in understanding how the *yakuza* has developed since the end of the Cold War. *Toppamono: My Life in Japan's Underworld* by Miyazaki Manabi is available in English in Japan. In German, the most fascinating book is *Japan nach Sonnenuntergang* by Wolfgang Herbert.

Chapter 14: The Future of Organized Crime

There is a wealth of material on China, but the starting point must be the academic papers and reports written by the Rutgers University academic Ko-lin Chin. See also *The Dragon Syndicates: The Global Phenomenon of the Triads* by Martin Booth and *Tongs, Gangs, and Triads: Chinese Crime Groups in North America* by Peter Huston. *The Triads as Business* by Chu Yiu Kong is also important. For material on Shanghai of the 1930s refer to *Old Shanghai: Gangsters in Paradise* by Lyn Pann. Otherwise, the two best-written introductions to what on earth is going on in the Middle Kingdom are James Kynge's *China Shakes the World: The Rise of a Hungry Nation* and Duncan Hewitt's *Getting Rich First: Life in a Changing China*. Both are equally illuminating but for different reasons.

INDEX

Abacha, Sani, 166
Abergil family, 118, 119, 120
Abu Dhabi, oil reserves in, 131
Abuja, Nigeria, airport scheme, 161–5
Access Asia, 335
Achebe, Chinua, 171
Action Program, 291
ADT, 192
advance fee frauds (419 scams), 161–8,
        177–82; anthem of ("I Go Chop Your
        Dollar"), 177–8; Banco Noroeste case,
        161–5, 167, 179–82; colonialist legacy
        and, 168–9; common forms of appeal
        in, 165; fraudsters' ability to evade
        prosecution for, 178–9, 180; statistics
        on, 166; technology and, 177, 178;
        victims' responses to, 165, 166–7, 168
Afghanistan, xiv, 131, 225; arms trafficking
        in, 197, 198; narcotics originating in,
        36, 176, 186, 222, 252, 326, 327; NATO-
        led intervention in, 226, 252; Soviet
        invasion of, 131
Africa, 67, 161–207, 331; arms trafficking to,
        6, 92, 187–8, 197–201; commodities sold
        on Western markets entangled with
        war in, 200–5; legacy of colonization
        in, 168–9, 177; Potemkin states in, 169,
        170. See also specific countries
African National Congress. See ANC
Agata, Mitsunori, 306–8, 311–12
Agland, Phil, 327
agriculture, 345; Bulgaria's lost revenue
        from, 10, 11, 31; labor needs in, 157, 343;
        Western restrictions on imports of, 10,
        11, 156
Ajman, 153–4, 155, 197
Akihito, Emperor of Japan, 295
al Qaeda, 147, 281; diamond trade and, 204;
        drug trafficking and, 226, 252
Albania, 18, 33; drug trafficking and, 45;

oil shipped to Serbia by, 31–2; stolen
        cars in, 13
Albanians, 35, 92; drug trafficking and, 36,
        41, 100; in Kosovo, 29, 42
Albany, N.Y., drug enforcement in, 232–4,
        237–9
Alberta, Canada, pro-American sentiments
        in, 218
alcohol: drugs compared to, 226–7;
        Prohibition and, 226
Allor, Peter, 269, 270, 271
The Americans (South African gang), 191–2
Amir, Menachem, 118–19
amphetamines, 6, 45, 70, 224, 263
Amsterdam, 222; cannabis smuggling in,
        206; as ecstacy center, 119, 206; as entry
        point for cocaine, 44, 175–6, 207
Anajemba, Amaka, 164, 168, 180, 182
Anajemba, Christian Ikechukwu, 164, 168
ANC (African National Congress), 175, 183,
        185, 190, 194
Angola: Bout's arms trafficking to, 197, 198,
        199; conflict or "blood" diamonds
        from, 199, 200–1, 203–4; "curse of oil"
        in, 48; wars in, 193, 200
anti-Americanism: in Brazil, 281; in
        Canada, 217–18, 219
Antient Free and Accepted Scottish
        Custom, 3
anti-Semitism, in Soviet Union, 101, 112, 113
Antwerp, 119, 201
apartheid, 188–94, 273; drug use and
        trafficking and, 186, 205; fall of, 183,
        186, 187–8, 193–4, 195; gang cultures
        and, 188–92; Group Areas Act and, 188,
        193; Nigerians in movement against,
        185; South African police force and,
        193–4; squalor of black living
        conditions in, 188; violence as legacy
        of, 187

355

Index

Index

Index

Index

Index

Index

Index

Index

Index

Index

enforcement and, 45; drug trafficking and, 44

Itera International Energy Corporation, 79, 92, 95

Ivanov, Dimitur, 8, 9

Jamaica, 187, 206

Jamundí, Colombia, massacre in (2006), 240–2, 243

Japan, xiv, 10, 114, 130, 224, 287–312, 322, 332, 338, 346; Americans' anti-Japanese sentiments and, 290, 291; anti-Chinese sentiments in, 309–10; *baburu* (bubble period) in, 289, 292–5, 302, 304, 310–11; Chinese counterfeit goods and, 334; Chinese mobsters in, 309, 311–12; cultural breakout of younger generation in, 300, 302; day laborers in, 295–6; Heisei recession in, 295; legal system of, 303–4; organized crime in, 288–312 (*see also yakuza*); Reagan's globalization initiative and, 289–90, 291; real estate speculation in, 289, 292–5; regional tensions and, 338–9; stock market boom in (mid 1980s), 292; subprime mortgage market collapse and, 344; urban landscape of, 288–9

Jerusalem Post, 118

Jews, 177; in former Soviet Union, 101, 112–13; Russian, immigration to Israel of, 100–3, 111, 112

Jiang, Mr., 314

JNA (Yugoslav People's Army), 21, 27, 28

joint-stock companies, in Bulgaria, 7–8

Justice Department (U.S.), 235, 321

Kabuki-cho, Tokyo, 306, 307–9; murder at The Parisienne in, 309, 311–12

Kafka, Franz, 73

Kaganovich, Lazar, 112

Kaohsiung, Taiwan, 340

Kapelyushny, Leonid, 90, 91

Kaptagon, 6

Karabas (Viktor Kulivar), 87–9, 90, 91, 92

Karachi, 122, 131, 134, 159

Karpachov, Oleg "Karpits," 103–4

Kathmandu, 132, 134, 155

Katrich, Antoly, 72

Kazakhstan, 46, 47–51, 78; caviar trade in, 48–51; independence and subsequent governance of, 48; oil and gas reserves in, 48

Ken-chan, 297–8, 299

Kerry, John, 150

key loggers, 268

KGB, 52, 54, 55, 56, 58, 91; oligarchs' dealings with, 68, 69

Khachidze, Dzhemal Konstantinovich, 55

Khan, Badshah, 137–9

Khatri, Mukesh, 123

Khordokovsky, Mikhail, 67

kibbutzim movement, 116, 117

Kim Jong-il, 338, 339

Kimberley Protocol, 204

Kintex, 6, 8

Kleiman, Gil, 103–4, 118

Knopp, Andras, 77–8, 80

Kobzon, Iosif, 114–15

Kondo, Tadao, 287–8, 289

Koreans, in *yakuza*, 300, 309

KOS (Yugoslav military counterintelligence), 28, 34, 35

Kosovo, 18, 29, 42; war in, 21–3, 25, 36, 37, 38, 41

Kosovo Liberation Army, 42

Krastev, Ivan, 5–6

Kravchuk, Leonid, 83, 92

Kremikovtsi, 9–10

Kroll Inc., 84

krysha (Russian protection agency or racket), 55, 59–60, 62

Kryshtanovskaya, Olga, 58

"Kubla Khan" (Coleridge), 121, 140

Kuchma, Leonid Danilovych, 83–6, 90, 92, 95, 96

Kukoc, Yerko, 43

Kulivar, Viktor. *See* Karabas

Kupchinsky, Roman, 80

Kuti, Fela, 168

Kuwait, 126

KwaZulu-Natal, 206

Kyulev, Emil, 5, 10

labor migration. *See* migrant laborers

Lala, Karim, 128, 129

Lamorde, Alhaji Ibrahim, 166

land sharking, 289, 292–4

Index

Index

Menem, Carlos, 28
mercantilism, 176
Mercer, Rick, 217
Mereilles, Fernando, 274
Merrill Lynch, 173, 174
methamphetamine, 311, 338
Mexico: Colombian narco-traffickers' allies
in, 250, 278; oil reserves in, 218
Miami, cocaine trafficking to, 246, 248
Miandad, Javed, 159
Middle East, 6, 18, 67, 339; as caviar market,
51, 52; U.S. policy toward, 148–9. *See
also specific countries*
migrant laborers, 153–7; Chinese, 284,
319–25; food prices and, 343; illegals
working in West, 156–7; inequalities of
globalization and, 156, 179, 322–3; in
Japan, 295–6, 311; in Shanghai, 327;
trafficking in, 15, 42, 90, 108, 155, 156,
157, 319–24; in UAE (United Arab
Emirates), 153–5; Western restrictions
on, 156, 322–3
Mihailev, Mladen (Madzho), 15
Mikhailov, Sergei, 63, 64, 65, 67, 72, 76–7,
111, 114
Milford, Jim, 249
Milosevic, Marko, 36, 37
Milosevic, Slobodan, 33, 35, 36, 38, 40, 148,
321, 322; Djukanovic's relations with,
23, 24, 25, 36–7; fall of, 40–1
Miyawaki, Raisuke (Toppamono),
292–3, 312
Miyazaki, Manabu, 290, 293
MK (ANC's military wing), 190
Mo Bangfu, 331–2, 340–1
mobile phones. *See* cell or mobile phones
Mobuto Sese Seko, 166, 200, 201
Mogilevich, Semion (Uncle Seva or Papa),
72–3, 75, 76, 77, 111, 114; ETG (Eural
Trans Gas) scam and, 77, 80
Mohammed, Sheikh. *See* Maktoum, Sheikh
Mohammed bin Rashid al-
Moldova, 79–80, 90, 96, 198; Transnistrian
relations with, 91–5, 105; women
trafficked out of, 105–6, 110
money laundering, 42, 167, 182, 345; in
Aruba, 279; in China, 329–30; of
Colombian narco-traffickers, 25, 250;
and difficulties of pursuing dirty
money, 149–50; in Dubai, 147–53;

FATF (Financial Action Task Force)
and, 147; in Hungary, 16; in Israel,
111–12, 116–17, 120; liberalization of
international financial markets and,
111, 120, 149–50, 172–3, 345; of Maxwell,
12; offshore banking centers and, 153,
345; of Russian oligarchs and
gangsters, 58, 68, 70, 76, 110, 111–12,
116–17; in UAE (United Arab
Emirates), 120; U.S. policy and, 147–9,
150, 151, 153; of *yakuza*, 311
Montenegrin Tabak Transit (MTT), 25
Montenegro, 21–6, 38; cigarette smuggling
in, 23–6, 34–5, 36, 40, 41; Clinton's
meeting with president of, 21, 23, 25;
no-fly zone over, 34; Serbian relations
with, 21–3, 24, 36–7; UN economic
sanctions and, 19, 23, 29, 30
Montgomery, Bill, 30, 31
Montoya, Diego, 242
Morais, Rogeriot, 267
Morecambe Bay, drowning of Chinese
cockle pickers in, 321, 324–5
Morocco, 102
Moscow, 63–4, 106; cars imported to, 64, 65;
flaunting of wealth in, 52–3, 66–7;
mob wars in, 59–63, 64–5. *See also*
Russia
Most, 69
Mozambique, 186, 193, 197
MPLA (Angola), 200
MTT (Montenegrin Tabak Transit), 25
Mugabe, Robert, 205
Mukhin, Alexei, 62
Multiart, 8
Multigroup, 4, 11, 12, 28, 30
Mumbai (formerly Bombay), 121–39;
anti-Muslim riots in, 124, 125, 136,
141; bombings in (March 1993), 123–4,
125, 136–42, 159; Dubai's historic
trading links to, 128, 130–1, 132; gang
warfare in, 142–6, 159–60; organized
crime in, 125, 127–30, 132–7, 138,
142–6, 159–60 (*see also* Ibrahim,
Dawood); police shoot-outs with
gangsters in, 144, 145–6; proxy conflict
between India and Pakistan in, 143;
special anti-crime squads in, 143–4;
textile strike in, 129–30, 133–4. *See
also* India

Index

Index

Index

Qiu Xiaolong, 318
Queiroz, Protógenes, 280, 282

Rabinovich, Vladimir, 111, 113
racial discrimination, enforcement of drug
    laws and, 234–6, 238, 262
Radio Free Europe, 80
Raijin, 338
Rajan, Bada (Big Rajan), 132
Rajan, Chhota (Little Rajan; born Rajendra
    Nikhalje), 132, 133, 135–6, 142–3, 159
Rashid, Sheikh. *See* Maktoum, Sheikh
    Rashid al-
rave culture, 224
RAW (Research and Analysis Wing,
    India), 142
razborka (Russian shoot-outs), 60, 69
Raznatovic, Zeljko. *See* Arkan
RCMP (Royal Canadian Mounted Police),
    216, 221, 230–1
Reagan, Ronald, 170, 172, 251, 289–90, 291
Rebaja Las Drogas, 250
Red Army, 52, 74
Red Command, 278
Reed, Karen, ix, x, xi, xvi
Refinetti, Domingos, 164, 167, 182
Renewal, 17
Reno, Janet, 235
Reynolds, James, 317
Ribadu, Nuhu, 171, 178, 179, 181–2
Rich, Marc, 147
Richey, Bill, 180, 182
RICO Act (Racketeer Influenced and
    Corrupt Organizations Act, U.S.),
    304–5
Rio de Janeiro, 278, 279, 280; *favelas* of,
    274–5
R.J. Reynolds, 25
Robinson family, 232
Rockefeller, Nelson, 233
Rockefeller drug laws, 233, 234, 237, 238–9
Rodrigues, Maria, 167
Rodríguez-Orejuela, Gilberto, 240, 247–8,
    249, 250–1. *See also* Cali cartel
Rodríguez-Orejuela, Miguel, 240, 247–8,
    251. *See also* Cali cartel
Romania, 19, 29, 34; oil shipped to Serbia
    by, 31, 32; Yugoslav trade with, 29
Rosenstein, Ze'ev, 117–18, 119, 120
RosUkrEnergo, 80

Rotterdam, cigarette smuggling and, 24,
    34, 35
Rough Trade, A (Global Witness), 204
Royal Canadian Mounted Police (RCMP),
    216, 221, 230–1
Ruml, Jan, 72
Rushaylo, Vladimir, 53, 54
Russia, 51–70, 177, 338, 346; banking in,
    65–6; Bout's return to, 198, 199;
    bureaucrats' collaboration with
    oligarchs and organized crime in,
    58–9; capital flight from, 112; as caviar
    market, 51–2; cybercrime in, 272, 273,
    274; drug trafficking and, 44, 70, 224,
    250, 251, 279; financial meltdown in, 51,
    61; gas deals and, 77–80; immigration
    to Israel from, 100–3, 111, 112, 117; legal
    system's collapse in, 58; oil and gas
    resources in, 56–7, 67, 90–1, 96; oil
    shipped to Serbia by, 32; Putin's
    market authoritarianism in, 67;
    transition from socialism to
    capitalism in, 54, 56–9, 61, 67;
    Transnistrian arms trafficking and, 92,
    94–5; women from, as prostitutes, 110,
    158, 309. *See also* KGB; MVD; Russian
    mafia; Russian oligarchs
Russian army, 65
Russian Federation, 49
Russian mafia, 16, 135; arms trafficking and,
    92; banking entered by, 65–6;
    conundrum in investigation of, 110–11;
    cybercrime and, 272; Czech police
    unit's offensive against and, 71–4;
    disproportionate number of Chechens
    and Georgians among, 113; drug
    trafficking and, 70, 250, 251, 279;
    emergence of, 53–67; in Israel, 113–17;
    Italian Mafia's differences from, 60–2;
    money laundering and, 68, 70, 76,
    111–12; Moscow mob wars and, 59–63,
    64–5; murders and assassinations
    carried out by, 62; oil and, 67, 74, 92;
    protection rackets and, 53–5, 58, 59–63,
    67, 68, 69–70; spread throughout
    Eastern Europe, 71–6; structure of, 55,
    61–3, 65; wealth flaunted by, 66–7;
    Western law enforcement's inability to
    prosecute, 76. *See also* Solntsevo
    Brotherhood

Index

Russian oligarchs, 53–5, 57–63, 67–70, 83, 338; bureaucrats' collaboration with, 58–9; commodities raided by, 57–8, 67; conundrum in investigation of, 110–11; disproportionate number of Jews among, 112–13; dispute-resolution process and, 59–60; in Israel, 110–17; Israeli citizenship taken by, 111; money laundering and, 58, 68, 70, 110, 111–12, 116–17; protection rackets and, 53–5, 58, 59–63, 66, 68, 69–70; Putin's market authoritarianism and, 67; Russian security services privatized by, 68–9; wealth flaunted by, 66–7

Rwanda, 202

Sacra Corona Unità (SCU), 24, 35, 279
SADF (South African Defence Force), 200
Sakaguchi, Nelson, 161–2, 163–5, 167, 180, 182
Samant, Dutta, 129
Samper, Ernesto, 249
Sanda, Umar Mamman, 163
santen hoshiki system, 308
São Paulo, 282–4; Chinese criminals in, 282–4; counterfeit goods in, 281–2; Operation Shogun in, 280; organized crime in, 275–6, 277, 280
Sarajevo, siege in, 33
Saudi Arabia, 29, 48, 174, 197, 218
Savimbi, Jonas, 200
Saxe-Coburski, Simeon, 3, 9
SBU (Ukrainian successor to KGB), 84
scams: of Nigerian fraudsters, 161–8, 173–4. *See also* advance fee frauds
Scandinavia, 273; drug trafficking in, 225
Scorpions, 198
SCU (Sacra Corona Unità), 24, 35, 279
Seagram's, 226
Secret Service (U.S.), 173, 220–1, 270
September 11 attacks (2001), 147, 148, 151, 262, 339–40
Serb Volunteer Guard (Tigers), 39
Serbia, 29–32, 33, 35, 92; assassinations of gangsters and businessmen in, 36–40; Chinese migrant laborers in, 321–2; discrepancies between rich and poor in, 37; drug trafficking and, 36, 119, 224; internecine battle among gangs in (Bloody Spring 2000), 40; Montenegrin relations with, 21–3, 24,

36–7; no-fly zone over, 34; oil smuggled into, 29, 30, 31–2; UN economic sanctions and, 19, 29, 30–1
Seven Stars, 111
Seychelles, 79–80
SEZs (special economic zones, China), 314, 318, 331
Shahal, Moshe, 115
Shakeel, Chhota, 133, 136, 137, 145, 160
Shakhnazarian, Artur, 51
Shan tribes, 325–6
Shanghai, 340; heroin and opium trade in, 326–8; organized crime in (Triads), 326–7
Shanghai Vice, 327
Sharansky, Natan, 115, 116
Sharjah, 127, 197
Sharma, Pradeep, 130, 143–4
Sharon, Ariel, 100, 116, 118, 120
shells (programs), 266–7
Shenzhen, China, counterfeit goods in, 331–3
Shetty, Sharad, 159, 160
Shinkansen (Bullet Train), 288–9
Shiv Sena (Shiva's Army), 124, 135, 141
Shushkov, Serhiy, 82, 84
SIC (Bulgarian distribution network for stolen cars), 14–15, 30
Sicar, Roberto, 253–4
Sicilian Mafia, 278–9, 299, 301, 302, 311. *See also* Italian Mafia groups
Sicilian Mafia, The (Gambetta), 299
Sidbury, Mark, 173
Siemens, 333
Sierra Leone, arms trafficking to, 197, 198, 199, 200
silver, 133
Simonsen family, 180, 182
Singapore, 340
Singh, Manmohan, 134
Sklar, Dick, 21, 23, 25–6
Skype, 272
Slovakia, 26; heating oil scandal and, 75–6
Smirnov, Igor, 91–2, 94
Smirnov, Vladimir, 94
smuggling, 344. *See also specific goods*
snakeheads: in Fujian, 319–25; use of word, 321. *See also* migrant laborers— trafficking in
Soares, David, 231–4, 237–9

Index

Index

United Nations. *See* UN

United States, xiv, 28, 30, 86, 111, 168, 181, 303, 332, 346; anti-Japanese sentiment in, 290, 291; Bulgaria and, 12; Chinese businessmen's and Party officials' children born in, 319; Chinese counterfeit goods and, 334; Chinese migrant laborers in, 319, 328–9; cocaine trafficking to, 44, 245–51, 262, 278; counterfeit goods and, 282; debt of, 11; drug policy of, 219–21, 222–3, 227, 232, 239, 251–2, 278; economic downturn of 1980s and, 289–90; enforcement of drug laws in, 231–9; heroin trafficking to, 171, 186, 207; Iraq war and, 199; marijuana trafficking to, 211–20, 227–8, 231; money laundering and policies of, 147–9, 150, 151, 153; Montenegro and, 21, 23; opening of emerging markets to goods from, 10; Plan Colombia of, 242–3, 254, 257–8, 261, 262; port security in, 339–40; proxy conflicts of cold war and, 200, 201; RICO Act in, 304–5; security of Pacific-Asia region and, 339; as spam target, 274; subprime mortgage market collapse in, 150, 344–5; *yakuza* ventures in, 311

UNODC (United Nations Office for Drug Control), 206–7, 224

Untouchables (leaders of China's 125 Gang), 325, 329

Uralmash, 70

Uribe, Álvaro, 242, 257, 258, 260, 261

Utsiev, Nazarbeg, ix–x, xi

Utsiev, Ruslan, ix–x, xi

Uzbekistan, 78, 252

Vaglenov, Stanimir, 7–8

Valenti, Jack, 282

Vancouver: decriminalization of marijuana possession in, 219; harm reduction program in (Four Pillars), 222; Hell's Angels in, 228–31; heroin use in, 222; Walters's visit to, 220–1, 222

Vasic, Milos, 42

VAT, carousel fraud and, 344–5

Vekselberg, Viktor, 68

Verloy, Andre, 197

Vicodin, 227

Vietnam, 177, 339

Vietnam War, 310

viruses, computer, 268–9, 270, 271, 272

VIS (Bulgarian distribution network for stolen cars), 14, 15

voice-over Internet Protocol (VoIP) telephone systems, 272

Volkov, Vadim, 60

Volkswagen, 334

Volovoy, Grigory, 94

Vorotyntsev, Ihor, 82, 83

vory (Russian criminal leaders), 55, 59–60, 61–2, 65

Walters, John P., 219, 220–1, 222–3

Wan Sui, 315

war on terror, 262, 339

Washington Post, 204

welfare systems, European, 26, 322–3

Western Union, 94

Wheeler, Dan, 211–17, 227–8

Williams, Amrit, 272

Williams, Ishola, 170

Williams, Tafida (alias of Bless Okereke), 161–3

Winer, Jon, xiv, xv, 69–70, 76, 120

women, trafficking in, 309, 326; in Eastern Europe, 15, 16–19, 41–2, 90, 309; as entry-level activity for criminals, 19; from former Soviet Union to Middle East (map), 98; recruiters in, 105–6; by Russian underground in Israel, 104–10; to UAE, 104–5, 155. *See also* prostitution

Wong Kin Cheung, 325–6, 329

Woolsey, James, 110–11

World Bank, xv, 170

World Economic Forum (2007), 310

World Jewish Conspiracy, 112

WTO (World Trade Organization), 173, 215, 332, 334

X., Mr. (Bokan's business partner), 29, 33

X-Force, 269, 271

Xiamen, China, 314

Xu Congrong, 315–16, 319, 329

Xu Li, 315

yakuza, 288–312; anti–organized crime law and, 296, 304–5, 306, 308; bad debts of,

Insert 1

Simeon Saxe-Coburski © Dr. Ivaylo Ditchev
Ilya Pavlov courtesy of *Capital Weekly*
Arkan © AP/PA Photos
Supporters of Milo Djukanovic © AP/PA Photos
Semion Mogilevich FBI Most Wanted Poster, April 2003, reproduced by permission
    of the FBI
Victor Kuliva "Karabas" © Misha Glenny
Tattoo. Image from *Russian Criminal Tattoo Encyclopaedia* by Danzig Baldaev,
    published by FUEL
Sergei Mikhailov © Reuters
Assassination attempt on Ze'ev Rosenstein © Michael Kremer
Bedouin smugglers, Negev Desert. Photo by Alon Farago © Wayward Lad Ltd.
Deepak Nachant protesting © Misha Glenny
Commander Rakesh Maria in Mumbai © *The Indian Express*
Dawood Ibrahim © *The Indian Express*
Inspector Pradeep Sharma in Mumbai © Misha Glenny
Aftermath of bombs in Bombay, March 1993 © AP/PA Photos
Drugs and guns in Cape Town © AP/PA Photos

Insert 2

Chief Emmanuel Nwude © AP/PA Photos
Nuhu Ribadu © Getty Images
Nelson Sakaguchi © Brazil Photo Bank
Cannabis growing in British Columbia © AP/PA Photos
David Soares © Misha Glenny
Shopfront advertising cannabis, Ottawa © Misha Glenny
Aftermath of *Mia Casita*, Jamundí © AP/PA Photos
Janneth Pachon © Misha Glenny
Mr. Pringle © Misha Glenny
Protógenes Queiroz © Misha Glenny
Jail riots, São Paulo, May 15, 2006 © Sipa Press/Rex Features
Mr. Agata © Misha Glenny
Pachinko game machines © Misha Glenny
Wolfgang Herbert © Misha Glenny
"Face" houses near Fuqing in Fujian Province © Misha Glenny
Pirated DVDs © Misha Glenny
Su Hangqi and her daughter © Misha Glenny

TEXT ILLUSTRATIONS

Map of e-mailing harvesting (p. 274): Property of Postini, Inc. © 2007 Postini, Inc.
Maps of the Balkans (p. 22), of the Caspian (p. 46), of Russia and the Middle East
(p. 98), and of the Arabian Sea (p. 122) by Paul Simmons